12th Edition

Plan Your Estate

Attorney Denis Clifford

Twelfth Edition   APRIL 2014

Editor   BETSY SIMMONS HANNIBAL

Cover Design   SUSAN PUTNEY

Book Design   TERRI HEARSH

Proofreading   IRENE BARNARD

Index   MEDEA MINNICH

Printing   BANG PRINTING

ISSN: 1931-7751 (print)
ISSN: 2332-6972 (online)
ISBN: 978-1-4133-2018-3 (pbk)
ISBN: 978-1-4133-2019-0 (epub ebook)

Please note

We believe accurate, plain-English legal information should help you solve many of your own legal problems. But this text is not a substitute for personalized advice from a knowledgeable lawyer. If you want the help of a trained professional—and we'll always point out situations in which we think that's a good idea—consult an attorney licensed to practice in your state.

Acknowledgments

Even more than most Nolo books, this one would never have seen the light of day without the generous efforts and contributions of many fine people. So my thanks to all those friends who helped me with this book, both putting it together and with previous editions over the years:

Betsy Simmons Hannibal, my current editor, brilliant, thorough, and a pleasure to work with. My previous Nolo editors, Jake Warner, Mary Randolph, Barbara Kate Repa, and Shae Irving.

Mark Peery of Greenbrae, California, a superb estate planning lawyer (and a great friend).

All my other friends and colleagues at Nolo.

Dorcas Moulton, Amanda Cherrin, and Naomi Puro, for their contributions to the cover painting on the original book.

Ken Fischer of Concord, California, a fine insurance agent; Bill Hudspeth of Austin Trust Co., Austin, Texas; Magdelen Gaynor, another fine estate planning attorney, White Plains, New York.

And my continued appreciation to other friends who also helped with other editions of this book: David Marcus; Paul Remack, R.G. Financial Service, San Francisco; Dave Brown; Peter Jan Honigsberg; Robert Wood of Athearn, Chandler & Hoffman, San Francisco; members of the Bay Area Funeral Society; Walter Warner; people who helped prepare the manuscript—Sandy Wieker, Christy Rigg, Cathy Cummings, and Bethany Korwin-Pawloski; and Keija Kimura, Carol Pladsen, and Linda Allison.

And last but not least, my heartfelt thanks to the many readers who have written me with suggestions, comments, corrections, and other thoughts for improving this book.

About the Author

Denis Clifford is a lawyer who specializes in estate planning. He is the author of several Nolo books, including *Make Your Own Living Trust* and *Quick & Legal Will Book*. A graduate of Columbia Law School, where he was an editor of *The Law Review*, he practiced law in various ways and became convinced that people can do much of their own legal work.

Table of Contents

Part II: Laying the Groundwork

Part III: Children

Part IV: Wills

Part V: Probate and How to Avoid It

Part VII: Reducing or Eliminating Estate Taxes

Part VIII: Imposing Controls Over Property

Part IX: Taking Care of Personal Issues

Part X: Family Business

Part XI: Going Further

Your Estate Planning Companion

I f you're like most people, you understand that estate planning is a good
idea. You know that estate planning
ensures that your property will pass to
the right people with minimal delay, red
tape, and cost. And if you have young
children, you likely know that you need
an estate plan to have a say in who will
care for your children if you're not around
to do it. Perhaps you even know that
you can use your estate plan to leave
specific instructions about your finances
and medical care in case you become
incapacitated and unable to make those
decisions for yourself.

You probably know all of that, and
yet, it's all too easy to put off actually
sitting down and making your plan. We
understand. Estate planning is not easy—
first, because it forces you to think about
your mortality, and second, because of
the legal complications and legal fees that
often come with it.

Plan Your Estate is here to help. This
book explains estate planning in plain
English, step by step, option by option.
Once you know your choices, you can
confidently move toward an estate plan
that fits your circumstances and wishes.

Plan Your Estate covers these estate
planning goals:

- **Leaving property.** If you have a modest
estate, you might use a simple will
or living trust, or both. You can also
use co-ownership, transfer-on-death
accounts, or beneficiary designations.
If you have a large estate, you might
also leave property to beneficiaries in
more complicated ongoing trusts. No
matter how you leave your property,
it is almost always better to have a
plan—if you die without one, state
law will decide who gets what.

- **Providing for young children.** If you
have young children, you'll want to
ensure that they will be well cared for
if you die before they become adults.
In your will, you can name guardians
to raise them and managers to look
after their inheritance. You'll also
want to buy life insurance to make
sure that your kids have money after
you're gone.

- **Planning for incapacity.** Part of estate
planning is preparing for what would
happen if you ever became unable to
make medical and financial decisions
for yourself. You can use a health

care directive to name someone who will make medical decisions on your behalf and to express your wishes about end-of-life care. You can also prepare a durable power of attorney that gives a trusted person control of your finances. Preparing these documents can save your family much heartache.

- **Avoiding probate.** Probate is a court-run process for wrapping up an estate. It's often expensive and time-consuming, yet rarely provides any benefit to the beneficiaries. Thankfully, with a little planning, probate is fairly easy to avoid. Trusts, pay-on-death accounts, joint tenancy, and other probate avoidance methods can keep most of your estate out of probate, saving your loved ones time and money.

- **Reducing estate tax.** Most people won't owe federal estate tax. But if you expect to leave over $5 million, you'll probably want to use your estate plan to reduce the tax that your estate will owe after your death.

If all this sounds overwhelming, please keep in mind that many people need only a simple estate plan. You may be able to prepare all your documents yourself. Or you might discover that you have some pretty complicated estate planning needs that will require advice from a lawyer. Most likely, you'll find yourself somewhere in between. No matter what your situation, with *Plan Your Estate* on your side you can go forward informed and empowered to make a smart and effective estate plan.

Congratulations on taking the first steps in planning your estate. It's an invaluable gift to yourself and to your loved ones—and it will feel great to get it done. Good luck!

Get Updates and More Online

When there are important changes to the information in this book, we'll post updates online, on a page dedicated to this book:

www.nolo.com/back-of-book/NEST.html

You'll find other useful information there, too, including author blogs, podcasts, and videos.

Selecting Your Estate Planning Goals

There are a number of ways to leave property to those you want to have it after your death. The peculiarities of our system of inheritance mean that substantial amounts of money and time can often be saved if property is labeled and transferred by certain legal methods rather than others. But to choose wisely among these methods, first you must clearly define your estate planning goals.

This book is divided into 12 parts; each part covers a different estate planning goal or purpose. This chapter gives you an overview of each goal, so you can select the ones that matter to you. It also presents a sample estate plan of a couple in their 50s, so you can get a feel for what kinds of decisions you may have to make and what types of documents you may end up with.

I urge you to read all chapters of every part that concerns you before you actually begin to formulate your own estate plan. Different aspects of estate planning are often intertwined. For example, it just doesn't make sense to decide what property should pass under your will—and so go through probate—until you understand that some of it might be better left by other probate avoidance methods. Similarly, if you are wealthy, you'll need to understand how estate taxes work before you can determine the wisest ways to transfer property to your loved ones. The point is that you need a good overview of all the parts of estate planning that concern you before you begin to make your plan.

Part I: Setting Your Goals

Use Part I to focus on your estate planning goals. After reading the first chapter, you should be able to decide which other parts of the book probably apply to your situation.

You should also take some time to mull over important personal concerns that can arise in estate planning—such as leaving unequal amounts of property to different children or avoiding potential conflicts. Chapter 2 discusses some of these concerns. Read this chapter unless you're very confident that your personal situation is clear and not conflicted.

"Thrift is a wonderful virtue, especially in an ancestor."

—Mark Twain

Part II: Laying the Groundwork

This part covers the primary concerns of any estate plan: what you own and to whom you want to leave it.

Obviously, you'll need to be sure of what you own. Also, sensible planning usually requires at least a rough idea of what your property is worth. Chapter 4 contains a worksheet you can use to list all your major items of property or just use as a safety check to make sure you haven't overlooked anything.

Your "estate" includes all the property you own, minus anything you owe (assets minus liabilities). You may find it useful to use the worksheet to make a rough estimate of the dollar value of your estate, which can be helpful both for general planning purposes and to predict whether or not your estate is likely to be liable for estate taxes. Of course, your estate will very likely have a different worth when you die, so precise figures aren't necessary.

You can't leave what you don't own. Ownership rules for single people are simple. Except as limited by contract (such as a partnership agreement or another form of shared ownership), you can leave all property you own outright. For these purposes, the fact that some institution has a claim on the property, such as a mortgage on a house or a loan lien on a car, doesn't create shared ownership.

Property ownership rules for a married person can be more complex. Read Chapter 3 before you start inventorying your property. Rules affecting ownership of property acquired during marriage may restrict your right to leave property. There are two basic systems that govern a married couple's property; which one applies to you depends on what state you live in. The majority of states follow the "common law" system where, in general, the owner of the property is the person whose name appears on the ownership document. The other system, applicable in nine states, mostly in the West, is "community property," where most property acquired during a marriage is owned equally by both spouses.

In common law states, laws limit a spouse's right to disinherit the other

Unmarried Couples: Who Owns What?

Unless an unmarried couple agrees to share ownership of specified property, each member of the couple owns only his or her own property. An agreement to own property together must often be in writing to be enforceable. In some states, an oral agreement is effective if it can be proved, but that can often be difficult. In short, it is best for unmarried couples to put any property-sharing agreement in writing.

If you're part of an unmarried couple where each person has kept all property separate (a written agreement to do this, listing the property of each person, is a good idea here as well), each of you is free to give your property to whomever you wish. However, if property ownership is shared, either under the terms of a written contract or in a tenancy in common or partnership, you're free to dispose of your share only, unless the contract or partnership agreement provides otherwise.

Property held by unmarried couples in joint tenancy goes to the survivor automatically.

For more information on property ownership problems of unmarried couples and sample property-sharing agreements, see *Living Together: A Legal Guide for Unmarried Couples*, by Ralph Warner, Toni Ihara, and Frederick Hertz (Nolo), a detailed guide designed to help unmarried couples minimize their entanglements with the law.

spouse. As explained in Chapter 3, in these states, a surviving spouse has the right to receive a certain portion of a deceased spouse's property, no matter what that spouse provided or intended. If you plan on leaving your spouse more than half your property, these laws can't affect you.

For most people, the heart of estate planning is deciding who gets what. You may have a very clear idea of who should inherit your property. If so, fine. Still, there are a number of issues that you may want to consider, from naming alternate beneficiaries to leaving shared gifts to forgiving debts. Chapter 5 discusses these and other concerns about your inheritors.

Part III: Children

If you have minor children, you'll want to plan for what would happen in the unlikely event that you and the other parent (if there is one) die before the children become legal adults. Indeed, for many new parents, concern for their child is what moves them to begin estate planning. Chapter 6 focuses on minor children, because a number of special estate planning issues affect them.

Most likely your first concern is who would raise the children if you couldn't. In your will, you can name someone to serve as the "personal guardian" for your children—the adult who would be responsible for raising them if neither parent could. Your nomination isn't automatically legally binding, but courts normally confirm the person you name if the other parent isn't available. Chapter 6 also discusses what you can do if you do not want the other parent to obtain custody.

The second big issue is who will manage any property you leave to your minor children. Minors cannot legally own more than a minimal amount of property without adult supervision. So, leaving property to your minor children requires you to choose a method for adult management. Chapter 6 explains the four legal methods you can use to impose adult supervision over property you leave to minors and the advantages and drawbacks of each.

Finally, Chapter 6 also addresses estate planning issues pertaining to adult children.

Part IV: Wills

Everyone should have a will, the most basic estate planning device. Chapter 7 explains why and shows you what you can accomplish in your will.

In your will, you name your "executor," the person with legal authority to administer the transfer of your will property. Chapter 7 discusses the responsibilities of an executor and presents some thoughts on selecting yours.

Wills do have one big drawback: Property left by a will must go through probate. So don't decide what property to transfer by your will until you've looked at transfer methods that avoid probate, which are discussed in Part V.

Legal Rights for Same-Sex Couples

Same-sex couples can marry in California, Connecticut, Delaware, the District of Columbia, Hawaii, Illinois, Iowa, Maine, Maryland, Massachusetts, Minnesota, New Hampshire, New Jersey, New Mexico, New York, Rhode Island, Vermont, and Washington. In these states, married same-sex couples receive the same state law rights as other married couples in that state.

Married same sex-couples are now also entitled to many of the same federal benefits as married heterosexual couples. These rights were recognized in 2013 when the Supreme Court declared Section 3 of the "Defense of Marriage Act" (DOMA) unconstitutional. The federal government now recognizes same-sex marriages performed in a U.S. state or foreign country that has legalized same-sex marriage—no matter where the couple lives. Federal rights now offered to married couples include filing a joint IRS tax return, receiving veterans benefits, and many others. Some federal agencies, including the Social Security Administration, still do not recognize the marriage of a same-sex couple if the couple's state of residence doesn't recognize it.

Colorado, Nevada, Oregon, and Wisconsin provide same-sex couples with some or most (depending on the state) of the property rights granted to married couples, but not the right to marry. These domestic partnership laws vary from state to state, so check your state's laws to learn what the specific rights are. Generally, to obtain these rights, a same-sex couple registers with a state agency.

Keep in mind that despite the rights available to same-sex couples in some states, relying on these laws should never be a substitute for doing your own comprehensive estate planning.

Whatever you decide about avoiding probate, you still need a will. At a minimum, a will is a backup device essential to the transfer of any property that somehow wasn't transferred by other methods, such as property you overlooked or that you unexpectedly acquire (e.g., a surprise inheritance or lottery winnings) after setting up your probate avoidance devices.

In almost all states, a will is the only document you can use to name a personal guardian for your minor children. Also, a will is best for transferring some types of property, like personal checking accounts or vehicles that may not be convenient to transfer by any other method.

Part V: Probate and How to Avoid It

Probate is the name given to the legal process by which a court oversees the distribution of property left by a will. The probate process is examined in detail in Chapter 8.

Probate proceedings are generally mere formalities, because there's rarely any dispute about a will, but they are nevertheless usually cumbersome and lengthy. During probate, your assets are identified, all debts and estate taxes are paid, fees for lawyers, appraisers, accountants, and for filing the case in court are paid, and the remaining property is finally distributed to your inheritors. The average probate proceeding drags on for at least a year before the estate is actually distributed.

The word probate has acquired a notorious aura. This is because in probate, it's common for lawyers, and sometimes other officials or executors, to charge large fees for what in most cases is routine, albeit tedious, paperwork. For example, if a father leaves his estate equally among his three children and no one contests the will, a lawyer might be paid a hefty sum just to shuffle papers through a bureaucratic maze.

Because probate lawyers are expensive, I've been asked many times by will beneficiaries if they can safely handle probate without an attorney. Unfortunately, except in California and Wisconsin, the answer is normally "no," at least not without considerable difficulty. In California, simple estates can be probated without an attorney by using *How to Probate an Estate in California*, by Julia Nissley (Nolo). Wisconsin has a simplified probate system, with court clerical assistance for completing the forms. Legally, it's permissible in most states (but not, for example, in Florida) for the executor named in a will to act for the estate, appear in probate court, and handle the proceedings without an attorney. But probate is a technical and tedious area of the law. Without good instructions, which are unfortunately nonexistent outside of lawyer texts (except, to repeat, in California and Wisconsin), the forms can seem very complicated to the uninitiated. Further, in some situations, there are court hearings to attend. In short, learning how to do probate from scratch normally takes considerable time and risks continuing frustration. Worse, the courts and clerks can be unhelpful, or even hostile, to laypeople.

A wiser choice is to reduce or eliminate probate fees by transferring property outside of probate. If you have a moderate estate, you can probably prepare probate avoidance devices and documents yourself, without an attorney. Chapters 9 through 14 explain the major probate avoidance methods:

- Living trusts allow you to retain full control over trust property while you live. After your death, your living trust property is transferred quickly to your beneficiaries.

- Joint tenancy is a form of shared property ownership with the key element that the surviving owner of joint tenancy property automatically inherits the share of a deceased owner. No probate is required.

- Pay-on-death designations let you name a beneficiary to quickly and easily receive, without probate, assets such as bank accounts or stocks when you die.

- Pay-on-death deeds and vehicle registrations pass real estate or vehicles to named beneficiaries without probate.
- Life insurance proceeds go directly to the policy beneficiary, without going through probate.
- Individual retirement programs, such as IRAs, profit-sharing plans, or 401(k) plans, allow you to leave any money remaining in the account to a named beneficiary. The money is transferred outside of probate.
- State law exemptions from normal probate allow smaller estates to go through a simplified probate procedure or avoid probate altogether. These rules apply to estates ranging from less than $5,000 to $200,000, depending on the state. A list of each state's rules is in Chapter 14.

Reading about probate avoidance doesn't mean that you must decide to pursue it. Some people intelligently decide that all the estate planning they want for now is a will.

Although you may find it surprising, limiting estate planning to making a will can, in the right circumstances, make good sense. For example, many younger people in good health often sensibly decide to postpone detailed estate planning for later. A will naming a personal and property guardian for minor children and leaving their relatively modest amount of property to a spouse, partner, and perhaps also a few close friends or relatives, is all they

Providing Ready Cash

One goal of estate planning can be to provide ready cash for immediate family needs or, later on, to pay any estate taxes or other debts. Particularly if you are your family's main provider, your survivors will need immediate cash for their living expenses, or for the "costs of dying"—hospitalization, funeral, and burial expenses—and other debts and taxes that are due promptly.

If most of your property is transferred by will, your family won't get it while probate moves on. Immediate family members can ask the probate court to release limited amounts for necessities, but it's wiser to plan to have money available without going to court and paying attorneys' fees.

If most of your property will be transferred outside of probate, there is much less reason to worry about arranging for ready cash, because cash is usually accessible promptly. However, if most of your assets aren't "liquid"—that is, cannot easily be converted to cash—you may still need to provide a source of ready cash. For example, if your worth is in real estate and shares of a private corporation that can't readily be sold, your family might have trouble obtaining cash for daily expenses. Traditional sources of cash are life insurance policies or money in a pay-on-death bank account.

want, and need, now. Since probate doesn't happen until death, a younger person should have plenty of time to plan to avoid it later in life.

In contrast, for older people with a reasonable amount of property, or people in ill health, it makes little sense to depend on a will alone. The amount of time and effort it takes to plan to avoid probate is just not that much—certainly far less than will be consumed going through the probate process, not to mention the significant costs saved.

Aside from avoiding probate altogether, if you significantly reduce the value of property transferred by probate, you'll likely reduce the attorneys' fee as well. A useful concept here is the "probate estate," the portion of your estate that must go through probate. Anything that is transferred by probate-avoiding methods is not part of the probate estate; it goes directly to inheritors without court proceedings. If you plan wisely, you can reduce considerably the size of your probate estate, or even eliminate it entirely.

TIP

Some reasons for probate. In unusual situations, probate can be useful. If your estate will have many debts or claims by creditors, probate provides a forum for resolving those claims with relative speed and certainty. And if creditors who are notified of the probate do not file claims within a set period (usually a few months), the claims are barred forever.

Part VI: Understanding Estate and Gift Taxes

Many people who engage in comprehensive estate planning want to know about estate and gift taxes. Will your estate be liable for taxes? If so, what can be done to reduce or avoid them? In Chapter 15, you'll learn how both federal and state estate taxes work and whether or not your estate is likely to be subject to a tax.

Estate Tax Uncertainty

The current estate tax rules were adopted by Congress in 2013 with the declaration that they are "permanent." Perhaps, but the reality is that these rules can be changed if Congress decides to, and that depends on political circumstances. For example, President Obama's proposed 2014 budget, released in April 2013, wanted to reduce the exempt amount to $3.5 million, without an annual inflation adjustment. This 2014 budget also proposed that the top estate tax rate be increased beginning in 2018 to 45%, from the current 40%. Congress is unlikely to accept any of these changes. Still, if you have a large estate, it's wise for you to keep on top of changes made to the federal estate tax laws and rules. To check on the latest information, go to Nolo's website at www.nolo.com.

In addition, a handful of states impose estate or inheritance taxes. Chapter 15 explains how estate and inheritance taxes work.

You will almost surely learn that no federal estate tax will be assessed against your estate. Federal law exempts a certain amount of property from tax. For 2014 the exemption is $5.34 million per person.

Chapter 15 explains this and other major federal estate tax exemptions. Another important exemption is what's called the "marital deduction," which provides that all property left or given to a spouse is exempt from estate or gift tax. However, the marital deduction does not apply to property a citizen spouse gives or leaves to a noncitizen spouse.

Chapter 15 also covers the concept of tax "basis" and how that applies to inherited property. Very briefly, the basis of property is the dollar value put on your ownership interest when determining the profit or loss from sale. To simplify here, we can say that the basis of property you own is the purchase price. However, if you inherit property under current federal law, your basis is not the cost to the person who left you the property, but the market value of the property when that person died. This is called a "stepped-up" basis. If you plan to leave property that has significantly increased in value since you purchased it, it's important to understand how this stepped-up basis works and can be used in estate planning.

To get a solid grasp of estate taxes, you also need to understand gift taxes, which are covered in Chapter 16. At first hearing, the phrase "gift taxes" sounds like something Scrooge came up with. How can you tax generosity? But if there were no gift taxes, estate taxes could be avoided simply by giving away property while you live instead of leaving it when you die. So the federal government, and a few states, impose tax on substantial gifts, currently, those above $14,000 to any person in one year.

> **CAUTION**
> **Separate taxes and probate.** Don't confuse avoiding probate with reducing estate or gift taxes. Unfortunately, avoiding probate doesn't have any effect on estate or gift taxes.

Definition of a Gift

A "gift" is property you transfer freely (not by sale or trade) to a person or an institution. Throughout this book, gift is used to describe both property you give away during your lifetime and property you leave at your death. This eliminates the legalese of "bequest," "devise," or "legacy."

Part VII: Reducing or Eliminating Estate Taxes

Chapters 17 to 23 cover major methods of reducing federal estate taxes, aside from tax-free gifts. These methods require using some form of irrevocable trust, or, sometimes, a number of trusts. I call these "ongoing" trusts because they function as independent entities for an indefinite time. This is in contrast to a probate avoidance living trust, which is normally operational only for a brief period, after the death of the person who set it up.

Because an irrevocable trust is an independent legal entity, it must obtain a federal taxpayer ID number. Trustees must keep separate trust financial records and file an annual trust income tax return, paying any taxes due. (See Chapter 17.)

Other marital estate tax–saving trusts are covered in Chapter 19. A "QTIP" trust enables a surviving spouse to postpone taxes otherwise due on property worth more than the federal estate tax threshold.

This chapter also explains "QDOT" trusts, which can be important if you are married to a noncitizen. As we've said, the marital deduction does not apply to property left to a noncitizen spouse. So normally any property over the federal estate tax threshold left by a citizen spouse to a noncitizen spouse is taxable when the citizen spouse dies. A QDOT trust enables the noncitizen spouse to postpone payment of any taxes due until after her or his death.

Whether you're married or not, if you're interested in making a large gift to a charity and also getting a tax break, you may want to investigate charitable trusts, covered in Chapter 20. With these trusts, you can leave property to charities and simultaneously obtain income tax as well as estate tax benefits. A charitable trust makes sense, from an estate tax perspective, only if your estate exceeds the federal estate tax threshold. However, Chapter 20 also provides useful information about charitable gifts, no matter how large your estate.

Still other kinds of ongoing trusts can be used by anyone, married or not, to save on estate taxes. These trusts, covered in Chapter 21, include:

- generation-skipping trusts, where you leave property in trust for grandchildren and avoid estate taxes on the trust property when your own children die
- irrevocable life insurance trusts, which can, in the right circumstances, save a bundle on estate taxes, and
- grantor-retained interest trusts, which can yield income and estate tax benefits if you transfer your home to a trust for a set period.

One other strategy that can sometimes lower a family's overall estate tax burden is the use of a "disclaimer." A disclaimer is simply a statement that you decline to accept property left to you—a legal way of saying "no thanks." Disclaimers can be used to direct gifts from a prosperous beneficiary who has ample resources to another person who has less. Aside from any personal goals this may achieve, it also may work to protect the prosperous person's estate from increased estate taxes. (Chapter 22 explains how to use disclaimers.)

Finally, some people use more than one kind of trust to achieve the most tax savings. (See Chapter 23.)

Part VIII: Imposing Controls Over Property

For one or more reasons, you may want to impose controls over property you leave—in other words, legally prevent the beneficiary from gaining unfettered ownership of the property. (Chapter 6 discusses controls you can use over property left to minors. This part covers restrictions on adult beneficiaries.) These types of controls require use of a trust.

You might want to impose such controls if you've remarried and want to balance the interests and needs of your current spouse with those of children from a former marriage. Chapter 24 explains how you can create a trust that leaves your spouse certain defined rights in trust property for his or her life, but preserves the principal for your children who receive the trust property when the surviving spouse dies.

Many issues can come up when trying to balance the rights of the spouse and the children. For example, can the surviving spouse sell trust property? What rights do the children have to see that the trust principal is being preserved? There is no generic solution to these questions. The answers must be worked out individually, fitting your specific desires and needs.

You may want a property control trust in a number of other situations, discussed in Chapter 25, including:

- **You want to help pay for a child's college or other schooling costs.** Here you'll need to decide whether you want to define what school costs include and what the criteria for being in school are, or if you'll let the trustee make those decisions.
- **You want to establish a "special needs" trust for someone with a disability.** Common problems include selecting the trustee and doing all that's legal to preserve the beneficiary's eligibility for government assistance.
- **You want to restrict a beneficiary's access to his or her inheritance.** If you believe an adult beneficiary can't responsibly handle money, you may want to set up a "spendthrift trust." It controls the beneficiary's freedom to use trust property, including the ability to pledge it as a loan.
- **You want to create a trust allowing the trustee to decide how property is distributed to adult beneficiaries.** With a "sprinkling trust," the trustee is authorized to distribute, within any limits set by the trust, unequal amounts of trust income or principal among the beneficiaries.
- **You want someone else to decide what happens to some or all of your property after your death.** This is called a "power of appointment." The person you

authorize can select your beneficiaries and decide how much of your property they receive, within any limits you've set.

Part IX: Taking Care of Personal Issues

When you're making plans for what happens to your property, don't overlook two important personal decisions that can affect what happens to *you*. The first is making arrangements for handling your financial and medical affairs if you become incapacitated and unable to make these decisions yourself. The second is what you want done with your body after you die. What are your choices, and how can you make your decisions binding?

To be sure your wishes are carried out if you become incapacitated, you'll need to prepare several documents. For health care, you can prepare documents that specify what type of medical care you want if you become incapacitated and cannot express your wishes, and that authorize someone you've chosen to make sure your wishes for health care are carried out. These documents normally become effective only if you become incapacitated and can't communicate your preferences for treatment.

To handle money matters if you become incapacitated, you can prepare a document called a "durable power of attorney for finances." In this document, you appoint someone to handle your financial affairs and make financial decisions for you. You can include any directions regarding your finances that you wish. Chapter 26 discusses these issues.

The options you have for disposing of your body after death are covered in Chapter 27. Subjects covered include death notices, donation of body parts for transplants or your entire body for medical research, funerals, cremation, burials, and how to leave binding written instructions. Doing this kind of planning can be a great gift to your loved ones, freeing them from burdensome tasks immediately after your death and almost always saving significant amounts of money.

Part X: Family Business Estate Planning

Small business owners have special estate planning concerns. Chapter 28 covers some basic issues: operation of the business after an owner's death, planning to reduce or eliminate any possible estate taxes on the business, and avoiding probate of business assets. Business estate planning is a complex field and I can delve into only the most central issues, but, at a minimum, this chapter should enable you to determine the areas with which you might want more help.

Protecting Assets in Case of Catastrophic Illness

 SEE AN EXPERT

Many people are concerned that if they become seriously ill, all their savings—indeed, all their assets—will be consumed to pay for health care. To address this valid concern, some people ask for a will clause, or a simple trust, or anything that will prevent their assets from being used for expensive medical bills. Unfortunately, this is not an easy matter to handle. No simple clause or trust can safely accomplish this. The best you can do is:

- Seek advice from an expert attorney in your state. The attorney must know applicable federal laws and regulations and also be up-to-date on your state's laws.
- If you're a member of a couple, research how you can best protect the assets of the person who doesn't become ill. Many states allow one spouse to shield his or her property from liability for medical bills of the other spouse. This is covered in depth in *Long-Term Care: How to Plan & Pay For It*, by Joseph L. Matthews (Nolo).
- Consider transferring some of your property to trusted family members before you become seriously ill. You need to be careful here and work with an expert in the field. Federal law prohibits giving away property and then applying for federal medical aid within five years of the transfer.

All this can be tricky and even dangerous. Both federal and state legal rules change rapidly. Nevertheless, a lawyer experienced in elder law issues in your state should be able to provide you with some measure of asset protection. This is likely to be less than you want, but the best you can do.

For tips on finding a lawyer, see Chapter 29.

Family Limited Partnerships

Some people believe that creating a "family limited partnership" can somehow eliminate all estate taxes, no matter how large the estate and how flimsy the "business." The notion is that the parents can transfer their property into a partnership business entity with their children and possibly grandchildren, sharing ownership as limited partners. The parents hope that as a result, the partnership will be transferred to younger generations tax free.

For such a plan to succeed, the IRS must be convinced that the limited partnership has some purpose beyond simply reducing estate taxes. Calling your home or stock investments a family business doesn't make them one. But if you own a real business, there can be estate tax advantages to creating a limited partnership for it and transferring minority interests to future inheritors. The pros and cons of this are discussed in more depth in Chapter 28.

documents you need. The chapter explores how to find a good lawyer and how to work with one, including making fair and sensible fee arrangements. You may also decide to do some legal research on your own; this chapter gets you started.

After your planning is done and the documents you want have been prepared, you'll need to know what to do with them. Chapter 30 covers how to store them, how to make copies, and when to revise your estate plan.

Doing conscientious estate planning while you're alive is a boon to your loved ones—but someone must still complete the process after your death. Chapter 31 gives you an overview of how your property will be transferred, depending on how you leave that property—by will, living trust, joint tenancy, pay-on-death account, or life insurance. It next discusses what happens if your estate owes taxes. The chapter also covers some important matters about ongoing trusts, including how they actually are put into gear, and the responsibility of the trustee to report to the trust beneficiaries.

Part XI: Going Further

Once you've determined, at least in outline, what your estate planning goals are and how you want to address them, you may want to see a lawyer or other expert.

Chapter 29 discusses the different types of lawyers and other experts who may be helpful, or necessary, for you to pin down the specifics of your plan and prepare the

Part XII: Sample Estate Plans

Now that you've read this first chapter, you should have some focus on the major issues you want to address in your estate planning. Part XII provides several examples of estate plans, to aid your understanding of how different goals and components can be melded into one plan.

In the hope of giving you a clearer notion now of what the end product of your efforts may be, here's one sample estate plan.

Abel Rublestam and Lynn Montgomery are married and in their 50s—he's 58, she's 51. They live in a common law property state. They have two children, Matt and Rebecca. Matt is married and has two young children. Rebecca is in graduate school.

Their property. The couple shares ownership of all their property. Their estate consists of a home worth $750,000 ($660,000 equity), securities (stocks and bonds) worth $280,000, money market savings of $350,000, life insurance on each spouse that pays $200,000 on death (for a total of $400,000), and their one-half ownership of the Montstam corporation, a family business. It's hard to determine the exact value of their business. As a rough guess, they decide it's worth at least $2,800,000. The current net worth of each spouse's estate, in 2014, is $2,290,000 and the net worth of their combined estate is $4,580,000.

Their estate planning goals. The couple wants to avoid probate. They decide they do not need to worry about possible federal estate taxes. Their combined estate of $4,580,000 is under half of the amount a couple can pass on to their inheritors free of estate tax. If the federal estate tax exempt amount is subsequently drastically reduced, they will revise their plan then.

They consider leaving more property to Matt, because of his family responsibilities. But they decide to leave equal amounts to both children. They don't want to seem to favor one child or one lifestyle. Also, they don't want to have to revise their plan if a major family event happens to one of their children—say, Matt has a third child or gets divorced, or Rebecca has a child.

Their plan. The couple prepares a living trust to avoid probate. Each leaves the other all his or her property. Both name their children as the final beneficiaries of their trusts.

They carefully transfer title to their home, Montstam stock, securities accounts, and money market funds into the living trust's name, having already checked that the bylaws of their co-op apartment association and the Montstam corporation permit this.

Each spouse names the other spouse as beneficiary of his or her life insurance policy.

When they're older, if their assets increase significantly in value, the couple intends to consider making yearly tax-free gifts to each of their children, but decide that they are not ready to do this now.

Each prepares a basic will. Then they prepare health care directives—a declaration and a durable power of attorney for health care for each of them. In their declarations, they each state that they do not wish to be placed on life support equipment if diagnosed with a terminal illness. In their durable powers of attorney for health care, each names the other as attorney-in-fact, with full authority to make medical decisions and to be sure that all wishes for health care are carried out. Finally, each prepares a durable power of attorney for finances, naming the other as attorney-in-fact.

Personal Concerns and Estate Planning

Underlying the creation of any estate plan are profound human concerns: a primal urge for order and the desire to pass on property to loved ones. A good estate plan is an accurate reflection of your deepest personal wishes. Although much of this book is about mechanics, methods, and documents, it's important to remember that no matter how well you deal with legal devices, your estate plan won't succeed unless you take feelings into account, too.

I make no claim to being an expert on the human psyche. Indeed, I am wary of "experts" (or anyone) who claim precise understanding of something as complex and mysterious as human beings. Happily, you usually won't need such an expert to cope with the human realities that can come up in your estate planning. You do need common sense and candor about the strengths, weaknesses, and genuine needs of close family members and, perhaps, friends as well. Legal aspects of estate planning are significant, of course, but should never interfere with what you know in your heart needs to be done.

Many people face no serious personal issues in their estate planning. They know whom they want to leave their property to. They do not foresee any possibility of conflict between their beneficiaries or threat of a lawsuit by someone claiming they were illegally denied their inheritance. On an emotional level, these people can happily focus on the satisfactions they expect their gifts to bring.

Other people's situations are not so clear and straightforward. They must deal with more difficult personal dynamics, such as potential family conflicts, dividing property unequally between children, providing care for minor children, or handling complexities arising from second or subsequent marriages.

Before beginning your legal planning, it's vital that you assess your personal circumstances and decide how you want to resolve any difficulties. If you're planning to leave all your property to your spouse or two compatible children, or are otherwise sure you don't face any personal issues, wonderful. You can safely go on to the next chapter that concerns you. If, however, you think you might face complications—or if you're not sure what kinds of problems can come up—read this chapter, which discusses a number of personal concerns that might arise.

Avoiding Conflict

Estate planning involves money—cash or assets that can be sold for cash. Money, as most of us learn as we get older, is strange stuff—or, more accurately, people can do strange things because of the desire for money. (If the love of money isn't *the* root of all evil, it's certainly somewhere under the tree.) So the first step in creating an estate plan is to recognize that if you plan unwisely, your plan may lead to bitterness, strife, and lawsuits rather than the happiness you surely intend. Avoiding conflict after your death to the extent reasonably possible should be a central goal of estate planning.

Start by asking yourself about the potential for conflict in your personal situation. If this potential exists, what can you do to eliminate or at least reduce it? One important thing to remember is that disputes are not always over property that is worth a lot of money. If different family members or other inheritors have deep emotional attachments to heirlooms, or what they stand for, or can't stand the idea of *that person* getting it, fighting can become fierce even if the heirlooms themselves won't make anyone rich.

John Gregory Dunne, in his autobiography *Harp* (Simon & Schuster), gives a telling description of one family's fight over heirlooms. His Aunt Harriet failed to specifically state who got what of her many items of personal property. Dunne wrote:

"In legal terms, Aunt Harriet became ... Estate of Harriet H. Burn," appraised and organized, room by room, into "8 carved Hepplewhite mahogany chairs" and "Coalport 'Kings Plate' china service for twelve" and "Repro. Victorian loveseat, blue brocade" and "Light blue upholstered settee, soiled." The house was sold, the belongings apportioned to the surviving children and grandchildren. There is something so metaphorical and final in the act of dividing up the possessions a family has accumulated over several lifetimes and more generations; for the first time I thought there might be a good argument for

primogeniture. It was not that the furniture and china and crystal and silver and linens had great worth; it was just that each piece, each object had a private history, a special meaning for one or the other of us. For a family, the process of apportionment is like psychoanalysis or the confessional box; long-buried resentments surface, old hurts and forgotten slights. In the end, a lawyer drew up the order of selection; his ground rules were worthy of Solomon:

"The order of selection will be determined as follows: each of you is requested to pick a number from one to ninety-nine and advise me of it by return mail: the person whose number is closest to the first two numbers of the Connecticut Daily Lottery on Tuesday, October 7, will have first pick, and so forth .... If the first person who selects property picks an item in an amount worth $1,400, the second person will be entitled to pick as many items as he or she wishes up to $1,400 in value. The third person would then have the right to choose property in the amount equal to the value selected by the person who preceded him or her and so forth until all items have been selected. In this way, each family unit will have an opportunity to select property, in turn and essentially of equal value."

The Connecticut State Lottery: God, if there is one, must have a sense of humor.

With some wise planning, the conflicts among the Dunne family could have been avoided. After all, well before Aunt Harriet died, a lawyer could have drawn up this distribution method, complete with the

Connecticut State Lottery. So even if you can't, or don't want to, decide before your death exactly who gets what, you can still create a binding method for peaceful and fair distribution of your property after you die.

Let's explore ways to avoid conflict by looking at three different family situations. However, here, at the beginning, I do want to recognize that in some situations, there's no way to prevent disagreements.

EXAMPLE 1: Choosing an Executor.
Patrick and Clara have five children. One, Sean, is a lawyer. Patrick and Clara admit to themselves, though they never reveal it to others, that Sean is their one grasping child, who has always wanted the most, materially, from his parents and the world. Indeed, by sheer persistence, Sean has already managed to acquire a substantial number of family heirlooms. Sean tells his parents he wants to supervise distribution of their property (after both die) as executor of their wills and successor trustee of their living trust, stating that he's obviously the most professionally qualified.

At first, Patrick and Clara aren't sure what to do. Their concern isn't that Sean will violate their wills and distribute their major items of property unequally. Rather, they worry that the personal possessions they have left to all their children won't be divided fairly. After considerable discussion, they decide they don't want Sean to

have sole authority to supervise the distribution of their estate. Basically, they conclude that while they love him as they do their other children, they simply can't rely on him to be able to put his own desires aside and distribute their heirlooms impartially. They'd prefer to have their daughter Maude, the kindest and most levelheaded of their kids, be both executor and successor trustee, which will allow her to preside over the division of the personal items. However, they're afraid of offending Sean, something they're determined not to do.

After much thought, they decide to have three executors and successor trustees—Sean, Maude, and another daughter, Maeve. (Patrick, Jr. lives in Europe and isn't interested, and Polly is preoccupied with her medical career.) A majority of executors can decide how the estate is handled. This solution may be a little awkward, and it sets up the possibility that Maude and Maeve may have to combine forces to cope with Sean (as they've had to do for 30 years), but Patrick and Clara feel it has a good chance of success. They plan to talk diplomatically to Maude, Maeve, and Sean to try to achieve some common understanding of what they want. But even if Sean is dissatisfied, the couple believes there is far less risk of serious family strife than if Sean were named sole trustee and executor.

EXAMPLE 2: A Child From a Previous Marriage. Sol and Bernice have two children in their late 20s, Abel and Alexis, and a combined estate worth about $750,000. Sol also has a 34-year-old daughter, Lilith, from his first marriage, whom he's seen very rarely since his marriage to Bernice. Sol wants to leave Lilith $200,000. "That's absolutely ridiculous," Bernice exclaims. "You're just trying to absolve yourself of the guilt you feel for being unable to see Lilith all these years." Sol retorts, "Isn't it my money?" Bernice points out that half of it is her money, because their property lists both their names as owners (see Chapter 3). Sol says, "Yes, but half of $750,000 is $375,000, so I can leave $200,000 to Lilith if I want to." But he soon admits that this approach would mean he would be leaving much less to his other two children. In short, Sol realizes that Bernice is right—his children from his present marriage would almost surely feel hurt.

Sol and Bernice decide to work through this problem together. After some lengthy talks, they decide that Sol will leave $40,000 to Lilith, and the rest to Bernice (assuming Bernice survives Sol). When Bernice dies, she will pass on everything that's left to Abel and Alexis. They then check with the two children to see if this seems fair to them as well. Happily, it does. Abel says, "Hey, it's your money, Pa."

Their daughter adds, "So enjoy." Both convince Sol and Bernice that they think the gift to Lilith is fair.

EXAMPLE 3: Family Heirlooms. Al is a widower with three children. Although there's no problem dividing his big-ticket items among his children equally—they all agree on that—all three children have expressed deep attachment to a number of relatively inexpensive family treasures. Al decides they have to talk it out. He gets all three children together and says, "You're going to have to work it out among you. Come up with something you all agree on and I'll do it. But don't make me guess, and don't leave me worrying that you'll be fighting amongst yourselves when I'm gone."

A family retreat is planned and carried out. It takes longer than any of them anticipate, but the kids stick with it, and eventually, a few flashes of temper and some weary hours later, they've worked out an agreement to divide some items of property and share others. Everyone is in good spirits. Al studies the agreement and secretly concludes that it's more complex than necessary, and in some small ways not completely fair. Still, his kids accept it, and that's what matters to him, so he includes it in his will.

EXAMPLE 4: Trouble Ahead. Freitel is 85 years old and in poor health. She lives in a retirement community in

Arizona. She has one son, Hugh, age 57. To her sorrow, she has not been close to Hugh for decades, and has become nearly estranged from him since his third marriage, to Kristin. Freitel believes Kristin dominates Hugh—always rather weak-willed—and that she has encouraged his worst materialistic tendencies.

Freitel has a substantial estate. During her 15 years of retirement, she has been very involved with her church, and also with a program to help poor children. She intends to leave the bulk of her estate to these charities, but worries what Hugh (read Kristin) might do. In one of her calls to Hugh (he almost never calls her), she mentions that she might leave some money to her church. Soon after, she receives calls from Hugh, and even Kristin, suddenly concerned about her health, including, not so subtly, her mental health. Freitel suspects that Hugh and Kristin might contest her will, possibly alleging that the church had gained "undue influence" over her. After talking her worries over with her closest friends, she reluctantly concludes that, given Hugh and Kristin's greed, it's unwise to try to further discuss her plans with them. Better to accept that they may fight her will. She decides to hire a lawyer experienced in will contests, so that she can do everything possible to ensure that her will stands up if attacked in court.

Leaving Unequal Amounts of Property to Children

Sometimes parents want to leave unequal amounts of property to their children but don't want to give the impression that they favor the child who is given more. Here are some examples of how people have handled this matter.

EXAMPLE 1: **A Disgruntled Child.** Jim's parents, Mort and Lisa, paid for his college and dental school education and helped him purchase his first house. Melinda, their other child, has always been an independent sort who, while a loving daughter, has prided herself on making it on her own. Now Mort and Lisa want to equalize their gifts by leaving considerably more to Melinda in their estate plan. Some hints of their thinking are enough to disturb Jim, and he argues that in balance, Melinda will wind up with more than half.

Mort and Lisa talk it over and decide they'll stick to their original plan. They think the dollar figures for each child are close to even overall, and that Jim is being a bit grasping. They also conclude that they won't discuss the subject with Jim again. But in their estate planning documents (a will and a living trust), they'll try to explain why and how they determined the distribution. They'll emphasize that they love both children equally and are determined to treat them equally.

Mort and Lisa hope that being fair and firm with Jim will gain his respect in the end.

EXAMPLE 2: The Struggling Musician. Ayyad, a widower with a moderate estate, has four grown children. Three are well established in conventional business careers with excellent future prospects. One is a serious, but impoverished, jazz musician. Because of his greater need, Ayyad considers leaving the musician most of his estate, but decides to confer with his children before finalizing that plan.

To Ayyad's surprise, he learns that two of his children don't agree with his plan. One has never much cared for his musician brother, thinking him irresponsible. (Besides, this child never liked his music, anyway.) Another child points out that she has two children and that, in today's market, neither her nor her husband's job is really secure. The musician, she reminds Ayyad, has provided him with no loving grandchildren. The daughter asks whether her children shouldn't receive some "rainy day" funds from their grandfather.

Ayyad says he'll think this over. He decides he doesn't want to talk it over further with his kids. This is, after all, his decision. He's gotten their input, but it's up to him to decide.

Finally, he decides to divide his total estate by percentages: 50% will go to the musician (Ayyad admires his son and thinks he is sincere, not indulgent), 12.5% will go to each of his other two children with no children of their own, and 25% to the daughter with children. If any of his other children has a child, or if the musician gains a measure of financial success, Ayyad plans to revise these percentages.

In an effort to soothe feelings, Ayyad writes a detailed letter explaining his decision and expressing his love and good wishes for each child. He attaches the letter to his living trust, where it will be revealed to his children after his death.

EXAMPLE 3: Unequal Earnings. Barbara and Barry have two grown children and a substantial estate. Their son is a doctor; their daughter is a part-time college student and environmental activist who wants a career helping make the world a better place, but isn't sure what that career is (or if it exists at all). Barbara and Barry consider leaving the bulk of their wealth to their daughter, figuring that their son is much more secure. But then, on reflection, they decide they don't want such an imbalance. Medicine, they reason, is surely changing, and may not be as lucrative in the future. Also, their son already has one child, with more hoped for. Who knows what his needs may become in the future. And anyway, they've been helping to support their daughter, and expect they may do so for several more years, until she's begun to carve out her niche.

Barbara and Barry decide, for the time being, to divide their estate equally between the two children. But they also agree to periodically review their plan, to see whether they now want to leave more property to one child.

EXAMPLE 4: A Special Needs Child. Ruth is a single mother in her late forties with three children: Ben, 20, Liz, 18, and Josh, 14. Josh has a serious physical disability that will require special care for his life. But exactly how much care is not clear when Ruth decides to prepare her estate plan.

Ruth owns a house with about $200,000 equity. She has total savings of roughly $75,000, plus a dwindling 401(k) account, currently worth $40,000. A successful graphic designer, she makes enough money to support her family and put aside modest yearly savings.

Ruth wants to leave all her property in trust for Josh, believing that he has the greatest need for her money. She discusses this with her two oldest children. Liz says honestly that she would like some financial help from home when she goes to college next year—but really, Liz understands and agrees with her mother's decision. Ben, however, proves difficult, indicating (though not clearly) that his mother

has always ignored him, and that he should be left at least some of her property, if not a full one-third share.

Ruth, surprised and somewhat hurt, discusses Ben's position with two close friends and Liz. Ruth concludes that Ben is equating money with love (and he's not the first person to do that). She decides on two courses of action: (1) She will leave her estate as she wants to, and (2) she will talk to Ben about the two of them going into therapy together (with Ruth paying) over the issue Ben has raised.

Kids First

Grateful Dead musician Jerry Garcia left a will designed to take care of what was most important to him: his four daughters, ages seven to thirty-one. To accomplish what he wanted, he ignored some sophisticated estate tax–saving strategies that would have delayed his children's inheritance or shifted money to his wife.

Garcia left his wife one-third of his separate property; she already owned one-half of their community property. Legally, property left to a spouse is free of all estate taxes. But Garcia didn't want all the taxes due on his estate to be paid only by his children, so he provided that any taxes due on his estate were to be paid before anyone, including his wife, received any of his property.

Providing Care for Minor Children

A prime concern of parents of minor children is who will take care of their children if the parents die. If both parents are involved in raising a child (together, or in the case of divorce or separation, with the participation of both), the principal worry is what happens if both parents die. Obviously, if there is only one parent, because the other is dead or has effectively abandoned the child, the sole parent is likely to be even more concerned that the child will be well cared for.

In either case, the primary issues are who will raise the child and who will be responsible for supervising property the parent(s) leave to the child. These issues are discussed in depth in Chapter 6. Here I want only to indicate some of the emotions that may arise when trying to resolve these issues.

EXAMPLE 1: **The Best Choice.** A married couple, Taylor and Sondra, have two grade school–age children. Taylor and Sondra discuss who will raise their children if they both die before the kids are adults. Taylor strongly promotes his sister, Beth, as the suitable guardian. Sondra thinks Beth is a snob and declares she doesn't want her children raised in that household. She suggests her older brother, Louis. Taylor retorts that Louis may be good with money, but he has a terrible temper and doesn't have the most stable marriage.

Fortunately, Taylor and Sondra are sensitive enough to realize they have to talk seriously to reach an agreement on who would make the best guardian. After considerable discussion, and a fairly successful effort to feel out the kids, they settle on Sondra's best friend, Hilda, whom they both trust and respect. Hilda has children about the same age and is willing to accept the responsibility for raising Taylor and Sondra's kids.

But both Sondra and Taylor agree that Hilda is not very sensible with money. They worry that she couldn't sensibly manage the money they would leave for the children. Hilda isn't overjoyed to hear this, but she is good-hearted. She accepts Sondra and Taylor's solution—she will be the children's personal guardian, and Louis will supervise the money left them until they're old enough to get it outright. Louis also agrees to this arrangement.

EXAMPLE 2: **Someone Who'll Accept the Job.** Marcie, a single parent, wants her best friend, Shoshana, to be the guardian of Katherine, Marcie's nine-year-old daughter, should Marcie die before Katherine is 18. To Marcie's surprise, Shoshana says she can't accept the responsibility. She has two kids of her own, and that's all she can handle. Marcie is hurt, and worries there's no one she trusts who will do the job. After some reflection and discussion with other friends, Marcie realizes that her brother Alex is willing to be guardian. Marcie is not overjoyed: Alex and she weren't really close as kids and still aren't. But she realizes that Alex is a trustworthy person and that Katherine would be well cared for with him. She concludes that her best estate plan is to stay alive until her daughter is an adult, but if she doesn't, she will rely on Alex.

Subsequent Marriages

People who've married more than once may face problems reconciling their desires for their present spouse and family with their wishes for children from their prior marriages. Individual situations can vary greatly, often depending on whether marriages occurred relatively early or late in life and on how well family members get along. But one thing is obvious: You must carefully consider—and do your best to reconcile—the conflicting needs within your family. These issues are covered in more depth in Chapter 24.

EXAMPLE 1: **Her Kids, His Kids.** Katerina and Pavel get married when they are in their 50s. Katerina has a son from her prior marriage. Pavel has three children, two daughters and a son. Katerina and Pavel both work. Pavel has a slightly higher income, and savings of $400,000 to Katerina's $130,000. They buy a house, with each spouse contributing half the down payment and equally sharing the monthly payments. Both spouses want to ensure that, when one spouse dies, the survivor gets to live in the house for the rest of his or her life. When both spouses die, they want the house to be divided equally, with one share going to Katerina's son and the other share divided between Pavel's three children. Similarly, by use of a marital property control trust (see Chapter 24), each spouse's assets will be left for the "use" of the surviving spouse, with "use" defined to mean the right to receive income the property generates or literal use of some property—for example, a car. Neither spouse can invade the other's principal.

Katerina and Pavel consider the wisdom of discussing their plan with all their children. Since they have chosen Eve, one of Pavel's daughters, to wind up their affairs after their death in the role of the successor trustee of their living trust, they have already discussed it with her. But because Katerina's son, Tad, has never accepted Pavel, and remains hostile to him, Katerina and Pavel sadly decide that talking their plan over with Tad will only provide an occasion for more rancor. So they simply don't tell him what they've agreed upon.

EXAMPLE 2: **The Impoverished Husband.** Angelina, in her 70s, is a wealthy widow with three grown children. She marries Arthur, also in his 70s.

They live in Angelina's house. Arthur, who has very little property, has two children from a prior marriage whom Angelina does not particularly care for. As she plans her estate, Angelina realizes she wants to allow Arthur to remain in the house if she dies before he does, but doesn't want him to be able to rent out the house, or be able to sell it and buy another one. She discusses her concerns with him. He is bothered that she doesn't trust him fully. She explains frankly that her children, who are delighted she has married Arthur, are nevertheless concerned that his children might end up with what they see as their inheritance.

Angelina decides to leave much of her property outright to her children. She will create a trust for the house, and leave enough money in the trust to pay for mortgage and upkeep on the house, plus a little extra to supplement Arthur's Social Security and small pension. The trust will be managed by the most responsible of her children. Arthur will have the right to live in the house for the duration of his life and receive the income produced by the trust.

Arthur agrees with this arrangement but asks what happens if he gets ill and must be hospitalized? Will he be thrown out of the house? His concern prompts Angelina to realize that there are aspects of the trust to pin down. She doesn't want to allow the possibility that Arthur can be thrown out of the house if he's in the hospital for a week. But also, if he moves permanently to a nursing home, she prefers that the house then be turned over to her children rather than remain in trust until Arthur dies. She discusses her concerns with Arthur. He's understanding but concerned himself about becoming ill and having to leave the house for a while and then not being able to return to it.

After considerable discussion, Angelina and Arthur agree that he will retain the right to live in, or return to, the house if he's lived away from it for up to eight consecutive months. If he's been away from it for a longer period than that, the house will come under management by the trustee, who can rent it out. But the trustee cannot sell it or live in it or allow other children to live in it while Arthur lives. Any income from the rental is added to the trust income available for Arthur.

Since Angelina is leaving much of her property outright to her children, outside this trust, she feels it is fair for them to wait to inherit the house until Arthur's death. He's in his 70s after all. Anyway, she may well outlive him, and she'll certainly keep the house herself until her death. Angelina then sees a good estate planning lawyer to prepare the trust she wants. With the lawyer's aid, Angelina pins down precisely how the trust will work.

Long-Term Care for a Child With Special Needs

Parents of children with mental or physical disabilities may need to provide care and support for those children whether they are minors or adults. Providing this care usually requires preparation of a "special needs trust" that coordinates contributions to the trust with rules on government benefits. This type of trust is discussed further in Chapter 25. Also, it may well be that in their estate planning, parents, like it or not, may need to concentrate most of their resources for their child with special needs, leaving less for any other children.

EXAMPLE: **Working It Out.** The Balfour family has a 15-year-old child, Bob, who will need care all his life. They have two other children, both of whom are healthy. The Balfours' primary estate planning concern is doing all they can to arrange for Bob's care after they die. They realize this means leaving Bob most of their modest estate. They discuss this with their 19-year-old daughter, Rebecca, who says "that's fine." Their other son, Jeb, resents Bob a little and isn't so acquiescent. But the Balfours decide that protecting Bob remains their top priority. They hope that, as Jeb matures, he will understand the difficulties Bob faces and that his resentment that Bob got more than his share (as Jeb defines it) of parental attention will fade.

There are many questions the parents must resolve about Bob. Who will be responsible for Bob's personal care after they die? How can they best leave money for his use? How will any money they leave be treated when determining eligibility for government benefits? After all, it makes no sense to leave money to Bob if it means he will be ineligible for government help until it's all used up.

The Balfours must choose a personal guardian to be responsible for Bob until he becomes a legal adult at age 18, and a financial guardian or manager to supervise any money they leave for him, as long as he lives.

The Balfours discuss these concerns themselves and then broaden their discussion to include Rebecca and other family members and close friends they are considering for these two tasks. Eventually, they choose Mrs. Balfour's younger sister to be Bob's personal guardian if needed. They name their closest friend, William, to be Bob's financial manager until Rebecca turns 30. After that, she will become Bob's financial manager.

To understand how to dovetail money they leave Bob in trust with government benefits, the Balfours do some preliminary research. They decide to establish a special needs trust for Bob. They use Nolo's *Special Needs Trusts*, by Stephen Elias and Kevin Urbatsch, to prepare a trust that will maintain Bob's eligibility for government assistance programs while establishing a trustee (the property manager) to control trust property used for Bob's benefit.

Concerns of Unmarried Couples

In almost all states, unmarried couples have no right to inherit each other's property, unless each member of the couple makes a will or legally leaves property to the other. (Exception: In a handful of states, same-sex couples who have registered as domestic partners may have the same inheritance rights as married couples in those states.) A central concern of most unmarried couples is to be sure they inherit each other's property. Happily, unmarried people—whether lesbian, gay, or heterosexual—have the right to leave their property to whomever they want, as long as they're competent. (Even if one or both have been legally married in the past, they have no obligation to their ex-spouses, unless specific support is still required by the divorce decree.) In case of serious legal threat by hostile family members, a couple may take action to establish by clear proof that they were competent when they prepared their estate plan.

EXAMPLE 1: **Videotape Evidence.** Ernest and James have lived together for many years. Aside from a few small gifts to friends or family, each wants to leave all his property to the other after death. They're concerned with efficiency and economy, but above all they want to be sure that their estate plan can't be successfully attacked by several close relatives who have long been hostile to their lifestyle. Ernest and James each prepare a living trust leaving their property as they desire. They videotape their signing and the notarization of the living trust to provide additional proof that they were both mentally competent and not under duress or undue influence when they signed.

EXAMPLE 2: **The Down Payment.** Solveig and Guido have one daughter, Renée, who has lived with Charles for several years. Renée asks her parents for a $50,000 loan for a down payment on a house. Solveig and Guido are not wealthy, but they have sufficient savings to make the loan and they want to help their daughter. They do want the loan repaid (with interest) and they want to be sure they are protected in case their daughter dies; they like Charles, but they don't want him to inherit the house and leave them stuck on the loan. To ease their worries, Renée executes a promissory note to Solveig and Guido for $50,000, plus 6% yearly interest. She also writes a will, expressly leaving her parents the full amount due on the promissory note, including interest.

Worries About the Effect of Inheriting Money

Sometimes people worry that someone they want to leave money or property to cannot handle it. In other words, they fear their gifts will have destructive results: The beneficiaries may be too young or too immature to handle the inheritance responsibly. Resolving these concerns always requires a careful examination of both the strengths and weaknesses of the potential beneficiaries. Sometimes it also involves putting one's own worries and prejudices under as objective a personal microscope as possible.

EXAMPLE 1: The School of Hard Knocks. Ely is quite wealthy and worried about the effects of his wealth on his children and grandchildren. He grew up poor, worked hard all his life, and made a small fortune. Shouldn't his kids, now in their 20s and 30s and just making their way in the world, be encouraged to continue to work hard, at least until they're old enough to keep a large inheritance in perspective? If Ely dies soon, and each child inherits over $1 million, will they lose their incentive to strive for goals they might strive for otherwise? Ely is not the type to question whether losing the incentive to strive might be a good thing. He had it, he wants his kids to have it. Ely wonders if his best estate plan wouldn't be to say, "Being of sound mind, I spent all I could and

I give the rest to charity"? And what about his grandchildren? Should he give money only to those who join his business? (The fact that none of his children did still rankles.)

No matter how much Ely learns about the intricacies of tax planning and probate avoidance, he needs to do some serious thinking and reflecting on the subject of his money and his family before he can hope to make a sound estate plan. Or put another way, Ely needs to better understand the complicated nature of his own emotions and expectations pertaining to his money. Once over this hurdle, he should be better able to make up a plan to benefit his children and grandchildren.

For example, perhaps Ely will realize that his insistence on making it the hard way is a tad extreme. If so, he may leave (or even give) moderate amounts of property to his children outright to help them cope better with parenting their young children. Ely will leave the rest of his estate in trust for his children. Each child will receive a moderate amount of income for a number of years, only getting the bulk of the property at the age Ely has chosen. (For example, Joseph Kennedy, Sr., established trusts for each of his children that didn't release the trust property until that child became 50 years old.)

Ely decides he doesn't want to hire, or pressure, a grandchild into his business by promises of additional inheritance. Instead, he creates an education trust for each grandchild, leaving each $100,000 for college or other educational costs.

EXAMPLE 2: **The Grasshopper and the Ant.** Sylvia, a wealthy widow, has two children in their 30s: Yvonne, the sensible one, and Colleen, who's always been improvident and often more than a little self-destructive. Sylvia wants to leave her estate equally to her two daughters. She'll give Yvonne's half to her outright, but she's troubled by the thought of Colleen receiving several hundred thousand dollars. Sylvia decides it's sensible to leave Colleen her money in what's called a "spendthrift" trust, where a trustee, someone other than Colleen, controls the money (principal), and Colleen receives only the trust income. (See Chapter 25.) She can draw on the trust principal only if the trustee agrees she needs it for educational, medical, or other essential needs.

Sylvia still faces three important problems: First, who is to be trustee of the trust? Second, should she tell Colleen what she's decided upon? Third, when should the trust end? Sylvia discusses both questions with Yvonne, who convinces her mother that, for reasons having to do with sibling rivalry, she—Yvonne—shouldn't be the trustee. Sylvia reluctantly agrees that, given the personalities involved

and the fact that Colleen will hate not getting the money outright, it's sure to be personally destructive if one sister controls the other's inheritance. So, Sylvia decides to appoint her younger brother as trustee. She also decides the trust will end when Colleen becomes 45, at which point she will get all the money outright. She hopes Colleen will be fully responsible by then. Finally, she decides to tell Colleen her plan, although she's not joyously anticipating that discussion. She softens the blow by also telling Colleen that if, over the coming years, she decides Colleen has matured and can handle money, she will change her estate plan and leave Colleen her money outright.

Disinheriting People, Including Children

Some parents want to disinherit a child, or children. Other people want to ensure that certain relations or ex-friends get none of their property. Legally, there is no need to expressly disinherit friends or relatives other than your spouse or children— most people inherit nothing unless you expressly leave them some property. However, your spouse normally has rights to a certain percentage of your property. (See Chapter 3.) It is legal to disinherit a child, however, if you take affirmative steps to do so. (See Chapter 6.) But deciding to disinherit a child is often not easy to do, emotionally.

EXAMPLE 1: The Bad Seed. Zorba and Kyria have three children—two daughters and a son—and a substantial estate. They are very close to the two daughters, but bitterly on the outs with their son, Nikos. Zorba and Kyria had originally intended to leave most of their property to each other, with some to the two daughters they're close to. Then, when the surviving spouse dies, the remaining property would be divided between the two daughters. But they have second thoughts. Do they really want to cut their son out entirely? This feels too harsh, too rejecting. And if they do cut Nikos out entirely, are they creating any real risk that he will be able to invalidate their estate plan? Although their lawyer tells them that they can legally disinherit Nikos with little danger of him overturning their estate plan, they decide that both parental charity and prudence dictate a different decision. Each will leave Nikos $25,000 and include a "no-contest" clause in their wills. This clause states that any beneficiary who challenges a will gets nothing if the challenge is unsuccessful. The parents expect that Nikos will take the certain $50,000 he'll receive from both parents rather than the risk and the cost of a lawsuit he's almost sure to lose. Also, despite the bitterness they feel towards Nikos, both Zorba and Kyria are relieved that they haven't allowed it to cause them to completely disinherit one of their own children.

EXAMPLE 2: The Charity. Peter has two grown children, both very prosperous. Peter decides he wants to leave most of his estate to his favorite charity—a cause he deeply believes in—and the rest to his children. He hints at this to them. One child is supportive; the other is very upset, arguing that property should stay in the family. Peter decides to stick to his plan, accepting whatever disapproval or conflicts it will cause. In his living trust, he states expressly why he has decided that the bulk of his property is best given to the charity, and that even though he has done this, he loves his children deeply.

Communicating Your Decisions to Family and Friends

Many of the examples I've just discussed demonstrate my belief that communication can usually, though certainly not invariably, resolve potential estate planning difficulties with family and friends. Happily, in many families, talking about the older generation's estate planning isn't difficult. Both the parents and the children want the planning to be out in the open so there will be no surprises down the road. Of course, there are certainly families where raising the subject of the parents' (or grandparents') estate plan may bring up tension or touch on old conflicts—and others where the response will not be easy to predict. Only you can decide whether, when, and how to talk about your plans, but here are some questions that may help with your thinking process:

- Whom do you want to talk to? Obviously, you need to talk to anyone you are naming to have responsibility for your minor children or for supervising the distribution of your property after you die. But what about some, or all, of your beneficiaries?

- What should you talk about? Do you want to tell people what you've already decided and why, ask for advice, or state that, within reason, you're open to suggestions? Do you want to discuss the mechanics of how your estate plan will work with your inheritors? (You should, of course, discuss this with your executor and successor trustee.)

- Do you want to give your inheritors copies of your estate plan?

Talking, of course, is not a guarantee of clear sailing. There are occasions when someone doesn't want to hear or talk and others when communication only reveals a deep and unbridgeable gulf. And, from the older generation's point of view, there can be risks involved with communication: If they promise money to beneficiaries, they may feel guilty if a future medical necessity eats up some—or all—of that money. They may also worry that revealing their plans will expose undesirable qualities like greed and hard-heartedness in those promised to inherit.

From the younger generation's viewpoint, it can be very difficult to open up estate planning discussions with parents. You certainly don't want to force a parent to talk about his or her property or plan. At the same time, you may need or want the reassurance that sensible planning has been done. For instance, you'll probably want to be sure that your parents have arranged for someone to handle their medical and financial affairs if they become incapacitated. There are many decisions to be made concerning this matter alone: Whom will they appoint to serve in this role? How do they each feel about the use of life-prolonging medical procedures, should one of them develop a terminal condition? What happens if they can no longer live independently or if maintaining their home becomes too burdensome? Questions can go on here—and it's almost certain that painful subjects will arise when you ask your parents about their estate plan. I can suggest no magic formula that makes broaching the subject easy. All you can do is be tactful and genuinely concerned and see if that opens any doors.

I do think it makes sense for all parents to at least indicate that they have done their estate planning. If not, it's a good idea for communication to be initiated by a child, especially if that child knows or suspects a parent, or parents, have not taken care of even the basics. Saying this is easy, but of course, there can be many barriers to candor, such as:

- a general societal code that death is an unmentionable, especially with one's own parents
- fear that motives can be misunderstood (a parent may fear being seen as trying to manipulate a child by offering inherited money for demonstrations of love; a child, in turn, may fear that raising the subject will be seen as pushy or greedy), and
- the sense that honor lies in not caring about a parent's property or that of any other loved one.

Still, the results of talking openly are usually positive. For example, I know of a situation in which a child who had done very well financially asked her parents to leave a disproportionate share of their estate to the other children. The children's discussion provided the impetus for their parents to do estate planning they'd intended to do for years. They were quite relieved to finally have it accomplished. Even where there are less dramatic results, I feel that communication, particularly among family members, is a healthy process that can aid in preventing later conflicts.

Special Property Ownership Rules for Married People

If you are married, special property ownership laws in your state may affect your estate planning. These laws determine what you own individually and what you own as a member of a couple, and may also give your spouse a right to claim a share of your property after your death.

If you and your spouse plan to leave all, or the lion's share, of your property to each other, it's not of much practical importance to understand who legally owns each item of property. After all, as long as the survivor will get all or most of the property, it's not important how it's labeled. However, if you plan to make substantial gifts of property to someone other than your spouse (especially if your spouse might prefer that you didn't), it's essential that you understand both who owns the property and whether there are any rules in your state that give your spouse the right to at least a minimum portion of it at your death. Otherwise, your decision to give property to someone other than your spouse may occasion a nasty conflict after your death.

RESOURCE

Learn more about the legal rights of same-sex couples. Nolo publishes two books that provide information about the legal rights of same-sex couples: *A Legal Guide for Lesbian & Gay Couples* and *Making It Legal: A Guide to Same-Sex Marriage, Domestic Partnerships & Civil Unions*, both by Frederick Hertz and Emily Doskow.

Same-Sex Couples

Same-sex couples can marry in California, Connecticut, Delaware, the District of Columbia, Hawaii, Illinois, Iowa, Maine, Maryland, Massachusetts, Minnesota, New Hampshire, New Jersey, New Mexico, New York, Rhode Island, Vermont, and Washington. In these states, married same-sex couples have the same state rights and responsibilities as other married couples.

In Colorado, Nevada, Oregon, and Wisconsin, same-sex couples can obtain many of the property rights of married couples (but not the right to marry itself) by registering with the state. The official term for the registered couple varies by state—some use "domestic partnership," and some use "civil unions." The property rights of domestic partners vary by state.

State law rights of married same-sex couples are covered in depth in *Making It Legal: Same-Sex Marriage, Domestic Partnerships & Civil Unions*, by Frederick Hertz and Emily Doskow (Nolo).

What You Need to Know

In the United States, there are two major types of marital property law systems. A minority of states, mostly in the West, have "community property" law. (Louisiana, which has a form of community property originally from French law, isn't covered in this book.) The other states and the District of Columbia follow the common law system.

If You're Unsure of Your Marital Status

Most people are quite certain of their marital status. If you're not, here's what you need to know.

The divorce decree. You're not divorced until you have a final decree of divorce (or dissolution, as it's called in some states) issued by a state court in the United States or, under limited circumstances, by the legally empowered authorities of a foreign country. (See below.)

If you think you're divorced but never saw the final decree, contact the court clerk in the county where you think the divorce was granted. Give the clerk your name, your ex-spouse's name, and the date, as close as you know it, of the divorce.

Legal separation. Even if a court has declared you and your spouse legally separated, and you plan to divorce, you are still married until you get the divorce decree.

Foreign divorces. Divorces issued to U.S. citizens by courts in Mexico, the Dominican Republic, or another country may not be valid if challenged, especially if all the paperwork was handled by mail. In other words, if you or your spouse got a quickie foreign divorce, you may well be still married under the laws of your state. On the other hand, foreign divorces where both spouses were present in person or through a representative may be recognized as valid in the United States. If you think that someone might make a claim to some of your property after your death, based on the invalidity of a foreign divorce, see a lawyer.

Common law marriages. In a few states listed below, a couple can become legally married by living together, intending to be married, and clearly presenting themselves to the world as a married couple. Even in states that allow such common law marriages, most couples who live together don't have common law marriages. Folk law notwithstanding, no magic number of years of living together automatically establishes a common law marriage. If you really do have a valid common law marriage, you must go to court and get a divorce to end it—there's no such thing as a common law divorce.

Common law marriages may legally be created in these states: Alabama, Colorado, District of Columbia, Iowa, Kansas, Montana, New Hampshire (for inheritance only), Oklahoma, Rhode Island, South Carolina, Texas, and Utah.

Common law marriages may have also been created in the following states, if the marriage was created before the date in parentheses: Florida (1/1/1968), Georgia (1/1/1997), Idaho (1/1/1996), Indiana (1/1/1958), Michigan (1/1/1957), Minnesota (4/26/1941), Mississippi (4/5/1956), Nebraska (1963), Nevada (3/29/1943), New Jersey (12/1/1939), New York (4/28/1933), Ohio (10/10/1991), Pennsylvania (1/1/2005), and South Dakota (7/1/1959).

If you think that you may have a common law marriage, see an attorney for advice.

Community Property and Common Law States	
Community Property	**Common Law**
Alaska*	All other states
Arizona	and the District of
California	Columbia
Idaho	
Louisiana	
Nevada	
New Mexico	
Tennessee*	
Texas	
Washington	
Wisconsin (called "marital property")	

* If agreed to in writing by husband and wife

In community property states, spouses share ownership of most property, even if only one spouse's name is on the title slip or deed. In these states, each spouse is free to leave his or her half of the property as desired, but has no control over the other spouse's half.

In the common law states, the spouse whose name appears in the ownership document owns that property. However, unlike community property states, these states provide that each spouse has a legal right to claim at least a minimum portion of the other's property at death, even if the deceased spouse left it all to someone else.

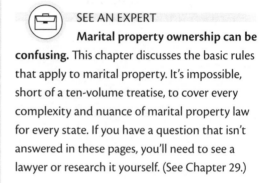

SEE AN EXPERT

Marital property ownership can be confusing. This chapter discusses the basic rules that apply to marital property. It's impossible, short of a ten-volume treatise, to cover every complexity and nuance of marital property law for every state. If you have a question that isn't answered in these pages, you'll need to see a lawyer or research it yourself. (See Chapter 29.)

If you think marital property laws could affect your situation, you need to know:
- which state is your "domicile," the legal term for where you permanently live.
  You can have only one domicile. The state of your domicile governs your marital property—except real estate in another state or country. If you have homes in two or more states, which you choose as your legal domicile can be important, both for property ownership and state inheritance tax purposes. Given a choice, it's usually best to opt for a state that imposes no, or low, property taxes.
- the property ownership laws of your home state, and of any other state or country where you own real estate. Real estate is controlled by the law of the state or country where it is located, no matter where you live.

Varying State Property Ownership Laws by Contract

If you and your spouse don't like the way state law defines your shared ownership of property, you can normally agree to change it at any time. To accomplish this, you and your spouse need to prepare a valid contract. If you make this kind of written agreement before marriage, setting out the terms by which your property shall be owned, it's called a "prenuptial agreement," or "prenup" for short. If you wait until after you're married, you'll make a "postnuptial agreement" or "postnup."

All contracts concerning marital property, including prenuptial contracts, must comply with your state's laws governing them. Generally, this means they must be in writing and both spouses must voluntarily agree to them after fair disclosure by both spouses of their property ownership and financial obligations. These agreements often explicitly cover inheritance and property ownership for estate planning purposes.

RESOURCE
Help with prenups.
To learn more about prenuptial agreements, including how to draft your own contract, see *Prenuptial Agreements: How to Write a Fair & Lasting Contract*, by Katherine E. Stoner and Shae Irving (Nolo).

CAUTION
Divorce means a new estate plan.
If you get divorced, reexamine your estate plan and bring it up to date. In most states, divorce automatically revokes gifts left to your former spouse in your will—but not in all states. Even in states where a divorce invalidates an earlier will's gifts to a divorced spouse, you still need to name a new beneficiary for that property. Also, in almost all states, divorce does not revoke a living trust, even if an ex-spouse benefits from it.

Resolving Conflicts Over Property Ownership

It's not crucial to define which spouse owns what property if you and your spouse plan to leave all or most of your property to each other, or in a way the other approves of. However, if you and your spouse discover any conflict over your property ownership that will significantly affect your estate planning, you need to deal with it.

It's best, of course, if you are able to resolve any disagreements between yourselves. If that doesn't work, you should consider getting professional help—from a mediator, lawyer, or therapist. If a mutually agreeable compromise isn't reached prior to death, there is real danger of a nasty court fight.

After resolving any problems, both spouses should sign an agreement setting forth their decisions.

SEE AN EXPERT

If you are unsure where you are domiciled. If you own two or more homes in the United States or live in both the United States and abroad, see a lawyer to discuss how this affects your estate planning. You must determine which state's or country's laws govern your marital property and what, if anything, you can do to change this if you so desire.

Marital Property in Community Property States

The basic rule of community property law is simple: During a marriage, all property earned or acquired by either spouse is owned in equal half shares by each spouse—except for property received as "separate property" by only one of them through gift or inheritance. This community property concept derives from the ancient marriage laws of some European peoples, including the Visigoths; these laws passed to Spain and then to many Western states through Spanish explorers and settlers. For estate planning purposes, there are no restrictions on how each spouse can leave his or her half of their community property. Neither is required to leave it to the surviving spouse, although, of course, many spouses do.

In community property states, separate property is property owned entirely by one spouse. Property owned by one spouse before a marriage remains separate property even after the marriage, as long as it's kept separate. Also, property one spouse is given or inherits is his or her separate property.

For many couples in long-term marriages, characterizing their property is relatively easy: It's all community property. Any property owned by either spouse before marriage is either long gone or so totally mixed with community property that it has long since lost its separate property status. Neither spouse has inherited or been given any substantial amount of separate property during the marriage, or if they have, it, too, has been mixed into the community pot. Still, even if you believe this to be your situation, read the next few pages to be sure.

What Is Community Property?

Unless a husband and wife agree to something different, the following is community property:

- **all income received by either spouse from employment or by other means (except by gift or inheritance to one spouse) during the marriage.** This generally refers only to the period when the couple is living together as husband and wife. From the time spouses permanently separate, most community property states consider newly acquired income and property as the separate property of the spouse receiving it.

At any time during the marriage, each spouse can arrange to keep his or her own income as separate property. All community property states allow spouses to treat income earned after marriage as separate property if they sign a written agreement to do so and then actually keep their income separate—for example, in separate bank accounts.

- **all property acquired with community property income during the marriage.** For example, if you are married and you use your salary (community property) to buy a car, that car is also community property, even if you take title to it in your name only.
- **all separate property that is transformed into community property under state law.** This transformation can occur in several ways, including when one spouse makes a gift of separate property to both of them. Generally, such a transfer must be done with a signed document.

EXAMPLE: Ned Terrlin owned a home for five years before he married Sally. He then signed a new deed for the house, listing the new owners as "Ned and Sally Terrlin, as community property." Ned has given one-half ownership of the house to Sally.

A common example of transformation of separate property is when it gets so mixed together with community property that it's no longer possible to tell the difference between the two. Lawyers call this "commingling."

EXAMPLE: When she got married, Felicity had a bank account with $85,000 in it, her separate property.

During her marriage, now in its 27th year, she maintained this account, depositing money she or her husband earned and making frequent withdrawals. No money in the account is separate property. The original $85,000 has long since been commingled with community property funds.

Community property can also be transformed into separate property by gifts between spouses. The rules for how to do this differ somewhat from state to state. Normally, if real estate is given, the gift must be in writing. And even for other property, the strong trend is to require that the gift must be made in writing.

What Is Separate Property?

The following property qualifies as separate property:

- all property owned by either spouse prior to marriage
- all property received by one spouse after marriage by gift or inheritance, and
- all property earned or accumulated by one spouse after permanent separation.

As mentioned, separate property stays that way so long as it is not:

- hopelessly mixed (commingled) with community property, or
- transferred in writing to shared ownership by the separate property owner.

Pensions

Generally, private pensions and military pensions are considered community property—at least the proportion of them attributable to earnings during the marriage. However, benefits from certain major federal pension programs, including Social Security and Railroad Retirement, aren't community property because federal law classifies them as the separate property of the employee.

Distinguishing Community and Separate Property

Most married couples have little difficulty determining what's community property and what is each one's separate property. However, these issues can get complicated. Divorce courts churn out a continual stream of decisions on the fine points of community versus separate property. Here are a few potential problem areas in estate planning.

Appreciated property. In most community property states, when the separate property of one spouse goes up in value, this appreciation is also separate property. However, sometimes one spouse owns separate property before a marriage, but both spouses contribute to the cost of maintaining or improving it during the marriage. The result can be that the property is part community, part separate. If the property substantially appreciates in value over the years, it can be difficult to determine what percentage of the current value of the property is separate property and what is community property.

A common example is a house that was originally owned by one spouse. Then for a length of time, say ten or 20 years, both spouses pay, from community funds, for mortgage, insurance, and upkeep. If the value of the house grew during the marriage, the couple can determine what portion of the present value is community property by agreeing in writing on any arrangement they decide is fair.

Businesses. If a family-owned business was owned by one spouse in whole or part before marriage and later grew, difficult ownership questions can arise. As with home ownership, the basic problem is to figure out what proportion (if any) of the increased value is community property. Again, a married couple can agree on any arrangement they want to. If both spouses work in the business, one sensible approach is to consider all the increase in value from the date of marriage as community property. However, if only the spouse who originally owned the business works in it, resolving ownership percentages can be more difficult. If it's likely the business would have grown in value anyway, much of the increase could reasonably be regarded as separate property.

Monetary recovery for personal injuries. As a general matter, personal injury awards or settlements are the separate property of the spouse receiving them, but not always. In some community property states, this money is treated one way (as community property) while the injured spouse is living and another way (as separate property) upon his or her death. Also, the determination as to whether it's separate or community property can vary when the injury is caused by the other spouse. In short, there's no easy way to characterize this type of property. If this issue concerns you, see a lawyer.

Income from separate property. Most community property states hold that income from separate property is also separate property. But a few states say that income from separate property is community property.

> **EXAMPLE:** Beth and Mike live in Idaho, where separate property income becomes community property. Beth inherits, as her separate property, a herd of 23 Angus cattle from her father. Those cattle go on to breed a herd of more than one hundred cattle. All the descendants of the original 23 animals are considered income from Beth's separate property, and therefore community property.

Inheritance Protection for Spouses in California, Idaho, Washington, and Wisconsin

In these four states—and in very limited circumstances—a surviving spouse may be entitled to inherit a portion of the deceased spouse's community or separate property. These laws are designed to prevent spouses from being either accidentally overlooked or deliberately deprived of their fair share of property.

To understand these rules, you need to know just a little bit about "quasi-community property." If you are married and acquire property in a common law state, and then move to California, Idaho, Washington, or Wisconsin, that property will be treated exactly like community property. This property is known as quasi-community property, except in Wisconsin, where it's called "deferred marital property."

Here's a brief summary of the rules that offer statutory protection for surviving spouses in community property states.

California. If the deceased spouse made an estate plan before marriage and didn't include the surviving spouse in a will or trust, the surviving spouse can claim one half of the deceased's community and quasi-community property. (Cal. Prob. Code §§ 21610 and following.)

Idaho. In some circumstances, if the deceased spouse gave away quasi-community property, or sold it for less than its value, the surviving spouse can demand that the property be returned to the deceased spouse's estate. The surviving spouse can then claim half of that property. (Idaho Code §§ 15-2-203 and following.)

Washington. If the deceased spouse transferred quasi-community property within three years of death to someone other than the surviving spouse, the survivor can, under certain conditions, claim a half interest in the property or in the proceeds from the sale of it. However, if the property was sold by the deceased spouse for a reasonable price, or with the consent of the surviving spouse, the surviving spouse cannot make a claim. (Wash. Rev. Code Ann. § 26.16.240.)

Wisconsin. Rather than take what the deceased spouse provided, the surviving spouse can elect to inherit up to one half of what's called the "augmented deferred marital property estate." This is the total value of the deferred marital property of both spouses, including gifts of deferred marital property made by the deceased spouse during the two years before death. (Wis. Stat. §§ 861.02 and following.)

 SEE AN EXPERT

Spousal protection laws are complicated. If you live in California, Idaho, Washington, or Wisconsin and you wish to learn more about these spousal protection laws, see an experienced estate planning lawyer. See Chapter 29 for tips on finding one.

Marital Property in Common Law States

Common law states protect spouses and keep them from being left out in the (property) cold when the other spouse dies. But they do it in a different way than community property states.

Who Owns What

In common law states, there's no rule that property acquired during a marriage is owned by both spouses. Common law principles are derived from English law, where in feudal times the husband owned all marital property; a wife had few

property ownership rights and couldn't even leave any property by will. Still today, in the common law states, the spouse who earns money or acquires property owns it separately and solely, unless, of course, he or she transfers it into shared ownership.

In common law states, the property you own for estate planning purposes, whether you are married or not, consists of:

- everything held separately in your name if it has a title slip, deed, or other legal ownership document (this always includes real estate, vehicles, securities and bank accounts, and your ownership interest in joint tenancy or other shared ownership property), and
- all other property you have purchased from your assets or income.

For example, if you earn or inherit money to buy a house, and title is taken in both your name and your spouse's, you both own it. But if your spouse earns the money to buy it, yet somehow title is placed in your name alone, you own it. Similarly, no matter who puts up funds to buy a house, if title is in your spouse's name, he or she owns it.

Despite the general rule stated here, these states have rules that prevent a spouse from disinheriting the other.

Family Protection in Common Law States

Common law states give a surviving spouse legal rights to claim a certain portion—usually one third to one half—of the other's estate.

Suppose, for example, that one spouse owns the family house, that the car and bank accounts are in his name alone and that he attempts to leave it all to a stranger (or worse, a lover). Can the stranger kick the surviving spouse out of the house, empty the bank accounts and so on? Of course, this rarely happens, but just in case, all common law property states prevent the surviving spouse from being completely, or even substantially, disinherited. While many of these protective laws are similar, they do differ in detail.

The methods that common law states use to protect families were developed hundreds of years ago by English courts, which were confronted with the same problem of a few people disinheriting their spouses. In response, they developed legal concepts called "dower" and "curtesy." Dower refers to the rights of a surviving wife; curtesy is the share received by a surviving husband. When the United States was settled, most states adopted these concepts. To this day, all common law states still retain some version of dower and curtesy, although many have dropped the old terminology and simply provide for "spousal inheritance rights" or something similar.

In most common law property states, a spouse is entitled to one third of the property left by the other. In a few, it's one half or some other standard.

Some states provide that all of the deceased spouse's property, including any that was transferred by means other than a will, is subject to the surviving spouse's claim. Other states take a different approach: They include not only all of the deceased spouse's property, but some or all of the separate property owned by the surviving spouse as well. (The total amount of property used to calculate the surviving spouse's share is called the "augmented estate.")

> **EXAMPLE:** Alice leaves her husband, Mike, $10,000, and her three daughters $90,000 each in her will. However, Alice also leaves real estate worth $500,000 to Mike by a living trust. The total Mike receives from this augmented estate, $510,000, is more than one half of Alice's total property, so he has nothing to gain by insisting on his right to make a claim against her will property.

A surviving spouse does not automatically inherit the share that's guaranteed by law; he or she must go to court and ask for it. So if a person leaves nothing to a spouse or leaves less than the spouse is entitled to under state law, the surviving spouse has a choice of either taking what the will or other transfer document provides, or rejecting the gift and instead claiming the minimum share allowed by state law. Taking the share permitted by law is called "taking against the will."

EXAMPLE: Leonard's will leaves $50,000 to his second wife, June, and leaves the rest of his property, totaling $400,000, to his two children from his first marriage. June can take the $50,000 or elect to take against the will and receive her statutory share of Leonard's estate. Depending on the state, this will equal about one third to one half of Leonard's total estate.

When a spouse decides to take against the will, the property that is taken must come out of what was left to others. In other words, somebody else is going to get less. In the above example, the children will receive much less than Leonard intended. So, if you don't provide your spouse with at least the statutory share under your state's laws, your gifts to others may be seriously reduced.

Family Allowances

Most states provide additional, relatively minor protections for spouses and children. These vary from state to state in too much detail to discuss here. Generally, however, these devices attempt to ensure that your spouse and children are not left out in the cold after your death, by giving them temporary protection, such as the right to remain in the family home for a short period or living expenses while your estate is being settled.

 SEE AN EXPERT
If you want to leave your spouse less than one half of your estate, see a lawyer. Put bluntly, if you want to leave your spouse little or nothing, and you haven't gotten your spouse's unforced and written consent to your plan, your estate may be heading for a legal mess. See a lawyer.

Moving to a Different State

A will or living trust valid in one state is, broadly speaking, valid in all. However, problems can develop when married people move from a community property state to a common law property state or vice versa. This is because the property each spouse owns (and is therefore free to leave or give away) may change. If spouses move from one state to another that follows the same property ownership system—for example, New York to Florida, or California to Texas—there is no need to worry about new marital property ownership rules.

Remember, technical property ownership rules are not a worry if spouses plan to leave all or most of their property to each other, or in a way the other spouse approves of.

Moving From a Common Law State to a Community Property State

What happens when a husband and wife acquire property in a common law state but then move to a community property state? California, Idaho, Washington, and Wisconsin (community property states) treat the earlier acquired property as if it had been acquired in a community property state. The legal jargon for this type of property is quasi-community property, except in Wisconsin, where it's called deferred marital property. Thus, if you and your spouse moved from any common law state into California, Idaho, Washington, or Wisconsin, all of your property is treated according to community property rules.

The other community property states don't recognize the quasi-community property concept for estate planning purposes and instead enforce the rules of the state where the property was acquired. So if you moved into any of the other community property states from a common law state, you'll need to assess your property according to the rules of the state where you used to live.

Moving From a Community Property State to a Common Law Property State

When spouses move from a community property state to a common law state, each generally retains a one-half interest in the property accumulated during marriage while living in the community property state. However, the courts have not been entirely consistent in dealing with the problem in situations where the property is in one spouse's name.

SEE AN EXPERT

Spousal disagreements. If you have moved from a community property state to a common law state and you and your spouse have any disagreement or confusion as to who owns what, check with a lawyer. See Chapter 29 for tips on finding a good one.

Inventorying Your Property

Preparing a thorough written inventory of your property is a good idea for thorough estate planning. It helps you:

- remind yourself of what you own
- determine what you owe
- estimate the current net value of your estate as an aid to estate tax planning
- pin down any shared ownership of property
- make a handy list to refer to when leaving gifts to beneficiaries in a will or living trust, and
- have your assets organized in case you later consult an estate planning lawyer.

That said, it's still up to you to decide whether you want to itemize your property in detail or simply estimate its overall worth. For some people, as much precision as possible is an important part of the process—we wouldn't dare say fun—of planning their estate. For others, giving the subject just enough thought to arrive at a decent ballpark estimate suffices. For example:

- If you want to leave all your property to one person, perhaps your spouse, or to your spouse for his lifetime use and then equally to your children, there is far less need to itemize all major items of property than if you wanted to leave separate gifts to a good-sized list of people.
- If you are confident that your net estate is worth less than the federal estate tax threshold, and is likely to remain so, there's no reason to estimate the value of your estate for tax purposes. (See "Federal Estate Tax Exemptions" in Chapter 15.)

EXAMPLE: Jane wants to leave all of her woodworking tools and equipment to her friend Alice, her car to her friend Amy, and everything else she owns (stocks, jewelry, money market funds, and personal and household possessions) to her longtime companion Mary. She knows her estate is worth no more than $400,000 (well under the federal estate tax threshold), that the state she lives in imposes no estate taxes, and that she has no significant debts. Jane decides there's no need for her to list separately each item of property, because with two easy-to-remember exceptions, she's leaving it all to Mary.

One caveat here. If you're a member of a couple and plan to leave most or all of your property outright to the other member, and your combined estates exceed the estate tax threshold, estate taxes will probably be assessed when the second spouse dies. So you may want to do some tax planning. (See Chapter 15 and Chapter 18.)

Instructions for the Property Inventory Worksheet

At the end of this chapter, there is a worksheet to help you inventory your property. As you'll see, you can record a wide range of property. Take a minute to get acquainted with its structure.

The following detailed description of the worksheet and the suggestions for completing it are for those who want or need to be thorough. It's up to you to decide how extensive and detailed your own listings need to be—or if you don't want to use the chart at all.

You May Be Worth More Than You Think

I've been surprised to learn that some people who have worked hard for years, and live a frugal life, find it difficult to admit that their assets could be worth more—sometimes substantially more—than the federal estate tax threshold.

This can occur with owners of appreciated real estate or a successful small business. When asked how much a residence or business is worth, the owner may think in terms of what was paid for it, plus a relatively small markup. I've seen situations where this estimate was hundreds of thousands of dollars off the mark. Or a person who has become so accustomed to the family furniture and paintings, may not consider the possibility that the heirlooms are now much-sought-after antiques or valuable art.

Section I: What You Own

In Section I of the chart, you list your assets—all the property you own. You can list four types of information for each item of property:

Column 1: a description of the item of property

Column 2: whether ownership of that item is shared and the type of shared ownership

Column 3: the percentage of any shared ownership property you own, and

Column 4: the net value of each item of property (or share of it) you own.

Now let's take a minute to review the information that should be entered in each column.

Column 1: Identify and Describe Your Property

Here you identify your property with sufficient detail so there can be no question what it includes. If you include any assets in an individual retirement program, such as an IRA or 401(k), take into account that you may spend some or all of these funds before your death. This worksheet divides your property into four groups:

Liquid assets. These include cash, savings, checking, and money market accounts, mutual fund shares, readily tradable stocks and securities, bonds, and certificates of deposit.

EXAMPLES:

- Certificate of Deposit #10235, Lighthouse Savings and Loan Association, Ventura, CA
- My savings account #18-17411 at Bay Bank
- 50 shares Transpacific Corporation common stock

Other personal property. This includes all your property except liquid assets, business interests, and real estate. This catchall category includes retirement accounts, automobiles, jewelry, furs, precious metals, artwork, antiques, tools, life insurance, collectibles, and so forth.

EXAMPLES:

- $10,000 El Dorado Drainage and Water System, District of Alameda, 1995 Bond Series C, 5% due June 1, 2015
- My IRA #442301299 at Wells Fargo Bank, Santa Barbara, CA
- 2005 Ford Mustang, Michigan license #123456
- All my fishing equipment
- Gold earrings with the small rubies in them purchased from Charles Shreve and Co. in 1981
- Daumier print captioned "Les beaux jours de la vie"
- Life insurance policy #A106004, You-Bet-Your-Life Insurance Co.
- All my carpenter's tools, including my power saws

If you are like most people, you have all sorts of minor personal possessions you don't want to bother itemizing. To deal with these, you can group a number of items in one category: "all my tools," "all my dolls," "my baseball cards," "my records, machines and equipment," "household furniture"—whatever. Of course, some items without large monetary value may have great emotional worth to you and your family: a photo album, an old music box, a treasured chair. List these individually as you desire.

As another alternative, you can conclude your list with one catchall item such as "all my other personal possessions and furnishings."

Frequent Flyer Miles

You may be able to leave frequent flyer miles as part of your estate. Some major U.S. airlines allow you to leave your accumulated miles in your will. Check with the airline's frequent flyer department to see if they allow this (there goes a couple of hours waiting on hold). If they do allow it, are any limitations imposed? For example, can you leave your miles to any beneficiary, or are your options limited? If you can leave your miles, it's a good idea to specifically state that you leave your frequent flyer miles with that airline to the beneficiary.

Business personal property. This includes all business interests, except any real estate used in that business.

EXAMPLES:

- My shares of stock in the Mo-To Corporation
- My business, dba Ace Stationery Store, Boca Raton, Florida
- My partnership interest in JTL Partnership Enterprises, Main Office, Detroit, Michigan
- My membership interest in the Gaelic Basketball Lounge Limited Liability Company
- All my copyrights and rights to royalties in the books with the following titles, currently published by Acme Press, Berkeley, California (titles listed)
- All my rights in U.S. Patent No. 2,230,240: three-way mirror and portable traffic light

SEE AN EXPERT

Special estate planning issues for intellectual property. Copyrights and patents are commonly known as "intellectual property." Unique estate planning problems can arise when dealing with this kind of property. Some issues are managerial: Will the beneficiary or beneficiaries be able to manage the asset? For instance, not everyone has the savvy to know how to market copyrighted materials, or develop a patent industrially. If your beneficiaries don't have the knowledge to make smart commercial use of intellectual property, you may be able to put a plan in place to help them. Another issue can be determining the value of intellectual property, especially for estate tax purposes. Sometimes it makes sense to give away

intellectual property while you live. Usually, it is tax wise to give a patent, but not a copyright. Because of these kinds of complexities, it's prudent to see a lawyer if your estate includes valuable intellectual property.

Real estate. This includes all business real estate, and all houses, co-ops or condominiums, mobile homes attached to land, and undeveloped or agricultural land. (The rules on when an attached mobile home becomes "real estate" vary from state to state. If this matters to you, see a lawyer.)

To describe real estate, simply list its address or location. This is normally the street address. If there's no post office address, as with undeveloped land, simply describe the real property in normal language like this: "my 120 acres in Lincoln County near the town of Douglas." You don't need to use the legal description from the deed.

EXAMPLES:

- 126 Oceanview Terrace, Mendocino, California
- My lot on Keeler Street, Middletown, Ohio
- 1001 Main Street (the Fullerton Hardware Building), Moose, New York

CAUTION

Contaminated property. If you own real estate that may be contaminated by any hazardous substances, you could be handing your inheritors a huge headache if you leave them that land. Under federal law, "responsible parties" are liable for the costs of cleaning up contaminated land. Responsible parties include past and current owners of the real estate, whether or not they caused the contamination, or even knew about it when they acquired the land. Federal and state laws contain a long list of contaminants, including petroleum products, dry cleaning solutions, and many other toxins.

Liability for contaminated land cannot be discharged in probate or through any other procedure transferring property to a beneficiary. This liability goes against the land itself and its current owner, period. So, to help your beneficiaries, as well as to be a law-abiding citizen, have an expert check out the condition of any land you own that may be contaminated, and then do what you must to rectify the damage.

Real property often contains items that are properly classified as personal property. For instance, farms are often sold with tools and animals. If you intend to keep both together (as one gift), indicate what this "together" consists of. It's best to specify the large-ticket items (tractor, cattle) and refer generally to the rest of the items as "personal property."

EXAMPLES:
- My 240-acre truck farm in Whitman County with all tools, animals, machines, and other personal property located there
- My fishing cabin on the Wild River in Maine with all the fishing gear, furniture, tools, and other personal property that are found there

- My ownership of the mobile home located at E-Z motor camp, and all possessions and furnishings contained in it.

Keeping Good Records

After taking inventory of your property, you might want to take the next step and get better organized for your family. *Get It Together: Organize Your Records So Your Family Won't Have To*, by Melanie Cullen and Shae Irving (Nolo), allows you to organize all your records and important paperwork for yourself and your survivors. You can document important information about everything from estate planning documents to tax records, financial records, government benefits, and much more. The book provides a comprehensive planner that you can readily update if your situation changes.

Column 2: Type of Shared Ownership

You need to be concerned with Columns 2 and 3 only if you own property with someone else. If you are single and own all your property outright, you can simply skip to the instructions for Column 4. However, if you are married or have entered into personal or business shared ownership transactions, please read what follows carefully. Before you can sensibly plan your estate, you must clearly understand what you own and therefore have the power to leave.

Your Digital Legacy

When you're thinking about making a plan for your property, don't forget to consider your digital legacy—that is, all of your accounts, blogs, social networking identities, and digital files that will be left online when you die. Although you can't leave most of these items through your will, you may still want to consider their fate. Here are some things to think about:

- Do you want someone to have access to your email accounts?
- What do you want done with your Facebook profile?
- Do you want someone to make final entries on your blog?
- Do you want any of your online communities to be notified of your death?
- Would you like someone to download any photos that you store online?
- What do you want done with your domain names?

If you have ideas about what should happen with your digital legacy after you die, you can leave instructions for your loved ones. For example, you might want to ask someone to archive the data from your blog, transfer your domain names to your children, or close your seller's accounts on websites like Amazon or eBay.

If you want your survivors to be able to log into your accounts as users, include log-in names and passwords with your instructions. If you choose not to leave log-in information, your estate representative may still be able to get limited access to your account. However, every company has its own guidelines and limitations about this, so getting access this way is bound to be a hassle.

You can write your instructions and log-in information in a letter; see "Explanatory Letters Accompanying Your Will" in Chapter 7. Store the letter with your other estate planning documents. Your wishes won't be legally binding, but your survivors will thank you for helping them wrap up the details of your life.

You probably know whether you own property with others. However, you may have to do some investigating to be sure about just how you and the other owners hold title to the property. Never guess. If you're not sure how you own an item of property, take the time to find out. For example, you may have to locate the deed to your house or your stock ownership records to clarify if you and your spouse own them in joint tenancy. You can check real estate records at the county property recorder's office.

If you are married, live in a community property state, and you and your spouse own both separate and community property, you may have some difficulty determining exactly what you and your spouse own. (I discuss this in Chapter 3.) For example, if you are unsure whether a $23,000 bank account is community property or your separate property, bear in mind that you and your spouse can resolve the confusion by jointly characterizing this account in either ownership category. To do this legally, however, it's important to put your conclusion in writing, signed by both of you.

Below I give you a summary of the different types of shared ownership. Some of these concepts may be new to you. If, after reading what follows, you don't understand exactly what a particular form of shared ownership means, you needn't worry. They are explained in more depth in later chapters. Simply note on your worksheet that the property is held in some form of shared ownership and

complete the "Shared Ownership" column later.

Here are the major types of shared ownership and the symbols you can use to record them:

- **Joint tenancy (JT).** Property held with a written ownership document identifying the owners either as "joint tenants" or "joint tenants with right of survivorship." Under these forms of ownership, each joint tenant owns an equal share of the property. The share of the first tenant to die must go to the survivors, even if there's a will or living trust to the contrary. (Joint tenancy is discussed in detail in Chapter 10.)

  Joint tenancy must be created by a written document. If you own property using the phrase joint tenants with right of survivorship, there is no question what type of shared ownership you have. But what about writings that are less clear? For example, suppose your real estate deed says "tenancy in common with right of survivorship"? In Oregon, this has the same practical effect as joint tenancy; in some other states, it surely doesn't. The point is—don't guess. If you're not clear what kind of legal animal you've got, check it out by doing your own research or checking with a lawyer knowledgeable about real estate law.

  Similarly, what if owners are listed simply with an "and" or an "or"? For example, two people may own real estate with the title listed as held by

"Smith and Jones." Or they may own real estate with title listed as "Smith or Jones." Is either of these joint tenancy? The answer is that it depends on the state in which the property is located. Under most states' laws, neither title by itself constitutes joint tenancy. If you hold ownership with another person with "and" or "or" in the title document, you need to know the specific rules of your state.

- **Tenancy by the entirety (TE).** A form of ownership, limited to married couples and recognized in a number of common law states. It is almost identical to joint tenancy and creates a right of survivorship between spouses. It must be created in writing. (See Chapter 10.)

- **Community property (CP).** In community property states (listed in Chapter 3), any property spouses earn or acquire during a marriage. Even if only one spouse's name is on the title document, if the property was bought with money earned during the marriage, it's community property. There are a few separate property exceptions, discussed below.

  Don't overlook the fact that you and your spouse may own partnership interests, corporate shares, or an interest in a tenancy in common that is also community property.

  You can leave your one-half share of community property to anybody you wish. Since the other one half of the community property belongs to your spouse, you obviously have no power to leave it by your will or living trust.

- **Community property with right of survivorship (CP/S).** A form of community property whereby the surviving spouse automatically inherits the property when the other spouse dies— in other words, community property that functions like joint tenancy property. This is available in Alaska, Arizona, California, Nevada, Texas, and Wisconsin.

- **Separate property (SP).** In community property states, all property that isn't community property but is held separately. Property that is given to or inherited by one spouse is his or her separate property. Likewise, property owned by each spouse prior to marriage remains separate property, if it's kept distinct from community property.

  In the common law states, separate property means all property that each spouse owns individually, including all property with one spouse's name on the title document, unless there is a written contract to the contrary.

- **Partnership (P).** Property owned by business partners, regulated by a partnership agreement (including shares in a limited partnership). Partnership agreements often contain detailed rules as to what happens to a partner's share at death.

- **Corporate shares (CS).** Shares of a small or closely held corporation (only a few owners) that may be freely transferable at death. However, your freedom to transfer them may also be regulated by corporate bylaws or a separate shareholders' agreement.

- **Limited liability company (LLC).** A type of business ownership allowing owners the advantages of both the corporate and partnership forms. An LLC must be established by formal documents under state law. Your ability to transfer your ownership interest in an LLC is most likely governed by the LLC's operating agreement.

- **Tenancy in common (TIC).** Any property held in shared ownership that isn't in another type of ownership—in other words, all shared property not owned in joint tenancy, tenancy by the entirety, community property, partnership, corporation, or LLC. Tenancy in common in common law property states may include considerable property spouses own together. You can own any percentage of tenancy in common property (0.005%, 95%, and so on)—owners' shares don't have to be equal, as they must be for joint tenancy property. If the ownership deed doesn't specify the type of shared ownership, it's probably tenancy in common, although, as mentioned above, in some states the word "or" may indicate joint tenancy ownership.

Unlike joint tenancy, where there is an automatic right of survivorship for joint tenants, you can leave your portion of property held as tenants in common as you choose, unless restricted by a contract.

EXAMPLE: Natalie and Jeremy Engels live in North Carolina, a common law property state. They hold several securities, their house, and a piece of land with both their names on the title documents, but no joint tenancy designation. They are presumed to own the property as tenants in common, with each owning a 50% share.

Column 3: Percentage of Shared Property You Own

In this column, list the percentage of each item of shared property you own. People who own property as tenants in common, or in a partnership or corporation, should be particularly careful—you can own any percentage of the property. Especially with a partnership, you must check your partnership agreement to be sure. With a tenancy in common, co-owners normally own equal shares (33.3% if you are one of three), unless there is a written agreement to the contrary.

TIP
Know your right to transfer. If you own an interest in a partnership, an LLC, or a small corporation, check your operating agreement or corporate documents to see if there are any restrictions on your rights to transfer your interest at death. Often, other business owners have an option to purchase your interest or shares. (See Chapter 28.)

Column 4: Current Net Value of Your Ownership

In this column, estimate the "net value" of each item listed. Net value means your equity in your share of the property. Equity is the market value of your share, less your share of any debts on it, such as a mortgage on a house, or the loan amount due on a car.

Making estimates normally doesn't require that you burden yourself seeking exact figures or expert appraisals. After all, the value of your estate will surely change some by the time you die. Here you need only ballpark figures. For example, if you have a reasonable grasp of market prices, and you believe that the net worth of your interest in your house, after you subtract the mortgage, is about $200,000, your car $5,000, and your stamp collection $35,000 if you put an ad in a philatelist's journal, use those numbers. Only with more complex types of property, in particular business interests, may you need expert help.

EXAMPLE 1: Clay owns a house with a market value of $550,000 as a tenant in common with his sister Ava; each owns half. Clay computes the net value of his share by first subtracting the amount of mortgages, deeds of trust, and liens from the market value, to arrive at the total equity in the property:

Market value:	$ 550,000
Owed on mortgage:	310,000
Lien against the property:	10,000
Total equity ($550,000 minus $320,000):	230,000
Net worth of Clay's (one-half) share:	$ 115,000

EXAMPLE 2: Stacey is sole owner of the Maltese Falcon Restaurant, a successful business she has run for 23 years. She has only a vague notion of its market value since she has never been interested in selling it. To competently plan her estate, she needs a reasonable estimate of the worth of the business. This can be difficult to make, particularly since the market value of her restaurant includes the intangible value of having an excellent reputation. Stacey talks to an accountant to help her arrive at a sensible estimate of the worth of the restaurant.

The last step in Section I of the Property Worksheet is to add up the net value of all your assets and list that sum in Part E.

Section II: What You Owe

In Section II, Liabilities, list any liabilities—debts—you haven't already taken into account in Section I. For example, in Section II, list any significant personal debts—the $10,000 loan from a friend or $5,000 unsecured advance on a line of credit. Also list all other liabilities, such as tax liens or court judgments. Remember, you have taken account of mortgages on your real estate and payments owed on your motor vehicle in Section I, so don't list them here.

Add up your estimate of all your liabilities and list that sum in Part D of Section II.

Section III: Your Net Worth

Finally, in Section III of the chart, estimate your current net worth. To get this figure, simply subtract your total liabilities listed in Section II from your total assets listed in Section I.

Your Property Worksheet

Remember, this chart is purely for your convenience. It can be as messy or as neat as you care to make it. Also, pencil is recommended (unless you're the type who does *The New York Times* crossword puzzle in ink).

Property Worksheet

Column 1	Column 2	Column 3	Column 4
	Type of Shared	Percentage	Net Value of
Description of Your Property	Ownership	You Own	Your Ownership

I. Assets

A. Liquid Assets

1. Cash

_____ _____ _____ _____
_____ _____ _____ _____
_____ _____ _____ _____
_____ _____ _____ _____

2. Savings accounts

_____ _____ _____ _____
_____ _____ _____ _____
_____ _____ _____ _____
_____ _____ _____ _____
_____ _____ _____ _____

3. Checking accounts

_____ _____ _____ _____
_____ _____ _____ _____
_____ _____ _____ _____
_____ _____ _____ _____

4. Money market accounts

_____ _____ _____ _____
_____ _____ _____ _____
_____ _____ _____ _____
_____ _____ _____ _____
_____ _____ _____ _____
_____ _____ _____ _____
_____ _____ _____ _____

Property Worksheet (continued)

Column 1 **Description of Your Property**	Column 2 **Type of Shared Ownership**	Column 3 **Percentage You Own**	Column 4 **Net Value of Your Ownership**
5. Certificates of deposit			
6. Mutual funds			
7. Tradable stocks and securities			
8. Government bonds			

Property Worksheet (continued)

Column 1	Column 2	Column 3	Column 4
	Type of Shared	Percentage	Net Value of
Description of Your Property	Ownership	You Own	Your Ownership

B. Other Personal Property (all your property except liquid assets, business interests, and real estate: houses, buildings, apartments, etc.)

1. Automobiles and other vehicles, including planes, boats, and recreational vehicles

___	___	___	___
___	___	___	___
___	___	___	___
___	___	___	___
___	___	___	___

2. Cameras, computers, and other electronic equipment

___	___	___	___
___	___	___	___
___	___	___	___
___	___	___	___

3. Precious metals

___	___	___	___
___	___	___	___
___	___	___	___

4. Household goods

___	___	___	___
___	___	___	___
___	___	___	___
___	___	___	___
___	___	___	___
___	___	___	___

Property Worksheet (continued)

Column 1 **Description of Your Property**	Column 2 **Type of Shared Ownership**	Column 3 **Percentage You Own**	Column 4 **Net Value of Your Ownership**
5. Clothing			
_____	_____	_____	_____
_____	_____	_____	_____
_____	_____	_____	_____
_____	_____	_____	_____
_____	_____	_____	_____
_____	_____	_____	_____
_____	_____	_____	_____
_____	_____	_____	_____
6. Jewelry and furs			
_____	_____	_____	_____
_____	_____	_____	_____
_____	_____	_____	_____
_____	_____	_____	_____
_____	_____	_____	_____
7. Artworks, collectibles, and antiques			
_____	_____	_____	_____
_____	_____	_____	_____
_____	_____	_____	_____
_____	_____	_____	_____
_____	_____	_____	_____
8. Tools and equipment			
_____	_____	_____	_____
_____	_____	_____	_____
_____	_____	_____	_____
_____	_____	_____	_____
_____	_____	_____	_____

Property Worksheet (continued)

Column 1 Description of Your Property	Column 2 Type of Shared Ownership	Column 3 Percentage You Own	Column 4 Net Value of Your Ownership
9. Valuable livestock/animals			
10. Money owed you (personal loans, etc.)			
11. Vested interest in profit sharing plans, stock options, etc.			
12. Limited partnerships			

Property Worksheet (continued)

Column 1 Description of Your Property	Column 2 Type of Shared Ownership	Column 3 Percentage You Own	Column 4 Net Value of Your Ownership
13. Vested interest in retirement plans, IRAs, death benefits, annuities			
___	___	___	___
___	___	___	___
___	___	___	___
___	___	___	___
14. Life insurance			
___	___	___	___
___	___	___	___
___	___	___	___
___	___	___	___
15. Frequent flyer miles (list airlines)			
___	___	___	___
___	___	___	___
___	___	___	___
___	___	___	___
___	___	___	___
16. Miscellaneous (any personal property not listed above)			
___	___	___	___
___	___	___	___
___	___	___	___
___	___	___	___
___	___	___	___
___	___	___	___
___	___	___	___
___	___	___	___

Property Worksheet (continued)

Column 1 Description of Your Property	Column 2 Type of Shared Ownership	Column 3 Percentage You Own	Column 4 Net Value of Your Ownership

C. Business Personal Property

1. Patents, copyrights, trademarks, and royalties

2. Business ownerships (closely held stock, stock options, partnerships, sole proprietorships, limited liability companies, corporations, etc.; list separately and use a separate sheet of paper if you need to elaborate)

Name and type of business

3. Miscellaneous receivables (mortgages, deeds of trust, or promissory notes held by you; any rents due from income property owned by you; and payments due for professional or personal services or property sold by you that are not fully paid by the purchaser)

Property Worksheet (continued)

Column 1 Description of Your Property	Column 2 Type of Shared Ownership	Column 3 Percentage You Own	Column 4 Net Value of Your Ownership
D. Real Estate			
Address _____ _____ _____	_____	_____	_____
Address _____ _____ _____	_____	_____	_____
Address _____ _____ _____	_____	_____	_____
Address _____ _____ _____	_____	_____	_____
Address _____ _____ _____	_____	_____	_____
Address _____ _____ _____	_____	_____	_____
E. Total Net Value of All Your Assets			$_____

Property Worksheet (continued)

Column 1

To Whom Debt is Owed

Column 2
Amount of Debt
You Owe

II. Liabilities (what you owe)

Many of your liabilities will already be accounted for because you listed the net value of your property in Part I of this chart. For example, to determine the net value of your interest in real estate, you deducted the amount of all mortgages and encumbrances on that real estate. Similarly, the value of a small business is the value after business debts and other obligations are subtracted. For this reason, the only liabilities you need to list here are those not previously covered. Don't bother with the small stuff—such as the phone bill, or what you owe on your credit card this month—which changes frequently. Just list all major liabilities not previously accounted for, so you can get a clearer picture of your net worth.

A. Personal Property Debts

1. Personal loans (banks, major credit cards, etc.)

_____ _____

_____ _____

_____ _____

_____ _____

_____ _____

_____ _____

2. Other personal debts

_____ _____

_____ _____

_____ _____

_____ _____

_____ _____

B. Taxes (include only taxes past and currently due; do not include taxes due in the future or estimated estate taxes)

_____ _____

_____ _____

_____ _____

Property Worksheet (continued)

Column 1

Column 2
Amount of Debt

To Whom Debt is Owed

You Owe

C. Any Other Liabilities (legal judgments, accrued child support, etc.)

_____ _____

_____ _____

_____ _____

_____ _____

_____ _____

D. Total Liabilities (excluding those liabilities already
deducted in Section I)   _____

III. Your Net Worth

Total Net Value of All Your Assets (Section I.E)   _____

Minus Total Liabilities (Section II.D)   _____

Net Worth   _____

Your Beneficiaries

Deciding which people or organizations you want to receive your property—who will be your beneficiaries—is obviously a main focus of your estate plan. This chapter raises some important concerns about choosing and naming beneficiaries. Even if you are sure who should receive your property and are tempted to skip ahead, I urge you to read at least the first half of this chapter, which covers important information everyone should take into account. Read the rest only if the subjects concern you.

If you already know who your major beneficiaries will be, you may want to write down their names when you start actually preparing your estate planning documents but for now, that's not necessary.

Types of Beneficiaries

The word "beneficiaries" means people or institutions you leave property to. There are different types of beneficiaries; the major types discussed in this book are:

- **Primary beneficiaries.** Those you leave identified gifts of property to.
- **Alternate beneficiaries.** Those named to receive a gift if the primary beneficiary can't receive it.
- **Life estate beneficiaries.** People who receive what's called a "life estate" interest in property, which means they have some rights to receive income from or use of the property during their life, but they never become legal owners of the property. Life estate

Some Thoughts About Gift Giving

What is a gift? That question can be more complex, and interesting, than you might think at first.

In our predominantly commercial culture, gifts, whether they are made during life or at death, are special. They are free, voluntary transfers of property, made without any requirement of receiving anything in return. The essence of gift giving is generosity, an open spirit. To say one makes gifts "with strings attached" is not a compliment.

Much of the satisfaction of estate planning comes from contemplating the positive effects your gifts will have on those you love. Sometimes, this satisfaction is quite focused—you know how much Judith has always liked your mahogany table, and now she'll get to enjoy it. Others are more general—your son can buy a house with the money you leave him, which you hope will relieve some of the financial and emotional pressures that have been weighing on him.

I mention the spirit of giving here because we've learned that it's easy to get entrapped by the details of estate planning and lose sight of your real purpose. So, if technicalities and legalities start to get to you, take a break and remember to whom you're giving your property and why.

If you wish to explore in profound depth what gift giving is, or can mean, read Lewis Hyde's *The Gift* (Vintage/Random House), a brilliant exploration of how gifts work in many cultures.

beneficiaries have no right to give away this property when they die.

- **Final beneficiaries.** Those named to inherit property after a life beneficiary for it dies.
- **Residuary beneficiaries.** Those named to receive property left under a will or trust that is not expressly left to other beneficiaries. Usually, an alternate residuary beneficiary is also named.

Primary Beneficiaries

Primary beneficiaries are usually named to receive a specific item of property. For example, a will might state: "I leave my car to my sister Joanne Corbett." Some people name many primary beneficiaries for different items. And some name none at all, simply leaving all their property to their residuary beneficiaries.

Simple Beneficiary Situations

If you know you want to leave all your property to one or a few people—say your spouse or children—you still may face some additional complexities. Do you want to name an alternate beneficiary, in case the person you've originally named dies before you do? Suppose you want to name two or more alternate beneficiaries. What happens if they wind up receiving your property? Does each one receive an equal share? If they inherit real estate, must it be sold unless all agree to keep it? In sum, even with a seemingly very simple

beneficiary situation, you'll almost always need to go further than just naming one person to receive all you've got.

Naming Beneficiaries in Your Estate Planning Documents Doesn't Require a Lawyer

If you are considering preparing your estate planning documents yourself, don't be put off by fears you must hire a lawyer, or use tricky legalese, to identify beneficiaries. You can safely name them in simple, plain English, using the names by which your beneficiaries are normally known.

Even if a beneficiary later changes his or her last name, that's no reason for you to revise your will or trust. For example, if a daughter later marries or divorces and decides to change her last name, you don't need to change her name as listed in your living trust or will. She, and others concerned, will know that you meant to name her.

Minors as Primary Beneficiaries

Estate planning issues concerning children are discussed in Chapter 6. Here, I briefly summarize the options available if you're considering leaving property to a minor child.

Minor children can own only a small amount of property outright in their own names. This amount, which is set by state law, varies from about $2,500 to $5,000.

Any property belonging to a minor above this amount must be legally controlled and supervised by an adult. So if you are contemplating leaving a substantial gift to a minor, you should choose an adult to be responsible for it. Your basic options are:

- Leave a gift to the other parent, who will use it for the children's benefit. If the parents get along and trust one another to manage money well, this is usually the simplest way to handle the matter.
- Leave the gift to the child, and name an adult to be responsible for supervising it. That adult can be one of the child's parents, but doesn't always have to be. When you have decided who the adult supervisor will be, your next step is to decide what legal form you want to use to make the gift. These issues are covered in Chapter 6.

Forgiving Debts

One form of gift is to forgive a debt, essentially leaving a gift to your debtor. Any debt, written or oral, can be forgiven.

> **EXAMPLE:** Bud loaned his daughter Kathlyn and son-in-law Tyrone $50,000 for a down payment on a house, but doesn't want them to be obligated to repay his estate after he dies. So, in his will, Bud includes a provision stating "I forgive the loan of $50,000 I made to Kathlyn and Tyrone Benson in 2006."

If you're married and forgiving a debt, be sure you have full power to do so. If the debt was incurred while you were married, you may only have the right to forgive half the debt (especially in community property states) unless your spouse agrees in writing to allow you to forgive his or her share of the debt as well.

Restrictions on Beneficiaries

There are two possible types of restrictions on gifts to beneficiaries:

- restrictions you, the giver, want to impose, and
- restrictions imposed by law.

Personal Restrictions

Most people simply leave their property outright to family, friends, or charities. However, sometimes a person wants to make a gift with restrictions or conditions on it, something like "if such and such happens, then the gift shall go to...." Sometimes, this is called "dead-hand control." The obvious risk is that circumstances are almost sure to change, so you must try to anticipate what is likely—or even possible—to occur in the future and provide for it. For instance, suppose you left a gift "to John, if he quits smoking." Who could ever tell if John fully quit smoking? He can't be watched around the clock each day. And how long is "quit"? These kinds of restrictions on gifts are probably unenforceable.

Sometimes, people think that imposing restrictions can be a simple matter of writing a couple of sentences when they name a beneficiary. For instance, some readers have wondered how to "write in a provision" to protect a beneficiary who has a disability, or to place limits on a heavy spender. The unfortunate truth is that to impose controls or restrictions on a gift, you need to create an irrevocable trust, which is a complicated matter that may require a lawyer. (See Chapter 25 for a discussion of creating trusts to control property after you die.)

 SEE AN EXPERT

Restrictions. If you're determined to place restrictions on a gift, see a lawyer. See Chapter 29 for tips on how to find a good one.

Legal Restrictions

With very few limits, you can leave your property to anyone you choose. While the few existing legal restrictions on beneficiaries rarely apply, let's be cautious and review them briefly:

- Some felons and anyone who unlawfully caused the death of the person who wrote the will (or living trust) cannot inherit under it.
- You cannot attempt to encourage or restrain some types of conduct of your beneficiaries. For example, you cannot make a gift contingent on the recipient's marriage, divorce, or change of religion.
- You cannot validly leave money for an illegal purpose—for example, to establish the Institute to Encourage Minors to Smoke.

Gifts to Caregivers in California

If you live in California and want to leave a substantial gift to any nonrelative who helps you with personal or health care, see a lawyer first. You can leave such a gift—but first you may need to have a lawyer sign a statement, verifying that you're acting freely and aren't being unduly influenced.

If you don't, the gift could be void— meaning the intended recipient won't get it. That's because of a California law that aims to thwart caregivers who take advantage of people who depend on them. Because of the law's broad terms, it could invalidate perfectly reasonable gifts that you really want to make. For example, a gift to a new neighbor who brings meals and helps you pay bills could be voided, as could a gift to a paid live-in caregiver who has become a good friend.

The law might come into play if you're 65 or older and you want to leave a gift of more than $3,000 (or less if your entire estate will be worth less than $150,000) to:

- a nonrelative you pay to help you, or
- a nonrelative who helps you without pay, if you've just recently struck up the relationship.

If you think you might be affected, see a lawyer who handles family or elder care matters and get a statement, called a "certificate of independent review," which states that you are freely making the gift.

Pets as Beneficiaries

Legally, pets are property (though many pet owners would, of course, disagree). This means that you can't leave money or property to them. Any money you try to leave directly to a pet would go, instead, to your residuary beneficiary. But that doesn't mean you can't ensure that your pets will have a good home and good care after your death.

Usually, the easiest thing to do is to arrange with a friend or family member to care for your pet. Then, in your will or living trust, you leave your pet to that person, along with some money to cover the expenses of your pet's feeding and care.

If you prefer to make more formal arrangements, most states allow you to establish a trust for your pet. The trust is a legally independent entity, managed by a trustee you name. You define the terms of the trust—including how your pet is to be cared for—in the trust document. Pet trusts can be desirable for people who feel they'd prefer not to leave their pet (and money for pet care) outright to someone. But creating a pet trust is more costly and complicated than simply leaving your pet outright.

SEE AN EXPERT

You'll need an attorney to prepare a pet trust. You can't prepare a pet trust on your own. You'll need to check with an attorney or do your own legal research, to learn whether you can validly use a pet trust in your state. If you can and want to do so, you should hire a lawyer to draft the document. (See Chapter 29.)

These issues are discussed in more detail in *Every Dog's Legal Guide*, by Mary Randolph (Nolo).

Life Estate Beneficiaries and Final Beneficiaries

A life estate beneficiary receives only a limited interest in property. This interest ends when the beneficiary dies. The person who originally left the life estate property names another beneficiary or beneficiaries, usually called the "final beneficiaries," to inherit the property outright when the life beneficiary dies.

> **EXAMPLE:** Mac leaves his brother Sam a life estate interest in Mac's house. Mac names his daughter Gay as the final beneficiary. Mac dies. Sam inherits the life estate interest in the house. (If Mac outlived Sam, the life estate interest would never take effect.) For the remainder of his life, Sam can live in the house, or rent it, but never becomes the legal owner. When Sam dies, the house will go outright to Gay.

Life estates are usually created by a trust. The rights of the life estate beneficiary and the final beneficiaries must be carefully defined in the trust document. Life estate trusts are generally used for imposing controls over property.

For example, someone in a second marriage may want to leave her spouse a life estate interest in property, with that property then going to her children from a prior marriage when the spouse dies. (See Chapter 24.) Or a parent may want to leave property to a child with a disability in a long-term managerial trust. (See Chapter 25.)

Alternate Beneficiaries

Most people name alternate beneficiaries to inherit property if their first choices die before they do. This is especially appropriate if you leave some gifts to older people or people in poor health. Also, you simply might not have the time, or inclination, before your own death, to revise your estate plan if a beneficiary dies before you.

On the other hand, this is one of the many estate planning issues where there are no absolutes. Some people decide they don't want the morbid bother of worrying about their beneficiaries dying before they do. Often, they leave their property to people considerably younger than they are—for example, their children. If a beneficiary dies before they do, they'll probably be able to modify their will, trust, or other document to name a new beneficiary. If they don't, the property will go to their residuary beneficiary (see below), who might, anyway, be the same person they would name as their alternate.

There can be alternate alternates, and indeed, as many layers of alternates as you care to create. Creating a second, third,

or more layers of alternates can get quite complicated. There are many "ifs" to work out—"If Joe dies and if Jane dies and if Jack and Jill die ..." then what? Resolving how to clearly draft a will or trust with many layers of alternates usually requires the assistance of a lawyer.

Residuary Beneficiaries

Whatever you decide about alternate beneficiaries, you should definitely name a residuary beneficiary or beneficiaries in your will, and in your living trust if you use one. A residuary beneficiary receives all property left under a document that isn't received by other beneficiaries, either because no beneficiary was named to get the property, or they didn't survive to inherit it. Your residuary beneficiary is your backup, to be sure your property goes to someone you've chosen.

If you prepare a living trust, the residuary beneficiary you name there receives only any remaining trust property not received by other beneficiaries. The residuary beneficiary you name in your will receives all property not left to other beneficiaries by any other method.

> EXAMPLE: Esther receives a surprise inheritance of $23,000 three weeks before she dies. She did not revise her will or living trust to leave this money to a primary beneficiary. The money is inherited by the residuary beneficiary of Esther's will.

A residuary beneficiary doesn't have to serve solely as a backup. Some people leave all of their property to their residuary. Others leave most to the residuary, naming only a few primary beneficiaries for modest gifts.

It's wise, and standard, to name an alternate residuary beneficiary so you have another backup in case your residuary beneficiary dies before you.

Gifts Shared by More Than One Beneficiary

Sometimes people want to leave shared gifts, particularly to their children. A shared gift is one left to two or more beneficiaries; each receives a portion of ownership of the property. This is different from leaving property with directions that it be sold and the profits divided between beneficiaries. With a shared gift, all the beneficiaries own the property itself.

> **EXAMPLE:** Virginia leaves her house to her three children—Alan, Patsy, and Philip—in equal shares. Each owns an undivided one-third interest in the house.

If you're considering leaving a shared gift, you should resolve some important questions first. What percentage of owner-ship does each beneficiary receive? You should spell out the percentages in your will or trust. If you don't, it's generally presumed that you intended equal shares, but this rule isn't ironclad. There's no good reason to be silent on this matter. If you want a gift shared equally, say so.

The next issue is control of the property. Generally, the beneficiaries must agree how to handle their shared ownership. They may all want to keep the property, or decide to sell it and split the proceeds. But if the beneficiaries can't agree how to use the property, they may end up in court. In most states, any co-owner can go to court and force a sale, with the net proceeds divided by percentage of ownership.

Informing Your Beneficiaries

Once you've made your estate plan, do you want to tell some or all of your beneficiaries that you've left them property? Do you want to tell them what you've left them? There is no law requiring you to tell your beneficiaries anything. Indeed, if you choose, you can arrange for a dramatic, or melodramatic, reading of your will after your death, just as you've seen in bad movies. At the least, you may sensibly decide there are good personal reasons, such as potential family conflict, for you not to reveal how you're leaving your property. But if there's little or no risk of trouble, why keep your gifts a secret? By informing your beneficiaries of what they'll receive, you can enjoy the pleasures that sharing that knowledge can bring.

If you don't think the beneficiaries can resolve any problems that arise, a shared gift is a bad idea. There's little you can do to forestall serious conflicts. You could try, by putting rules governing what the shared owners can do in your will or trust. For instance, you could specify that "The house cannot be sold unless all three of my children agree to the sale." But often other problems follow. If two kids want to sell the house, but one doesn't, who manages the house? Must it be rented at market value? Can the child who wants to keep the house live in it? If so, must that child pay the others rent? And what happens if one child dies? The difficulties of dealing with these types of complications mean it is rarely sensible to try to impose long-term control on shared gifts.

The final issue to consider is what happens if a beneficiary of a shared gift predeceases you. Here things can become quite complicated. To return once more to the house Virginia wants to leave to her three children, what are her options if she wants to name alternate beneficiaries?

- She can specify that a deceased beneficiary's share is to be divided between her surviving children.
- She can name three separate alternate beneficiaries, one for each child—for example, each of their spouses.
- She can provide that a deceased child's share is to be divided equally between that beneficiary's own children, or, if there are none, between her surviving children.
- She can name another alternate beneficiary (a friend or another

relative) to receive the interest of any child who dies before she does.

Juggling and resolving these types of contingencies can get confusing, especially if you want two or more layers of alternate beneficiaries. Still, many people want to work out having alternates for shared gifts, which, of course, is fine. If pinning down how it will work gets too tricky, see a lawyer—or consider making your alternate beneficiary plan for shared gifts less complicated.

Establishing a Survivorship Period

A survivorship period requires that a beneficiary must survive you by a specified time period to inherit. The purpose of a survivorship period is to ensure that if the beneficiary dies soon after you do, the property will go to the alternate you've selected, rather than to the people the beneficiary chose to inherit his or her property.

Survivorship periods are commonly used in wills. Since probate takes months, you're not tying up your property by imposing a short survivorship period—45 to 60 days is common.

Using the same reasoning, establishing a survivorship period of more than a few weeks isn't usually desirable for property transferred by living trust, since a principal advantage of a living trust is that property can be transferred quickly to the new owners. (See Chapter 9.) There's no sense in setting up a living trust to allow quick transfer of property and then frustrating that result by requiring beneficiaries to wait many months to inherit.

Explanations and Commentary Accompanying Gifts

If you wish, you can provide a brief commentary when leaving a gift in a will or a living trust.

> **EXAMPLE:** "I leave $40,000 to my business associate, Mildred Parker, who worked honestly and competently with me over the years, and cheerfully put up with my sporadic depressions and weirdnesses."

There are times, particularly in family situations, when an explanation of the reasons for your gifts can help avoid hurt feelings or family fights.

> **EXAMPLE:** "I leave my house at 465 Merchant St., Miami, Florida, and all stocks and bonds I own as follows:
> - 40% to my son Theodore Stein
> - 40% to my daughter Sandra Stein Smith, and
> - 20% to my son Howard Stein.
> I love all my children deeply and equally. I leave 20% to Howard because he received substantial family funds to go through medical school, so it's fair that my other two children receive more of my property now."

Another approach is to write a letter stating your views and feelings, and attach the letter to your will or living trust. If you have a lot to say, a letter is a better way to go than trying to include it all in your will or living trust. Including lengthy personal explanations in legal documents can render those documents confusing. Further, a will becomes a matter of public record and so would your comments. If you don't want to expose your sentiments to anyone who chooses to look at a probate court file, a letter protects your privacy.

Your letter isn't officially a part of a legal document, and has no legal effect. It is prudent for you to state in your letter that you understand this, to eliminate any possibility someone could claim you intended the letter to somehow modify the terms of your legal documents.

RESOURCE
WillMaker can help you write your letter. If you need a little help writing your letter, the "Letter to Survivors" in Quicken WillMaker Plus can help you get started. It prompts you for a range of information that you might want to write about—you include as little or as much as you want. To learn more about WillMaker, go to www.nolo.com.

Short of libel, the scope of your remarks is limited only by your imagination. Some writers have expressed, at length and in their own chosen words, their love for a mate, children, and friend. By contrast, Benjamin Franklin left his son William, who was sympathetic to England during our Revolution, only some land in Nova Scotia. Franklin's will stated, "The fact he acted against me in the late war, which is of public notoriety, will account for my leaving him no more of an estate than he endeavored to deprive me of." And the German poet Heine wrote a will leaving his property to his wife on the condition that she remarry, so that "there will be at least one man to regret my death." William Shakespeare cryptically left his wife his "second best bed," a bequest that has intrigued scholars for centuries.

Disinheritance

You can disinherit most people simply by not leaving them property. Indeed, "disinheritance" isn't the apt word, since no one except your wife (in common law states) and children (in some situations) have any legal claim on your property.

Disinheriting a Spouse

If you live in one of the 41 common law states or the District of Columbia, you cannot disinherit your spouse. These states allow a spouse to claim a significant portion of your estate despite your wishes, although many states do allow a spouse to waive these rights in a written marital property agreement.

By contrast, in community property states, a spouse has no legal rights to inherit any of the other spouse's property. Or, put another way, each spouse has the right to leave his or her one half of the community property and all his or her separate property as he or she sees fit.

Unmarried Couples

Unmarried couples living together have no statutory rights to inherit any of each other's property, except lesbian or gay couples registered as domestic partners in Colorado, Illinois, Nevada, New Jersey, Oregon, or Wisconsin. However, in any state, each member of an unmarried couple can leave his or her separate property to anyone he or she wants to, which of course can include the other person.

Disinheriting a Child

The rules for disinheriting a minor child are discussed in detail in Chapter 6. Here I briefly summarize them.

In all states, you have the power to disinherit any or all of your children, if you do so expressly. However, if you fail to mention a child in your will, that child may have a legal right to claim part of your property. Some states' laws protect only children born after the will was written. Other states protect any child not mentioned in the will.

The goal of these laws is to prevent children from being unintentionally over-looked. You don't have to leave your children property as primary beneficiaries. The point is to establish that you considered each child when leaving property. Many spouses validly leave all their property to the other spouse, naming their children as alternate beneficiaries. This shows that the children weren't overlooked.

If you want to disinherit a child, you must state that explicitly in your will. There is no legal requirement that you state a reason, but you can if you wish.

No-Contest Clauses

A "no-contest clause" in a will or living trust is a device used to discourage beneficiaries of your estate plan from suing to void the plan and claiming they are entitled to more than you left them. Under a no-contest clause, a beneficiary who unsuccessfully challenges a will or living trust forfeits all his or her inheritance under that document.

Leaving People a Minimal Amount

You may have heard that some lawyers recommend leaving a minimal amount, usually one dollar, to certain close relations. This is not legally necessary and is a bad idea. Doing so burdens your executor with trying to track down these beneficiaries, and then getting them to sign a receipt for one dollar. And all this when they had no rights to any of your property to begin with.

No-contest clauses might be sensible if there's a risk that a beneficiary might challenge your will or living trust, claiming that you were incompetent or unduly influenced. The risk of losing all property left to a beneficiary may by itself deter a potential challenger from suing.

In most situations, a no-contest clause isn't necessary, since there is no reasonable risk of lawsuit by a beneficiary. Also, you don't have to be "fair" when distributing your property. Absent fraud, duress, or mental incompetence, you can leave it however you want to, with the exceptions for your spouse or children noted above.

SEE AN EXPERT

Thwarting fights over your will or living trust. See a lawyer if you fear that a beneficiary or would-be beneficiary might contest your will or living trust. There may be a number of things you can do to establish that you are competent to make your estate plan and to protect your estate from lawsuits, or at least increase the odds that your side will prevail. You can ask your lawyer about including a no-contest clause in your will or trust. However, traditionally, courts have interpreted no-contest clauses strictly and narrowly—so they don't always work as intended. In several states, including California, laws impose restrictions on the scope of no-contest clauses.

Simultaneous Death

Many couples, married or not, who leave their property to each other wonder what would happen to the property if they were to die at the same time. (Another common concern—what happens to children if both parents die simultaneously—is discussed in Chapter 6.) Imposing a survivorship period on beneficiaries—who include a spouse—takes care of this issue.

> **EXAMPLE:** Hermancia's and Ed's wills leave their property to each other. Each one's will imposes a 45-day survivorship period on all beneficiaries. Hermancia names their daughter Raquel as her alternate beneficiary. Ed names Raquel and his brother Malachy as his co-alternate beneficiaries, each to receive 50%.
>
> Hermancia dies. Ed dies 25 days after she does. Because Ed did not survive 45 days after Hermancia, he never became owner of her property. It goes directly to Raquel. Malachy does not inherit any of the property originally owned by Hermancia. (He does, of course, inherit half the property owned by Ed.)

If no survivorship period is imposed and you and your spouse die almost simultaneously, your property could pass to your spouse, and then immediately to your spouse's inheritors. That might not be the result you want. To eliminate this possibility, you can use a "simultaneous death" clause, which provides that when it's difficult or impossible to tell which spouse died first, the property of each spouse is disposed of as if he or she had survived the other.

How, you may ask, can simultaneous death clauses logically work? How can you be presumed to have outlived your spouse for your will's purposes and she also be presumed to have outlived you for her will's purpose? Yes, it is a logical paradox, but in the real world it works. Under the law, each estate is handled independently of the other. Each spouse's will is read as if the other spouse's will didn't exist. This allows both spouses to achieve the results each wants in the event of simultaneous death. As Oliver Wendell Holmes put it, "The life of the law has not been logic: it has been experience."

Property You Give Away by Will or Trust That You No Longer Own at Your Death

Before your estate can pay any cash gifts you leave, it must pay all your last debts and taxes, including estate taxes. After that, if your estate doesn't have enough money available to pay your cash gifts, there's trouble. This necessitates what's called an "abatement" in legalese. An abatement means a reduction of gifts when there isn't enough to go around. Specific provisions in your will governing how a shortfall of cash is to be handled will be enforced; otherwise, the matter is normally resolved by your executor.

There's an obvious way to avoid this sort of nasty postdeath mess—don't leave more cash than you're confident you'll have. And if your cash resources drop below this amount, revise your cash gifts.

Children

When you're working on your estate plan, the word "children" can have two meanings. The first is "minors"—people who are not yet 18. The second meaning is offspring of any age; parents who live long enough can have children who are in their 40s, 50s, or older. This chapter focuses primarily on minor children because of the special problems inherent in planning for them. It also discusses ways to leave property to a young adult child when you're concerned that the child may not be sufficiently mature to handle money responsibly.

Most parents of minor children are understandably concerned about what will happen to their children if disaster strikes and the parents die unexpectedly. If both parents are raising the children, the major concern is usually simultaneous death of the parents. If you're a single parent and the other parent is deceased, has abandoned the child, or is unavailable for some other reason, you'll want to arrange for someone else to care for, and quite possibly, help and support the child if you die while the child is a minor.

Providing for your minor children if you die involves two distinct concerns:

- Who will raise the children if you can't—that is, who will be each child's personal guardian?
- How can you best provide financial support for your children? What money or property will be available?

Who will handle and supervise it for the child's benefit? And what legal method is best for managing it?

These concerns are addressed in depth in this chapter.

You don't need to appoint a personal guardian for adult children, nor is a property guardian legally required. However, you may not want to allow your children to receive substantial amounts of property outright while they're still in their 20s or even early 30s. This chapter explains how you can impose mature adult supervision over gifts you leave to young adult children.

Finally, if you want to disinherit a child—not common, but it does happen—this chapter covers special rules you must follow.

Revise Your Estate Plan When a Child Is Born or Dies

If, after preparing your estate plan, you have an additional child, revise your plan by providing for the new child. If you don't, that child has a legal right to inherit a percentage of your property state law whether you want that or not. You should also, of course, make sure that all property left to a deceased child is redirected to other beneficiaries.

Naming Someone to Take Custody of Your Minor Children

If two legal (biological or adoptive) parents are willing and able to care for a minor child, and one dies, normally the other has the legal right to assume sole custody. If the parents are married, or even if they are divorced, as long as both parents are cooperating to raise their child, this rule presents no problem. But what happens if both parents die? Or a sole parent dies?

If no legal parent is available, some other adult must be legally responsible for raising the child. This adult is called the child's "personal guardian." No personal guardian is required if the child is "emancipated," which means the child has achieved the legal status of an adult; normal grounds for emancipation are marriage, military service, or factual independence validated by court order.

Use a will to name your child's personal guardian. Except in a couple of states, you cannot use a living trust or any other document for this purpose. If you have minor children, this is an obvious reason why a will is essential.

It's important to understand that the person you name as a minor's personal guardian in a will doesn't actually become the legal guardian until approved by a court after your death. The judge has the authority to name someone else if the judge is convinced it is in the best interests of the child. In short, children

are not property, and naming a personal guardian in a will doesn't have the same automatically binding effect as a provision leaving a lamp to someone. However, if no one contests your choice for your child's personal guardian, a court will almost certainly confirm this person. In practice, a court will reject an unopposed nominee only if there are obvious grave and provable reasons, such as alcoholism, a serious criminal background, or provable child abuse. I presume that as a responsible parent you wouldn't select a guardian with such problems.

Choosing the Personal Guardian

You may well know who your child's personal guardian should be. But this isn't always an easy decision. I know people who've struggled hard to decide who is their best choice. Keep in mind the obvious: You can't draft someone to parent your kids. Be sure any person you plan to name is ready, willing, and able to do the job.

You should always name an alternate personal guardian as well, in case your first choice is unable or unwilling to serve.

Where two parents are involved in raising their kids, they should agree on the person that they want to appoint— naming different people could result in a nasty conflict if both parents died simultaneously.

In some situations, you may want to name different guardians for different children. Naming different personal guardians for different children is certainly

Naming a Couple as Coguardians

In many cases, it's a poor idea to name more than one person to serve as guardian for your children. Naming multiple guardians raises the possibility that they may disagree about the best way to raise a child, resulting in conflict and perhaps even requiring court intervention. However, there is one situation in which naming two guardians makes good sense: when you want to name a couple to care for your children together.

If you know a couple—for example, your sister and her husband—who are willing and able to take good care of your children, it's fine to name them both. The couple will act as your children's surrogate parents. Both of them will be allowed to do things for your children that require legal authority, such as picking up your children from school, authorizing field trips, or taking them to the doctor.

Keep in mind, however, that if you name a couple as guardians, they must be able to

agree on what's best for your children. Any severe difference of opinion between them could require court intervention—and this would be difficult for the couple and upsetting to your kids. Also, if you name a couple that parts ways while you are still alive, you should revise your will to name one or the other to care for your children or to choose a different couple to act as guardians.

The main point is that you must choose carefully when naming a couple as personal guardians for your children. Select a couple that can make joint decisions without conflict, has a unified parenting style, and is likely to stay together a long time. If you have any reservations about the longevity of the couple's relationship or any concerns about either person's parenting style, you may be better off just naming one of them—for example, name just your sister. If you like, you can explain the reasons for your choice in your will or in a separate letter.

legal. A court would likely follow this arrangement, unless there's persuasive proof that it would be harmful to a child.

EXAMPLE: Irene is a single parent with two sons, aged 14 and 15, from her first marriage, and a daughter, Bo, age four, from her second. Her first husband has never taken any interest in the children. Her second ex is a decent, though from Irene's view, well below superb, father to Bo, and

has also tried to be a decent father to the boys. Irene's brother, Biff, is close to her sons, and she and they feel he would be the best personal guardian for them. But Biff isn't wild about raising a young child. Also, Irene recognizes that if she named Biff as guardian of Bo, and she died while Bo was a minor, the result would probably be a court fight with Bo's father, who would likely prevail. So Irene names her second ex as personal guardian of Bo, and Biff as guardian of her boys. She attaches a statement to her will explaining why she believes this is best for the children.

Choosing a personal guardian does not automatically mean you're also selecting that person to manage any money you leave for your children. If you're worried that the person you name as personal guardian isn't good with money, you can name someone else for the latter job. There are obvious risks of conflict in having one person have legal authority to raise a child and another to manage money used to support and educate the child. If you decide to divide authority between two people, be sure that both people you want to name are willing to accept their roles. If the two potential guardians genuinely accept this arrangement, your major problem is solved.

If You Don't Want the Other Parent to Become Personal Guardian

A parent raising a child may not want the other parent to get custody, for any of a number of reasons. Here are a couple of examples:

- I don't want my ex-husband, who I believe is dangerously mentally unstable, to get custody of my children if I die. How can I prevent him from becoming personal guardian?

- I have legal custody of my daughter and I've remarried. My wife is a far better mother to my daughter than my ex-wife, who mostly ignores her and is occasionally mean to her. What can I do to try to make sure my present wife gets custody if I die?

There is no definitive answer to these types of questions. Assuming a contested case was presented to a court, a judge's decision would very likely turn on both the facts of each situation and the judge's own beliefs. A general rule is that one parent cannot succeed in appointing someone other than the other legal parent to be personal guardian, unless the second legal parent:

- has legally abandoned the child, or
- is unfit as a parent.

If the other parent seeks custody after your death, it's usually quite difficult to prove that the parent is unfit, absent serious problems, such as alcohol abuse, a history of child molestation or violence, or mental illness. Your negative opinion of the other parent is never enough, by itself, to prevent custody. If you want to name someone other than the other parent as personal guardian for your children, be sure that person knows that this may lead to a custody fight.

It's unlikely that anyone except the child's other parent would win custody against your wishes. For instance, if you name your best friend Betty to raise your children if you can't and Betty can be proved to be a caring adult, it's unlikely that someone else, such as the child's grandmother or uncle could gain custody over your choice.

It can be a good idea to attach a letter to your will explaining your choice for personal guardian. Here's an example of such a letter:

Sample Letter Explaining Your Choice for Guardian

I have nominated my partner, Peter N., to be the personal guardian of my daughter, Melissa, because I know he would be the best guardian for her. For the past six years, Peter has functioned as Melissa's parent, living with me and her, helping to provide and care for her, and loving her. She loves him and regards him as her father. She hardly knows her actual father, Tom D. She has not seen him for four years. He has rarely contributed to her support or taken any interest in her.

Date: January 15, 20xx

Signed by: *Juanita R.*

It is also possible to explain your choice of guardian in your will.

SEE AN EXPERT

Potential custody fights. If you don't want the other legal parent to gain custody, it's wise to discuss the details of your situation with a lawyer who specializes in family law. If there's a disputed custody proceeding after your death, a judge has wide discretion in deciding how much weight, if any, to give to a written statement about your child's custody that you make before you die. A good lawyer should help guide you to prepare the most persuasive case you can. This might include preparing your best statement of why the other parent shouldn't get custody, and identifying people who will back up your statement by their court testimony, if necessary. See Chapter 29 for tips on finding and working with a lawyer.

If You Name Your Same-Sex Partner as Guardian

If you coparent your children with a same-sex partner, you probably want to nominate your partner as the personal guardian of your children. The likelihood of the nomination being respected will depend on where you live and what the legal relationship is between you and your partner and between your partner and your children.

If your children have another legal parent, perhaps from a prior relationship, the court will choose that parent over your partner unless you provide a good reason not to. (See previous section.)

If you live in any of the states that recognize same-sex marriage, domestic partnership, or civil unions, and your children were born after you and your partner entered into a legal relationship under the laws of that state, then you and your partner are both legal parents under state law, and there's no reason a court in your state wouldn't respect your partner's legal right to continue parenting your children after your death, with or without a nomination in your will. (Of course, you should always make the nomination and explain your reasons for it, as discussed below.)

It's likely that courts in other states would also respect the legal relationship between your partner and the children, but it's not quite as secure. For this reason, many attorneys recommend that even if you are married, registered, or have entered into a civil union, you still use an adoption to secure the legal relationship between a nonbiological parent and a child born to that parent's partner. An adoption decree may be more acceptable to another state than a legal relationship based solely on your state's law, which may not be recognized in other states.

If you live in a state that doesn't offer any legal relationship for same-sex couples, then the court will make the final decision about who will care for your children. The court will consider your choice for personal guardian, but it may not understand or fully respect your relationship with your partner. For these reasons, take advantage of the opportunity to fully explain to the court why you named your partner to care for your children. You might say, for example, "I name my life partner, Ruth Williams, as the personal guardian for our son, Matthew Price, because we conceived and raised him together and she is his only other parent." Or, "I name my husband, Richard Bennett, as personal guardian for

our daughter, Jane Bennett-Hines, because he is her other legal parent, as recognized by the state of California."

RESOURCE

Learn more about same-sex families. For a detailed discussion of parenting issues for same-sex couples, see *A Legal Guide for Lesbian & Gay Couples*, by Frederick Hertz and Emily Doskow (Nolo).

Naming an Adult to Manage Your Child's Property

Minor children cannot own property outright, free of adult control, beyond a minimal amount—usually in the $2,500 to $5,000 range, depending on the state. This means there must be an adult legally responsible for all property owned by a child. This person may be called a "custodian," "trustee," or "property guardian," depending on the method you select for leaving property to your child. For now, let's simply call this adult your child's "property manager." If you have minor children, a vital part of your estate plan is selecting their property manager.

In addition, you may wish to choose an adult to manage any property you leave your younger adult children. You, like many parents, may not want property to be turned over to children when they become legal adults at age 18. If you wish, you can have that property supervised by a more mature person until the children become 25, or even 35 or older, and are (presumably) more responsible.

Taxation of a Child's Income

Income received by a minor is subject to the "kiddie tax." This tax can also apply to young adults from the age of 18 through 23. The kiddie tax applies to annual "unearned income"—that is, money from investments, interest, or other nonwork sources. Here's how it works:

- For a child under 18, the first $1,000 of unearned income is not taxed. The next $1,000 of unearned income is taxed at the child's tax rate. But all unearned income over $2,000 is taxed at the highest tax rate of the child's parent(s).

- The kiddie tax also applies to 18-year-olds whose earned income (i.e., from a job) is less than 50% of their overall income.

- The kiddie tax also applies to young people ages 19 through 23 if they are full-time students, if their earned income is less than 50% of their overall income.

This kiddie tax has eliminated income tax incentives for parents, or others, to transfer income-producing property from themselves and their own high tax brackets to a child younger than 18.

For more information about filing requirements for children, read IRS Publication 929, *Tax Rules for Children and Dependents*, available at www.irs.com.

Leaving Property to Your Spouse for the Benefit of Your Children

One alternative for parents of minor or young adult children is for each to leave property outright to the other spouse to be used for their child's benefit. This approach makes sense if the parents trust each other, but obviously isn't a good choice if the other parent is not available or is financially imprudent. Even if you leave all property to your spouse, it's always wise to name a backup child's property manager. This takes care of the remote possibility that you and your spouse might die simultaneously.

Choosing a Property Manager for Your Child

When deciding on your minor child's property manager, here's a sensible rule: Name the same person you choose to have custody of the children (their personal guardian) unless there are compelling reasons to name someone else. For example, choose a different person if you're concerned that the personal guardian doesn't have sufficient financial or practical experience to manage property prudently.

You should also name an alternate property manager in case your first choice can't serve. Again, name the same person you designated as the child's alternate personal guardian unless there are strong reasons to choose someone else.

The duty of the property manager is to manage the property you leave for your children honestly and in the children's best interests. This means using it to pay for normal living expenses and health and education needs. If you pick someone with integrity and common sense, your children's property will probably be in good hands. If substantial funds are involved, the property manager can pay for help to handle the more technical aspects of financial management. For instance, it's routine for a property manager to get an accountant's help for complicated tax and accounting matters.

Obviously, it's important to name a property manager who is sincerely willing to do a job that may, depending on the ages of your children, last for many years. It's also wise to choose someone that the other members of your family respect and accept. You want your children to inherit money, not family arguments.

Except as a last resort, don't name a bank or other financial institution to be property manager. Most banks won't manage accounts they consider too small to be worth the bother; as a rough rule, this means accounts worth less than $250,000. And even for larger estates, they charge hefty fees for every little act. In addition, it's my experience that banks are simply too impersonal to properly meet a child's needs. It is far better, I think, to name a human being you trust, rather than a bureaucracy. But if you can't find any adult who's willing and competent to be your child's property manager, normally it's better to name a financial institution than

to make no choice at all, which amounts to leaving the matter up to a court. You'll need to check around with different banks and private trust companies to see which ones will accept the job and seem most likely to do it for reasonable fees.

Selecting Different Property Managers for Different Minor Children

In some situations, you may want to name different property managers for different minor children. Doing this is legal. And unlike naming a personal guardian, it doesn't require court approval.

How Your Children's Property Should Be Managed

Your next task is to choose which legal method you want to use to leave property to your minor or young adult children. There are four basic options for leaving property to minor children:

- a custodianship, under the Uniform Transfers to Minors Act
- a child's trust
- a family pot trust, or
- a property guardianship.

The Uniform Transfers to Minors Act

You can leave gifts to your child (or to any minor) in your will or living trust under what is called "the Uniform Transfers to Minors Act" (UTMA), a law that has been adopted by every state except South Carolina and Vermont. Under UTMA, your child's property manager is called a "custodian." The custodian's management ends when the minor reaches age 18 to 25, depending on state law.

Here's how leaving a gift using the Uniform Transfers to Minors Act works. In either your will or living trust, you identify the property and the minor you are leaving it to. You then appoint the adult custodian to be responsible for supervising the property until the age the child must receive the property (see the chart on the following page). You provide that the custodian is to act "under the [your state's] Uniform Transfers to Minors Act." You can also name a "successor custodian" in case your first choice can't do the job.

The custodian has great discretion to control and use the property in the child's interest. Among the specific powers the UTMA gives the custodian are the right, without court approval, "to collect, hold, manage, invest, and reinvest" the property, and to spend as much of it "as the custodian considers advisable for the use and benefit of the minor." The custodian must also keep records so that tax returns can be filed on behalf of the minor and must otherwise act as a prudent person would when in control of another's property. A custodian does not, however, need to file a separate income tax return. The custodian is entitled to be paid reasonable compensation from the gift property. No court supervision of the custodian is required.

Each gift under the Uniform Transfers to Minors Act can be made to only one minor, with only one person named as custodian. A child who reaches the age the act specifies for termination gets the remaining balance of the gift. The custodian must also furnish an accounting of all funds distributed.

A limitation of the UTMA is that, in most states, custodianships end at age 21, and even at 18 in others. Particularly if your children are already teenagers and your estate is substantial, you may want property management to last longer. If so, you may wish to use child's trusts, which allow you to designate an older age at which property management ends.

Trusts for Children

There are two major types of trusts you can use to provide property management for property you leave to your children: a "child's trust" or a "family pot trust." (Other, more sophisticated trusts, such as a "special needs" trust for a child with a disability, or a "spendthrift" trust for a child who simply can't handle money, are discussed in Chapter 25.) With a child's trust, you leave specified property to one child; that property is held separately from any property you leave for other children. If you have more than one child, you can create a child's trust for each child. In contrast, with a family pot trust, you leave property collectively for two or more children in one

States That Have Adopted the Uniform Transfers to Minors Act

State	Gift Must Be Released When Minor Reaches Age	State	Gift Must Be Released When Minor Reaches Age
Alabama	21	New Jersey	21 (can be reduced to no lower than 18)
Alaska	18 (can be extended up to 25)	New Mexico	21
Arizona	21	New York	21
Arkansas	21 (can be reduced to no lower than 18)	North Carolina	21 (can be reduced to no lower than 18)
California	18 (can be extended up to 25)	North Dakota	21
Colorado	21	Ohio	21
Connecticut	21	Oklahoma	18 (can be extended up to 21)
Delaware	21	Oregon	21 (can be extended up to 25)
District of Columbia	18 (can be extended up to 21)	Pennsylvania	21 (can be extended up to 25)
Florida	21	Rhode Island	21
Georgia	21	South Dakota	18
Hawaii	21	Tennessee	21 (can be extended up to 25)
Idaho	21	Texas	21
Illinois	21	Utah	21
Indiana	21	Virginia	18 (can be extended up to 21)
Iowa	21	Washington	21 or 25
Kansas	21	West Virginia	21
Kentucky	18	Wisconsin	21
Maine	18 (can be extended up to 21)	Wyoming	21
Maryland	21		
Massachusetts	21		
Michigan	18 (can be extended up to 21)		
Minnesota	21		
Mississippi	21		
Missouri	21		
Montana	21		
Nebraska	21		
Nevada	18 (can be extended up to 25)		
New Hampshire	21		

States That Have Not Adopted the UTMA

At present, the UTMA has not been adopted in South Carolina or Vermont.

Even if you live in one of these two states, it is theoretically possible for you to use the UTMA in your will, if the minor or custodian resides in an UTMA state when you die (or if the gift property itself is located in an UTMA state). But for most parents, all these are and will likely remain in the state where they live. Even if they are in an UTMA state now, you don't know where they will be when you die. Committing yourself to this kind of updating is an unnecessary burden, because you can easily use a child's trust instead.

common fund; any amount of trust property can be spent for any child.

A trust is a legal entity under which an adult, called a "trustee," has the responsibility of handling money or property for someone else—in this case, your child or children. So if you create a trust, your child's property manager is called the "trustee" or "successor trustee." The trust document sets out the trustee's responsibilities and the beneficiary's rights.

A child's trust or a family pot trust can be established by either will or living trust. If established as part of a living trust, the property placed in trust avoids probate. If you use your will, the property must go through probate before it's turned over to the trust.

Both a child's trust and a family pot trust are legal in all states. All property you leave to a beneficiary for whom a trust is established will be managed under the terms of the trust document. If you create either type of trust, any property inherited by a minor beneficiary will be managed by the trustee until the beneficiary reaches the age when he or she is entitled to receive the trust property outright.

The trustee's powers are specified in the trust document. Normally, the trustee may use trust assets for the education, medical needs, and living expenses of the beneficiary or, with a pot trust, beneficiaries. With a family pot trust, the trustee doesn't have to spend the same amount on each beneficiary; this flexibility is one of the pot trust's main advantages.

With a child's trust, you can select the age the beneficiary must reach before trust property is turned over to him or her. So a child's trust is commonly used when a large amount of money is left for a child, and the giver doesn't want that child to inherit the property outright before a mature age, perhaps 30 or 35. A child's trust can also be used for property you leave to minors or young adults who aren't your children—your grandchildren, for example.

If a Child Never Inherits Property or Receives It When Older

If you arrange for property management for a minor or young adult, but that person never inherits the property, no damage is done. Likewise, if the beneficiary has already passed the age at which management was slated to end, the management provisions for that beneficiary are simply ignored. For instance, suppose you identify a favorite niece to take property as an alternate beneficiary and create a child's trust for that property until the niece turns 30. If the niece never inherits the property because your primary beneficiary survives you, no child's trust will ever be established for her. Similarly, if the niece does inherit the property, but is 31 when you die, she will receive the property outright, and the trust provisions will never take effect.

CAUTION

A child's trust shouldn't last a lifetime. If you want a child's trust to last beyond age 30 or 35, you need to face the likelihood that their problem goes deeper than their youth, and they may never be able to manage their own finances. You may need a more complicated trust.

Most family pot trusts last until the youngest beneficiary becomes 18. By that age, with all beneficiaries legal adults, it makes less sense to treat them all as one family unit. But you could have a pot trust last until the youngest beneficiary becomes 21, or even older, if you're sure that you want to keep your children's property lumped together this long. Also, some pot trusts are drafted so that they convert to individual trusts when the youngest child reaches 18.

A pot trust is most often used by parents with younger children. These parents want to keep family money together, capable of being spent on any child as needs require. The trustee, like a parent, decides how much money shall be spent on each child. If one child has a serious illness or other extraordinary needs, the maximum family resources possible are there for him or her.

Although family pot trusts clearly have the appeal of flexibility, they can make the trustee's job tougher as compared with a child's trust, where each child's property is legally separate from the trust property of other children. With a pot trust, the trustee may literally be called on to choose between one child's need for expensive orthodontia and another's desire to go to a pricey college.

If there is a wide age gap between children, a pot trust is less desirable. If one child is 16 and another is two, and the trust ends when the youngest becomes 18, the oldest must wait until age 32 to receive any property outright, which may not be what the parents want. Further, it's likely to be harder to balance needs between children of widely varying ages. How much of the pot should be spent for the eldest's college needs? How much retained for the youngest? When children are closer together in age, these types of troubling differences are less likely to arise.

Some parents whose children are young and close in age decide a pot trust is best for the children now. Then, when a child grows older—say the eldest reaches 16—the parents (assuming they are still alive) may decide to pull property for that child out of the pot trust and create a new child's trust or an UTMA custodianship.

Which Is Better for You, the UTMA or a Child's Trust?

We've already discussed some key factors in deciding which method is most appropriate for your family. But because this issue can be so important, let's examine it in more detail.

As a general rule, the less valuable the property involved and the more mature the child, the more appropriate the UTMA is because it is simpler and often cheaper, from a tax point of view, than a trust. There are several reasons for this:

- Because the UTMA is built into state law, financial institutions know about it and should make it easy for the custodian to carry out property management duties. In states where the UTMA allows for property management until 21 or 25, setting up an UTMA custodianship can be particularly sensible if you leave property worth less than $100,000 to your child. Normally, amounts of this size will be fairly rapidly expended for the child's education and living needs and are simply not large enough to tie up beyond age 21.

- Another factor can be the age of the child at the time you create your will or living trust. If your daughter is now two years old, it will obviously take far more money to support her until adulthood than if she is currently 17. For instance, $100,000 left to a two-year-old may be used up before she gets to college, but $100,000 left to a 17-year-old should cover at least some of her college costs or whatever else she plans to do in the next four years.

- Using the UTMA can also be desirable because trust income tax rates are now higher than individual rates. Annual income above $5,000 retained in a child's trust at the close of its tax year is taxed at higher rates than is property subject to the UTMA, which is taxed at the child's individual tax rate. Any trust income spent for the child's benefit during the year will be taxed at the child's rate, not the trust rate. But for income held in the trust, a higher tax rate applies.

- A child's trust is desirable when you want to extend the age at which a beneficiary receives property to well beyond when that child becomes a legal adult. As a rough cutoff point, if you're leaving more than $100,000 to a child, a child's trust is desirable.

Unlike UTMA custodianships, with a child's trust, no age limit is imposed by state law. With a family pot trust, any termination age is theoretically possible, but as we've discussed, they usually end when the youngest child turns 18, so they also aren't suitable for imposing longer age limits on beneficiaries. By contrast, child's trusts can be, and often are, established for young adults already older than 18 or 21, when a parent (or other older adult) believes the child is not yet a good bet for responsibly handling property.

> **EXAMPLE:** Marilyn, a single parent, creates a living trust leaving her estate, worth $720,000, equally to her two children, Todd, age 25, and Carolyn, age 27. Carolyn has always been frugal, if not parsimonious, with money. She has been saving money from the time of her first allowance. Todd is the flip side of the coin. He runs through whatever cash he has at the blink of an eye and, from Marilyn's perspective, often goes beyond generosity to recklessness with money. So in her living trust, Marilyn leaves Carolyn her half of Marilyn's estate outright. However, Todd's half

is left in a child's trust, with Marilyn's brother—a stable type if ever there was one—as trustee. Todd will not receive any trust property outright until he becomes 35. By that age, Marilyn hopes he will have become sensible enough to manage a large amount of money.

Naming a Property Guardian

It is rarely wise to leave property to your children to be supervised by a property guardian. There are several reasons:

- The property must go through your will, which means it will go through probate.
- Property guardians are often subject to court review, reporting requirements, and strict rules as to how they can expend funds. All this usually requires hiring a lawyer and paying significant fees, but in my view, does little to guarantee that the property manager will do a good job. And those lawyer fees, of course, come out of the property left to benefit the minor.
- Property guardianship must end at age 18.

All this said, your will should still name a property guardian as a backup, to handle any property that for some reason isn't covered by a trust or custodianship.

Specifically, naming a property guardian in your will provides a supervision mechanism in case:

- Your minor children earn substantial money after you die, or receive a large

gift or inheritance that doesn't, itself, name a property manager.
- You and your spouse leave property to each other to use for your children, naming the children as alternative or residuary beneficiaries without bothering to add an UTMA designation or establish a child's trust or pot trust. If both spouses die simultaneously, the property will be managed by the property guardian.
- You failed to include in an UTMA custodianship, child's trust, or pot trust some property you want your children to inherit. This can occur because of oversight or, more likely, because you didn't yet own the property when you established your will or living trust and didn't amend that document later.

Creating a child's trust, pot trust, or a custodianship under your state's UTMA is really quite simple to do, so normally the children's property guardian will be used only for the backup purposes listed above. However, if you want to postpone estate planning or keep it to the bare minimum, it is far wiser to name a property guardian than ignore the issue altogether. Having your minor child's property supervised by a property guardian you name in your will is certainly preferable to having a judge appoint someone for the job. So, for example, a young couple, both healthy and unlikely to die for decades, may not want to deal with other supervision methods now. But if they do both die, they don't want a court deciding who'll manage the property they leave for their children. So, they create wills, where each names a property guardian to manage property for their children's benefit if both die simultaneously.

Comparison of the Four Major Ways to Leave a Child or Young Adult Property

On the next page is a chart that summarizes the rules for and reasons to use each of the four major methods for leaving gifts to your minor or young adult children.

Tax-Saving Educational Investment Plans

Federal law provides two different plans you can use to save for a child's education. (You can use them for other young relatives, too.) If you establish one of these plans, future educational expenses should, in theory, eat up less of your own estate. However, choosing the best plan is not always simple. Both types of plans have drawbacks, and even after you choose the type of plan you'll probably have some investment decisions to make. To make these choices, you'll need to do some fiscal homework.

529 Plans

A "529" plan is a tax-free investment account established to pay for the higher education expenses of a named beneficiary. The beneficiary must be a "family member," so in addition to your own children, you can use this type of plan for a grandchild, favorite niece or nephew, or other young relation.

How 529 Plans Save on Taxes

Income accumulates in a 529 plan free of taxes. Even better, no income tax is assessed on money paid from a 529 plan for the beneficiary's higher education expenses. (Qualified expenses include tuition, books, fees, supplies, and equipment necessary to attend college, graduate school, or an approved vocational institution. Authorized expenses can also include special services for a student with disabilities.)

For any one beneficiary, you can contribute up to $14,000 per year free from gift tax. (Contributions can be made only in cash.) A couple can give up to $28,000 per year. Any amount over those limits given to one account within a year is subject to federal gift tax. (See Chapter 16.) However, you can contribute up to $70,000 in one year ($140,000 for both spouses) and face no tax if you live five more years and make no additional contributions during those five years. If a beneficiary does not attend college, you can name a new beneficiary from the eligible family group. But if you or the beneficiary ever withdraw money from a 529 plan for noneducational purposes, taxes and penalties apply.

Choosing a 529 Plan

These plans are called 529 plans because they were created by that section of the

Leaving Gifts to Your Minor or Young Adult Children

	Gift Under UTMA	Child's Trust	Property Guardian	Family Pot Trust
Availability	All states but SC and VT	All states	All states	All states
Amount of Property	If maximum age for release of gift is 18 in your state, then use is often best for older children or for smaller gifts under $50,000 (depending on current age of child). If age for release is 21 or 25, useful for gifts of $100,000 or more, especially to make sure money will be managed to last through college.	Often good for gifts of any amount if UTMA age for release of gift in your state is 18, or if UTMA isn't applicable in your state. Often good for gifts in excess of $100,000 if UTMA applies in your state and age for release of gift is 21 or perhaps even 25.	Last resort no matter what the amount	Any amount
Paperwork	No trust tax returns required, but minor must file a yearly return based on money actually received. Custodian must give accounting when property is turned over to child.	Trustee must file yearly income tax returns for trust.	Usually substantial because reports must be presented to court	Trustee must file yearly income tax return for trust.
Court Supervision	None	None	Guardian must make regular reports to court.	None
Termination	In most states, custodian must turn over property to child at age specified or by statute, usually 18–21 (25 in AK, CA, NV, OR, TN, and WA)	You specify the age at which the minor gets control of the trust property.	Guardian must turn property over to child at age 18.	Usually, when youngest child reaches age 18 or 21
Uses of Property	Custodian has broad statutory power to use property for child's living expenses, health needs, and education.	Trustee normally has power to use any of child's trust property for minor's need for living expenses, health needs, and education.	Heavily limited and regulated by state law	Trustee can spend any trust property for any beneficiary.

Internal Revenue Code. (Sometimes they're also called "qualified tuition programs.") But state law controls the plans, and you can only invest in a state-authorized plan. Each state has a separate plan, managed by an investment company or companies selected by that state. Managers range from TIAA-CREF to Vanguard to J.P. Morgan to various lesser-known financial institutions.

Some state plans allow you to invest only if you live in that state, but most states allow anyone to invest in their plan. (About half the states allow residents to deduct state plan contributions from their state income tax, which could be an incentive to buy a homegrown plan.) You can invest in more than one 529 plan if you like—and indeed, there is a rather bewildering array of plans to choose from.

Whatever plan or plans you choose, you are basically investing in securities—stocks and bonds. But some states' 529 managers have a far more "aggressive" (risky) investment strategy than do managers of other states' plans. And the fees and costs for different plans vary widely. So you'll need to do some homework before selecting a 529 plan that's right for you.

Types of 529 Plans

There are two types of basic 529 plans.

Savings plans. With a savings plan, you make contributions to an investment account established for a minor's education costs. The account functions much like an IRA or a 401(k) account; your money is placed in mutual funds or similar investments.

You hope the value of these assets rises substantially by the time the minor starts college.

Prepaid plans. With a prepaid plan, you pay in advance for all or part of the costs of a public college education in your state. These plans are not an investment; what you've paid into the plan is what will be available for college costs. A prepaid plan may be converted to pay for the costs of out-of-state and private colleges. "Independent" 529 plans are available as pay-in-advance plans for private colleges.

Possible Drawbacks of 529 Plans

There can be serious drawbacks to 529 plans. The first of these is high fees. Investors pay annual expenses for management of 529 funds. Many funds' annual administrative charges exceed 2%, significantly higher than for other types of investments. Before you select a 529 plan, investigate all management fees—some can be well hidden. It's also important to check out the plan's disclosure rules: How easy will it be for you to find out how the company is actually handling your money?

Second, each state offers its own plan, and these plans vary dramatically. Some state plans exempt withdrawn funds from state income taxes, others do not. Some states penalize their citizens if they invest in another state's plan. Finally, and crucially, the types of allowed investments vary widely among state plans.

For many, the biggest drawback of a 529 plan is limited investment choices.

With a 529 plan, you can invest only in the options allowed by the state, which could be just one or two mutual funds. Some people prefer to put money for a young person's education in accounts that allow them to select whatever investments they think are wisest. Commonly, these folks make a gift to a child under the Uniform Transfers to Minors Act (UTMA) and name one parent as custodian (manager) for that gift. However, money earned in an UTMA account is subject to income tax, and in some circumstances it may also reduce the child's eligibility for other forms of financial aid. So when deciding between a 529 plan and an UTMA gift, you must determine whether investment freedom outweighs other costs. If you need help, a good accountant or other financial adviser can help you with this analysis.

Because 529 plans are essentially securities investments, they come with the stock market pitfalls we've all become aware of. As the legendary Wall Street investor Bernard Baruch observed, the only thing certain about the stock market is that "prices will fluctuate." Still, 529 accounts remain popular; well over $100 billion has been placed in these accounts to date.

Coverdell Accounts

With a Coverdell account (also called an Educational Savings Account), you can contribute up to $2,000 per year, though contribution amounts phase out for folks with six-figure incomes. Further, this $2,000 limit is the total amount that can be set aside in any one year for any one beneficiary. In other words, three different family members cannot each contribute $2,000 per year for one beneficiary. Combined, they can contribute no more than $2,000.

Contributions are not tax deductible when you make them. However, money in the account is not taxed when (or if) it grows, and no tax is due when you make qualified withdrawals from the account to pay for a child's education expenses. (In this way, a Coverdell account functions much like a Roth IRA.)

A parent managing a Coverdell account can use the money for any investment desired. Investments are not restricted as they are in 529 plans.

While the $2,000 limit restricts the appeal of a Coverdell account, it may be the right plan for some. For example, these accounts can work well for families with young children and not much money: Each year, for each child, the parents put whatever they can afford into a Coverdell account—up to $2,000 per child. At that rate, the total saved could be quite helpful when a child attends college (even if it can't foot the entire bill). Coverdell accounts can also be useful for grandparents or other relatives who want to contribute something toward a child's education while you invest in a 529 account or save in other ways for higher education costs.

Naming Children as Beneficiaries of Life Insurance

Some may think I've put the legal cart before the financial horse here—all this discussion about how to leave property to your children before any talk of how to acquire some valuable property to begin with. Well, this is a book on how to dispose of an estate, not about how to acquire one. Indeed, if I were a master of that, maybe I wouldn't have bothered writing the book. So all I can offer here is some general advice.

If you don't have the luxury of putting significant amounts aside, the best way to be sure cash will be available for the children if you die is to purchase some term life insurance. Term is the cheapest form of life insurance. Younger parents can obtain a significant amount of coverage for relatively low cost, for the obvious reason that statistically they are unlikely to die soon, so the risk to the insurance company is low. (Life insurance is discussed in depth in Chapter 12.)

If you name your children as beneficiaries, or alternate beneficiaries, of your policy, and you die while the children are minors, the insurance company cannot legally turn over the proceeds directly to them. If you haven't arranged for another method of adult supervision over the proceeds, court proceedings will be needed to confirm the children's property guardian. This means this property guardian can become enmeshed in the time-consuming court reporting requirements state laws typically impose. It also means the prop-

erty guardian can only spend money under the terms of state law.

Here are your options for avoiding problems:

- Name the children as policy beneficiaries and name a custodian under the UTMA. Most insurance companies permit this and have forms for it. Essentially, you fill out a separate form for each minor, providing the usual UTMA information—the beneficiary's and the custodian's name, state, and age of termination, if you get to choose. If you want the proceeds to go to more than one child, you'll need to specify the percentage each one receives.

- Leave the proceeds to your child or children using a child's trust or a pot trust as part of a living trust. You name the living trust (or the trustee, if that's what the insurance company prefers) as the policy beneficiary in the living trust. In the trust, you name minors as beneficiaries of any insurance proceeds that trust receives and create the child's or pot trust to handle those proceeds. You'll need to give a copy of your living trust to the insurance company.

It may not be possible to leave insurance proceeds to a child's trust established by a will. Some insurance companies balk at this, on the grounds the trust won't come into existence until you die, and the policy beneficiary must be in existence when named. Rather than try to persuade an insurance company that this can be done, it is better to use the UTMA or create a living trust to achieve your goals. A living trust avoids this problem because the trust is effective as soon as you create it.

Leaving Property to Children Who Are Not Your Own

If you want to leave property to minor or young adult children who aren't your own, you have the following choices:

- Leave the gift outright to the child's parent or legal guardian, and rely on the parent to use the gift for the benefit of the child.
- Leave the gift in your will or living trust through the Uniform Transfers to Minors Act. This is best suited for gifts under $100,000.
- Leave the gift through your living trust or will, by creating a child's trust for that gift. You can create a child's trust for any young adult beneficiary who you believe is not presently capable of managing property wisely. Name the trustee of this child's trust, to manage all property in it. Doing this makes sense for large gifts—roughly, above $100,000. This plan can make good sense for gifts to grandchildren, particularly if the trustee is the child's parent and will supervise that child's trust.

> **EXAMPLE:** John, an elderly widower, wants to leave some antique furniture from his living trust to his 13-year-

old grandniece, Sally. He decides to make the gift using his state's Uniform Transfers to Minors Act. He names Sally's mother, Mary, to be the custodian. Her husband, Fred, is the alternate custodian. In his living trust, John makes the following gift: "Sally Earners shall be given the following furniture: my Hoosier cabinet, my two oriental rugs, and my three stained glass lamps; Mary Earners is to be custodian under the Minnesota Uniform Transfers to Minors Act. If Mary Earners is unable to serve or continue serving as custodian, the successor custodian shall be Fred Earners."

- The least desirable method is to leave the gift outright in your will. If the child is a minor when you die, court proceedings will be necessary to appoint a property guardian to supervise the gift. And since you are not the child's parent, you can't even appoint or suggest a property guardian for him or her in your will.

Disinheritance

To an outsider, it may seem sad that a parent would want to disinherit a child, but it's surely been known to happen. Whatever the reasons, it's legal for a parent to do so.

At the same time, legal rules protect children, and children of a deceased child, from being accidentally disinherited. The legalese for accidentally overlooked children is "pretermitted heirs." In most states, your children have a statutory right to inherit from you if you unintentionally leave them out of your will or fail to make one. Grandchildren do not have any statutory right to inherit if their parent (your child) is still alive, so there is no need to disinherit them if you don't want them to inherit. However, children of a deceased child (your grandchildren) may have the same inheritance rights as that child.

CAUTION

Special rule for Floridians. The Florida Constitution (Art. 10, § 4) prohibits the head of a family from leaving his or her residence by will to someone other than spouse or child, if either exists.

If you want to disinherit a child, you should specifically state that in your will. You can also achieve a functional dis-inheritance by leaving a child a miniscule amount of property in your will. But do not try to disinherit a child simply by omitting that child's name from your will. If a child's name is omitted, it may not be clear whether you meant to disinherit that child or whether you accidentally overlooked that child. As stated, "overlooked children" have statutory inheritance rights in most states.

Even if you transfer all your property by a living trust and want to disinherit a child, you must use a will to accomplish that. The reason is simple: some state laws require disinheritance to be accomplished by a will, and only by a will.

Similarly, the laws of each state protect your children who are born after your will is made ("afterborn children") by entitling them to a share of your estate. How much a child gets depends on whether you leave a spouse and how many other children you have.

What if you provide for your children outside your will—by leaving them property from your living trust, for example—but didn't mention them in your will? They could, at least in theory, claim to be accidentally overlooked heirs and demand additional shares of your estate. In defining whether a child is overlooked, and therefore entitled to receive a share of your estate, some state's laws specifically refer to omitting a child from a "will." Read literally, these statutes don't allow property left to a child by a living trust (or other method) to be considered to determine if a child has been overlooked.

So, to be absolutely safe, even if you generously provide for your children outside of your will, you should list the names of all your children (and children of a deceased child) in your will and make some provision for them.

Remember, for the pretermitted heir issue to become a problem, a child must file a lawsuit contesting your will and estate plan. If you trust that your children aren't going to sue, you don't have to worry about this.

Children Conceived After a Parent Dies

Rapidly advancing medical technology now makes it possible for a child to be conceived after the biological mother or father dies. (In legal terms, these are known as "posthumously" conceived children.) If sperm or embryos are frozen before a father's death and later used to begin a pregnancy, a child could be born to a father who has been dead for years. Similarly, a fertilized embryo could be carried by another woman well after the embryo donor's death.

Complications from this development have already made it to courts in a handful of states, with inconsistent results. For example, a Massachusetts court ruled that twins conceived through artificial insemination using a late husband's sperm could be entitled to inherit from his estate under the state's intestacy laws. However, in similar circumstances, an Arizona court ruled that its inheritance laws excluded a child conceived after a father's death. In contrast, a federal appeals court ruled that a posthumously conceived child was entitled to payments from the deceased father's Social Security.

The rights of a posthumously conceived child may be important for reasons other than inheritance—for instance, the surviving parent may want the baby to qualify for government or other benefits that come only with being the child of the deceased parent.

California has taken the lead in adopting laws governing children conceived after a parent's death. Specifically, California law provides that a child conceived after death will be deemed to be the child of the deceased person and born during his or her lifetime if all of the following are proved by clear and convincing evidence:

- The decedent specified in writing that his or her genetic material should be used for posthumous conception of a child.
- The writing is signed by the decedent and dated.
- A person has been designated by the decedent to control the use of the decedent's genetic material.
- Written notice was given to the decedent's executor, within four months of the decedent's death, that the decedent's genetic material was available for posthumous conception.
- The child was conceived within two years of the date of issuance of decedent's death certificate.

(Cal. Prob. Code § 249.5.)

This is a rapidly changing area of law and technology. If you are planning for the possibility of a posthumously conceived child, you'll want to consider what his or her property rights will be. You'll need to know your state's law (if any) on the subject to figure out what you think is best. It's essential that you consult a knowledgeable estate planning lawyer to discuss these matters.

Wills

A will is what many people think of when they first consider estate planning. This makes sense. Everyone should have a will, whether or not they make a more extensive estate plan. And quite a number of people decide that a will is all the planning they need, at least for the time being.

As you undoubtedly know, a will specifies who gets property covered by that document when you die. A will can also serve other vital purposes, such as appointing a personal guardian to raise your minor children if you and the other parent aren't available.

Property left by a will must normally go through probate. As I've mentioned, probate is usually costly and burdensome. So a substantial portion of this book is devoted to explaining how to avoid this process. (Probate is discussed in more detail in Chapter 8.) However, despite the downside of probate, every estate plan should at least include a "backup" will to cover things that probate avoidance devices don't take care of.

A Will as the Centerpiece of Your Estate Plan

Many people reasonably decide to make a will the centerpiece—or even, in some cases, the only piece—of their estate plan. They decide that, for the foreseeable future, a will accomplishes their estate planning goals. They can sensibly postpone more complicated, and perhaps more costly,

estate planning work. You may be this kind of person if:

- No matter what your age or health, you simply don't want the bother of more extensive estate planning. Quite a few people say, "Yes, I guess I should probably do full-scale estate planning, but I never seem to get around to it, so I'd better at least make a will now and think about the full-scale plan later." After all, a will achieves the basic goal of distributing your property as you see fit, with as little disturbance to you as possible. Sure, a will is likely to lead to probate, but the goal of probate avoidance, as smart as it is, should never obscure the more important goal of seeing to it that your property goes to the people and organizations you want to receive it.

- You're healthy and, statistically, unlikely to die for decades. If you just want to be certain your basic wishes for your property are carried out in the very unlikely event you die unexpectedly, a will achieves this goal with considerably less paperwork than a living trust. And as you acquire property, and people close to you are born and die, it can be a lot easier to make a new will than to amend a living trust.

- Your primary estate planning goal is to ensure, to the best of your abilities, that if you die, your minor children are well cared for. A will allows you to name a personal guardian (something that, in most states, can't be done by any other document), while also allowing you to create a method for adult supervision of any property you leave to your children. Years later, of course, if you accumulate considerable property, you may want to engage in more thorough estate planning.

A Backup Will With a Comprehensive Estate Plan

If you prepare a thorough estate plan and arrange to avoid probate for all your property, do you still need a will? Yes. It's always desirable to have at least a simple will, which I call a backup will, as part of your estate plan for one or probably more of the following reasons:

- **To leave property generally best left by will.** Some types of property are not suitable to leave by living trust, and often don't work well with other probate avoidance devices either. The most common example is your car. Living trusts do not work well for cars, because most insurance companies are unwilling to insure a car owned by a trust; the companies claim they can't tell who is authorized to transfer the car. Occasionally, another probate avoidance device can be used for a car—owning it in joint tenancy, or holding title in a transfer-on-death registration. But most people simply leave their car or cars as part of their will property.

- **To dispose of suddenly acquired property.** Anyone may end up acquiring valuable property at or shortly before death, such as a sudden gift or inheritance, poker winnings, or even a lottery prize. Of course, it's wise to promptly revise your estate plan to name a specific beneficiary to inherit this property. But what if you don't get around to it before you die? If you have a will, that property will go to your residuary beneficiary, who, by definition, takes "the rest of your property"—that is, everything that isn't left to some specific named beneficiary. Unfortunately, there's no easy way to leave leftover property through a living trust, because property must be formally added to the trust for it to be subject to the trust provisions.

- **To dispose of property not transferred by a probate avoidance device.** If you buy property but don't get around to planning probate avoidance for it— by placing it in your living trust, for example—a will is a valuable backup device, ensuring that the property will go to whomever you want to have it (your residuary beneficiary), and not pass under state law. Similarly, if somehow you've failed to transfer some of your existing property to a probate avoidance device—for example, because you didn't properly complete transfers of title, a will directs that property to your residuary beneficiary.

- **To name a personal guardian for your minor children.** If you have minor children, you need a will to achieve the vital goal of naming a personal guardian for them. You can't use any other device for this purpose (except a living trust in a couple of states). Also, in your will, you can appoint a property guardian for your children to manage any of their property not otherwise legally supervised by an adult. (See Chapter 6.)

- **To leave property you don't currently own but expect to receive.** If someone has left you property by will and that property is still enmeshed in probate when you die, you can't arrange to transfer it by a probate avoidance device such as a living trust, because you don't have title to the property. But under your will, that property goes to your residuary beneficiary. Similarly, if you expect to get money from a lawsuit settlement, only a will can be used to transfer that property. Of course, no one knows what property they might receive shortly before death, which is one reason you always need a will.

- **To disinherit a child or spouse.** You can expressly disinherit a child in your will. (See "Disinheritance" in Chapter 6.) You can disinherit a spouse in your will only if you live in a community property state. (See Chapter 3.)

- **To name your executor.** In your will, you name your executor, the person with legal authority to supervise distribution of property left by your will, and to represent your estate. It is a good idea to have an executor even if you have also set up a living trust and named a successor trustee to manage it when you die, because banks and other financial institutions can be reassured to know an executor exists. The successor trustee and executor are often the same person.

- **In case probate is not required.** Some states don't require probate, or greatly simplify probate, for small or modest estates. (See Chapter 14.) If your estate qualifies for simplified treatment, there may be no need to use a series of probate avoidance devices—a will might do the job. And in some states, even larger estates can make use of simplified probate. For example, California allows estates worth up to $150,000 to be transferred by a will without any probate. Property transferred by probate avoidance methods doesn't count toward this $150,000 limit. So, in California (and many other states), a will can be a handy method for making small gifts—that treasured antique clock to a niece or $3,000 to a fondly remembered employee—once you have arranged to transfer the bulk of your estate outside of probate.

Choosing Your Executor

Your executor should be the person you trust the most and who's willing to do the job. If you plan to prepare a living trust, it's generally best that your executor be the same person you choose to be the successor trustee of your trust. If possible, it's best to name an executor who lives in your state or near it. Some states place extra rules and restrictions on out-of-state executors.

It's simpler to name just one executor, but you can name coexecutors, or even several executors, if you have good reason for it. There can be compelling reasons—family harmony is one common example—for selecting more than one executor.

Some conservative estate planners recommend selecting a bank to be your executor. I strongly recommend against this, unless you have no other option. Your executor is your link to the future, in charge of distributing your property after your death. You want someone human, with genuine concern, not an impersonal institution that charges fees for every small act. If your most trusted friend is your banker, name her or him as executor, but not the bank itself.

Your executor is responsible for arranging probate and supervising the transfer of your will property to your beneficiaries. This may be simple or complicated. Locating the property may not be easy. More commonly, distributing property can become difficult. For instance, if a will writer leaves general instructions to divide property—such as heirlooms or personal photos—between beneficiaries, the executor may become embroiled in all sorts of personal dramas.

Also, if your estate is over the estate tax threshold, your executor is responsible for filing a federal estate tax return—and also a state one, if it is required. (See Chapter 15.) Of course, the executor doesn't have to actually prepare these tax forms personally. They are complicated forms, and the executor will usually hire an expert to do the work.

RESOURCE

What an executor does: the full picture. For a comprehensive and accessible guide to an executor's duties, see *The Executor's Guide: Settling a Loved One's Estate or Trust*, by Mary Randolph (Nolo). The book covers in depth each legal, financial, and practical matter that an executor may have to handle after a death. It also explains the steps you can take while you are still alive to make your executor's eventual job easier.

What Makes a Will Legal?

Drafting a legal will isn't nearly as complicated as many people fear. The requirements are:

- You must be at least 18 years old.
- You must be of "sound mind." The fact that you're reading and understanding this book is, as a practical matter, sufficient evidence that you meet this test.
- The will must be typewritten—either typed on a typewriter or printed out from a computer.
- The will must have at least one substantive provision. The most common one leaves some or all of your property to whomever you want to have it.
- You must appoint at least one executor.
- You must date the will.
- You must sign the will in front of two witnesses. (Colorado allows wills to be notarized or witnessed (Colo. Rev. Stat. § 15-11-502).) Witnesses need only be:
  - adults (people over 18) and of sound mind, and
  - people who won't inherit under the will—will beneficiaries cannot be witnesses.

Witnesses watch you sign your will and then sign it themselves. They must be told that it's your will they are signing, but they don't have to read it or be told what it contains.

There's no requirement that a will be recorded or filed with any governmental agency, nor need a will be notarized.

Still, you may want to use a notary when signing your will and having it witnessed. In most states, having the witnesses sign a brief statement called a "self-proving" affidavit, which is then notarized, can eliminate any need for a witness to testify at subsequent probate proceedings.

What a Will Looks Like

Years ago, when I was a partner in a small law firm, I learned that some clients were disappointed that their wills didn't look more impressive; a few sheets of typed paper seemed lacking in "gravitas." So I began stapling each will in a blue cover binder and attaching a red ribbon and red wax seal. Some clients appreciated these touches—although they were certainly not legally required. If you want extras like these, you can purchase them yourself for far less than if you buy them from a lawyer.

Types of Wills

There are various types of wills. To help clear up any confusion, I briefly cover the main ones here.

Handwritten Wills

A handwritten will (called "holographic" in legalese) must be written, dated, and signed entirely in the handwriting of the person making the will. It does not have to be witnessed. Handwritten wills are not legal in many states. I definitely don't recommend them, even in the states where they're legal.

Handwritten wills aren't recommended because probate courts traditionally have been very strict when examining them after the death of the writer. Since a handwritten will isn't normally witnessed, judges sometimes fear that it might have been forged. Also, a judge may require proof that the will was actually and voluntarily written by the deceased person, which sometimes isn't easy to do. In short, given the tiny bit of extra trouble it takes to prepare a typed will and have it witnessed, it's reckless not to do it.

Pour-Over Wills

A "pour-over" will is one that directs that the property subject to it goes to (is "poured over" into) a trust. For example, sometimes people make their living trusts the beneficiaries of their wills. When the will property is poured over to the trust, the trust document controls who receives that property.

Living Overseas

You do not have to live in the United States to prepare a will that is valid in this country. To prepare a valid will if you live abroad, you must meet the requirements listed above and maintain legal residence in a U.S. state. If you live overseas temporarily because you are in the armed services, your residence is the home of record you declared to the military authorities.

If you live overseas for business, education —or just for the fun of it—you probably still have sufficient ties with a U.S. state to make it your legal home ("domicile" in legalese). For example, if you were born in New Hampshire, lived in New Hampshire, and are registered to vote there, then your residence is New Hampshire for will-making purposes.

> **CAUTION**
> **If your choice is not clear.** If you do not maintain continuous ties with a particular state, or if you have well-established homes in both the United States and another country, consult a lawyer before preparing your will.

When a Pour-Over Will Is Undesirable

It's usually not a good idea to use a pour-over will with a basic probate avoidance living trust. Pour-over wills do not avoid probate. All property that is left through a will—any kind of will—must go through probate, unless the amount left is small enough to qualify for exemption from normal probate laws. Probate is most definitely not avoided simply because the beneficiary of a will is a living trust.

It's generally better to simply use a standard backup will to take care of your leftover (not in a living trust) property. In the backup will, you can name the people you want to get the property and skip the unnecessary extra step of pouring the property over to the living trust after your death.

When used as a backup will, a pour-over will actually has a disadvantage that standard wills don't: It forces the living trust to go on for months after your death, because the property left through the pour-over will must go through probate before it can be transferred to the trust. Usually, the property left in a living trust can be distributed to the beneficiaries, and the trust ended, within a few weeks after the person's death.

When You May Want a Pour-Over Will

There are, however, two situations in which you might want to use a pour-over will. The first is if you set up an AB disclaimer trust to possibly save on estate taxes. With this device, the spouses want up to the maximum amount of property allowed under the federal estate tax exemption to eventually wind up in the trust of the deceased spouse. (See Chapter 18.) So each spouse writes a pour-over will, leaving his or her will property to the AB disclaimer trust. (After one spouse dies, the other spouse should amend her or his will or prepare a new one.)

Also, if you set up, as part of your living trust, a child's trust to provide management for property left to a young beneficiary, you may want any property that child inherits through your will to pour over into that trust. Otherwise, you would create two trusts for the child: one in the will and one in your living trust.

Statutory Wills

A statutory will is a fill-in-the-blanks, check-the-boxes will form authorized by state law. California, Maine, Michigan, New Mexico, and Wisconsin have statutory wills. In theory, statutory wills are an excellent idea—inexpensive, easy to complete, and reliable. Unfortunately, in practice, statutory wills are so limited in scope they aren't useful for most people. The choices provided in the statutory forms are quite narrow and cannot legally be changed—that is, you can't customize them to fit your situation or, indeed, change them at all. For example, the Michigan form allows you to make only two cash gifts (aside from household property); everything else must go to your spouse or children.

Normally, statutory wills are useful only if you are married and want all or the bulk of your property to go to your spouse (or, if she predeceases you, in trust for your minor children). Because of the limitations of statutory wills, the movement to introduce them in other states has stalled. No state has adopted a statutory will since the late 1980s.

Ethical Wills

An "ethical will" is a document or materials in which a person expresses the beliefs and experiences that have mattered most in his or her life. The intent is to communicate core values to loved ones. Such a statement can have real worth to those close to you.

While you could legally include an ethical will statement in your regular will—that is, the one you use to leave your property to others—it's wiser to prepare a separate document. Trying to sum up what's in your soul may turn out to require many pages and take considerable time. Better not to enmesh that profound searching with the task of preparing your conventional will. More practically speaking, you'll want to avoid including anything potentially confusing or ambiguous in your legal will.

As long as you don't contradict the provisions of your legal will, your options for expressing yourself are limited only by the time and energy you have for the project. You could do something as simple as use your explanatory letter to set out a concise description of your basic values.

Or, if you feel inspired, you may leave something much more detailed for your loved ones. Many survivors are touched to learn about important life stories, memories, and events. You might also consider including photographs or other mementos with your letter. If writing things down seems like too much effort, you could use an audio- or videotape to talk to those who are closest to you. A little thought will surely yield many creative ways to express yourself to those you care for.

RESOURCE
More information about ethical wills. If you want to go beyond writing down some of your experiences and values in your explanatory letter, there is a growing body of websites and literature that can help you explore different ways of making an ethical will. You might begin by visiting www.celebrationsoflife.net. The site offers some basic free information and sells ethical will-writing kits.

CAUTION
Don't use your will to control behavior. For some, an ethical will means putting provisions in their legal will that attempt to reward beneficiaries for acting in certain ways—or to punish them if they don't. For example, a will writer might want to provide cash incentives to younger beneficiaries if they work for favorite causes. Usually, trying to establish this type of control over others is at best futile and at worst destructive. If you weren't able to pass on your values and morals by example while you lived, it's very unlikely that you can do so through gifts

of your property after your death. Moreover, the mechanics of imposing moral conditions on your gifts are inherently complicated. Among the issues that must be resolved are: Who is to determine whether the beneficiary is fulfilling your moral requirement? How is that to be determined? For how long must the beneficiary do what you want before they receive your gift? Functionally, you must create an irrevocable trust if you want to try to require certain behavior from your beneficiaries. The trustee of that trust would be responsible for determining if your requirements had been met. Setting up this type of trust requires an expert lawyer and will be a complicated and costly process.

Other Types of Wills

You almost surely want a formal, witnessed will, either as your primary estate planning device or as a backup to a living trust. But you may also have questions about other types of wills, such as:

- **Oral wills.** Oral wills (also called "nuncupative" wills) are valid in a minority of states and, even where valid, are acceptable only if made under special circumstances, such as the will maker's perception of imminent death on the battlefield or in some other highly unusual circumstance. Clearly, they are not to be relied on as a serious estate planning device.
- **Electronic wills.** An electronic will refers to an original will that is created and stored exclusively in an electronic format. Nevada authorizes electronic

wills, and both a Tennessee appellate court and an Ohio probate court upheld electronic wills even though there was no specific authorization for it in Tennessee or Ohio law.

In Nevada, the will must use advanced technology to create a distinctive electronic signature and at least one other way to positively identify the will maker, such as a fingerprint, retinal scan, or voice or face recognition technology. While it's true that such technology is developing rapidly, there are currently no readily available or acceptable methods for making an electronic will that's trustworthy and valid. It's likely that Nevada is laying the groundwork for a time when such wills will be easy to prepare. When that time comes, other state laws are sure to follow this one.

- **Video or film wills.** Video or film wills are not valid under any state's law. But films of a person reciting will provisions, such as to whom they are leaving property, can be useful evidence if a will is challenged, to demonstrate that the will maker was of sound mind and didn't appear crazy or under undue influence.

 SEE AN EXPERT

Avoiding lawsuits over your will. If you truly fear a will contest based on your lack of sound mind or the undue influence of a beneficiary, ask a lawyer about using videos or films to help establish that you were thinking clearly when your will was signed.

- **Joint wills and contracts to make a will.**
A joint will is one document made by
two people, usually a married couple.
Each leaves everything to the other,
and then the will goes on to specify
what happens to the property when
the second person dies.

  A similar method for controlling
both spouses' property is called
a "contract to make a will." Each
spouse agrees by contract to make a
will and not revoke gifts to specified
beneficiaries, even after one spouse
has died. Joint wills and contracts
to make a will prevent the survivor
from changing his or her mind about
what happens to the property, even if
circumstances change drastically.

  I do not recommend using a
joint will or contract to make a will
to control property of a surviving
spouse. If you want to impose
controls over property you leave to
your spouse, the sensible way to do it
is through a trust. (See Chapter 25.)

- **Living wills.** A living will (commonly
called a "health care directive") has
no relation to a conventional will
at all. Essentially, a living will is a
document in which you state whether
or not you want your life artificially
prolonged by use of life support
equipment. Depending on state law,
other issues related to health care can
also be covered. They are discussed
in Chapter 26.

When to Consider a Contract to Make a Will

An agreement to leave certain property to the other person who signs the contract can be valid but is usually not wise unless it is part of a thoughtfully prepared prenuptial agreement or living-together contract made between partners.

A typical instance of an unwise contract to make a will arises when someone provides services—care or live-in nursing—in return for an agreement that the person receiving the care will leave property to the person providing the care. Tying up your property like this so you cannot change your will, even if circumstances change, isn't desirable for many reasons. Most lawyers prefer to establish a trust in these situations.

SEE AN EXPERT
Making promises binding.
If you face a situation in which you want to guarantee now that someone will receive money from your estate, you'll need to see a lawyer. However, if you're about to get married and you want to make these promises in a valid premarital contract, you can get a head start by reading *Prenuptial Agreements: How to Write a Fair & Lasting Contract,* by Katherine Stoner and Shae Irving (Nolo). The book will help you decide what provisions to include in your contract and show you how to draft an agreement for your lawyers to review.

What Property Cannot Be Transferred by Will?

In almost all cases, property that is transferred by a binding probate avoidance device can't also be transferred by will. In other words, once you place property in one of the following forms of ownership, listing that property in your will has no effect:

- property in a living trust that goes to the beneficiaries named in the trust document
- joint tenancy property. At your death, your share automatically goes to the surviving joint tenants (but if all joint tenants die simultaneously, you can leave your share by will).
- money in informal bank account trusts or pay-on-death accounts. The person you designate as beneficiary on the account document inherits the funds.
- real estate transferred by transfer-on-death deeds and vehicles transferred by transfer-on-death registrations. The property or vehicle goes directly to the beneficiary you name on the deed or registration.
- life insurance proceeds payable to a named beneficiary or beneficiaries that go directly to the named beneficiaries
- funds remaining in retirement plans, including pensions, 401(k)s, IRAs, and profit-sharing plans, payable to named beneficiaries who get these assets no matter what your will says, and

- property that is promised to someone in a prenuptial agreement, living-together contract, partnership agreement, corporate shareholder agreement, or other contract.

Washington state has passed a law called the "superwill statute" that varies some of the rules above. If you like, you can leave the following types of property in your will:

- your share of joint tenancy bank accounts
- pay-on-death bank accounts
- property in your living trust, and
- money in individual retirement accounts (but not 401(k) accounts).

If you live in Washington and set up one of these probate avoidance devices, but later use your will to change the beneficiary, the property goes to the person you name in your will. However, if you designate a new beneficiary after you make your will—for example, by updating the paperwork for a pay-on-death bank account or amending your living trust—the gift in the will has no effect. (Wash. Rev. Code § 11.11.020.)

Explanatory Letters Accompanying Your Will

In addition to preparing your will, you may want to leave a letter explaining your motives and desires in leaving your property. At the beginning of your letter, you should expressly declare that it is separate from your will; this prevents confusion for those who are handling your affairs after death. While the letter has no legal or binding effect, it can give you some peace of mind while you live, and also soothe potential slights or hurts of surviving family members or friends.

I wouldn't attempt to instruct you on how to express the feelings of your heart. What follows are some suggestions of topics you might wish to cover.

> **RESOURCE**
> **WillMaker can help you write your letter.** If you need a little help writing your letter, the "Letter to Survivors" in Quicken WillMaker Plus can help you get started. It prompts you for a range of information that you might want to write about—you include as little or as much as you want. To learn more about WillMaker, go to www.nolo.com.

Explaining Why Gifts Were Made

You may have thought much about why you're leaving a specific item of property to a beneficiary. In a letter, you can set forth your thoughts. For example, you could write why you've left that boat to your old fishing buddy or that necklace to your niece.

Explaining Disparities in Gifts

You may wish to explain your reasons for leaving more property to one person than another. This can be particularly valuable if you leave more property to one child than another. Ideally, while you live, you could call together those involved, explaining to them why you plan to leave your property as you will be doing. However, as the ideal may not be (once again) feasible or prudent, explaining your reasons in a letter can be far preferable to silence and mystery. Among the common reasons some people decide to leave different amounts of property are:

- One child has already received more money from a parent than other children—say, for purchase of a house or to cover the costs of education.
- One family member has greater need than others.

Explaining Your Choices for Executor

You may name whomever you wish as your executor, but you may also be concerned that one or more of your loved ones will feel overlooked or left out if they aren't given the job. You can try to soothe injured feelings by leaving a letter that explains your choices. Even if the truth is not easy for family or friends to hear, they will know that you gave your decision careful thought.

Expressing Positive Sentiments

You may wish to express loving emotions, gratitude, or other positive feelings when leaving a gift to a beneficiary. As for negative emotions, I suggest that you leave them out of your will *and* your explanatory letter. The old maxim states, "Don't speak ill of the dead." The wise corollary is that the dead shouldn't speak ill of anybody else. Legally, of course, you can express whatever you like, except that if you libel someone, your estate would be responsible for any damages.

Obviously, there are near-infinite reasons you might want to express positive feelings in a letter, including:

- appreciating the service and care someone—a doctor, a car mechanic, a teacher, whoever—gave you
- appreciating the fun and love a friend provided, or
- expressing gratitude and respect for someone who aided you when you were in trouble.

Providing Care for Your Pet

As discussed in Chapter 5, you can't leave property directly to your pets. Usually, the wise thing to do is to use your will to leave your pet and a sum of money to a friend who has agreed, in advance, to take the animal. If you like, you can use a separate letter to express feelings you have about your pet, and how you want it cared for.

 SEE AN EXPERT

Pet trusts. A majority of states allow trusts for pets. *Every Dog's Legal Guide*, by Mary Randolph (Nolo) provides a list of these states and a discussion of the pros and cons of establishing a pet trust. If your state allows pet trusts and you want to create one, you'll need to see a lawyer to have the trust properly drafted. See Chapter 29 for tips on finding and working with a lawyer.

Instructions for Your Digital Legacy

You may want to leave instructions about your digital legacy—your online accounts, information, identities, and files—that will be left when you die. If you know what you want to happen with them, you can leave guidance and login information in your explanatory letter. (Read more about this in "Your Digital Legacy" in Chapter 4.)

Can My Will Be Successfully Challenged?

The fact that many people worry about the possibility of lawsuits over their wills shows how fear-ridden estate planning has become. Fortunately, the reality is that will challenges, particularly successful ones, are rare. The legal grounds for contesting a will are limited to extreme circumstances. Basically, your will can be invalidated only if you were underage when you made it, if you were clearly mentally incompetent (not of "sound mind"), or if the will was procured by fraud, duress, or undue influence.

A person must be pretty far gone before a court will rule that he or she lacked the capacity to make a valid will. For example, forgetfulness or even the inability to recognize friends doesn't by itself establish incapacity. It's important to remember that courts presume that the will writer was of sound mind; a challenger must prove incapacity. Similarly, a will is rarely declared invalid on grounds it was procured by fraud, duress, or undue influence; this requires proof that some evildoer manipulated a person in a confused or weakened mental or emotional state to leave his or her property in a way the person otherwise wouldn't have. If a will maker is improperly influenced, however, a court is the right place to remedy the injustice.

SEE AN EXPERT

If you fear a lawsuit. If you think someone might contest your will, it's best to prepare in advance to prevail against any lawsuit. Or if there are special circumstances, such as a seriously debilitating illness, that you believe might raise questions about your competency and the validity of your will, it's also prudent to see a lawyer. This can mean having the lawyer come to see and perhaps even physically help you. For example, in many states, if you're too ill to sign your own name, you can direct that a witness or an attorney sign it for you. In any unusual physical or mental circumstances, it's prudent to have a lawyer's assistance, especially if substantial amounts of property are involved. Someone could possibly claim that if you were too ill to sign your name, you weren't mentally competent. In any subsequent court challenge to the will, the lawyer's testimony that you appeared to be in full possession of your faculties could be very important.

Keeping Your Will Up to Date

If important circumstances change, you may need to revise your will.

Does Divorce Automatically Revoke a Will?

In some states, if you get divorced after making a will, the provisions that left property to your former spouse are automatically revoked. But that's not true in all states and it's not true for some kinds of property such as ERISA pension benefits. In any case, you should always revise your will and bring your estate plan up to date after a divorce. Never rely on a state law for your estate planning, especially for matters concerning an ex-spouse. (See Chapter 30.)

What Happens If I Have a Child or Marry After I Make a Will?

If you have a child or get married after you make your will, you must revise your will—and your estate plan—to reflect your new situation. If you don't, your estate may become entangled in laws designed to protect spouses or children. (See Chapter 6.) In any case, you'll probably want to revise your estate plan to provide for the new child or spouse.

Is My Will Valid If I Move to a New State?

A will signed in one state remains valid if you move to another state. However, it's often advisable to draft a new will after a permanent move. If you're married and move from a common law property state to a community property state or vice versa, the marital property ownership laws of your new state may affect your will. (See Chapter 3.) Or your new state may have a different form for a self-proving will affidavit than your old one did. (See "What Makes a Will Legal?" above.) You may also want to appoint an executor who lives in your new state.

Probate and Why You Want to Avoid It

Many people aren't sure what probate actually is, except that it involves lawyers and courts in transferring property after one's death. One thing they do know is they want to avoid it. That's a sound instinct. In most instances probate is a costly and time-consuming business, providing no benefits except to attorneys.

What Is Probate?

Probate is the legal process that includes:

- filing the deceased person's will with a local court (depending on the state, the court may be called the "probate," "surrogate," or "chancery" court)
- identifying and inventorying the deceased person's property
- having that property appraised
- paying off debts, including estate tax—if any
- having the will "proved" valid to the court (this is almost always a routine matter; indeed, it's so routine that it's done without a formal hearing in many states, unless there is a contest, which is extremely rare), and
- eventually, distributing what's left as the will directs.

If the deceased person didn't leave a will, or if the will isn't valid and the deceased didn't leave the property in any other way, such as through a living trust or joint tenancy, the estate must still go through probate. The property is distributed to immediate family members as state law (called "intestate succession" law) dictates.

People who defend the probate system (mostly lawyers, which is surely no surprise) assert that probate prevents fraud in transferring a deceased person's property. In addition, they claim it protects inheritors by promptly resolving claims creditors have against a deceased person's property. In truth, however, most property is transferred within a close circle of family and friends, and very few estates face creditors' claims. Whatever bills the deceased had—often not many—are readily paid out of the property left. (According to a study by the American Association of Retired People (AARP), the great majority of creditors' claims are filed by the funeral industry, which has learned to use probate as a collection device.) In short, most people have no need of probate's so-called benefits. The system usually amounts to a lot of time-wasting and expensive mumbo jumbo of use to no one but the lawyers involved.

The actual probate functions are essentially clerical and administrative. In the vast majority of probate cases, there's no conflict, no contesting parties, none of the normal reasons for court proceedings. Likewise, probate doesn't usually call for legal research, drafting, or lawyers' adversarial skills. Instead, in the normal, uneventful probate proceeding, the family or other inheritors of the dead person provide a copy of the deceased person's will and other needed financial information. The attorney's secretary then fills in a small mound of forms and keeps track of filing deadlines and other procedural technicalities. In some states, the attorney makes a couple of routine court appearances; in others, the whole procedure is normally handled by mail.

There is so much money in the probate business that some lawyers hire probate form preparation services to do all the real work. In most instances, the existence of these freelance paralegal services is not disclosed to clients, who assume that lawyers' offices at least do the paperwork they are paid so well for.

A typical probate takes up to a year or more, often much more. I once worked in a law office that was profitably entering its seventh year of handling a probate estate—and a very wealthy estate it was. By contrast, property transfers by other legal means, such as a living trust, can usually be completed in a matter of weeks.

Probate usually requires both an executor and someone familiar with probate procedures, normally a probate attorney. The executor, appointed in the will (usually a spouse, relative, or friend of the deceased), is responsible for making sure that the will is followed. The executor hires a probate lawyer to do the paperwork. After that, the executor does little more than sign where the lawyer directs, while wondering why the whole business is taking so long.

Probate Fees

For their services, the lawyer and the executor are each entitled to a hefty fee from the probate estate. However, many executors don't accept a fee, especially if they inherit much of the property anyway.

Court Filing Fees

Probate court filing fees impose an additional cost to the process, beyond attorneys, and executor's fees. For example, the fee to file a petition for probate in California is $435.

Annually, probate fees amount to hundreds of millions of dollars, perhaps over a billion. In many states, the fees can be whatever a court approves as "reasonable." (In 1997, the U.S. Tax Court allowed an attorney's probate fee of $1,600 per hour for a total of $368,100, declaring that the fee "was reasonable under New York law.") In a few states, the fees are a percentage of the estate subject to probate. Either way, probate attorney fees for an uncomplicated estate with a value of $500,000 (these days, often little more than a home, some savings, and a car) can amount to $10,000 to $15,000 or more. And, in addition, there are court costs, appraiser's fees, and other possible expenses. Moreover, if there are any "extraordinary" services performed for the estate, the attorney or executor can often ask the court for additional fees. Some lawyers even persuade (or dupe) clients into naming them as executors, enabling the lawyers to hire themselves as probate attorneys and collect two fees—one as executor, one as probate attorney.

Is a probate lawyer really necessary? One obvious way to reduce probate fees would be for your executor to appear in court without an attorney ("in pro per") as the representative of your estate. Unfortunately, a few states don't permit the executor to act without a lawyer. And some judges make things difficult for an executor who tries to go it alone. The only states in which it's a reasonable choice for most people are California (see *How to Probate an Estate in California,* by Julia Nissley (Nolo), an excellent self-help book designed for, and used by, thousands of nonlawyers) and Wisconsin, which has an established in pro per procedure. In other states where in pro per action is theoretically possible, there are no comprehensive published materials, nor is other help available to nonlawyers. Without help, learning to complete the forms, understanding the intricacies of court petitions, estate inventories, "proof of service" declarations, and so on, is likely to be very difficult. To make matters worse, court clerks and judges are likely to be unsympathetic (to put it mildly), so any mistake is likely to cause delay, and possibly embarrassment. Still, handling probate without a lawyer is not impossible. Legal secretaries and paralegals typically copy necessary forms and follow procedures set out in lawyer practice manuals. These are usually available at public law libraries, and many people have successfully used them.

In all states (including California and Wisconsin), rather than trying to save money by having your estate probated without an attorney, it generally makes more sense to see if you can avoid probate at least for the bulk of your property. This approach involves transferring the big-ticket items of your property—for example, your house and stock portfolio—outside of probate, leaving only less valuable items to be passed by your will. (As you know, I recommend that you always have a least a backup will.)

If the value of the property transferred by your will is relatively low, probate may not be required. Most states exempt small will estates from probate. The limits vary from state to state. (See Chapter 14.)

Excessive Probate Fees

Marilyn Monroe's estate offers an extreme example of how outrageous probate fees can be. She died in debt in 1962, but over the next 18 years, her estate received income, mostly from movie royalties, in excess of $1,600,000. When her estate was settled in 1980, her executor announced that debts of $372,136 had been paid, and $101,229 was left as the final assets of the estate, for distribution to inheritors. Well over a million dollars of Monroe's estate was consumed by probate fees.

Finally, if some of your estate will be subject to probate, you can try to reach an agreement with an attorney to do your probate for less than the conventional fees. If the probate of your estate is routine, it may be profitable for the attorney even at a fee lower than the conventional rate. If you do arrange a reduced fee, put something in writing, even if it's only a letter confirming this arrangement. However, you cannot bind your attorney to handle the probate of your estate for a reduced fee. In fact, you don't have the power to select the attorney at all. The law gives this authority to the executor.

Avoiding Probate

In response to the manifest waste perpetrated by the probate system, a number of legal methods have been developed to avoid probate entirely. Because leaving property in a will usually results in probate, probate avoidance methods involve arranging, prior to death, to transfer property by other legal means. The major probate avoidance methods are:

- revocable living trusts (Chapter 9)
- joint tenancy and tenancy by the entirety (for married couples) (Chapter 10)
- "pay-on-death" and "transfer-on-death" designations, most often used for bank accounts, but also available for securities (stocks and bonds), vehicles in some states, and real estate deeds in several states (Chapter 11)
- life insurance (Chapter 12)
- retirement accounts that go to a designated beneficiary (Chapter 13)
- state laws that exempt from probate certain amounts of property left by will (Chapter 14), and

- gifts you make while you're still alive (Chapter 16).

Below is a summary chart of the pluses and minuses of each method. Deciding which method, or combination of methods, is best for you is a major part of estate planning. So please read all the chapters on probate avoidance methods before you make final choices.

Informal Probate Avoidance

Some people ask, "Why not just divide up a deceased relative's or friend's property as the will directs and ignore the laws requiring probate?" Indeed, some small estates are undoubtedly disposed of this way, directly and informally by family members.

EXAMPLE 1: An older man lives his last few years in a nursing home. After his death, his children meet and divide the personal items their father had kept over the years. What little savings he had were long ago put into a joint account with the children, so there's no need for court proceedings. If the father owned no other property, the children have, in effect, "probated" his estate.

EXAMPLE 2: Several decades ago, my grandmother died in her 80s, a few years after her husband. I don't know what formal documents they left regarding their property, but I do know what happened to the household furnishings of their modest home on the outskirts of New York City. I was

Transfer Device	Avoids Probate?	Major Advantages	Drawbacks
Will	No, except in limited circumstances for small estates (see Chapter 14)	Simple and easy to prepare; can serve other purposes, such as naming guardian for minor children. Often a good interim device to use until later in life.	Normally puts property in probate where inheritors face attorneys' fees and other costs, and time delays.
Living Trust	Yes	Complete control over property while alive; flexibility in providing for beneficiaries. Allows for property management in case of incapacity.	More trouble to establish than a will. Initial attorneys' fees can be higher.
Joint Tenancy	Yes	Can be simplest probate avoidance device to create.	Fine for long-term couples owning property together, but usually not a good substitute for a living trust later in life, because each joint tenant can normally sell their interest. There may be gift taxes involved in creating joint tenancy and putting property in joint tenancy. May mean partial loss of stepped-up tax basis.
Tenancy by the Entirety	Yes	Easy to create	Available only in some common law states; limited to married couples. Can be a problem if one spouse becomes incapacitated.
Community Property With Right of Survivorship	Yes	Easy to create	Available only in Alaska, Arizona, California, Nevada, Texas, and Wisconsin.
Pay-on-Death Bank Accounts	Yes	Very easy to create; no additional costs	Limited to bank accounts and some government securities. Not a good idea when small children may inherit, since a property guardian will have to be appointed. (See Chapter 6.)

Transfer Device	Avoids Probate?	Major Advantages	Drawbacks
Transfer-on-Death Car Registration	Yes	Easy to do	Available only in Arizona, Arkansas, California, Connecticut, Delaware, Illinois, Indiana, Kansas, Missouri, Nebraska, Nevada, Ohio, and Vermont.
Transfer-on-Death Registration for Securities	Yes	Easy to do	Not available in Texas.
Transfer-on-Death Deeds for Real Estate	Yes	Easy to do	Available only in Arizona, Arkansas, Colorado, District of Columbia, Hawaii, Illinois, Indiana, Kansas, Minnesota, Missouri, Montana, Nebraska, Nevada, New Mexico, North Dakota, Ohio, Oklahoma, Oregon, Virginia, Wisconsin, and Wyoming.
Naming Beneficiary to Pension Plan or Retirement Account	Yes	Generally easy to do	Limits can be imposed by specific policy or plan.
Life Insurance	Yes	Good way to provide quick cash for beneficiaries or to pay estate taxes. Proceeds don't go through probate.	If family members will not need immediate cash (or if they don't rely on you for support), the expense of policy may not be justified.
State Law Exemptions to Normal Probate	Yes	Can work well if state allows this method to be combined with other probate avoidance methods.	Only relatively small amounts of property qualify. Rules vary for each state. (See Chapter 14.) You have to understand your state's laws; research or hiring an attorney may be required.
Dying Intestate, Without Creating Any Property Transfer Method	No	No effort required	Usually a terrible choice. Property will be distributed according to state laws, which is likely not to be as you wish. Your executor (administrator) will be appointed by a judge. Guardian for your minor children will be selected by a judge.

informed that the house was open to family—indeed, had been open for a couple of days—and I could go and take anything I wanted. I took my grandfather's favorite reading chair and their dining room table, both of which I use to this day. There was never any trouble about where their household furnishings went, nor accounting of it, let alone court proceedings.

For this type of informal procedure to work, the family must be able to gain possession of all of the deceased's property, agree on how to distribute it, and pay any creditors. Gaining possession of property isn't difficult if there's nothing but personal effects and household items. However, if real estate, securities, bank accounts, or other property bearing legal title papers, such as cars and boats, are involved, informal family property distribution can't work. Title to a house, for example, can't be changed on the say-so of the next of kin; someone with legal authority must prepare, sign, and record a deed transferring title to the house to the inheritors.

One good rule is that whenever outsiders are involved with a deceased's property, do-it-yourself distribution by inheritors is not feasible. For instance, creditors can be an obstacle. A creditor concerned about being paid can usually file a court action to compel a probate proceeding.

Another stumbling block can be getting family members to agree on how to divide the deceased's possessions. If there's a will, it may not be a problem, since the will

acts as a legal blueprint for distribution. If there is no will, things can be trickier. One alternative is for the family to look up and agree to abide by the state intestate succession rules, which specifically cover situations in which there is no will. Or, in either case, the family may simply adopt their own, mutually agreed-on settlement. For example, if, despite a will provision to the contrary, one sibling wants the furniture and the other wants the tools, they can simply trade. All inheritors must agree to the estate distribution if probate procedures are bypassed. Any inheritor who is unhappy with the estate distribution can, like creditors, file for a formal probate.

In sum, informal probate avoidance, even for a small estate, isn't something one can count on. Realistically, probate avoidance must be planned in advance.

Planning to Avoid Probate

Because probate has justifiably come to be viewed as an unnecessary device designed to fill lawyers' coffers, some have concluded that probate must be avoided for every last bit of one's property. In our view, this is too rigid. True, most people who take the time to plan their own estate decide they want to avoid probate, at least for the major items of property they own. As we've said, this is fine, but prepare a backup will as well.

But do you want to plan to avoid probate now? Many younger people sensibly elect to put off planning to avoid probate until they are at least in middle age. For example, a younger couple may decide that making wills accomplishes their principal needs, which are to leave most or all property to each other and to provide money and a guardian for their children if they should die at the same time. They understand that using probate avoidance methods will require some paperwork now, and perhaps some legal fees. Since it's highly unlikely they will die soon and suddenly (should they become ill, they'll normally have time to plan), and because they haven't yet accumulated a great deal of property, they decide to wait a few decades before engaging in probate avoidance planning.

When You May Want Probate

If your estate owes a lot of debts, probate may be a good idea. Most estates don't involve complex creditor problems. Most deceased people leave little more than conventional household debts: mortgages, utilities, magazine subscriptions, auto loans, credit cards. Probate is not necessary to handle these debts. But if there's a significant risk that many creditors, especially those owed large sums, will make claims against your estate, probate can be advisable, especially if your executor will contest one or more of these claims.

If you own a failing business, or are involved in complicated financial transactions or complex litigation, probate can provide benefits because it provides a ready-made court procedure for resolving creditors' claims faster than by normal lawsuit. Creditors who are notified of the probate proceeding must file their claims promptly with the probate court, often within four or six months after probate begins, or they needn't be paid. This is a much shorter deadline than would otherwise apply and can allow beneficiaries to take their property (or what's left) free of anxiety about future creditors' claims.

If you believe someone may challenge your estate plan in court, probate can be the most efficient way to resolve the conflict. Any estate planning device, whether it be a will, living trust, or any combination of legal methods, can be attacked by a lawsuit after your death. Fortunately, the legal grounds for attack are quite limited. The challenger must prove the estate plan is a result of someone's illegal act, such as fraud, duress, or undue influence over the deceased person, or the challenger must establish that the deceased person was mentally incompetent when the documents were signed. These legal theories are hard to prove, although easy to allege. If you believe there's a risk that your estate may be subject to legal attack, even by someone who has little chance of success, probate may be advisable as part of your plan to defeat that attack. Under probate law, only a brief time is allowed for attacking a will, and the people who witnessed the signing of the will should be able to testify that you were of sound mind.

SEE AN EXPERT
Lawsuit fears. If you're worried about a lawsuit, you should discuss your estate planning with an attorney. Together, you can decide on your best course of action. (See Chapter 29.)

Debts, Taxes, and Probate Avoidance

If an estate is probated, debts and taxes are paid before property is distributed to inheritors. If duly notified creditors don't make their claims within the allotted time, they're simply cut off. But without probate, obviously, courts can't ensure that debts get paid. Fortunately, for most estates, there's no indication that judicial policing is needed. Many people leave no significant debts, and even if some do, they normally leave sufficient assets to pay them. It's important to realize that the primary financial obligations most people do have—mortgages on real estate or loans on cars—don't need to be paid off promptly after the owner dies. Normally, the person who inherits the asset becomes liable for the mortgage or loan. In other words, mortgages or car loans pass with the property and don't need to be paid off separately.

If no probate occurs to cut off creditors' claims, all the deceased's property remains liable for debts, including any estate tax. This is true even after the property is transferred to inheritors. If only one person will inherit from you, that person will be responsible for paying your debts and any estate tax from the inherited property. If there are several inheritors, the responsibility for paying debts and taxes can, theoretically, become more confusing, but this confusion can be eliminated in advance by earmarking money in your estate plan to pay debts. One way to do this is to allocate, in a living trust, specific assets (a bank account, or a particular stock) to pay debts and taxes. If you don't have a suitable asset available to do this, consider purchasing insurance to provide cash.

If you're concerned about estate taxes, read Chapter 15 to learn whether any federal or state tax will likely be due at your death. The vast majority of estates will not owe estate tax because only estates worth well over $5 million are subject to the tax. If estate taxes aren't likely to be assessed on your estate, this is, obviously, one less thing to worry about. If estate taxes seem likely, plan to leave enough cash or property that can easily be sold to cover them.

Probate Reform

Why is probate so time-consuming and expensive? Why is probate court approval required for so many routine actions when there's normally no conflict whatsoever? Aside from the mystique of professionalism and good old greed, the history of probate supplies most of the answer. Probate became legal business through a quirk of English history. In medieval England, wealth and power resided almost exclusively in the ownership of land. It passed, by feudal law, to the eldest son. Inheritance of land was a political matter of direct concern to the king, so land transfers after a death were done through the king's courts.

The proceedings were technical, formal, and costly. Personal property (everything except real estate) was transferred by much simpler ways. When the United States became independent, it followed the traditional British legal system for land inheritance. But instead of distinguishing between land and personal property, our new nation tossed everything into the new "probate" court. Over 200 years later, all types of property can still be transferred through these formal judicial proceedings.

Over the years, there have been countless efforts to reform probate by making it easier or cheaper, or to simply do away with it. But because a complicated probate system means substantial fees for lawyers, the legal profession continues to fiercely defend it.

Lawyers' assurances that probate is necessary sound increasingly hollow. Even the British eliminated tedious, expensive probate proceedings over half a century ago. In 1926, England reformed its probate system to provide that the person named in the will as the executor (normally a nonlawyer) files a simple form listing the estate's assets and liabilities with the local probate office, which appraises the inventory and assesses any estate tax due. If the papers are in order, as they

should be in all routine probates, a "grant of probate" is issued in as little as seven days. Without any court proceedings, the executor then handles all the estate's problems—paying the bills, collecting assets, and distributing gifts to inheritors. Only if there's a problem, such as a will contest or a contested debt claim, is the matter referred to the Principal Registry, the functional equivalent of our probate courts.

In most countries in Western Europe, probate is even simpler. Wills are presented to a notary when signed. A notary, under this system, is a quasi-judicial official who's responsible for ensuring the validity of documents. Upon death, the deceased person's successor named in the will performs the probate functions without any judicial supervision. If there are disputes such as contests of the will or disputed creditors' claims, they are handled like any other legal conflict.

Will our probate system be reformed soon? Any improvement is likely to be slow and grudging. True, most people favor probate reform, in a vague way. And there's some real pressure on a number of state legislatures to adopt genuine probate reform, on the order of the simplified estate distribution system used in England or other countries. HALT (Help Abolish Legal Tyranny), a Washington, DC-based law reform organization, is one leader in this movement. Unfortunately, though, probate reform isn't a hot, glamorous issue that deeply moves many voters; without lots more public pressure, politicians (many of whom are either lawyers or sensitive to the lobbying of lawyer groups) are unlikely to become seriously interested in it.

Much of what passes currently for probate reform merely simplifies probate procedures for lawyers, but keeps the overall system, particularly the fees, intact. For example, under names like "Independent Administration of Estate Act," or "Unsupervised Administration Law," a number of states have passed laws simplifying probate procedures. But because these laws don't improve nonlawyer access, the result is that lawyers have continued to do the vast majority of probates, charging their same high fees while doing less work.

There's more at work to prevent probate reform than lawyer greed, however. Ours is a society professing devotion to equality, but also to freedom, and that leaves us a little confused about money, especially inherited wealth. We don't have any blood aristocracy, but the grandchildren of wealthy people like Rockefeller, Vanderbilt, or Kennedy and thousands of others inherit money taxed at a far lower rate than any English lord or French duke can.

It's not an exaggeration to say that a principal role for American lawyers is to legitimate wealth. Corporate lawyers are the clergy of money and present themselves accordingly. They dress in dull garb, display grave demeanors, and occupy somber offices. Wherever the millions originally came from—whether hard, honest toil or robber baron's thievery—lawyers will be standing by. Even if money is filthy to start with, after a couple of generations of lawyers get through with it, it becomes more respectable and, when a few suitable charities are involved, almost holy. And the inheritors receive the money in clear conscience. After all, they didn't have anything to do with any earlier shenanigans.

Probate has been an essential part of this sanctification process. The idea seems to be that if you make the legal process surrounding the transfer of money on death complex and formal, it keeps attention off who decided what the rules are for inherited money anyway.

But despite inertia and greed, there is one real incentive to probate reform, and that's the fact that many middle-class people are learning to avoid the system. An endearing trait of Americans is that they are as good at avoiding rules as economic interests are at inventing them. As is discussed in more detail in later chapters, the living trust is currently the most popular of a small flock of safe, easy probate avoidance schemes—so popular, indeed, that unless lawyers make probate simpler, cheaper, and fairer, Americans may succeed in killing it through almost universal avoidance.

Living Trusts

A living trust is an efficient and effective way to transfer property at your death—without probate. Essentially, a living trust is a legal document (a few pieces of paper) that controls the transfer of any property you have placed in the trust; when you die, the beneficiaries you've named in that document receive trust property. If this sounds a lot like a will, you're right. A living trust allows you to do the same basic job as a will, with the huge plus of avoiding probate.

One big advantage of living trusts is that they are extremely flexible: You can transfer all your property by living trust or, if appropriate, use a living trust to transfer only some assets, transferring the rest by other methods. Also, living trusts normally are not made public at your death. Wills, on the other hand, become part of the public record during the probate process.

Living trusts are called "living" (or sometimes "inter vivos," which is Latin for "among the living") because they're created while you're alive. They're also called "revocable" because you can revoke or change them at any time, for any reason, before you die. While you live (as long as you are mentally competent), you still effectively own all property you've transferred to your living trust and can do what you want with that property, including selling it, spending it, or giving it away.

A basic probate avoidance living trust can also be combined with other types of trusts. For example, you can create a living trust that first avoids probate and then continues for years after your death to save

on estate taxes, control property left to someone with special needs, or provide for your spouse and children from a previous marriage. (Ongoing trusts used to save on estate tax or control property are discussed in detail in Chapters 17 through 25.)

No Trust Tax Return Required

You do not need to maintain separate trust tax records or obtain a taxpayer ID number for your living trust. As long as you live, all transactions that are technically made by the trust are reported as part of your personal income tax return. Aside from some paperwork necessary to establish a probate avoidance living trust and transfer property to it, there are no serious drawbacks or risks involved in creating or maintaining the trust.

The estates of most people won't have to pay federal estate taxes, so the job of a living trust is simply to avoid probate. Here's a summary of how a living trust works to accomplish that.

You begin by creating the living trust document. In it, you name yourself as trustee to manage the trust property and a successor trustee (usually a family member or close friend) to distribute the property when you die. You also name the trust beneficiaries, who receive the property when you die. You then formally transfer property into the trust's name. When you die, the successor trustee simply obtains the property from whomever holds it and transfers it to the named beneficiaries. No probate or other court proceeding is required.

Does Everyone Need a Living Trust?

Most people who plan their estates eventually turn to a living trust to transfer some, and often the bulk, of their property. If you want to arrange to avoid probate now, because you're elderly, seriously ill, or own lots of valuable property and don't want to risk it going through probate, a living trust is probably the best probate avoidance device.

But despite my enthusiasm for living trusts, not everyone needs one. The reason is twofold. First, some people don't really need to plan to avoid probate now. Second, other probate avoidance methods may fit a particular estate planning situation better. Good estate planning can't be reduced to one universal formula. To make good decisions, you need to understand what a living trust can and cannot do and how it can be used with other estate planning methods in devising your overall plan. Norman Dacey, in his pioneering work *How to Avoid Probate* (Crown), essentially asserted that living trusts should be used by all people in all situations. A number of lawyers now make the same claim in advertisements and seminars. These claims are much too broad.

You may not need a living trust, at least not right now, if you're in one of these categories:

- **You are young, healthy, and unlikely to die for a long time.** People in their 30s, 40s, and sometimes older usually have the primary goals of seeing that their property will be distributed as they want and that their young children will be cared for in the highly unlikely event they die suddenly. A will, perhaps coupled with life insurance, often achieves these goals more easily than does a living trust. A will is simpler to prepare and easier to revise than a living trust. While using a will normally means property goes through probate, this occurs only after death. As long as a person is alive, the fact that probate will be avoided is of no consequence. Because very few young, healthy people die without any warning, it can make good sense now to make and revise a will for a number of years. Later in life, when the prospect of death is more imminent, and the person has (hopefully) accumulated more property, a living trust can be established to avoid probate.

- **You can transfer assets more sensibly by other probate avoidance devices.** Living trusts aren't the only game in town; joint tenancy, transfer-on-death accounts, and life insurance are among the other methods you can use to leave property outside of probate. And the laws in some states allow certain amounts or types of property (and occasionally property left to certain classes of beneficiaries, such as a surviving spouse) to be transferred without probate even if a will is used. (See Chapter 14.) None of these methods has the breadth of a living trust, which can be used to transfer virtually all types of assets. However, each can be easier to use, and equally efficient, in particular circumstances. For example, adding a pay-on-death designation to a bank account is very simple, and it costs nothing. At your death, the money in the account will go to the person you named, without probate.

- **You have, or may have, complex debt problems.** If you have many creditors, probate provides an absolute cutoff time for notified creditors to file claims. If they don't do so in the time permitted, your inheritors can take your property free of concern that these creditors will surface later and claim a share. A living trust doesn't create any such cutoff period, which means your property could be subject to creditors' claims for a much longer time.

- **There's no one you trust to oversee your trust after your death.** One crucial element in having a living trust work effectively is someone you fully trust who serves as your successor trustee. No court or government agency makes sure your successor trustee complies with the terms of your living trust. So, if you don't have a

spouse, child, other relative, friend, or someone else you believe is truly trustworthy to name as successor trustee, a living trust isn't for you.

- **You own little property.** If you don't own much of monetary value, probate fees won't amount to that much anyway. There isn't much point in bothering with a living trust and probate avoidance.

- **You are involved in a divorce proceeding.** To protect the rights of each spouse, your state may have very specific rules about what you can do regarding a living trust after separation but before your divorce is final. For instance, under California law, during a divorce proceeding a spouse cannot transfer property into a living trust.

Living Trusts Explained

Don't let the word "trust" scare you. True, the word can have an impressive, slightly ominous sound. Historically, monopolists used trusts to dominate entire industries— for example, the Standard Oil Trust in the era of Teddy Roosevelt's "trust-busting." And while many people don't know exactly how a trust works, they do know, vaguely, that trusts have traditionally been used by the very wealthy to preserve their riches from generation to generation. (Indeed, isn't one version of the American dream to be the beneficiary of your very own trust fund?) Trusts may even appear to some as a particularly obnoxious form of lawyers' black magic, somehow enabling

Be Wary of "Free" Living Trust Seminars or High-Pressure Salespeople

There are lots of ads these days for free seminars on living trusts. Usually, these events are nothing more than elaborate pitches for paying a lawyer (or some nonlawyer entity or service) $1,000 or more to write a living trust. Sometimes salespeople contact prospective customers by phone and pressure them to make an appointment to buy a living trust. Is it worth it? Almost invariably, no.

Seminar sponsors try to sell the idea that much of your estate is likely to be gobbled up by estate tax and probate costs unless you set up trusts now to avoid some of the tax and buy life insurance to pay the rest. In truth, most people don't have estates large enough to owe estate tax. (See Chapter 15.) Further, there are many ways to avoid probate, and you should evaluate them all before deciding what's best for you.

The sponsors won't tell you this, but instead usually hustle:

- lots of life insurance to pay for supposed estate tax, and
- a fill-in-the-blanks trust that they claim will avoid probate while reducing estate tax—a version of what I call an AB trust.

Before buying a trust from a salesperson or seminar, ask yourself a few important questions: Do you really need to avoid probate now? Is your estate likely to be liable for estate tax? If so, and you are married, what type—if any—of AB trust makes sense? Is your situation too complex for a standard form? Buying a trust from a seminar is a bit like buying aluminum siding from a door-to-door salesperson. If you really need exactly what the person is selling, you can satisfy yourself by checking references and making certain that the company provides a quality product and that the price is fair. But that takes a lot of work, and there are better ways to find legal help. (See Chapter 29.)

people to escape tax or other financial obligations. The reality is—as it tends to be—more mundane.

What Is a Living Trust?

Living trusts are, in basic concept, simple. You create a legal entity called a trust and transfer property. You keep control over it while you're alive, and at your death, it goes to the people you've named to inherit the property.

To create a trust, you must sign a document that specifies:

- the "trustee," who has the authority to manage the trust property; you name yourself as the trustee
- the "successor trustee," who turns the trust property over to the beneficiaries after your death
- the property that is subject to the trust
- the "beneficiary" or beneficiaries of the trust, who receive the trust property at your death, and

- other terms of the trust, including the fact that you can amend or revoke it at any time.

How a Living Trust Works

The key to a living trust established to avoid probate is that you, the grantor, aren't locked into anything. You can revise, amend, or revoke the trust for any (or no) reason any time before your death, as long as you're mentally competent. You appoint yourself as the initial trustee, to control and use the trust property as you see fit. If you become mentally incapacitated, your successor trustee steps in and manages the trust property for your benefit, for as long as you live. If you regain your mental capacity, you regain the authority to manage your living trust property.

And now, for the legal magic of the living trust device: Although a living trust is really only a legal fiction during your life, it assumes a very real presence for a brief period after death. When you die, the living trust can no longer be revoked or altered. And because property held in a living trust does not need to be probated, the successor trustee can immediately transfer that property to the trust beneficiaries.

Some paperwork is necessary to complete transfer of the trust property to the beneficiaries, such as preparing new ownership documents. Still, these matters can normally be handled in no more than a few weeks, without a lawyer. Once the trust property is legally received by the beneficiaries, the trust ceases to exist.

A Mini-Glossary of Living Trust Terms

The person who sets up a living trust (that's you) is called the **grantor**, **trustor**, or **settlor**. These terms mean the same thing and can be used interchangeably. You can also set up a trust with your spouse; in that case, you are both grantors.

The grantor creates a written **trust document** or instrument, containing all the terms and provisions of the trust.

All the property you own at death, whether in your living trust or owned in some other form, is your **estate**.

The property you transfer to the trustee, acting for the trust, is called, collectively, the **trust property**, **trust principal**, or **trust estate**. (And, of course, there's a Latin version: the trust corpus.)

The person who has power over the trust property is called the **trustee**.

The person the grantor names to take over as trustee after the grantor's death (or, with a trust made jointly by a couple, after the death of both spouses) is called the **successor trustee**.

The people or organizations who get the trust property when a grantor dies are called the **beneficiaries** of the trust. (While a grantor is alive, technically he or she is the beneficiary of the trust.)

EXAMPLE: Travis intends to leave his painting collection and his house to his daughter, Bianca, but he wants to have complete control over the house and the collection until he dies, including the right to sell any painting in the collection if he chooses. At the same time, he doesn't want the $450,000 value of this house and the $250,000 value of the collection to be subject to probate. Travis reasons that it's pretty silly to pay thousands of dollars in probate fees just to have his own house and paintings turned over to his daughter.

So Travis establishes a living trust, with the house and paintings as the trust's assets. He names himself as trustee, with full power to control the trust property. Bianca is named as the successor trustee, to take over after he dies. He also names Bianca as the trust beneficiary.

When Travis dies, Bianca, acting as successor trustee, turns the paintings over to the beneficiary, herself, as directed by the terms of the trust. And, as trustee, she prepares and records a deed transferring the house from the trust to herself. The trust then ceases to exist. All probate proceedings, delays, and costs are avoided. And because the estate is worth less than the federal estate tax threshold, no federal estate tax is assessed.

Living Trusts and Income Taxes

As I've said, during your life, a living trust doesn't exist for income tax purposes. The IRS treats the trust property as it does any other property you own. So, you don't have to maintain separate books, records, or bank accounts for your living trust. And because, while you live, the trust isn't functionally distinct from you, your living trust can't be used to lower your income tax.

Selling Your Home From a Trust: Tax Breaks

Many people put their homes—their most expensive asset—into their living trusts. If you do, you won't lose any tax benefits:

- You can still deduct mortgage interest.
- You can sell your principal home once every two years and exclude $250,000 of capital gains from income taxation. A couple can exclude $500,000.

Living Trusts and Estate Taxes

Let me say it loud, clear, and in capital letters: LIVING TRUSTS DESIGNED TO AVOID PROBATE DON'T REDUCE ESTATE TAXES. I emphasize this because when some people hear the word "trust," they feel it must mean "tax savings."

A living trust designed to avoid probate can, however, be combined with a second trust that might save on estate tax. Read about estate taxes in Chapter 15.

Living Trusts and Minor Children

You can leave property to minors using a living trust. Many married people name their spouse as beneficiary of their trust, and their minor children as alternate beneficiaries. If you leave property in your trust to minors as any type of beneficiary, you impose adult management over that property in the trust document. The different methods of adult management are discussed in Chapter 6.

You can use a living trust to leave life insurance proceeds to minor children. You do not transfer ownership of the policy to the trust, but name it as beneficiary of that policy. In the trust, you name the children as beneficiaries for any insurance proceeds the trust receives. As with other types of property, you must set up a method of adult management for the life insurance benefits.

Living Trusts for Couples

A living trust can work as effectively for a couple as for a single person. And any couple, married or not, can use one living trust to handle both their shared and individually owned property. Because most couples who use living trusts are married, the discussion that follows is cast in terms of "spouses" and "marital property." However, the concepts discussed apply equally to unmarried couples.

The fact that a couple can create a shared living trust to cover the property of both doesn't mean they must. In some circumstances, it may make sense for each spouse to make a separate living trust. For example, if each spouse owns mostly separate property, a combined living trust may make little sense. But if spouses share ownership of much or all of their property, as is usually the case, it's generally preferable that they use one living trust for their property.

If you live in a community property state, in which spouses equally own most property acquired after marriage, you and your spouse almost certainly own property together. Even in the other (common law) states, where one spouse may legally be the sole owner of much property, spouses who have been married for many years typically regard most or all property as owned by both. (See Chapter 3 for a list of common law and community property states and an explanation of both systems of property ownership.) Unmarried couples can also share ownership of property, if they choose, and register any ownership/title document in both their names as co-owners.

Setting up two separate living trusts for shared property owned by a couple is generally undesirable, because ownership of the shared property must be divided. That's a lot of trouble. Worse, it can lead to unfair and undesired imbalances—for example, one spouse's stocks might go up in value while the other's decline.

Fortunately, there is no need for spouses to divide property this way. Instead, a couple can create one trust and transfer the shared property to it. (You can also put individually owned property into the trust.) Each spouse has full power to name the beneficiaries of his or her portion of the property put in trust.

When the first spouse dies, the trust is split in two. One trust contains all property of the deceased spouse. The other contains all property of the surviving spouse. The deceased spouse's property is transferred to the beneficiaries he or she named in the trust document. One beneficiary is commonly the surviving spouse, but children, friends, and charities may also inherit property.

The diagram below shows how this type of marital living trust works. In this example, the husband and wife transfer their shared ownership property into one living trust. The husband is the first spouse to die, the "deceased spouse." The wife is the "surviving spouse."

How a Shared Living Trust Works

1. Husband and wife transfer shared property to trust. (Each spouse can also transfer individually owned property.)

2. Husband dies. Shared trust property is divided in half.

3. Husband's one-half ownership of shared property, and any individually owned property, goes to his beneficiaries. All property owned by wife, including her half of shared property, remains in her trust.

4. Wife's property stays in her living trust.

Revocable Living Trust
Husband's and wife's shared property

→ **Husband's** → Other beneficiaries

→ **Wife's**

Revocable Living Trust
Wife's property

↓

Revocable Living Trust
Wife's property
(including property received from husband)

Living Trusts and Your Debts

Property in a revocable living trust is not immune from attack by your creditors while you're alive. You have complete and exclusive power over the trust property, so a judge is not going to let you use the living trust (which you can revoke at any time) to evade creditors.

On the other hand, if property is put in a trust that you can't revoke or change (called an "irrevocable trust"), it's a different legal matter. (See Chapter 17.) Property transferred to a bona fide irrevocable trust cannot be reached by your creditors. The key words here are "bona fide." If an irrevocable trust is set up only to defraud creditors, it's not bona fide.

If It Sounds Too Good to Be True...

Some "authorities" have inaccurately stated that property in a revocable living trust can't be grabbed by your creditors during your life. They argue that, for collection purposes, a revocable living trust is legally distinct from its creator. I know of no law or case that supports this position.

 SEE AN EXPERT
Shielding property. If you're concerned about protecting your assets from creditors, see a lawyer.

Major Decisions in Creating a Living Trust

Let's look a little deeper into the key decisions you'll need to make if you want to create a living trust, whether you do it yourself or get help from a lawyer.

Initially, you must make four major decisions:

- What property will be in the trust?
- Who will be the successor trustee? (You, or you and your spouse, are the initial trustee or trustees.)
- Who will be your beneficiaries?
- If you transfer most of the value of your estate by living trust, how will any debts and taxes outstanding at your death be paid?

Choosing Property to Put in the Living Trust

You can place all your property in your living trust, or transfer some, or even most, of it by other means, such as a will or joint tenancy. In general, if you decide to use a living trust to avoid probate, it's sensible to transfer all your big-ticket items to it, unless they are covered by another probate avoidance device. Thus, if you and your spouse already own your house in joint tenancy, you've already arranged to avoid probate of the house.

EXAMPLE: Mr. and Mrs. Tramsey share ownership of a house with an equity of $300,000, held in joint tenancy, personal possessions worth $20,000,

U.S. government bonds worth $80,000, stocks worth $100,000, and a savings account with $60,000 in it. Each wants to leave his or her half of the house, personal possessions, cars, and stocks and bonds to the other. Because the house is already in joint tenancy, the survivor will become the sole owner free of probate. (See Chapter 10.) To take care of the personal possessions and the stocks and bonds, the Tramseys decide to create a revocable living trust.

However, when it comes to their savings account, they both decide that, at death, each will leave his or her half directly to their son, not to the surviving spouse. They learn that the simplest way to transfer bank accounts outside of probate is by using a pay-on-death account. (See Chapter 11.) So, the Tramseys divide the money in their savings account in half, and each spouse then creates a separate pay-on-death account, naming their son as beneficiary, to receive the money in that account when he or she dies.

Many people do put real estate into their living trust. Some special issues come up when real estate is involved:

- **Property taxes.** In some states, transferring real estate to a new owner can result in property being immediately reappraised for property tax purposes. By contrast, if the property is not transferred to new owners, it usually won't be reappraised for a set period of years, or (in a few states) at all. Because you and your living trust are considered the same basic entity while you're alive, there's no real change in ownership and therefore no reappraisal. If you want to be absolutely sure that this is true in your state and county, check with your local property tax collector.

- **Homestead protection.** State homestead protections, which typically protect your equity interest in a home from creditors up to a designated amount, should not be lost if you transfer real estate to a living trust. If you are not seriously in debt, there is no need to worry about this one. However, if you're in debt and concerned that a creditor may try to force a sale of your house, check your state's homestead rules carefully. (You can find these rules in *How to File for Chapter 7 Bankruptcy*, by Stephen Elias and Albin Renauer (Nolo).) Bankruptcy laws have changed—generally, for the worse. To learn about these changes, read *The New Bankruptcy: Will It Work for You?*, by Leon Bayer and Stephen Elias (Nolo).

- **Mortgage holder and homeowners' insurance.** Don't bother notifying your mortgage holder or homeowners' insurance company that you have placed your home in your living trust. While you live, you remain the owner of your home for all real-world purposes. Under federal law, your mortgage cannot be called because you transferred your home to a living trust. Also, your insurance policy will still cover your home. But if you tell your bank or insurance company about the transfer, they might raise problems and questions that you'll have to waste time answering. Don't risk the possible hassles.

Choosing the Trustees of Your Living Trust

You must make two choices when it comes to naming a trustee to manage the trust property: Who will be the initial trustee, and who will take over as the successor trustee when the first trustee dies or becomes incapacitated?

Your Initial Trustee

As discussed, the initial trustee of your living trust is usually you, the person who set it up. Serving as trustee is how you continue to absolutely control your trust property.

If you and your spouse (or significant other) set up a trust together, you'll both be cotrustees. When one spouse dies, the other continues as sole trustee.

SEE AN EXPERT

One spouse as trustee. It's possible, but very unusual, to have only one spouse be the original trustee of a shared living trust. If you're interested in doing this, see a lawyer.

Naming someone else as initial trustee. If you want to name someone besides

yourself to be your initial trustee because you don't want to, or cannot, continue to manage your own assets, it greatly complicates matters. You'll probably need much more detailed controls on the trustee's powers. In addition, under IRS rules, if you aren't a trustee of your own living trust, separate trust records must be maintained, and a trust tax return must be filed. However, completing this return need not be particularly onerous; all the IRS requires is filing the face page of the fiduciary return (Form 1041) and a summary listing of items of trust income and expense. These items are actually reported on the trust creator's regular Form 1040 income tax return.

Naming cotrustees. You can name two people (or even more) to serve as initial trustees. This can be desirable if you want or need someone else to manage the trust property for you while you live but you don't want the IRS complications that come with a separate trustee. You name yourself and someone else as trustees and authorize either to act for the trust. Since you are, legally, one of the trustees, the IRS does not require that separate trust records be kept or trust tax returns filed.

Your Successor Trustee

It's also essential that you name at least one successor trustee. Your successor is the person who makes your trust work after you die, by distributing its assets to your beneficiaries. With a shared marital trust, the successor trustee takes over after both spouses die. Also, the successor trustee is normally authorized to take over management of the trust if you (or you and your spouse, with a shared marital trust) become unable to handle it yourself.

You should also name an alternate successor trustee, in case the successor trustee dies before you do or for any other reason can't serve.

The Job of the Successor Trustee

The primary job of the successor trustee is to turn trust property over to the beneficiaries you have named. No court's approval is required, and normally this task is not difficult if the property and beneficiaries are clearly identified. Still, some effort is required.

The successor trustee obtains several certified copies of the death certificate of the grantor and presents one, with a copy of the living trust document and proof of her own identity, to financial institutions, brokers, and other organizations that have possession of trust assets. Institutions that deal with financial assets—from title companies to stockbrokers—are familiar with living trusts and how they work. They should not balk at accepting the authority of the successor trustee.

If any documents of title must be prepared to transfer trust property to the beneficiaries, the successor trustee prepares them. For example, to transfer real estate to the beneficiaries, the successor trustee prepares, signs, and records (in the local land records office) the following documents:

- a deed showing the beneficiaries as the new owners, and
- a short statement (declaration) stating that the original trustee (the grantor) has died and the successor trustee has taken over.

In addition to dealing with property subject to formal ownership (title) documents, the trustee supervises the distribution of all other trust assets—household furnishings, jewelry, heirlooms, collectibles—to the appropriate beneficiaries. The trust ends when all beneficiaries have actually received the trust property left to them in the trust document.

Notifying Trust Beneficiaries

A number of states have passed laws requiring the successor trustee of a living trust to notify all trust beneficiaries when the trust has become irrevocable—that is, when the grantor dies. Currently Arizona, Arkansas, California, Colorado, District of Columbia, Florida, Georgia, Iowa (sometimes), Kansas, Kentucky, Maine, Massachusetts, Michigan, Missouri, Nebraska, New Hampshire, New Mexico, North Dakota, Oregon, Pennsylvania, South Carolina, Tennessee, Utah, Vermont, Virginia, West Virginia, and Wyoming impose this notification requirement. In many of these states, the successor trustee must also provide a copy of the trust to the trust beneficiaries, at least to those who request a copy.

This notification requirement is based on provisions in the Uniform Trust Code. These provisions are currently being studied by other state legislatures, meaning that many states will likely adopt similar laws soon.

> **CAUTION**
> **Successor trustees advised to notify all beneficiaries.** Whatever state you live in, your successor trustee would be wise to notify all trust beneficiaries, in writing, that the trust has become irrevocable and to provide other basic information about the trust. Here are some facts commonly included in the notice:
> - the name and date of death of the trust creator
> - the date on which the creator signed the trust
> - the name, mailing address, and phone number of the successor trustee, and
> - a statement that the recipient (a trust beneficiary) can receive a copy of the trust by notifying the trustee.
>
> It's sensible to send out this type of notice even if it's not legally required. There's rarely a plausible reason to keep the trust's beneficiaries in the dark about the fact that the trust has become irrevocable and its basic terms. A successor trustee who keeps the terms of a trust secret is liable to incur suspicion or wrath—or even lawsuits—from the trust's beneficiaries.

Choosing Your Successor Trustee

Your successor trustee should be the person you feel is most trustworthy to do the job and who's willing and able to do it. Often a principal beneficiary, such as a spouse or adult child, is named as successor trustee. However, if you believe the beneficiary (much as you love him

or her) will be troubled by the practical details and paperwork, it is preferable to name someone else.

When you prepare a backup will, name your successor trustee to serve as executor, too. If a different person fulfills each function, conflicts could arise.

Choosing Successor Cotrustees

Legally, you can name as many successor cotrustees as you want, with power divided between them as you specify. However, because of coordination problems and possible conflicts among multiple trustees, it's generally best to name a single successor trustee. This isn't invariably true, however. For example, you might name two or more children as successor cotrustees, to avoid being seen as favoring one child over others. This can be especially appropriate if the children are equal beneficiaries of the trust. And if the children all get along, doing this rarely causes a problem. However, if the children are prone to conflict, you do none of them a favor by having them share power as trustees. It's better just to name the most reliable one and let the chips fall where they may.

Choosing a Bank as Successor Trustee

In my experience, it is usually a bad idea to name a bank or financial institution as successor trustee. There are plenty of horror stories involving the indifference or downright rapaciousness of banks acting as trustees of family living trusts. Think of it this way: Your successor trustee is your link with the ongoing life of your loved ones. You want that link to be a human being you trust, not a corporation dedicated to the enhancement of its bottom line. However, if there is no human being you believe will act honestly and competently as your successor trustee, and after reviewing the other probate avoidance devices discussed in this book, you are still determined to establish a living trust, you'll need to select some financial institution to do the job. Probably the best choice here is a private trust company. These companies generally offer more humane and personal attention to a trust than a bank and can be more reasonable about fees.

Naming Trust Beneficiaries

Beneficiaries, of course, are simply the people or organizations you choose to inherit your trust property. You can select anyone you want to be beneficiaries of your living trust. And generally, you can leave each beneficiary whatever trust property you want.

Certain trusts require you to name certain types of beneficiaries. For example, if you set up a probate avoidance trust combined with an AB disclaimer trust, you must name a life beneficiary (your spouse) and final beneficiaries, who receive property after the death of the second spouse. Each spouse can name his or her own final beneficiaries. Commonly, both spouses name the same final beneficiaries—their children—but that's not mandatory. Spouses in second

or subsequent marriages often name their children from prior relationships.

If you create a shared living trust with your spouse, each of you can name your own beneficiaries. Commonly, each spouse names the other as the sole beneficiary, with their children as alternate beneficiaries. In other situations, people may wish to divide their property between their spouse and children. And, of course, you can choose other beneficiaries: relatives, friends, or charities.

> **EXAMPLE:** Malcolm and Ursula create a shared living trust. They have been married for 30 years; neither was previously married. They have one child, Suzanne. Each spouse leaves the bulk of his or her property to the other. Each also leaves some smaller gifts to relatives, friends, and charities. Both name Suzanne as their alternate beneficiary and residuary beneficiary. They both name Suzanne's husband, Tom, as alternate residuary beneficiary.

You can leave different percentages of different trust properties if you wish, by spelling that out in your trust document.

> **EXAMPLE:** "The grantor's children, John Balesteri, Ellen Balesteri Walsh, and Sophia Balesteri, shall be given the interests stated below in the specified trust properties:
> The apartment house at 673 North Maine Street, Pittsburgh, PA:
> - 40% to John Balesteri;
> - 30% to Ellen Balesteri Walsh;

• 30% to Sophia Balesteri.

The apartment house at 19 Stone Street, Pittsburgh, PA:

• 30% to John Balesteri;

• 35% to Ellen Balesteri Walsh;

• 35% to Sophia Balesteri."

Arranging for Payment of Debts and Taxes

Many people don't leave any substantial debts or income or estate tax obligations when they die. (Leaving a house with a mortgage isn't a concern here; the mortgage simply passes with the house.) If you fit into this category, you can go on to other concerns.

When you die, your successor trustee will pay whatever bills you owe, either from property you earmarked in your trust document for this purpose or from trust property generally. Either way, no beneficiary will suffer a substantial loss.

However, if you transfer the bulk of your property by living trust and will likely have significant debts, including estate taxes, it's best to identify trust assets that you want used to pay off these obligations. First, of course, you'll need to make a realistic appraisal (or at least a decent guess) of what you'll owe, for both regular debts and taxes, at your death. (See Chapter 15.)

Creating a Valid Living Trust

Some people have a lawyer prepare their living trust. If your estate plan calls for combining a living trust with sophisticated ongoing trusts designed to minimize taxes, it's likely you'll need a lawyer to prepare these trusts for you. But other people can safely prepare living trusts themselves, using good do-it-yourself materials. In fact, even if you fully intend to pay a lawyer to draft documents, it's still a good idea to educate yourself about living trusts and even to prepare a draft trust.

 RESOURCE

Making your own living trust. To learn more about living trusts or to prepare your own, turn to one of these Nolo resources:

• *Make Your Own Living Trust*, by Denis Clifford (Nolo). This book contains all the forms and instructions you need to make two kinds of trusts: a simple probate avoidance trust, or a trust for couples that could save on estate taxes, called an AB disclaimer trust.

• *Nolo's Online Living Trust*. This online program allows you to make an individual or shared living trust online. Just log in, answer questions about yourself and your property, and print. Comes with detailed help and instructions. Find *Nolo's Online Living Trust* at www.nolo.com.

• *Living Trust Maker*. This software program is very similar to *Nolo's Online Living Trust* (above), except that instead of making your trust online, you use software downloaded to your computer.

However you decide to proceed, there are two crucial steps in creating a valid living trust:

1. Preparing the living trust document.

2. Transferring title to property into the name of your trustee (that's you) as trustee of your living trust.

We'll look briefly at each step, to give you an idea what creating a living trust involves.

Preparing Your Living Trust Document

No law specifies the form a living trust must take. As a result, there is no such thing as a standard living trust. Indeed, there are a bewildering variety of living trust forms, including some attorney-created forms that contain vast piles of verbiage that serve little real-world purpose.

Something simple is all you need. Your living trust document must define all the terms of the trust. It names the trustee and successor trustee and your beneficiaries and lists the trust property. You list the trust property on one or more "schedules" attached to the main trust document. You need only identify each item of property in a way that your successor trustee and beneficiaries unambiguously know what you're referring to. No legal rules require property to be listed in any particular form.

You should sign the trust document in front of a notary public. Unlike wills, no witnesses are required.

> ! **CAUTION**
> **Don't rely on a bank guarantee for your signature.** Some banks provide guarantees for customers' signatures on bank and other important documents. Some readers have asked whether they can use a bank guarantee for their

living trust, in place of notarization. The answer is no. After your death, it's vital that your living trust be accepted by many institutions, from title companies to county land records offices to stockbrokers. These institutions are not used to seeing living trust signatures validated by a bank guarantee. If any institution refuses to accept your living trust for this reason, there is little or nothing your successor trustee will be able to do about it. Getting a bank guarantee may, for some people, be easier than locating a notary. Unfortunately, this convenience is irrelevant. You must have your signature notarized.

Finding a Notary

How do you find a notary, if you don't already know one? Hopefully it won't be hard. Many banks have notaries, as do most real estate offices and title insurance companies. It usually costs less than $20 to have a document notarized. Many law offices have notaries also, but they may charge a heftier fee. In most areas, you can find a notary that will travel to you, but you can expect to pay significantly more for that service. To search for a notary, look in the yellow pages (hardcopy or online) or search other online listings, like Yelp.

I've received reports that some people have been told that a lawyer must review a living trust (or any legal document) before it can be notarized. This is absolutely wrong. There is no law requiring that a lawyer has to look over a living trust before notarization or at any other time.

Transferring Trust Property Into the Trustee's Name

An essential step in making your trust effective is to transfer ownership (title) of property to the trustee. If you don't, your successor trustee won't be able to transfer it to your beneficiaries. To achieve this, you register title to trust property, if the item has a title document, in the trustee's name—for example, "Ellen Yurok, as trustee for the Ellen Yurok Trust."

Many estate planning lawyers insist on doing this work. They don't necessarily do it to raise their fees (though that is one result) but because they believe that clients can't be relied upon to do the job right. I think that with clear instructional materials, you can do this work yourself. But even if you decide to let a lawyer do it, you'll benefit from gaining a basic understanding of what's involved.

Naming the Trust as Beneficiary

If you simply name your living trust itself as the beneficiary to receive specified property after you die, you do not have to reregister title to that property. For example, if you want your living trust to receive the proceeds of your life insurance, designate your successor trustee as the policy beneficiary. But do not transfer ownership of the policy or account into the trustee's name. While you live, you, not the trust, are the legal owner of the policy. The trust is simply who you've named to receive benefits payable on your death.

For purposes of transferring title into the trustee's name, there are two types of property: those with ownership (title) documents and those without.

Property Without Ownership (Title) Documents

Many types of property don't have title documents, including all kinds of household possessions and furnishings, clothing, jewelry, furs, tools, most farm equipment, antiques, electronic and computer equipment, works of art, bearer bonds, cash, precious metals, and collectibles. You transfer these items to the trust simply by listing them on a trust schedule. In addition, you can use a "Notice of Assignment" form, a simple document that states that the property listed on it has been transferred to the trustee's name. In New York, state law requires that you use such a separate document. (N.Y. Est. Powers and Trusts Law § 7-1.18.)

Property With Ownership (Title) Documents

It is vital that all items of trust property that have ownership documents (title papers) be registered in the trustee's name. Your living trust won't affect any property with an ownership document that is not reregistered in the trustee's name.

Property with title documents includes:

- real estate, including condominiums and cooperatives
- bank accounts

- stocks and stock accounts
- most bonds, including U.S. government securities
- corporations, limited partnerships, and partnerships
- money market accounts
- mutual funds
- safe deposit boxes, and
- vehicles, including cars, most boats, motor homes, and planes.

CAUTION
Note for Colorado readers. In Colorado, if you want to hold real estate in your living trust, state law makes it advantageous to transfer title to the property into the name of the trust itself, rather than the trustee. (Colo. Rev. Stat. §§ 38-30-108, 38-30-108.5.) Colorado law does not require that trust assets be held in the trust's name, but it is becoming the accepted way to proceed. So if you create a living trust and want to transfer Colorado real estate to it, you should take title in the name of, for example, "The John Doe Revocable Living Trust dated January 12, 2014."

Usually, it costs nothing or very little to make these transfers. A very few localities, however, do impose hefty transfer and recordation tax. Also, there may be special local forms that must be completed for the transfer to be recorded. For example, in California, transfers of real estate must be reported on a "Preliminary Change of Ownership" form, available at county recorders' offices. No fee or tax is required to file this form.

Gift Tax Worries

Transferring property into a living trust does not create gift tax liability. Because your living trust can be revoked at any time before you die, you don't make a gift simply by transferring property to the trust. Therefore, no gift tax can be assessed on trust property before you die. (See Chapter 16 for a discussion of gift taxes.)

Creating an Abstract of Trust

An "abstract of trust," sometimes called a "certification of trust," is a kind of shorthand version of your trust document. The purpose of an abstract is to show that your trust exists, without revealing the heart of it—what property is in it and whom you've named as beneficiaries. Some people do not want to reveal this information to financial institutions that require proof of the trust's existence before transferring property into the trustee's name. So they submit an abstract instead of a copy of the entire trust document.

The majority of states have laws requiring that specific information be contained in an abstract or certification of trust. These states are: Alabama, Alaska, Arizona, Arkansas, California, Delaware, District of Columbia, Florida, Georgia, Idaho, Indiana, Iowa, Kansas, Maine, Michigan, Minnesota, Mississippi, Missouri, Nebraska, Nevada, New Hampshire, New Mexico, North Carolina, North Dakota,

Ohio, Oregon, Pennsylvania, Rhode Island, South Carolina, South Dakota, Tennessee, Texas, Utah, Vermont, Virginia, Washington, West Virginia, and Wyoming. The easiest way to find out what form is required, if any, is to ask the financial institution you're working with.

Keeping Your Living Trust Up to Date

You need to keep your living trust up to date by making appropriate changes if you acquire or dispose of major items of property or find that, for one reason or another, you want to change your beneficiaries or successor trustees. You can do this kind of work yourself, or you can have a lawyer do it for you. But because a lawyer may not know of changes in your personal life that would result in your wanting or needing to amend your living trust—changes such as divorce, marriage, having a child, selling a major trust asset— it's up to you to keep your trust current.

You can amend or revoke your living trust at any time. However, often a shared living trust document can be amended only by both spouses. This prevents one spouse from pulling a fast one with trust property in the event of a dispute or divorce. When one spouse dies, his or her portion of the trust becomes binding and irrevocable, and the successor trustee distributes the property according to the trust's terms. The surviving spouse can now amend or revoke

his or her own portion of the trust, like any other single person.

If You Move to Another State

Your living trust remains legal and valid if you move to a different state after establishing it. Revocable living trusts are valid and used in every state.

However, if you're married, and you move from a community property state to a common law state or vice versa, you may want to check the marital property ownership laws of your new state to make sure that the property you believe is yours really is.

Amending Your Trust

You must amend your living trust by a signed document and have it notarized. Amendments are usually for simple, clear changes—such as adding a new beneficiary, deleting a beneficiary, changing a successor trustee, or deleting property from the trust. Amendments are not appropriate for making major revisions or wholesale changes in your living trust. In that case, revoke the old trust and prepare a new one.

Adding Property to Your Trust

Many living trust forms specifically give you the right to add property to your trust. You can do so simply by listing the new property on the appropriate schedule and transferring title to it (if it has a title document) to the trustee's name.

Just because you've added property to your trust does not mean you've provided for who will receive it after your death. So you may need to amend your trust to name a beneficiary for newly added property.

Selling or Refinancing Trust Property

If you decide to sell or refinance property owned by your trust, you can either:

- sell or refinance it directly out of the trust (acting in your capacity as trustee, you sign the title document or otherwise authorize the sale by completing a bill of sale, sales contract, or other document), or
- in your capacity as trustee of the living trust, first transfer title of the trust property back to yourself as an individual (from yourself as

trustee), and then sell or refinance the property in your own name.

Use the way that is most convenient. If real estate is involved, what is most convenient is generally what the title company requests.

If you remove property from your trust, be sure to amend the document, so that it doesn't appear to give away property that's no longer in the trust.

Revoking Your Living Trust

You can revoke your living trust at any time, for any reason. Revocation must be done in a signed document. A basic shared trust or AB disclaimer trust can usually be revoked by either spouse any time. The reason either spouse can revoke a living trust—but it takes both to amend it—is that revocation simply returns both spouses to the status quo.

Joint Tenancy and Tenancy by the Entirety

This chapter explains what joint tenancy is and how it works and explores the advantages and drawbacks of using joint tenancy to avoid probate. The chapter also explains the workings of tenancy by the entirety, which is similar to joint tenancy and available in most, but not all, states for married couples only.

The purpose of joint tenancy is to avoid probate. To simplify and generalize, joint tenancy can be desirable for people, usually a couple, who want to share ownership of property. By contrast, it is rarely sensible for a sole owner to transfer property into joint tenancy with another owner to avoid probate.

What Is Joint Tenancy?

Joint tenancy is one way co-owners, called "joint tenants," can own property together. Under some circumstances, it is a useful probate avoidance tool, because all property held in joint tenancy carries with it the "right of survivorship." This means that when one joint tenant dies, his or her ownership share of the joint tenancy property is "automatically" transferred to, and becomes owned by, the surviving joint tenant, without the need for probate.

> **EXAMPLE:** Ron and Linda own their house and a stock account in joint tenancy. At Ron's death, ownership of his half share of the house and stock account automatically goes to Linda,

who becomes 100% owner of this property, without probate.

The automatic right of a surviving joint tenant or tenants to inherit is basic to this form of ownership. You cannot leave your interest in joint tenancy property to anyone but the other joint tenants. If you leave it in your will to someone else, that provision has no effect. However, in almost all states, you can easily terminate a joint tenancy ownership while you and all the other joint tenant owners are alive, changing your share into a form of property called "tenancy in common." You can then transfer or leave your share to whomever you wish.

Simultaneous Death of Joint Tenants

Many joint tenants, as well as married tenants by the entirety, are concerned about what will happen to their property if they die simultaneously. After all, if there's no surviving owner, the right of survivorship that's central to joint tenancy has no meaning. To deal with this highly unlikely—but still potentially worrisome—possibility, in your will, you can name a beneficiary to inherit your share of the property in the event of simultaneous death. Or, if you don't, the property would still pass under your will, to your residuary beneficiary.

Other forms of shared ownership, such as tenancy in common or community property, don't create a right of survivorship, and you can leave your share of them by will or living trust.

Any number of people can own property together in joint tenancy, but they must all own equal shares (except in Connecticut, Ohio, and Vermont, where owners can provide otherwise in the deed). The owners share equally in all income, profits, and losses from their property. If an ownership document specifies different percentages or shares of ownership, it's a tenancy in common, not a joint tenancy, and there's no right of survivorship for the co-owners.

Unequal Ownership of Property

If you want to own property in unequal shares, you must do it as tenants in common (except in Connecticut, Ohio, and Vermont). For example, two people living together may decide to own property in unequal shares because one person initially has more money to invest in the property than the other. Contracts and forms to create a tenancy in common are contained in *Living Together: A Legal Guide for Unmarried Couples*, by Ralph Warner, Toni Ihara, and Frederick Hertz (Nolo), and *A Legal Guide for Lesbian & Gay Couples*, by Frederick Hertz and Emily Doskow (Nolo). Property held in tenancy in common does not avoid probate automatically. To avoid probate, each owner can put his or her interest in the property into a living trust. (See Chapter 9.)

It's common for real estate to be owned in joint tenancy, but any type of property can be owned in this manner and avoid probate. Bank accounts, automobiles, boats, and mobile homes are all routinely held in joint tenancy for just this reason.

States That Restrict Joint Tenancy

Alaska has abolished joint tenancy for real estate, with the exception for married couples noted below. A few other states restrict joint tenancy, but you can still use it (or an equivalent substitute). Here are the rules you should know:

Alaska	No joint tenancies are allowed for real estate, except for a husband and wife, who may own property as tenants by the entirety.
Oregon	A transfer of real estate to a husband and wife creates a tenancy by the entirety, not joint tenancy.
Tennessee	A transfer of real estate to a husband and wife creates a tenancy by the entirety, not joint tenancy.
Wisconsin	No joint tenancies are allowed between spouses after January 1, 1986. If you attempt to create a joint tenancy, it will be treated as marital (community) property with right of survivorship.

Joint Tenancy Bank Accounts

A joint tenancy bank account can be a useful means of avoiding probate, especially when two people are already a family unit and are sharing income and expenses. Most banks have standard joint tenancy account forms, and all common types of bank accounts, including checking, savings, and certificates of deposit, may be owned in joint tenancy. To open such an account, all people involved sign the account papers as "joint tenants with right of survivorship." (Some banks abbreviate this "JTWROS.") When one joint tenant dies, the other can obtain all the money in the account, with no need to go through probate.

In most joint tenancy bank accounts, any owner can withdraw any or all of the money in the account at any time. If the purpose of the account is for shared expenses—as the family account of a husband and wife—this isn't normally a problem. If it may raise difficulties, ask whether the bank will let you require two signatures for withdrawals on a joint tenancy account. Many will.

A joint tenancy bank account is generally not a good idea if your only purpose is to leave your own money at death to someone else. By changing the ownership document for the account to list the other person as a joint owner, you give that person complete legal access to the account now. The other person can remove all the money in the account at any time while you're alive. As

just mentioned, you could try to protect yourself by requiring that both of you must sign to validly withdraw money, but this means you'll have to get someone else's signature each time you want to withdraw your own money from the account.

There's a better way to do it. If your goal is to avoid probate for money in your own account, a pay-on-death account allows you to retain full and exclusive control over your money while you live, and still have the account avoid probate. (See Chapter 11.)

If you're considering creating a joint bank account by adding someone's name to your individual account, you may wonder if you have to concern yourself with gift tax. Happily, no legal gift is made by creating a joint bank account or depositing money in it. However, a gift is made by the depositor if the other person takes money out of the account. Under current IRS rules, the other person could remove up to $14,000 per year without there being any gift tax liability. (The rules for gifts and gift taxes are discussed in Chapter 16.)

Joint Tenancy Safe Deposit Boxes

A joint tenancy safe deposit box can be a good place to keep important papers—wills, funeral instructions, burial or body donation directions, and documents relating to veteran, union, or company pensions or benefits, or individual retirement programs, such as IRAs. This is true because either joint tenant can normally obtain instant access to the documents when they are needed.

Keep in mind that access to the safe deposit box will be limited or absent on weekends and holidays. So it won't be the best place to keep documents that someone might need immediate access to, such as your health care directive or instructions for final arrangements.

If you decide to get a joint tenancy safe deposit box, be sure to specify on the bank account cards whether or not the co-owners share ownership of all contents of the box. This can be particularly important if you keep valuable objects, such as jewelry, in the box. In some states, joint tenancy rental of a safe deposit box gives both joint tenants access to the box, but doesn't necessarily create ownership rights to that box's contents unless it's clearly spelled out. So if you don't want the other person with access to the box to own certain property in it, be sure it's clear that the joint tenancy in the safe deposit box is for access only. And of course, you would also want to leave the property in the box by your living trust or will.

> **CAUTION**
> **Don't store estate planning documents in a safe deposit box that may be sealed after an owner's death.** In some states with state inheritance tax, safe deposit boxes are sealed by a bank as soon as it is notified of the death of an owner. The contents cannot be released until the box is inventoried by a government official. So if your state has an inheritance tax (see Chapter 15), check with your bank's officials to see whether the safe deposit box will be sealed upon death of a joint tenant and how one gets the box unsealed. Usually this can be done reasonably quickly and easily. Generally, however, a safe deposit box isn't a good place to store documents that you want to be readily available at your death, including your living trust, will, or instructions for your final arrangements.

Tenancy by the Entirety

"Tenancy by the entirety" is a form of property ownership that is similar to joint tenancy, but is almost always limited to married couples. It has almost the same advantages and disadvantages of joint tenancy and is most useful when a couple acquire property together. If you do not live in a state that specifically allows tenancy by the entirety, you cannot use it.

Like joint tenancy, property owned in tenancy by the entirety does not go through probate when one spouse dies; it automatically goes to the surviving spouse.

If property is held in tenancy by the entirety, neither spouse can transfer her or his half of the property alone, either while alive or by will or trust. It must go to the surviving spouse. Also, in general, tenancy by the entirety property is better protected than joint tenancy property from creditors of just one spouse. If someone sues one spouse and wins a court judgment, in most states the creditor can't seize and sell the tenancy by the entirety property to pay off the debt. And if one spouse files for bankruptcy, creditors cannot reach or sever the property held in tenancy by the entirety.

States That Permit Tenancy by the Entirety

Alaska*	Missouri
Arkansas	New Jersey+
Delaware	New York*
District of Columbia	North Carolina*
Florida	Ohio**
Hawaii	Oklahoma
Illinois*	Oregon*
Indiana*	Pennsylvania
Kentucky*	Rhode Island*
Maryland	Tennessee
Massachusetts	Vermont
Michigan	Virginia
Mississippi	Wyoming

* Allowed only for real estate

** Allowed for real estate only and only if created before April 4, 1985

\+ Also available to registered domestic partners or civil union partners

CAUTION

The IRS can override tenancy by the entirety protections. The Supreme Court has ruled that if one spouse owes federal taxes, the IRS can go after that spouse's interest in tenancy by the entirety property. The IRS can impose a lien and force a sale of the property.

This is a concern only if you own tenancy by the entirety property and one spouse is in serious tax trouble with the IRS. The overwhelming majority of couples who own tenancy by the entirety property will never have to worry about this.

Joint Tenancy in Community Property States

This section is of interest only to married people who live in or own real estate in a community property state: Alaska (if the couple prepares a written agreement), Arizona, California, Idaho, Nevada, New Mexico, Tennessee (for inheritance purposes), Texas, Washington, or Wisconsin.

Most property accumulated by either spouse during a marriage is the community property of both. Spouses can, and commonly do, hold their community property in joint tenancy with each other to avoid probate when the first spouse dies. Doing this can make good sense. However, for certain important income tax reasons, it's important to be able to show the IRS that community property held in joint tenancy for probate avoidance purposes is still community property.

Alaska, Arizona, California, Nevada, Texas, and Wisconsin expressly permit spouses to hold property "as community property with right of survivorship." In other words, in these states you can obtain all the benefits of community property ownership, plus the important advantage that if the deceased spouse's share of community property is left to the surviving spouse, that property doesn't have to go through probate. Instead, the surviving spouse owns it automatically.

States have unique rules about what makes community property agreements valid. All states require them to be in writing. They may need to be witnessed or notarized. You may also need to record (file) them in the county where you live and where any real estate that's covered is located.

> ⚠ **CAUTION**
>
> **Be sure you understand what you're doing.** If you want to create a community property agreement, be sure to check your state's current rules. If you don't, your agreement may not have the effect you intend.

In the other community property states, there's no statutory authorization for holding community property in joint tenancy. In these states, a standard method of achieving this goal is to hold title in joint tenancy and prepare a separate document, signed by both spouses, declaring that identified property "retains its character as community property, despite our holding title to this property in joint tenancy, which we do solely for convenience, to avoid probate." Why this rigmarole? Because some title companies refuse to permit transfers of real estate into "community property held in joint tenancy," maintaining the two legal forms are inconsistent. Because in the real estate world, sadly, the law is often whatever title companies

say it is, it's safer in these states to go the two-document route: Hold title in joint tenancy, and have a separate document stating the property remains community property. Interestingly, neither title companies nor the IRS have any objection to this. It's the all-too-frequent legal story: What you cannot do directly, because of institutions, courts, or misapplication of legal technicalities, you can do indirectly—if you know how.

Although the vast majority of spouses in community property states who hold property in joint tenancy do so with one another, one spouse might wish to place property into joint tenancy with some-one else. If the property is the separate property of the transferring spouse, there's no ownership problem, since it's his or her property to do with as he or she wishes. (Possible tax disadvantages are discussed below.) However, if the property is community property, serious ownership problems can develop between the surviving spouse and the surviving joint tenant. The reason for this is simple: Each spouse automatically owns one half of all community property, whether or not his or her name appears on property ownership documents. Thus, a spouse has authority to transfer only half of the community property into joint tenancy with someone else.

> **EXAMPLE:** Mrs. Abruzzi, who has one daughter, owns a house as her separate property. She marries Mr. Mykenas. For several years, they use their community property income to make mortgage

payments on the house. Mrs. Abruzzi decides to transfer the house into joint tenancy with her daughter to avoid probate at her death. When Mrs. Abruzzi dies, Mr. Mykenas could claim that part of the house was community property because community funds were used for mortgage payments. Half of the community property portion of the house is his. Mrs. Abruzzi had no legal right to transfer his portion to her daughter.

Tax Concerns Affecting Joint Tenancy

Before deciding whether you want to use joint tenancy in your estate planning, you should understand the possible tax implications. The major concerns are estate taxes, gift taxes, income tax "basis" rules, and property tax reappraisals. I know wading through this probably sounds dreary, but hang in there—you can make it through. And you do need to know this material before you can intelligently resolve whether or not you want to use joint tenancy.

Federal Estate Taxes

Owning property as a joint tenant or tenant by the entirety doesn't affect your taxable estate for federal estate tax purposes. The federal government includes the value of the deceased's jointly owned property in the taxable estate. How that value is determined depends on whether the joint tenancy owners were married or not.

If You're Married

The tax rule for marital joint tenancies is simple. When a husband and wife own property as joint tenants or tenants by the entirety, one half of the market value of the property, as of the date of death of the joint tenant, is included in the federal taxable estate of the first spouse to die. It doesn't matter what amount of money either spouse actually put up to buy the property.

> **EXAMPLE:** Lou and Isabelle are married and live in New York. During their marriage they purchased real estate as tenants by the entirety. Isabelle actually paid the entire down payment for the property from her savings. Mortgage payments were shared more or less equally by both spouses. Isabelle dies. The IRS rules provide that 50% of the market value of the property on the date of her death is included in her taxable estate. This is true even if she in fact put up more than 50% of the total cost of the property.

Either spouse may transfer separately owned property into joint tenancy with the other spouse without any liability for gift taxes. No gift taxes are assessed against any gift made between a husband and wife (as long as the spouse receiving the gift is a U.S. citizen), no matter how much it is worth.

Unmarried Joint Tenancies

The IRS rules defining the worth of a nonmarried joint tenant's share in joint tenancy property are trickier than for married couples. Under the IRS rules, if you own joint tenancy property with someone who isn't your spouse, the value of your interest is based on how much you contributed for the costs of the jointly owned property. If the deceased put up all the money to purchase a piece of joint property, the full market value of the property (at death) is included in the taxable estate. If you paid half the cost of acquiring the property, 50% of its worth is included in your taxable estate.

But here's where matters get sticky. The IRS presumes that the first joint tenant to die contributed all of the money for the purchase of jointly owned property, "less any part that is shown to have originally belonged to... (another) person." (I.R.C. § 2040.) The IRS also presumes that the first joint tenant to die paid for all capital improvements, if any. The surviving joint tenants can overturn these presumptions by proving that the survivors made cash or other contributions toward buying or maintaining the property. To the extent the surviving tenants can prove that they put up part of the purchase price, mortgage payments, or other expenses, the value of the joint tenancy property interest included in the deceased's taxable estate will be proportionately reduced. Therefore, one risk for unmarried people holding property in joint tenancy is that, unless they keep good records, the full value of the jointly owned property could be subject to estate taxes twice: when the first joint tenant dies and then again when the survivor dies.

EXAMPLE: Decades ago, Phil and his sister Patsy bought a house as joint tenants. They each contributed half the purchase price and paid off the mortgage equally, but any records that can prove that have long since vanished. Patsy died in 2014. The full 2014 market value of the house was included in her taxable estate, since the IRS presumes she contributed all the purchase price and Phil has no proof to rebut this presumption. Phil, the surviving joint tenant, owns the entire house until he dies in 2015. The full 2015 market value of the house is included in his taxable estate, because he now owns all the property. Had Phil and Patsy kept records, only half the value of the house would have been included in Patsy's taxable estate.

Joint Tenancy as a Taxable Gift

If you create a joint tenancy, you may be making a taxable gift (except between married couples). To understand the basics of how gift taxes can affect joint tenancy, all you need to know is that the federal government currently assesses taxes against any gift over $14,000 made to any person, other than one's spouse, in a calendar year. (See Chapter 16.)

Gift taxes can affect joint tenancy because the IRS takes the position that, except for joint bank accounts (discussed below), a taxable gift is made when joint tenancy is created if the owners don't pay equally for the property. So if you put up all the money to purchase property, but list another person as a joint tenant, you've made a legal gift of half ownership of the property. If the value of that gift exceeds $14,000, you must file a gift tax return and gift taxes are assessed. In other words, if a sole owner of property worth more than $28,000 transfers ownership into joint tenancy with another person, a taxable gift has been made, because the half given away is worth more than $14,000.

> **EXAMPLE:** Martha transfers her house, worth $300,000 (all equity), into joint tenancy with her son Richard solely to avoid probate. The IRS position is that she has made a taxable gift of one half the value of the house (less the $14,000 exempt amount).

However, to remind you, if you open a bank account in joint tenancy, with one person actually making all or most of the deposits, there's no taxable gift. Only if a new co-owner actually withdraws money is there a legal gift. This exception also applies to buying a savings bond in joint tenancy. Only when a person takes possession of more than his or her original contribution (by withdrawing money from the bank account, or selling an interest in the bond) is there a taxable gift.

Normally, no gift taxes must actually be paid when a gift of joint tenancy is made. Any tax assessed is deducted from the giver's estate/gift tax credit. (See Chapter 16.) In other words, you won't have to spend any cash out of pocket to pay gift taxes, but you must still prepare and file a gift tax return, a hassle to many people.

Joint Tenancy and Federal Income Tax Basis Rules

In most cases, someone who inherits joint tenancy property gets a break on income taxes if he or she eventually sells the property. To understand this, you need to understand the tax concept called "stepped-up" basis.

Put simply, the "basis" of property is the overall dollar amount your interest in that property cost you. To determine the profit or loss if you sell the property, deduct your basis from the selling price. For example, Gus buys stock for $50,000, which is his tax basis for the stock. Two years later, Gus sells the stock for $70,000. His taxable profit is sale price ($70,000) less basis ($50,000), leaving $20,000 profit.

The basis is not always simply equal to the owner's original purchase price. For example, the basis of real estate can be its purchase price plus the cost of any capital improvements.

> **EXAMPLE:** Ardmore buys a house for $200,000 and puts $37,000 into capital improvements. Thus the property's basis is $237,000. If Ardmore sells the

house for $350,000, his taxable profit (sales price minus basis) is $113,000.

Under federal law, the basis of inherited property is changed to its market value on the date the owner dies. If the market value has increased from the price the deceased owner paid for the property, the basis to the inheritor is "stepped up" to the higher death-date value. In other words, if B inherits property from A, B's basis in the property is its market value when A died, *not* its basis to A.

> **EXAMPLE:** Grant's basis in his house was $120,000. Grant died and left the house to Serena under his will. The market value of the house when Grant died was $550,000. When Serena inherited the house, her tax basis for it was stepped up to that market value of $550,000. If Serena sells the house for that amount, she has no taxable gain.

If the market value of property has risen substantially above the original owner's basis, it's clearly desirable for an inheritor of that property to receive a stepped-up basis to the value as of the date of the owner's death. In the above example, if Serena had only received Grant's basis in the house of $120,000 and she then sold the house for the market value of $550,000, she would have a taxable profit (or capital gain) of $430,000. Instead, because of the stepped-up basis, she has no taxable profit.

Okay, now to apply this to joint tenancy. The general IRS rule for joint tenancy is that a surviving joint tenant gets a stepped-up basis only for one half the value of the property, the half owned by the deceased owner. The half owned all along by the surviving joint tenant retains its original tax basis. (A different rule applies to couples in community property states.)

> **EXAMPLE:** Ellen and Julie buy an investment property (a rental house) for $100,000 and hold it in joint tenancy. Each contributes the same amount to the down payment and operating expenses. When Ellen dies, the property is worth $200,000. The basis of Ellen's half of the property is stepped up to $100,000. The basis of Julie's half remains at $50,000, her share of the original purchase price. So Julie's new total net basis becomes $150,000.

This rule does not create any special problem when expenses of buying the joint tenancy were shared equally, or it was created between spouses. But, as we've discussed, if one of the owners did not contribute an equal share to the purchase price (except for spouses), federal tax law includes in the estate of the first joint tenant to die the full market value of the property, less any part the surviving owner can prove he or she paid for. So if someone transfers solely owned property into joint tenancy as a gift, the entire value of that property will be included in the giver's taxable estate. And because the entire value is included in that estate, all of the property will receive a stepped-up basis.

EXAMPLE: Mary transfers her house, worth $250,000 (all equity), into joint tenancy with her son, Ed, who pays nothing for his share (it's a gift). When Mary dies, the house is worth $340,000. The full value of the house—$340,000—is included in her taxable estate, because Ed didn't contribute any cash for the property. And because the full value of the house is included in Mary's taxable estate, all of that property receives a stepped-up basis. So Ed's basis is now $340,000.

Sharp-eyed readers may have noticed a problem here. Wasn't Mary supposed to file a gift tax return when she originally transferred the house into joint tenancy with Ed? Yes, that's what the law requires. Since gift tax was assessed, doesn't Ed become the full legal owner of half the property, so that only half of its value is included in Mary's estate, and only half of it receives a stepped-up basis? The answer is, no. Despite Mary's filing the gift tax return, the IRS includes all the value of the property in her estate and all the property receives a stepped-up basis. Mary's estate does receive a credit for the gift tax previously assessed.

Community Property Held in Joint Tenancy

The stepped-up tax basis rules are different for married couples who live in a community property state. In these states, both shares of community property held in joint tenancy are entitled to a stepped-up basis upon the death of a spouse, no matter what contributions were made to the initial purchase. Thus, if a husband and wife own community property real estate in joint tenancy purchased for $200,000 and worth $2 million at the husband's death, both the husband's and wife's shares get a stepped-up basis of $1 million.

But to get the full stepped-up basis, you must be able to prove to the IRS that the joint tenancy property is community property. Otherwise, only the half of the deceased spouse gets the stepped-up basis. So if you're married and do not live in a state that expressly allows community property to be held in joint tenancy (community property with right of survivorship), be sure you can prove it retained its character as community property.

Joint Tenancy Property Acquired Before 1977 in Common Law States

If you live in a common law property state and you acquired joint tenancy property before 1977, the tax basis rules were and remain different. If the property was acquired prior to 1977, the full value of joint ownership property is included in the value of the estate of the first owner to die. So the surviving owner receives a stepped-up basis for the whole property. (This rule applies to all joint tenants, not only married couples.)

In some circumstances, this can result in significant income tax savings for the surviving joint owner, if subsequently the property is sold.

EXAMPLE: Rob and Sue bought a farm for $30,000 in 1971, as tenants by the entirety in Iowa. Rob died in 2009. Under the pre-1977 tax law, the full current value of the property, $3,400,000, is included in Rob's taxable estate. However, no estate taxes must be paid because all Rob's interest in the farm goes to his wife, under the rules of tenancy by the entirety, and all property left to a surviving spouse is free of estate tax.

Because the full value of the farm was included in Rob's taxable estate, all of it receives a stepped-up basis to its value at Rob's death. So Sue's basis in the farm is now $3,400,000. If she immediately sells the property for the market value, she should have no taxable gains. By contrast, if Rob and Sue had bought the farm after 1977, and the same figures applied, only Rob's half of the property would get a stepped-up basis, in this case, $1,700,000. Sue's half would retain her share of the original basis, which is one half of $30,000, or $15,000. So Sue's total basis would be $1,715,000. If she immediately sells the property, her taxable gain would be $1,685,000.

The moral: Anyone who bought property in joint tenancy before 1977 has a big tax incentive to keep that form of ownership, rather than transferring the property to a different form of ownership, such as placing it in a living trust.

State Income Tax Basis Rules

State tax basis rules can also be quite complicated. However, in general, there's little need to worry about these rules. State income taxes take small enough bites that, in our opinion, they aren't worth bothering about when you're doing estate planning. Also, joint tenancy applies most often to real estate, and land obviously can't be moved from a high-tax state to a low- or no-tax one.

TIP

More legal worries. If you have a large estate and want to be extremely cautious and review the impact of your state's basis rules on your estate plan, see a tax lawyer or another tax expert.

Local Property Taxes

In some areas of the country, real estate is reassessed for local property tax purposes every time it changes hands. This usually means that taxes go up, sometimes by a lot, if your property hasn't been reassessed recently.

In general, creating a joint tenancy interest in real property isn't a "change of ownership" if the original owner is one of the new joint tenants. In California, for example, there is no property tax reappraisal if you transfer your property into joint tenancy with yourself and others. However, as a general rule, if the original owner isn't one of the new joint tenants, then any creation of a joint tenancy interest is a change of ownership, and the property will be reassessed. Before relying on this advice, however, contact your local property tax assessor and determine the specific rules for what types of transfers trigger the reassessment of property.

> **EXAMPLE 1:** Mrs. Jefferson owns two pieces of real estate. She transfers title to the first to herself and her husband, Raymond, as "joint tenants with right of survivorship." She transfers title to the second to herself and her daughter, Lila, also as "joint tenants with right of survivorship." There has been no change of ownership in either of these transfers for reassessment purposes in almost all states.
>
> However, when Mrs. Jefferson dies, there may be a reappraisal, depending on state property tax rules.

> **EXAMPLE 2:** Mrs. Jefferson gives a third lot to her son and his wife ("Raymond Jefferson and Jane Jefferson, as joint tenants with right of survivorship"). There has been a change of ownership, since the original owner, Mrs. Jefferson, isn't one of the new joint tenants. This is likely to trigger a property tax reassessment.

Drawbacks of Joint Tenancy

As part of deciding whether to use joint tenancy, there are certain possible risks you should consider.

Any Joint Tenant Can End the Joint Tenancy

As long as all joint tenants are alive, any of them can terminate the joint tenancy, whether or not the other owners consent to it. (But, to repeat, this is not true for tenancy by the entirety property.) Some states require a joint tenant who wants to end the joint tenancy to go to court and get formal court partition (division) of the property. In other states, any joint tenant has the power to end it without court rigmarole and can retain his or her interest, now held as a tenant in common, to do with as he or she wishes. In either case, if there's a sale, the new owner takes his or her interest as a tenant in common with the remaining original owners. If the new and old owners can't resolve a conflict, either can ask a court to partition the property into equal parts. If that isn't feasible, the court will order a sale with the proceeds divided in equal shares.

The risk that a co-owner may sell his or her share of the property may not be serious for couples or close friends who purchase property together with money they each contribute. In this situation, if a divorce, separation, or other reason to end the joint tenancy occurs, each joint tenant simply gets her or his fair share. However, if solely owned property is transferred into joint tenancy by an older person in the form of a gift, the situation is quite different. The older person has given up ownership of half the property. And unlike putting property into a living trust, he or she can't change his or her mind later and take it back.

> **EXAMPLE:** Sid transfers his house into joint tenancy with his nephew Joe. Then the two have a bitter fight. Sid wants to regain sole ownership of the house. Joe says, "Nothing doing. I'm half owner, legally, and there's nothing you can do about it." And there isn't.

So, one question to answer before you transfer property into joint tenancy is: Do you absolutely trust that your joint-tenant-to-be won't sell the property or do anything with the ownership interest that's adverse to you? If you have any doubts, joint tenancy isn't for you.

TIP

A living trust may be a better way to transfer property ownership. To eliminate the risk of giving property to someone in joint tenancy who would then sell his or her interest in the property or turn into someone you don't get along with, I advise people in Sid's situation to create a living trust. Then name whomever you want as beneficiary for the house. If you have a falling out later, you can simply amend the trust and change beneficiaries.

Creditors and Joint Tenancy

Creditors of any joint tenant may go after (legally "attach" or "foreclose") that tenant's individual interest, but not the other joint tenants' interests. But a court may order the whole property sold to reach the debtor's share.

Generally, upon the death of one owner, the surviving owner takes the property free of any responsibility for the deceased's debts. But, in a number of states, a creditor of the deceased owner can go after the property if:

- the deceased person had pledged his interest in the property as security for a loan
- the creditor sued, got a judgment, and initiated legal steps to collect the money before the deceased died, or
- the creditor can show that the joint tenancy arrangement was a scheme set up solely to defraud creditors.

Incapacity

Any form of shared ownership can become difficult if one owner becomes incapacitated. The other owners may need someone with legal authority to act for the incapacitated owner, particularly to sell the property or refinance it.

The best way to authorize someone to act for you if you become incapacitated is by use of a durable power of attorney for finances (discussed in Chapter 26). To be secure, owners of joint tenancy property should each prepare a durable power of attorney. Otherwise, a court proceeding may be required if one owner becomes incapacitated.

When Joint Tenancy Makes Sense

Don't interpret our comments about the risks of joint tenancy as a damning indictment against using it under all circumstances. In some situations, owning property in joint tenancy certainly does make sense. For people who value simplicity (joint tenancy is easy to create), and whose situations don't involve the drawbacks and risks we've discussed, joint tenancy can work fine.

Buying a House

Any two people, most commonly a married couple, can sensibly use joint tenancy to buy a house together if each person wants the other to receive his or her interest in the house on death. Indeed, buying a house in joint tenancy or tenancy by the entirety is probably the most common way this form of ownership is used.

> **EXAMPLE:** Susan is in her 60s; her mother Kate is in her 80s. They have lived together for four years and decide to buy a house together. They want to make sure that the survivor has full and exclusive rights to the property when one dies and that some grasping relations cannot validly contest the survivor's rights. The easiest way for them to achieve their goal is to buy the property in joint tenancy.

Transfers Into Joint Tenancy When Death Is Imminent

If a sole owner of property is likely to die soon, transferring that property into joint tenancy can be a useful last-minute probate avoidance device if no previous estate planning has been done.

> **EXAMPLE:** Avram, who is old and in rapidly declining health, lives in a co-op apartment in Manhattan. Avram wants the apartment to go to his daughter, Molly, whom he trusts totally—and he wants to avoid probate. He also loathes paperwork and wants the transfer accomplished as simply as possible. Avram can simply transfer ownership of the property into joint tenancy with his daughter. It requires less paperwork than a living trust. He doesn't worry about filing a gift tax return, since by the time it's due, he'll probably be no longer living. And since Molly didn't contribute any cash for the purchase of the co-op, it will all receive a stepped-up basis to the market value at Avram's death.

Transfers of solely owned property into joint tenancy are less desirable if the original owner is likely to live an appreciable time. In this situation, a gift tax return must actually be filed (well, it's supposed to be); then there's more paperwork and possible subsequent estate tax credit calculations when the original owner dies. For long-term

Individual Grant Deed

RECORDING REQUESTED BY

AND WHEN RECORDED MAIL TO

Name
Address
City &
State

Alfred Smythe
123 Easy Street
El Dorado Hills, Ca.

This Order No. _____ Escrow No. _____

SPACE ABOVE THIS LINE FOR RECORDER'S USE

MAIL TAX STATEMENTS TO

Name
Address
City &
State

Alfred Smythe
123 Easy Street
El Dorado Hills, Ca.

𝕴𝖓𝖉𝖎𝖛𝖎𝖉𝖚𝖆𝖑 𝕲𝖗𝖆𝖓𝖙 𝕯𝖊𝖊𝖉

Alfred Smythe

GRANTS to

Anthony Smythe and Alfred Smythe, as Joint Tenants

all the real property situated in the   City of El Dorado Hills

County of   Bloomfield   , State of California, described as follows:

[property described and identified]

Said property to be owned in joint tenancy by Alfred Smythe and Anthony Smythe

Dated   July 1, 20XX

_____   /s/ Alfred Smythe

_____   /s/ Anthony Smythe

STATE OF CALIFORNIA

County of _____

On _____ before me, a notary public, personally appeared _____

who proved to me on the basis of satisfactory evidence to be the person(s) whose name(s) is/are subscribed to the within instrument and acknowledged to me that he/she/they executed the same in his/her/their authorized capacitiy(ies), and that by his/her/their signature(s) on the instrument the person(s), or the entity upon behalf of which the person(s) acted, executed the instrument.

I certify under PENALTY OF PERJURY under the laws of the State of California that the foregoing is true and correct.

WITNESS my hand and official seal.

FOR NOTARY SEAL OR STAMP

_____
Signature of Notary Public

MAIL TAX STATEMENTS AS DIRECTED ABOVE

planning with solely owned property, a living trust remains a better method.

Creating a Joint Tenancy for Property With Documents of Title

Joint tenancy is commonly used for many types of property with documents of title, including real estate, stocks, vehicles, bank accounts, and safe deposit boxes. There are two ways property with documents of title can be placed in joint tenancy:

- two or more people buy or acquire property and take title in joint tenancy, or
- a person who owns property transfers title into joint tenancy with another person or people.

The Language Required

To create a joint tenancy, the title document must contain words that clearly demonstrate the owners' intention. In most states, joint tenancy may be created by putting the phrase "in joint tenancy" or "as joint tenants" in the ownership document. In some states, it's traditional or required to use one of the phrases "joint tenants, with right of survivorship" or "in joint tenancy with right of survivorship." This is sometimes abbreviated "JTWROS." Sometimes, the following is used: "Joint tenancy, not as tenants in common, and with right of survivorship." Simply listing the owners' names joined by "and" or "or" is

not nomally adequate to create a joint tenancy, although a few states allow it.

If you decide to transfer some of your existing property into joint tenancy, you must learn your state's law to learn the exact wording needed. If you're transferring real estate, any reliable title company or lawyer can tell you what wording to use. You'll find that a few states have special requirements governing how a joint tenancy is created. For example, in Florida, a joint tenancy can be created only in an instrument of transfer—a deed made when property is sold or given away. In Texas, the joint tenancy owners must also sign a separate written contract agreeing to the joint tenancy.

Do You Already Own Property in Joint Tenancy?

You may not remember how you took title to a piece of real estate, your car, or your bank account. To see if shared ownership property is held in joint tenancy, look on the deed (for real estate) or the title slip (for other kinds of property, such as cars). If it doesn't say the co-owners own the property "as joint tenants" or "with right of survivorship" or similar language, the property isn't held in joint tenancy.

In a number of other states, specific language must be used to create the joint tenancy. In Ohio, for instance, the document must state "for their joint lives, remainder to the survivor of them." In

South Carolina, joint tenancy for real estate must use the words "as joint tenants with rights of survivorship, and not as tenants in common." And in Oregon, you can't use the words "joint tenancy," but you can create the functional equivalent by expressly indicating that co-owners have a right of survivorship.

Real Estate

To demonstrate how simple creating joint tenancy can be, we've included a deed used to transfer solely owned real estate into joint tenancy. (See above.) In this deed, Alfred Smythe has created a joint tenancy in real estate between himself and his son Anthony.

Creating Joint Tenancy for Personal Property Without Documents of Title

You can also create joint tenancies for property without documents of title, such as valuable paintings, jewelry, or even for your shoes. All you and the other co-owners have to do is declare in a signed document that you all own the property "in joint tenancy" or "as joint tenants." The document doesn't need to be filed with the county land records office, unlike deeds putting real property in joint tenancy. However, you should have your signatures notarized.

> **EXAMPLE:** Guy and Danielle have been together for years. They have acquired a considerable amount of household furnishings, including appliances, furniture, and glassware. Each wants the other to receive all their property when one of them dies. They want to avoid probate and the possibility that a member of either one's family could claim any of their property. So, Guy and Danielle write up and sign a joint ownership document, stating that all the household furnishings listed in it are their joint tenancy property.

Pay-on-Death Designations, Registrations, and Deeds

With a pay-on-death or transfer-on-death designation, you formally name another person or persons to receive certain property, or whatever is left of it, when you die. Property left with a pay-on-death (POD) designation avoids probate. When you die, the property goes directly to the named beneficiary. (You do not leave pay-on-death property through your will or other transfer device. To accomplish the transfer, you need only the POD designation.)

Pay-on-death designations have become widely used, particularly for bank accounts and government securities. Also, every state except Texas has adopted laws allowing the use of transfer-on-death registration for securities—stocks, bonds, or stock brokerage accounts. An increasing number of states also allow transfer-on-death registration for motor vehicles and transfer-on-death deeds for real estate. Finally, individual retirement programs, such as IRAs, 401(k)s, or profit-sharing plans, allow you to name someone to receive any funds left in the account at your death; this use of a POD designation is discussed in Chapter 13.

Pay-on-death accounts avoid probate with a minimum of paperwork. Normally, an institution, such as a bank or the U.S. Treasury Department, provides you with one simple form on which you designate the beneficiary, and that's it. The beneficiary, of course, has no rights to any of the property until your death.

Pay-on-Death Bank Accounts

Pay-on-death bank accounts may be called by various names by different banks in different parts of the country. Common names, aside from "POD" account, include "informal trust," "bank trust account," and a "Totten trust" (perhaps from an old New York case, *Re Totten,* although some commentators have suggested the name is derived from the German "Tod," meaning death).

Whatever it's called, it works the same way. You open an account in your name, as depositor, and name your beneficiary—the person you want to receive whatever money is in the account when you die. Sometimes you list yourself as trustee for the benefit of your beneficiary. As long as you live, the beneficiary has no rights to any money in the account. You can spend it freely—indeed, spend it all, if you want to or need to. After your death, the beneficiary can promptly obtain whatever money remains in the account simply by presenting the bank with proof of identity and a certified copy of the death certificate.

> **EXAMPLE:** Ray Jones wants to leave cash, probate free, to his two daughters. He simply opens a pay-on-death trust certificate of deposit account as "Ray Jones, depositor, as trustee for Michelle and Mary Jones, equal beneficiaries." After he dies, his daughters go to the bank, present a copy of his death certificate and proof of their identities

to bank officials and then withdraw and divide equally all money in the account.

Advantages of POD Bank Accounts

There are normally no risks in creating a POD bank account. Unlike joint tenancy bank accounts, there's no danger that the beneficiary will withdraw any money from the account while you're alive. In addition, you can close the account or change the beneficiary at any time. You can deposit or withdraw any amount desired (subject, of course, to any penalties the bank applies on early withdrawal, if you have a CD account).

Because you retain complete control over the account until death, establishing a pay-on-death account isn't a gift and, therefore, doesn't involve gift tax concerns. Only when the beneficiary gets the money at your death does legal ownership of that money change.

Choosing Beneficiaries

There are few restrictions on whom you can name as a POD beneficiary (sometimes called a "payee"). But there are some issues that may concern you.

Multiple Beneficiaries

You can name more than one beneficiary for a POD account, except with certain government securities. You simply list all beneficiaries on the account form. Each will inherit an equal share of the money in the account unless you specify differently.

> **CAUTION**
> **Be careful when leaving unequal shares.** In a very few states—for example, Florida—you cannot change the equal shares rule. If you're concerned about this issue, check your state's laws or open a separate account for each beneficiary.

Alternate Beneficiaries

Normally, with a POD account, you cannot name alternate beneficiaries. If you name only one beneficiary and he or she doesn't outlive you, the POD designation no longer works, and the funds in the account will pass to the residuary beneficiary of your will. If you name more than one POD beneficiary, and one dies before you, all money left in the account goes to the surviving beneficiaries. The lesson here is clear: If you're concerned about what happens if a POD beneficiary doesn't survive you, a POD account isn't for you, unless you're prepared (and able) to create a new account if a beneficiary does predecease you.

Children as Beneficiaries

It's fine to name a minor—a child under 18—as a POD beneficiary. However, as I've discussed in Chapter 6, if you do this you should consider what might happen if that child is still a minor when you die. Depending on your state's laws, you can choose between the following options:

- You can name an adult "custodian" for the property, under the Uniform Transfers to Minors Act (valid in every state except South Carolina and Vermont). All you need to do is name the custodian as the POD payee of the account. This custodian then has the legal responsibility to manage and use the money on behalf of the child. Then, when the child reaches the age required or permitted under your state's UTMA, the property is turned over to the child.

  > **EXAMPLE:** Mary-Kate wants to make her grandson, Mike, the POD payee of a bank account. Mike is six years old. So Mary-Kate names Mike's father, Claude, as custodian of the money in the account. On the bank's form, Mary-Kate writes, in the space for the POD payee, "Claude du Monde, as custodian for Mike du Monde under the Florida Uniform Transfers to Minors Act." If Mike is not yet 21 when his grandmother dies, Claude will be legally in charge of the money until Mike's 21st birthday.

- If you create a child's trust as part of your estate planning, you can name the trustee of that trust as the beneficiary for the POD account and direct that money from the account be used for the benefit of the child.

- If state law allows it, money left to a minor can simply be turned over to the beneficiary's parents. The parents hold the money for the benefit of the child until the child reaches age 18. Unfortunately, at present, only five states follow this sensible approach.

Opening a POD Account

An appealing aspect of a POD account is that it's so easy to open. Most banks, including most credit unions, have standard forms for opening this kind of account; they will do the paperwork for you. A POD account may either be a newly opened account or an existing account to which you add a beneficiary designation. Banks don't normally charge extra fees for holding your money in a POD account.

Generally, any regular bank account, including checking, savings, or certificates of deposit accounts, may be used as POD accounts. In practice, these accounts are usually savings accounts, since it's more likely there will be substantial funds in a savings account at the depositor's death than in a checking account. And because most checking accounts don't pay interest, they aren't suitable places to keep substantial sums.

Estate Taxes

The money in a POD account is included in the taxable estate of the depositor. So a POD account works only as a probate avoidance device and will not save on federal or state estate tax, assuming your estate is large enough to owe them. (See Chapter 5.)

Before You Open a POD Account

If you decide to open a POD account, there are a few concerns you should be aware of and ask about at your bank:

- **Early withdrawal penalties.** If the type of bank account you choose for a POD account requires holding a deposit for a set term or paying a substantial penalty for early withdrawal—as would be the case, for example, for a six-month certificate of deposit—the penalty is usually waived if the depositor dies before that term expires and the beneficiary claims the funds.
- **Spouse's share of estate.** If you try to disinherit your spouse, the person you name as POD payee may not get all the money in your account. The reason is simple. In many states, if your spouse goes to court and claims a share of your estate, some funds deposited in a POD account may be paid to the spouse.
- **Special state rules.** A few states—generally those with state inheritance or estate taxes—throw up barriers to collecting a POD bank account after the depositor dies. Ask at your bank if there are any special state rules on collecting a POD account before you set one up.

Naming a Payable-on-Death Beneficiary for Government Securities

You can hold U.S. Treasury Department securities (T-bills) in a pay-on-death account form. The Treasury Department, or your investment adviser (if you have one), can provide you with the correct form. In that form, you register ownership of your securities in your (the purchaser's) name, followed by "payable on death to [whomever you name as beneficiary]." If a minor (or an incompetent adult) is beneficiary, that status must be stated on the registration.

There can be only one primary owner and one beneficiary for these government securities. So a POD account will not work for government securities if you want the money divided between different beneficiaries.

Naming a Beneficiary for Stocks and Bonds

In every state except Texas, you can add a transfer-on-death designation to brokerage accounts or to individual securities (stocks and bonds) under the Uniform Transfers-on-Death Securities Registration Act.

If you register your stocks, bonds, securities accounts, or mutual funds in a transfer-on-death form, the beneficiary or beneficiaries you designate will receive these securities promptly after your death. No probate will be necessary. Your broker can provide the forms you'll need to name a beneficiary for your securities account.

CAUTION

Your broker isn't required to cooperate. Although most stockbrokers and corporate transfer agents offer transfer-on-death registration (where legally permitted), the law doesn't require them to do so; it simply allows them that option. Of course, if they don't offer you that option, you can threaten to switch brokers or sell your shares, which may well overcome resistance.

Even if you live in Texas, you can use a transfer-on-death registration for securities if any of the following is true:

- The stockbroker's principal office is in a state that has adopted the law.
- The issuer of the stock or the stockbroker is incorporated in a state that has adopted the law.
- The transfer agent's office is located in a state that has adopted the law.
- The office making the registration is in a state that has adopted the law.

If you want to avoid probate but can't use a transfer-on-death designation for your securities, it's usually better to use a living trust rather than joint tenancy. With a living trust:

- the beneficiary of the living trust has no right to the securities while you live, and
- you can change the beneficiary or end the living trust if you wish.

With joint tenancy, you cannot decide to remove the joint tenant as co-owner, and that person is legal co-owner of half of the stock/securities.

Vehicle Registration

Currently, a number of states allow you to register cars in transfer-on-death form: Arizona, Arkansas, California, Connecticut, Delaware, Illinois, Indiana, Kansas, Missouri, Nebraska, Nevada, Ohio, and Vermont. If you live in one of these states and want to use transfer-on-death registration for your vehicles, contact your state's motor vehicles agency for the appropriate form. Other states are considering legislation to allow transfer-on-death car registration. It may soon become a widely used probate avoidance method.

Simplified Vehicle Transfer

If your state doesn't allow transfer-on-death registration for vehicles, it may still offer a simple method for transferring ownership after a death. Sometimes, these streamlined methods are available only to a surviving spouse or only if the value of the vehicle is below a certain amount. For details and forms, your best bet is to contact your state's motor vehicles agency. To find a link to that agency's website, you can look on the Response Insurance website, at www.response.com/tips_tools and click on "State Motor Vehicle Links."

In California, transfer-on-death registration is also available for small boats, called "undocumented vessels," which include the myriad of small pleasure boats that aren't required to have a valid marine document from the U.S. Bureau of Customs. Only one owner and one beneficiary may be listed. (Cal. Veh. Code § 9852.7.)

Transfer-on-Death Deeds for Real Estate

In some states, you can prepare and record a deed now that will transfer your real estate only after you die. The states that allow transfer-on-death real estate deeds are Arizona, Arkansas, Colorado, District of Columbia, Hawaii, Illinois, Indiana, Kansas, Minnesota, Missouri, Montana, Nebraska, Nevada, New Mexico, North Dakota, Ohio, Oklahoma, Oregon, Virginia, Wisconsin, and Wyoming.

The deed should expressly state that it does not take effect until your death, and name the person(s) to receive title to the real estate after your death. Most states require certain specific language. A transfer-on-death deed must be written, signed, notarized, and recorded (filed in the county land records office) just like a regular deed. But unlike a typical deed, you can revoke a transfer-on-death deed at any time before your death.

RESOURCE

Make your own transfer-on-death deed. Nolo offers transfer-on-death deeds for those states that allow them. To get one, go to www.nolo.com and search for "transfer-on-death deed."

CAUTION

Don't try this unless you know your state law authorizes it. You can't use a deed to transfer real estate at your death unless your state law (or the state law where the real estate is located) specifically authorizes this type of transfer method. If your state law doesn't allow transfer-on-death deeds, you must use a valid transfer device, such as a will, living trust, or joint tenancy.

Life Insurance

L ife insurance has long been a part of estate planning in the United States. Indeed, one of the reasons some people fear the phrase "estate planning" is that it may be a cover for hard-sell visits by life insurance agents. Life insurance does not need to be a part of every person's estate plan. It can be very useful, however, especially for parents of young children and those who support a spouse or a special needs adult or child. It can also provide cash to pay debts and estate taxes.

Do You Need Life Insurance?

In addition to helping support dependents, life insurance can help solve several other common estate planning problems. These include:

- **Providing immediate cash at death.** Insurance proceeds are a handy source of cash to pay the deceased's debts, funeral expenses, and income or estate taxes. (Federal estate taxes are due nine months after death, so cash to pay them doesn't have to be raised immediately.)
- **Probate avoidance.** Normally, the proceeds of a life insurance policy avoid probate because you name your beneficiary in the policy instead of in your will. This means that the proceeds can be transferred quickly to survivors with little red tape, cost, or delay.
- **Estate tax reduction.** When an insurance policy is not legally owned

by the person who is the insured, the proceeds are excluded from the insured's taxable estate. This can significantly reduce the estate tax liability of the insured's estate. Obviously, though, this is a benefit only for people whose estates are large enough to owe estate tax in the first place.

Having indicated some of the reasons life insurance can be desirable, let me again emphasize that simply buying some is not an adequate way to plan an estate. Many, if not most, people who have no minor children or financially strapped dependents simply don't need life insurance. Those who decide to purchase insurance should know exactly why they are buying it, the best type of policy for their needs, and of course, should buy no more than they need. As a group, Americans certainly believe in life insurance, holding over two trillion dollars' worth—far more, per capita, than any other country.

Here are some questions to ask yourself to help evaluate your life insurance needs.

Long-Term Needs

To determine whether it makes sense for you to purchase insurance to provide financial help for family members over the long term, consider:

- How many people are really dependent on your current earning capacity over the long term? If the answer is "no one," it's doubtful that you need life insurance.

- How much money would your dependents really need, and for how long, if you died suddenly?

Short-Term Needs

Now, assess whether you need life insurance for short-term needs:

- How long is it likely to be, after you die, before your property is turned over to your inheritors? If most of your property will avoid probate, there's usually little need for insurance for short-term expenses, unless you have no bank accounts, securities, or other cash assets. By contrast, if the bulk of your property is transferred by will, and therefore will be tied up in probate for months, your family and other inheritors may need the ready cash insurance can provide. While a probate court will usually promptly authorize a family allowance or otherwise allow a spouse or other inheritor access to estate funds, it can still be nice to have insurance proceeds available.

- What other assets will be available to take care of immediate financial needs? Aside from buying insurance, there are other, cheaper, ways of providing ready cash, such as leaving some money in joint or pay-on-death bank accounts, or placing marketable stocks and other securities in joint tenancy.

- Will your estate owe substantial debts and taxes after your death? If so, your estate will need enough cash to pay these bills. Lawyers and financial advisers call cash and assets that can quickly be converted to cash "liquid." If your estate is made up almost entirely of "nonliquid" assets (e.g., real estate, collectibles, a share in a small business, or jewelry) there may be a major loss if these assets must be sold quickly to raise cash to pay bills, as opposed to what they could have been sold for later if there had been enough liquid money from insurance or other sources to meet all pressing bills. Obviously, if your estate has significant funds in bank accounts or marketable securities, you won't need to purchase insurance for this purpose.

- If you are sole owner of a business, how much cash would it need on your death? Do you want, and expect, that some of your inheritors will continue the business? If so, do you think there will be a sufficient cash flow so the new owners can successfully maintain the business? How much is your death likely to reduce cash flow? How much will it affect the value of the business, if it must be sold? Do you need insurance proceeds to cover any cash flow shortage of the business? (Chapter 28 discusses estate planning for business in more detail.)

  If you don't plan to have your inheritors continue the business, the

Buying Insurance

If you don't own life insurance and think you want it, you need to talk to an insurance salesperson or broker. Normally, a salesperson sells for one company only, while a broker can place your policy with one of several. In theory, this would seem to be a reason to prefer a broker, but in practice, the integrity of the person you are dealing with is far more important than is the legal relationship to an insurance company or companies.

If you do contact an insurance salesperson, look for a person who will function as an ally, offering additional information and proposing alternatives—not forcing you. If you get too much quick-sell pressure, contact someone else. And here's one more tip: Some salespeople either don't recommend that you buy term insurance or they try to talk you out of it, for no other reason than they get a much higher commission from selling you whole life or universal.

Before you contact anyone who sells insurance, you should have a good idea of what kind of policy you need and how much it should cost. Insurance costs can vary considerably from company to company.

Many states survey life insurance companies and publish the premiums charged for various policies in different parts of the state. You can find out if your state does this by visiting your state's department of insurance website. To find it, use an Internet search engine such as Google, and type in the term "department of insurance" or "insurance commissioner."

You can also contact a free life insurance rate-shopping service, which will provide information on the costs of different companies' policies. Often free quotes are given only for term insurance policies. Companies that offer free quotes for term insurance by phone or online include:

- Quicken InsWeb Market, 916-853-3300 www.insweb.com
- QuickQuote, 800-867-2404, www.quickquote.com, and
- Insure.com, www.insure.com.

Other companies provide online forms you can complete and submit to the quote service. You will usually receive quotes from these companies within a week:

- SelectQuote, 800-670-3213 www.selectquote.com, and
- InsuranceQuote Services, 800-352-9742, www.iquote.com.

You may get more personalized service from a phone conversation than you can with the constraints of a Web form. Still, the websites can provide information to help you select what type of insurance you want, and how much dollar coverage you need.

These quote service organizations often make money if you buy a policy that they recommend, so use any information that they give you as a starting place.

questions are simpler: Will there be enough cash so the business can stay alive until it is sold? Is there really anything to sell? For many personal service businesses, the answer is no—the business ends when the person providing the service dies.

Types of Life Insurance

If you are interested in life insurance, any salesperson will be delighted to explain the bewildering array of policies available to you. But unless you educate yourself first, it's all too easy to get mesmerized by insurance policy lingo and end up paying too much for a policy that may not even meet your needs. Basically, for estate planning purposes, there are two main types of life insurance: term, which provides insurance only for a set period, and some form of "permanent" insurance, which the company can never cancel as long as the premiums are paid. Over time, permanent insurance builds a cash value, which produces returns for the policyholder. However, although permanent insurance policies do function as one type of investment, maximizing your investment return is not the purpose of insurance. If that's what you want, look elsewhere.

Permanent insurance includes whole life, universal life, and variable life (all discussed below). Any of these types of life insurance can be purchased with one lump sum, called a "single-premium payment," which can be a useful estate planning device if you have sufficient

funds and want to lock in your life insurance now. I explain each in the sections that follow.

TIP

A trustworthy insurance agent is a must. There are a bewildering number of variations of life insurance policies. I can tell you about the basic forms and offer two pieces of advice: First, many of the variations are of the "bells and whistles" type, with minor differences that don't mean nearly as much as some insurance agents may claim. Second, when it comes to selecting a policy or fine-tuning your needs, your choice of an insurance agent is crucial. Unless you are prepared to do an immense amount of research yourself, you'll have to rely somewhat on the advice of your agent. So you surely need one you trust. I'm fortunate to have a fine insurance agent (now a good friend) and can attest to the value of working with someone you trust and like.

Term Insurance

Term insurance provides a preset amount of cash if you die while the policy is in force. For example, a five-year $130,000 term policy pays off if you die within five years—and that's it. If you live beyond the end of the term, you get nothing (except, of course, the continued joys and sorrows of life itself). With term insurance, you pay for only life insurance coverage. The policy does not develop reserves.

Term insurance is the cheapest form of coverage over a limited number of years.

How Safe Is Your Insurance Company?

As some surprised and angry insurance policy owners have learned, insurance companies can encounter serious financial trouble, and even go broke. For instance, a few insurance companies invested heavily in junk bonds and "go-go" real estate deals during the 1980s, and paid the price of insolvency when glimmers of fiscal (and societal) sanity returned to these economic areas in the 1990s.

There is no national or federal insurance guarantee fund for life insurance companies similar to FDIC insurance for bank depositors. However, all states and the District of Columbia have a state department with some regulatory power over life insurance, as well as some sort of industry-sponsored state guarantee fund. While these funds offer most life insurance policyholders the reasonable hope that they won't lose everything they invested if their insurer goes broke, you certainly don't want to have to wait for state regulators to take charge of an insolvent company, investigate, and finally—and it can take a while—determine how much money you get back.

To avoid this sad scenario, you can check the reliability of the insurer you plan to buy a policy from. Several major companies rate the financial stability of insurance companies. It's prudent to check your insurance agency against one—and even better, two—of these rating systems, to be sure the company you're interested in got top grades. You'll probably have to pay a small fee to obtain a specific company's rating.

The names of the major rating companies are:
- Weiss Ratings (the most rigorous of the bunch) www.weissratings.com
- A.M. Best, www.ambest.com
- Moody's Investors Service, www.moodys.com, and
- Standard and Poor's, www.standardandpoors.com.

You should be able to locate the reports of these companies at a large public library or online. If not, your insurance agent should be able to assist you with locating their business offices and phone numbers. Each company has a slightly different code for its rating—for instance, Weiss Research's top rating is "A+" whereas Standard and Poor's top rating is "AAA." Each company will provide you its rating code system.

As a candid life insurance man once said, "It provides the most bang for the buck, no question—over the short term."

Life Insurance Costs

Curiously, the cost of life insurance has gone down from prices a decade or two ago. My trusty insurance agent cited two main reasons for this: (1) People are living longer, and (2) increased competition, including more variety within each basic type of insurance. So if you've owned a policy for some time, you may want to see if you can replace that policy with one that's cheaper.

Term life insurance is particularly suitable for younger people with families, who want substantial insurance coverage at low cost. Since the risk of dying in your 20s, 30s, or 40s is quite low, the cost of term insurance during these years is as reasonable as life insurance prices get.

Term policies offered by different companies can have some fairly significant differences. For example, some policies are automatically renewable at the end of the term without a medical examination, often for higher premiums, and some are not. Some have premiums set for a period of years, while others guarantee a premium rate for only the first year—after that, the rate can go up. Some can also be converted from a term to whole life or universal policy during the term, again without needing to requalify.

Permanent Insurance

Permanent insurance is automatically renewable without a new physical examination of the insured. With a permanent policy, your premium payments for the first few (or more than a few) years cover more than the actuarial cost of the risk of your death. The excess money goes into a reserve account, which is invested by the insurance company. Unless the company is disastrously managed, these investments yield returns—interest or dividends. A proportion of these are passed along to you. These returns can be used to add to your policy reserves or borrowed against, after a set time. And if you decide to end the policy, you can cash it in for the "surrender value."

Returns that accumulate are not taxable, unless the money is actually distributed to you. Certain partial withdrawals can even be made without paying tax. By contrast, the interest on bank accounts is subject to tax in the year it is paid, even if left untouched in the account.

Whole Life Insurance

Whole life (sometimes called "straight life") insurance provides a set dollar amount of coverage that can never be canceled, in exchange for fixed, uniform payments.

Whole life often is not the best choice for younger people with small children, who don't have adequate savings to cope should a main income provider die. People in this group usually can't afford initially expensive permanent policies.

Universal Life Insurance

Universal life insurance combines some of the desirable features of both term and whole life insurance, and offers other advantages. Over time, the net cost usually is lower than whole life insurance. With universal life, you build up a cash reserve, as with whole life. But you can also vary premium payments, amount of coverage, or both, from year to year.

Variable Life Insurance

Variable life insurance refers to policies in which cash reserves are invested in securities, stocks, and bonds. In a sense, these policies combine an insurance feature with a mutual fund. Since over the past decade overall prices on the stock market have risen dramatically, variable life policies have usually produced the best returns. But of course, there's a potential downside to this also. These policies are almost sure to bring unpleasant surprises when financial markets decline.

Variable Universal Life Insurance

Variable universal life insurance is a type of whole life insurance that combines the premium payment and coverage flexibility of universal life insurance with the investment opportunity (and risk) of variable life insurance.

Single-Premium Life Insurance

With single-premium life insurance, you pay up front all premiums due for the full duration of the policy. Normally, any policy with a savings feature can be purchased with a single premium. Obviously, this requires the expenditure of a large amount of cash—$5,000, $10,000, or often much more, depending on your age and the dollar amount of the policy.

One reason to commit so much cash to buying an insurance policy is that it enables you to give the fully-paid-for policy to new owners. For the wealthy, there can be major estate tax savings if someone other than the insured owns the policy.

Survivorship Life Insurance

Survivorship life insurance (also called "second-to-die" or "joint" insurance) is a relatively new type of insurance. It provides a single policy that insures two lives, usually spouses. When the first spouse dies, no proceeds are paid. Indeed, the policy remains in force, and premiums must continue to be paid, as long as a spouse lives. The policy only pays off on the death of the second spouse.

Why would any couple want such a policy? Mainly as part of an estate plan for wealthier couples who expect that substantial estate taxes will be assessed on the death of the second spouse. (See Chapter 18.)

This kind of insurance can also be desirable if one member of a couple is in less than good health. If the other spouse is in reasonably good health, the couple can usually obtain survivorship life insurance.

Because two lives are insured, premiums for survivorship life policies are comparatively low compared to policies on one person's life. It's those old insurance companies' actuarial tables again: The odds of two people dying in X time period are less than of one doing so. But, of course, cost also depends on the age and the health of the insured couple.

SEE AN EXPERT
The federal tax statute governing survivorship life insurance is somewhat ambiguous. Because this is a complex area, you need to check with a good estate planning lawyer with current knowledge of the tax rulings on this type of policy. Also, discuss this issue with your insurance agent to be sure your survivorship policy will have the effect you intend. It may be best to have the policy owned by a life insurance trust.

First-to-Die Life Insurance

"First-to-die" life insurance is, as the name indicates, the reverse of survivorship insurance. With a first-to-die policy, two (or occasionally more) people, usually business partners or co-owners, are insured under one policy. Because these policies are usually maintained as part of a business buyout agreement, usually the company or partnership itself buys

and maintains the policy. When the first insured dies, the policy pays off, with the funds typically paid to the company or partnership. Effectively, this means payments go to the other owners of the business.

A first-to-die policy is significantly cheaper than individual policies for two, or several, business owners. Obviously, insuring against only one death exposes an insurance company to lower risks than if several people are separately insured for the same amount.

When one business owner dies, the proceeds of a first-to-die policy can be used to pay off the worth of the deceased owner's interest, under a buyout clause. Or, if the deceased owner's beneficiaries wish, and are allowed, to participate in the business, the funds can be used for the costs of whatever adjustments and problems the business faces because of the death of an owner.

EXAMPLE: Paul, Gabe, and Liz are equal partners in a flower store. Their partnership agreement provides that if a partner dies, the two surviving partners can buy out that partner's interest according to a set valuation formula. The business does not have a great deal of ready cash. Almost all the available cash the partners had was consumed by opening the business and operational costs.

The partnership buys a first-to-die policy covering the lives of the three partners. The partners have made a rough guess of how much the business is worth now, and have paid for a policy that pays off about half this value. In theory, they need coverage for only one-third of the value, but they hope and expect their business will increase, and so want to include some allowance for increased value of a deceased partner's interest.

If a partner dies, the life insurance pays the proceeds to the partnership. The value of the deceased partner's interest is determined from the formula. The two surviving partners pay this amount to the deceased partner's inheritors. If there are any insurance proceeds left over, the partners can use them however they agree upon. And when everything is wound up, the two surviving partners own the business 50-50.

Annuities

Basically, an annuity is a policy in which an insurance company contracts to pay the policy beneficiary a certain cash amount each year, or month, instead of one lump sum upon death. There are all sorts of annuity policies and combinations of annuity payment plans with cash value life insurance policies. Some people who don't trust their own ability to hold onto money even purchase an annuity policy when times are good, naming themselves as

beneficiary. They thus provide themselves with a set income for life, beginning at a specified age.

Life Insurance and Probate

The proceeds of a life insurance policy are not subject to probate unless you name your estate as the beneficiary of your policy. If anyone else, including a trust, is the beneficiary of the policy, the proceeds are not included in the probate estate and are paid to the beneficiary without the cost or delay of probate. Unless your estate won't have ready cash to pay anticipated debts and taxes, there is no sound reason for naming your estate as the beneficiary of an insurance policy.

CAUTION
Think again before naming your estate as a life insurance beneficiary. The problem of a deceased person having substantial debts and no liquid assets is rare. In most instances, estates contain enough cash, or other assets that can be sold for cash, to pay debts and taxes. Unless life insurance proceeds are used for estate costs, they will be distributed to someone, eventually. So it seems foolhardy to reduce the amount inheritors receive from your life insurance because of probate costs—or add to the time your inheritors must wait before they get this money.

Choosing Life Insurance Beneficiaries

As you know, when you buy life insurance, you name the policy's beneficiaries—those who will receive the proceeds when you die. As long as you own the policy, you can change beneficiaries, provided that you are mentally competent. You can't, however, change an insurance beneficiary by naming someone else in your will or living trust. If you want to change a beneficiary, contact your insurance agent or company, and complete the appropriate form.

Special Rules for Community Property States

If you live in a community property state and buy a policy with community property funds, one half of the proceeds are owned by the surviving spouse, no matter whom the policy names as the beneficiary. This result can be varied by a written agreement between the spouses, in which one spouse transfers all interest in a particular insurance policy to the other spouse. Again, contact your insurance company for the proper form.

Minor Children as Beneficiaries

If you want your minor children to be the beneficiaries of your life insurance policy, you need to arrange for the proceeds to be managed and supervised by a competent adult. If you don't, and your children are not legal adults at your death, the insurance company would require that a court appoint a property guardian for the children before releasing the proceeds. As discussed in Chapter 6, this is not desirable because it necessitates attorneys' fees, court proceedings, and court supervision of life insurance proceeds left to benefit your children—costs and hassles the children surely won't benefit from. There are two ways to prevent this:

- Name your living trust (or successor trustee, depending on which the insurance company prefers) as the beneficiary of the policy. In the trust document, you name the minor children as beneficiaries of any money the trust receives from the insurance policy. You also establish within the trust a method to impose adult management over the proceeds, which can be either a child's trust or an UTMA custodianship.
- Leave the proceeds for the benefit of your children simply by using your state's UTMA directly. You name as policy beneficiary an adult "custodian" for your minor child or children.

Grandparents or other friends or relatives who name minors as beneficiaries of their life insurance policies can also use these methods.

Finally, you could rethink your plan to name minors as beneficiaries of your life insurance policy. Instead, name a trusted adult beneficiary who you are confident will use the money for the children's benefit.

Reducing Estate Tax by Transferring Ownership of Life Insurance Policies

This section is important only if your estate is likely to have to pay federal estate tax. (See Chapter 15.)

Whether or not life insurance proceeds are included in the deceased's taxable estate, and so subject to federal estate tax, depends on who owns the policy when the insured dies. If the deceased owned the policy, the full amount of the proceeds is included in the federal taxable estate; if someone else owned the policy, the proceeds are not included.

Proceeds Payable to a Spouse Are Exempt From Federal Estate Tax

If a surviving spouse is the beneficiary of a policy owned by the deceased spouse, no federal estate taxes will be assessed against the proceeds, no matter how much they are. This is because all property left to a surviving spouse is exempt from federal tax. (See Chapter 15.)

EXAMPLE: Melissa purchases and owns a life insurance policy with a face value of $200,000, payable to her son, Jeff, as beneficiary. Melissa's business partner, Juanita, owns a second policy, covering Melissa's life for $400,000, payable to Juanita. She will use these proceeds to pay Jeff, Melissa's sole inheritor, the worth of Melissa's interest in the business. Melissa dies. All the proceeds of Melissa's policy, $200,000, are included in her federal taxable estate. However, none of the $400,000 from the policy Juanita owns is part of Melissa's federal taxable estate, because Melissa did not own the policy.

Income Taxation of Insurance Proceeds

Cash policy proceeds payable to a beneficiary after an insured's death are exempt from federal income taxes. However, if the proceeds are paid in installments, any interest paid on the principal is taxable income to the recipient. Likewise, the proceeds of an insurance policy are exempt from state income tax in most states.

There are two ways you can transfer ownership of a life insurance policy. One, you can simply give the policy to another person or persons. Or, you can create an irrevocable life insurance trust and transfer ownership to that entity. Here we'll primarily focus on the first method. The second, I discuss briefly here and in more depth in Chapter 21.

If you choose to transfer a life insurance policy, you must do it with the knowledge of, and with forms approved by, the issuing company. The transfer won't be legally effective if the insurance company has no record of it.

You have the right to assign or give ownership of your life insurance policy to any other adult, including the policy beneficiary. (The only exceptions are some group policies, which many people participate in through work, and which don't allow you to transfer ownership.)

Transferring Ownership to Other People

Transferring ownership of your policy to another person or persons involves a trade-off: Once the policy is transferred, you've lost all your power over it, forever. You cannot cancel it or change the beneficiary. To make this point bluntly, suppose you transfer ownership of your policy to your spouse, and later get divorced. You cannot cancel the policy or recover it from your now ex-spouse. Nevertheless, in many situations, the trade-off is worth it, as, for example, when you transfer policy ownership to a child (or children) with whom you have a close and loving relationship.

The IRS has some special rules about determining who owns a life insurance policy when the insured dies. Gifts of life insurance policies made within three years of death are disallowed for federal estate tax purposes (and often for state tax purposes, too). This means that the full amount of the proceeds is included in your estate as if you had remained owner of the policy.

EXAMPLE: Louise gave her term life insurance, with proceeds of $300,000, payable on death, to her friend, Leon, in 2012. She dies in 2014. For federal estate tax purposes, the gift is disallowed, and all the proceeds, $300,000, are included in Louise's taxable estate. If Louise had transferred the life insurance policy more than three years before her death, none of the proceeds would have been included in her taxable estate.

The message here is obvious: If you want to give away a life insurance policy to reduce estate taxes, give the policy away as soon as feasible. (And then don't die for at least three years.)

Another IRS regulation provides that a deceased person who retained any "incidents of ownership" of a life insurance policy is considered the owner. The term incidents of ownership is simply legalese for keeping any significant power over the transferred insurance policy. Specifically, the proceeds of the policy will be included in your taxable estate if you have the legal right to do any one of the following:

- change or name beneficiaries of the policy
- borrow against the policy, pledge any cash reserve it has, or cash it in
- surrender, convert, or cancel the policy, or
- select a payment option—decide if payments to the beneficiary can be a lump sum or in installments.

Transferring a Policy Will Not Affect Premium Payments

Transferring ownership of a life insurance policy from the insured person to someone else will not change the premium payment amount. The transfer has no effect on the life expectancy of the insured, which is what the insurance company is betting on.

Gift Tax Concerns

When a life insurance policy is transferred from the original insured owner to a beneficiary, the transaction is regarded as a gift by the tax authorities. So, under current gift tax rules, if a policy with a present value of more than $14,000 is transferred to one person, gift taxes will be assessed. (See Chapter 16.) Even so, the amount of gift tax assessed will be far less than the tax cost of leaving the policy in your estate. This is because the proceeds payable under a policy when the insured dies are always considerably more than the worth of the policy while the insured lives.

> EXAMPLE: In 2014, Eugene transfers ownership of his universal life insurance policy to his son, David. The cash surrender value of the policy when he transfers it is $22,000. Under IRS rules, $8,000 worth of this value is subject to gift tax. Eugene dies four years after giving his son the insurance policy, which pays $300,000. None of this $300,000 is included in Eugene's federal taxable estate. (Nor are the proceeds considered income to David, for federal income tax purposes.)

How to Transfer Ownership of Your Policy

You can give away ownership of your life insurance policy by signing a simple document called an "assignment" or a "transfer." To do this, notify the insurance company and use its assignment or transfer form. Also, the policy itself will usually have to be changed to specify that the insured is no longer the owner. There's normally no charge to make the change.

After the policy is transferred, the new owner should make any premium payments. If the previous owner makes payments, the IRS might contend that the previous owner was keeping an incident of ownership, so the proceeds of the policy must be included in the deceased owner's federally taxable estate—precisely what you're trying to avoid. If the new owner doesn't have sufficient funds to make the payments, you can give her money to be used for these payments.

Life Insurance Trusts

An irrevocable life insurance trust is a legal entity you create while you live for the purpose of owning life insurance you previously owned personally. (These trusts are covered in more depth in Chapter 21.)

Once you transfer ownership of life insurance to the trust, it owns the policy, not you. So the proceeds aren't part of your estate.

Why create a life insurance trust, rather than simply transfer a life insurance policy to someone else? One reason can be that there's no one you want to give your policy to. In other words, you want to get the proceeds out of your taxable estate, but you want to exert legal control over the policy and avoid the risks of having an insurance policy on your life owned by someone else—perhaps a spouse or child you don't trust to pay policy premiums. For example, the trust could specify that the policy must be kept in effect while you live, eliminating the risk that a new owner of the policy could decide to cash it in.

EXAMPLE: Marcie is the divorced mother of two children, in their 20s, who will be her beneficiaries. Neither is sensible with money. Marcie has an estate of $700,000, plus universal life insurance which will pay $5 million at her death. She wants to be sure her estate will not be liable for estate taxes and, so, desires to transfer ownership of her policy. However, there's no one Marcie trusts enough to give her policy to outright. With the controls she can impose through a trust, however, she decides it's safe to allow her sister, the person she's closest to, to be the trustee of a life insurance trust for the policy. She creates a formal trust, and transfers ownership of the life insurance policy to that trust. After Marcie's death, her sister will handle the money for the children under the terms of the trust document.

There are strict requirements governing life insurance trusts. If you want to gain the estate tax savings, the following must be met:

- The life insurance trust must be irrevocable. If you retain the right to revoke the trust, you will be considered the owner of the policy, and the proceeds will be taxed as part of your estate upon death.
- You cannot be the trustee.
- You must establish the trust at least three years before your death. If the trust has not existed for at least three years when you die, the trust is disregarded for estate tax purposes, and the proceeds are included in your taxable estate.

SEE AN EXPERT

Get legal help for a life insurance trust. If you want to explore using a life insurance trust, you'll need to see a lawyer. Tax complexities must be considered: How will future premium payments be made? If the person establishing the trust makes the payments directly, or even indirectly, how could that affect estate taxes? Personal concerns also have to be carefully evaluated. Who will be the trustee? Or, suppose you have a child after the trust becomes operational? Or a child gets divorced? Or marries or remarries? There aren't any standard answers to these questions. You have to carefully work out what you want.

Retirement Benefits

When they retire, most people are entitled to payments from one or more retirement programs, such as Social Security, military plans, private or public employee pensions, union pensions, or individual retirement plans.

When you do your estate planning, you need to take into account any retirement benefits you or other family members have coming. For example, a married couple should consider each spouse's retirement income. If a surviving spouse can expect generous monthly pension checks that will cover living expenses, with a little left over, the other spouse may understandably decide to leave at least some money and property directly to children or friends. Similarly, buying a life insurance policy on the life of a breadwinner makes great sense if there will be little continuing income should he or she die and much less sense if a generous pension is in the offing.

Financial planning for retirement can be complicated, and I don't get into that subject here. This chapter covers the basics of how common kinds of retirement benefits—Social Security, individual retirement plans, and pensions—are transferred after death, and the impact of choosing beneficiaries to inherit these benefits.

RESOURCE

Going beyond finances. While financial planning is essential, a truly successful retirement is about much more than money. *Get a Life: You Don't Need a Million to Retire Well*, by

Ralph Warner (Nolo), provides thoughtful advice on enjoying a fulfilling retirement—emphasizing relationships and personal interests rather than just the accumulation of wealth.

Social Security

The most extensive retirement program in the United States is the federal Social Security system. Despite periodic anxieties that the program will run out of money, it has always managed to make regular payments to millions and continues to do so. For years, payments began at age 65. That age is now gradually increasing, until it will reach age 67 in 2027. The payment age for 2012 through 2020 is 66 years.

It is possible to receive reduced payments as soon as your reach age 62. But there are often serious drawbacks to this. If you are still working, Social Security will subtract one dollar from your monthly check for every two dollars you earn. (You must earn over a minimal amount, roughly $13,000.) By contrast, if you wait until you reach full retirement age, there's no limit on how much money you can earn and still receive your full check.

If your spouse is already receiving Social Security and you are at least 62, you may also be eligible to receive a monthly benefit from your spouse's earnings. This is in addition to what your spouse already receives and your own Social Security benefits. (The Social Security Administration usually advises a person approaching age 62 of this benefit. If not, contact your local Social Security office.)

Social Security also provides payments to many surviving relatives of covered wage earners, even if these people are not entitled to payments based on their own earnings record.

Relatives usually eligible to receive some benefits based on a deceased wage earner's record include:

- a surviving spouse
- a former spouse (in some circumstances)
- unmarried children up to age 18 (or 19 if the child is a full-time high school student)
- students with disabilities, in some situations
- dependent grandchildren and great-grandchildren, and
- dependent parents over age 62.

In addition, Social Security pays a magnanimous one-time death payment of $255 to the surviving spouse or child eligible for benefits.

RESOURCE
More information about Social Security benefits. *Social Security, Medicare & Government Pensions*, by Joseph Matthews (Nolo), thoroughly discusses Social Security payments, so that you can find out exactly what you and your family members can expect to receive in the way of Social Security survivor payments.

Individual Retirement Plans

In addition to depending on Social Security, savings, and investments, many people contribute regularly to one or more individual retirement plans to ensure that they will have enough income when they get older. In fact, retirement plans are becoming major assets of many people. Nevertheless, retirement plans are not primarily designed to be estate planning devices. There may be nothing left in your retirement account when you die. But in case there is money left over, it's important to consider the possible effects on your estate plan.

There are many complex rules governing what you can and can't do with funds in an individual retirement plan. Here, I'll cover only the basics about using these plans in estate planning.

RESOURCE
More information about individual retirement plans. For a thorough explanation of the rules governing retirement plans, particularly how you, or a beneficiary after you die, can withdraw money without getting into trouble, see *IRAs, 401(k)s & Other Retirement Plans: Taking Your Money Out*, by Twila Slesnick and John C. Suttle (Nolo).

Traditional Individual Retirement Plans

Individual retirement plans, such as IRAs (individual retirement accounts) or SEP-IRAs

(Simplified Employee Pension IRAs, formerly called profit-sharing plans or Keogh plans) are retirement plans you fund yourself. The money you contribute is tax deductible (within limits); you don't pay tax on the principal or earnings until you withdraw them after retirement. You are in charge of how the money is invested.

A SEP-IRA is for the self-employed. By contrast, an IRA can be created by any income earner through annual contributions. Currently, annual contributions of up to $5,000 ($6,500 if you're age 50 or older) are tax deductible if you aren't covered by a company retirement plan. The amount is indexed for inflation and will periodically rise in $500 increments.

If you participate in an employer-sponsored retirement plan, you are entitled to the full tax deduction unless your income is above a certain level. This income ceiling may change each year. Contact your plan administrator to learn the current limit.

Whether or not you participate in an employer-sponsored plan, you can contribute more than the annual tax-deductible amount to an IRA, but you can't take the tax deduction on the overage.

If you are self-employed, the Tax Relief Act of 2001 raised the contribution amounts for SEP-IRAs according to your income and also established a catch-up program. See your accountant or tax preparer to learn more about these changes.

If you withdraw money early—usually before age 59½—a penalty is imposed, unless you are disabled or the money is used for educational expenses or for first-time home buying (this amount has a limit).

You must begin to take money from your account when you reach age 70½. Then the percentage of the total that you must withdraw each year is determined by your statistical life expectancy. (The IRS determines the withdrawal percentage by using the "Uniform Lifetime Table.") In theory, this means that all of the funds in the program will be used up by the time you die. And, of course, you can withdraw more than the minimum required amount if you decide to and deplete the account that way.

TIP

Withdrawal amounts are different if your spouse is more than ten years younger. If your spouse is the sole beneficiary of your retirement plan and is more than ten years younger than you, distribution rules are slightly more favorable. Withdrawal percentages are calculated on the basis of both your and your spouse's life expectancies. Because your spouse is younger, your combined life expectancies will be longer than your own life expectancy. Therefore, you will be required to withdraw a lesser percentage from your retirement fund each year than if only your life expectancy were used to determine the percentage. (The IRS determines these percentages by using what it calls the "Joint Life and Last Survivor Table.")

All money remaining in an individual retirement program (if there is any) at the death of the owner goes to a named beneficiary or beneficiaries, without probate. You simply specify the beneficiary or beneficiaries on the account documents. The money can be paid in a lump sum or in installments.

Roth IRAs

Roth IRAs differ from the traditional IRAs just discussed. You fund a Roth IRA with money that has already been taxed. Like regular IRAs, the money is allowed to grow tax free until it is withdrawn. But when you do withdraw it, no further tax is due as long as the money was in the account for at least five years.

The biggest difference, for estate planning purposes, between regular IRAs (and most retirement plans) and a Roth IRA is that you don't have to start withdrawing money from a Roth IRA when you reach age 70½. In fact, you can still contribute to it after that age and leave the money intact for your heirs.

The tax penalty for withdrawing funds before age 59½, however, does apply to a Roth IRA, with several exceptions. Again, there is no penalty if you are disabled. There is also no penalty if funds are paid to a beneficiary upon the death of the individual. And you may take money out penalty free to buy a first-time house, not only for yourself, but also for a child, grandchild, or parent. You may also use Roth money to pay for education expenses for yourself, your spouse, or children and grandchildren of you or your spouse.

Annual contribution limits are the same as the limits for traditional IRAs. However, individuals who earn over a certain amount are restricted to lesser amounts.

RESOURCE

Retirement plan resources from the IRS. If you want detailed (and complex) information about retirement plans, you can download the following publications free of charge from the IRS website, www.irs.gov:

- IRS Publication 590 covers individual retirement arrangements (IRAs).
- IRS Publication 560 covers retirement plans for small businesses, such as profit-sharing plans.

To find these forms on the IRS website, enter the publication number into the search box on the home page.

401(k) Accounts

Many employers now offer employees 401(k) plans or 403(b) plans. (The 401(k) is for businesses, the 403(b) for nonprofit corporations and government workers.) Employees defer a portion of their wages, contributing them to the retirement plan. Many employers match these funds or at least make some contribution to the account. It's up to the employees whether or not to participate.

Money in your account is invested, according to your direction, in investments offered by the plan administrator. That money grows (at least you hope it grows) tax free over the years until you withdraw it. In some cases, you can retire at age 55 and take money out without penalty. You must begin withdrawing it at age 70½. At your death, the beneficiary you named receives whatever funds are left in the account. If you are married, the beneficiary must be your surviving spouse unless your spouse signed an agreement giving up this right.

If the money contributed to the plan was never taxed, every withdrawal is subject to income tax. If part of the contribution consisted of money that was taxed previously, a formula will be used to figure out what portion of the withdrawal is subject to income tax. The interest that has been accruing in the account tax free is also subject to income tax.

Educational Savings Accounts (Formerly Educational IRAs)

Two types of tax-saving education accounts—529 plans and Coverdell accounts—are authorized by federal law. With each, you name the young people for whom you are saving, and funds you contribute are not considered part of your taxable estate. The beneficiaries are considered the owners of the account, even though you can retain management rights over account investment. These plans are discussed in more detail in Chapter 6.

Pensions

A pension, unlike an individual retirement program, is not under your control. Your company sets up a pension plan, and determines what rights you receive. You may acquire the right to receive payments— perhaps generous ones—and this right may extend to your surviving spouse or perhaps other beneficiaries, depending on the pension program. But you don't have any say over how the money in a pension fund is invested, and you have only limited say (at most) over how and when you receive benefits.

Specific Pension Programs

There are many types of pensions: military, railroad, union, and so on. The benefits these programs provide depend on the specifics of each program. Check the rules of each program that applies to you.

No law requires an employer to offer a pension plan. Some are generous, some are miserly, and some don't even bother to say "tough luck, friend."

SEE AN EXPERT
When you are ready to retire, you'll be fortunate if your pension plan office provides tax assistance. For instance, money contributed during certain years may be taxed at different rates. It is truly necessary to get the tax help you need. A onetime visit to a good accountant will pay off in the long run.

ERISA Laws

The Employee Retirement Income Security Act (ERISA), a federal law covering pensions and some other retirement programs, requires that every pension plan spell out who is eligible for coverage. Plans do not have to include all workers, but they cannot legally be structured to benefit only top executives or otherwise discriminate—for example, by excluding older workers.

If you are eligible to participate in your employer's pension program, you are entitled to several documents:

- **A summary plan description.** Explains the basics of how your plan operates. ERISA requires your employer to give you this document within 90 days after you begin participating in a pension plan. It also requires your employer to provide you with any updates to the plan.

  This document will tell you the formula for vesting in the plan, if it is a plan that includes vesting. A vesting plan means that you must work for a certain required period to be eligible for benefits. A formula is used to determine your benefits and the contributions that your employer will make to the plan. The summary will also tell you whether or not your pension is insured.

- **A summary annual report.** Your employer must provide a yearly accounting of your pension plan's financial condition and operations.

- **Survivor coverage data.** If you request it, you should also receive a statement of how much your plan would pay to a surviving spouse or beneficiary should you die. Your plan administrator is required to give you a detailed, individual statement of the pension benefits you have earned if you request it in writing or are going to stop participating in the plan because, for example, you change employers. You have the right to one such statement per year.

SEE AN EXPERT

Courts have now expanded ERISA to require that pension benefits go to a surviving spouse after the pension recipient has died. Problems abound in community property states (listed in Chapter 3) due to remarriage after divorce or death of a nonparticipant spouse. If you are in this situation, you should seek expert advice. (See Chapter 29.)

CAUTION

Divorce does not remove a former spouse as beneficiary. For all retirement plans controlled by ERISA, divorce does not automatically remove an ex-spouse as beneficiary of the other spouse's plan. The plan holder must amend the plan and name a new beneficiary. Any state law that automatically revokes a spousal beneficiary designation upon divorce is void for ERISA plans.

RESOURCE

Publications on pension plans. IRS Publication 575 discusses the rules for many pension plans, but it's not easy reading.

A number of brochures on pensions, which are easier to understand, are available from The American Association of Retired People (AARP), 601 E Street NW, Washington, D.C. 20049, 888-687-2277, www.aarp.org, and from The Pension Rights Center, 1350 Connecticut Avenue NW, Suite 206, Washington, D.C. 20036, 202-296-3776 or 1-888-420-6550, www.pensionrights.org.

If you want help understanding the details of your pension or retirement plan and can't get what you want on your own, you'll need to see a pension plan expert, or a lawyer knowledgeable in this specialized field.

When You Retire

Upon retirement, you may have several choices as to how you will receive your retirement benefits.

Here are your main options:

- **Regular payment upon retirement.** Many people receive a monthly sum from a pension plan, in addition to any funds they receive from an individual retire- ment program like an IRA or 401(k).
- **Lump sum payment.** Some pensions, 403(b)s, or other retirement programs allow employees to take the entire amount in their retirement accounts (based on age and amount contributed) plus interest and account earnings, in one lump sum.

- **Rolling pension funds into an IRA or other retirement fund.** If you retire before you are 70½ and your pension plan allows it, you can roll over your pension funds, putting them in an IRA and deferring income tax until later.

Retirement Plans and Estate Planning

Retirement accounts may contain money when the account owner dies. Sometimes, they are a significant part of an estate. If so, choosing who will inherit these retirement funds may be an important estate planning decision.

You can (and should) name a beneficiary or beneficiaries for an individual retirement plan: an IRA, profit-sharing, 401(k), or 403(b) account.

Keep in mind, however, that these plans are meant to be for one's retirement, not inheritors. A long-living owner is likely to have used up all or most of the funds in a retirement plan. So a retirement account only becomes part of a deceased owner's estate if he or she dies earlier than predicted by the IRS life expectancy tables, causing some assets to remain in the plan.

If you die with funds in a retirement account, the important issue becomes how your beneficiary will receive payment. Generally, a lump-sum payment is undesir- able, because that money is subject to income tax in that year. Better to spread payments over as many years as possible, so the tax bite is smaller.

For that reason, there is a tax advantage to naming a "designated beneficiary" to receive your retirement plan. According to the IRS, a designated beneficiary must be a natural person, as opposed to an entity such as a charity or corporation. (Some trusts can be designated beneficiaries if certain conditions are met, including that all trust beneficiaries are natural persons.) If any of your beneficiaries are not natural persons or eligible trusts, all funds in the account must be distributed within five years.

Naming Your Spouse as Beneficiary

Many married people name their spouse as the beneficiary of their retirement funds. They want to support their spouses, and in larger estates, defer estate tax. Leaving assets to the surviving spouse postpones tax, under the marital deduction, until the death of the surviving spouse.

If you have a 401(k) or 403(b) plan, you must name your spouse as the beneficiary unless the spouse signs a waiver. Most pension plans follow the same rule, imposed by federal law. Different laws apply to individual retirement programs like IRAs or profit-sharing plans: You can name anyone you choose as beneficiary. However, in community property states, the spouse has a legal interest in money the other spouse has earned unless that spouse signs a document giving up the interest. This can affect both individual retirement plans and pension funds.

Your spouse-beneficiary can leave the account in your name and spread distributions over his or her life expectancy. (If you died before you were 70½, your surviving spouse can wait until the year you would have reached that age to begin making withdrawals.) A spouse also has the option to roll the plan over to a new IRA in the spouse's own name. This allows the spouse to make no withdrawals until she or he reaches 70½. This defers income tax for the surviving spouse, allowing the account to grow.

If your estate is large enough to face estate tax, you can still leave any funds remaining in your retirement accounts to your spouse. Your personal estate tax exemption can be applied to property left to other beneficiaries.

EXAMPLE: Randolph dies in 2014, with an estate of $5.5 million, including $900,000 in a profit-sharing plan. His spouse, Rose, is the beneficiary of these funds, so they will not be subject to estate tax because of the marital deduction. Randolph had placed his other assets in a living trust, with income to go to Rose. Since the amount of these assets ($4.6 million) is under the personal exemption of $5.34 million for 2014, no estate tax is due when he dies. (See Chapter 15.)

Naming Others as Beneficiaries

Some people choose to name someone other than their spouse—often their child—as the beneficiary of a retirement account. The rules for nonspouse beneficiaries are a little different.

One beneficiary. If you name just one nonspouse as beneficiary, after your death, payments can be spread out over the beneficiary's life expectancy, as determined by the IRS tables. The law also allows a nonspouse beneficiary to transfer the plan assets into a new IRA, as long as the IRA is established in the name of the deceased. Again, payments are made according to the beneficiary's life expectancy. The assets must be transferred directly from the old account to the custodian of the new IRA. The beneficiary may not take possession of the funds at any time or those funds will be considered distributed and taxable.

The benefits to a beneficiary of creating this type of IRA are twofold: It avoids lump-sum payments from the deceased's plan, if that plan required prompt distribution on death (as many pension plans do), and it may allow the beneficiary more investment options than were available under the deceased's plan.

A nonspouse beneficiary can never roll over the deceased's account funds into a new IRA in the beneficiary's name and cannot receive funds from the account until she or he reaches age 70½.

Multiple beneficiaries. If you name multiple beneficiaries for one retirement plan, distributions must be based on the life expectancy of the oldest beneficiary. However, the beneficiaries may be able to split the account so that each beneficiary gets a separate share. This requires consent of the plan administrators, which may not be easy to get, and must be done between September 30 of the year following your death and December 31 of that year. If the accounts are split, payments are made according to each individual beneficiary's life expectancy.

If you are attempting to equalize gifts you leave to your children (as many folks do), and retirement funds seem likely to be part of your estate, remember the income tax consequences. The beneficiary of a retirement program (except funds in a Roth IRA) will have to pay income tax on any money received.

> **EXAMPLE:** Trish wants to be completely fair and equal to her two children. She leaves her house, worth $300,000, to her son. She designates her daughter as the beneficiary of her SEP-IRA, also worth $300,000 now. The daughter's inheritance is not equal to her brother's even if the SEP-IRA is still worth $300,000 at Trish's death, because it is reduced by the income tax she will pay.

Naming Your Living Trust as Beneficiary

If you make a living trust, should you name it as the beneficiary of your retirement plan? Usually, this is not a good idea. Here's why.

No probate benefits. Because no probate is needed to transfer funds in a retirement account to the named beneficiary in the first place, there is no need to name your living trust as beneficiary in an effort to avoid probate.

Possible higher mandatory withdrawals. If your spouse is the sole beneficiary of your living trust and is also more than ten years younger than you, you can spread out withdrawals over a longer period of time. Many people prefer this option, because lower withdrawals mean lower income tax payments.

In addition, IRS provisions that give a surviving spouse favorable rights over a deceased spouse's retirement accounts are not available if a living trust is the beneficiary, even if the surviving spouse is the only primary beneficiary of that trust.

Naming an Irrevocable Trust as Beneficiary

Occasionally, designating an irrevocable trust to receive what's left in your individual retirement accounts at your death can make sense. You can accomplish this by naming the trustee of the trust as the beneficiary.

One possible reason to do this is if the beneficiaries are minors and need their money managed by a trustee. The same is true if the beneficiary is incapable—for whatever reason—of managing money. If the trust is properly structured and irrevocable, payments can be received

based on the life expectancy of the oldest beneficiary.

However, once the trust ends, all funds remaining from the individual retirement account must be distributed to the beneficiary in that year. So if you leave your retirement account to a child's trust that ends when the child becomes 25, that is the year of final payout; payments could not be spread over the rest of that child's life expectancy.

Naming an AB Disclaimer Trust as Beneficiary

An AB disclaimer trust is a special type of living trust used by some couples to avoid probate and possibly reduce estate taxes. (See Chapter 15.) For many people, a retirement plan is a major asset, and their AB disclaimer trusts might not be fully funded unless remaining plan assets are placed in the trust. But the law does not allow a trust to "own" a retirement plan while the plan creator lives; it must be owned by a person. So to fund the AB disclaimer trust, that trust is named as the beneficiary of the retirement plan. All beneficiaries of the trust must be natural persons. After death, distributions from the plan are directed to the trust every year, until the plan funds are depleted. Distributions to trust beneficiaries are made as the trust directs. However, there can be income tax drawbacks to naming a living trust as beneficiary. For more information, see Chapter 18.

Probate and Taxes

No matter what the assets in your estate are, you want to avoid probate and minimize any taxes that may be owed to the government when you die. Funds left in your retirement plans at your death are no exception.

Probate

Money in an individual retirement plan (such as an IRA, a Roth IRA, or a 401(k) account) that is left to a named beneficiary at the owner's death does not go through probate. The plan administrator pays the funds directly to the named beneficiary.

If a surviving spouse or another beneficiary is entitled to receive pension payments under the terms of a pension earned by a deceased worker, those don't go through probate either. Again, they're paid directly to the recipient.

Estate Tax

The money you leave in an individual retirement plan—for example, the remaining balance in an IRA, a profit-sharing account, 401(k) plan, or pension—is subject to federal estate tax for as long as these taxes are imposed (see Chapter 15). It doesn't matter how the funds are paid out, whether in a lump sum or over time. The value of the plan at your death is part of your estate for estate tax purposes.

If the value of your estate exceeds the amount of the personal estate tax exemption, estate taxes will be assessed. Of course, if a surviving spouse inherits the retirement benefits, this money is not taxable, because of the unlimited marital deduction.

Income Tax

Generally, no income tax is due on inherited money. For example, if you leave a bank account to your son, he won't have to report it as income. Rules are different for some tax-advantaged retirement plans, however. Someone who inherits the funds in an individual retirement plan, such as a traditional IRA or 401(k) account, must pay income tax on the money. That's because when the money was socked away in the account over (usually) many years, the contributions were tax deductible, and the income accumulated without being taxed.

The money in one of the new Roth IRAs, however, is not taxed when the beneficiary inherits it. That's because contributions to the Roth IRA are not tax deductible when made. Income from contributions that have been in the account for at least five years is not taxed when it's withdrawn, either before or after the death of the account owner.

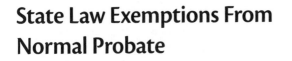
State Law Exemptions From Normal Probate

As a general rule, property left in a will must go through probate. However, there are exceptions; many states allow "small estates" to be transferred free of probate or under a very simplified probate process. Because of the way the laws are written, however, not only small estates can benefit. Many good-sized estates—worth hundreds of thousands of dollars—legally qualify as "small," and are therefore eligible for special transfer procedures that speed property to inheritors.

There are two basic kinds of probate shortcuts for small estates:

Affidavit procedure—no court required. If the total value of all the property you leave behind is less than a certain amount, the people who inherit your personal property—that's anything but real estate— may be able to skip probate completely. The exact amount varies tremendously— from $5,000 to $150,000, depending on the state.

If your estate qualifies, an inheritor can prepare a short document stating that he or she is entitled to a certain item of property under a will or state law. This paper, when signed under oath, is called an affidavit. When the person or institution holding the property—for example, a bank where the deceased person had an account—receives the affidavit and a copy of the death certificate, it releases the money or other property.

Simplified court procedures. Another option for small estates (again, as defined by state law) is a quicker, simpler version of probate. In some states, these procedures are easy to handle without a lawyer. In other states, you may need a lawyer, and may face at least some attorneys' fees, court costs, and delays.

Most states have both kinds of procedures; some offer just one. A brief summary of each state's laws is provided below, along with the state statute to help you look up the details yourself. If you want to make your research easier, you can find full details for each state in *The Executor's Guide*, by Mary Randolph (Nolo).

Will Your Estate Qualify?

If you're sure that you will leave behind property worth much more than your state's dollar limit, you probably assume that the simple procedures described in this chapter won't be available to your inheritors. But that might not be true. Even if the value of your estate is much bigger than your state's limit, you may still be able to take advantage of the simpler procedures.

The reason is that when adding up the value of your estate to see whether it is under the dollar limit, many states exclude large chunks of assets. For example, many states don't consider the value of vehicles, real estate, or real estate located in another state. Perhaps more important, many states don't count the value of property that won't go through probate—say, because you've placed it in a living trust or pay-on-death account or because you own it in joint tenancy with someone else. Considering the many exemptions, it's conceivable that in some states, an estate worth hundreds of thousands of dollars could qualify for small estate procedures.

If There's No Dollar Limit

When determining which estates qualify for simplified probate, a number of states don't specify a dollar amount as an upper limit. Instead, they grant small estate status to estates that will be used up by paying certain high-priority debts: the family allowance mandated by law, reasonable funeral and burial expenses, and medical costs of the last illness. The reasoning is that if there's nothing left for other creditors, there's no need for a probate court proceeding. Obviously, estates of very different size will qualify, depending on the debts of the deceased person.

If you plan ahead and learn about your state's rules (keeping in mind, of course, that they may change before your death), chances are good that you can adjust your affairs so that you will leave a small estate as your state defines it.

> **EXAMPLE:** Jerold, a California resident, dies owning a car worth $23,000 and a half-interest in the following assets, worth almost $400,000:
> - an IRA worth $75,000

- a pay-on-death bank account with $12,000 in it
- $30,000 worth of stocks, and
- a house worth $650,000, which he and his wife own as community property with right of survivorship.

The limit for small estates in California is only $150,000, but vehicles, payable-on-death accounts, and property that goes to a surviving spouse aren't counted toward that limit. From the list above, only the stocks count, allowing Jerold's estate to qualify for small estate procedures.

Using These Rules to Plan

Understanding your state's definition of a small estate is an essential step in a plan to avoid probate. Once you have that information, you'll know how much effort you need to devote to other probate avoidance methods.

For example, say you discover that your state allows estates worth up to $70,000 to be transferred by affidavit, and only property that is subject to probate counts toward that limit. You'll know that as long as your most valuable items avoid probate, your executor will be able to use the small estate procedures for the miscellaneous assets that you leave through your will.

TIP
Talk to your executor. Even if your estate qualifies for a simplified probate

procedure, it won't do you any good unless your executor knows that the option is available. Too many confused or intimidated executors simply turn everything over to a lawyer, and inheritors pay the price.

Summary of State Law Exceptions to Normal Probate

Alabama

Affidavit Procedure: No
Simplified Probate: $25,000 personal property
Statute: Ala. Code §§ 43-2-690 and following

Alaska

Affidavit Procedure: $100,000 for vehicles; $50,000 for other personal property
Simplified Probate: Up to value of homestead allowance, exempt property, family allowance, expenses of death, and last illness
Statute: Alaska Stat. §§ 13.16.680, 13.16.690, 13.16.695

Arizona

Affidavit Procedure: $50,000 real estate; $75,000 personal property
Simplified Probate: Up to value of homestead allowance, exempt property, family allowance, expenses of death, and last illness
Statute: Ariz. Rev. Stat. Ann. §§ 14-3971.B, 14-3971.E, 14-3973, 14-3974

Arkansas

Affidavit Procedure: No

Simplified Probate: $100,000 plus limited amounts for surviving spouse or dependents
Statute: Ark. Ann. § 28-41-101, § 28-41-103

California

Affidavit Procedure: $150,000; special affidavit for real estate worth less than $50,000
Simplified Probate: To surviving spouse, community property petition, no dollar limit; otherwise $150,000
Statute: Cal. Prob. Code §§ 13050, 13100 and following; §§ 13200 and following; §§ 13500 and following

Colorado

Affidavit Procedure: Net estate, $60,000
Simplified Probate: No fixed dollar limit
Statute: Colo. Rev. Stat. §§ 15-12-1201, 15-12-1203

Connecticut

Affidavit Procedure: No
Simplified Probate: $40,000 personal property
Statute: Conn. Gen. Stat. Ann. § 45a-273

Delaware

Affidavit Procedure: $30,000 personal property only. Beneficiaries can only be spouse, grandparents, children, or other specified relations, trustee, or funeral director.
Simplified Probate: No
Statute: Del. Code, Tit. 12 § 2306

District of Columbia

Affidavit Procedure: No (except if entire estate is no more than two cars, and all debts and taxes are paid)

Simplified Probate: $40,000

Statute: D.C. Code Ann. §§ 20-351 and following

Florida

Affidavit Procedure: No (except for very small estates that meet certain requirements)

Simplified Probate: $75,000 property in Florida subject to probate; also available if deceased person has been dead more than two years

Statute: Fla. Stat. Ann. §§ 735.201, 735.301

Georgia

Affidavit Procedure: No

Simplified Probate: When there is no will, estate owes no debts, and all heirs have agreed on how to divide the property

Statute: Ga. Code Ann. §§ 53-2-40 and following

Hawaii

Affidavit Procedure: $100,000 personal property, can also transfer motor vehicles, regardless of value

Simplified Probate: $100,000 personal property

Statute: Haw. Rev. Stat. §§ 560:3-1201 and following; §§ 560:3-1205 and following

Idaho

Affidavit Procedure: $100,000 personal property

Simplified Probate: No fixed dollar limit

Statute: Idaho Code §§ 15-3-1201 and following; §§ 15-3-1203 and following; §§ 15-3-1205

Illinois

Affidavit Procedure: $100,000 personal property

Simplified Probate: $100,000 real and personal property if all heirs and beneficiaries consent in writing

Statute: 755 Ill. Comp. Stat. §§ 5/25-1, 5/9-8

Indiana

Affidavit Procedure: $50,000 personal property only

Simplified Probate: $50,000

Statute: Ind. Code §§ 29-1-8-1, 29-1-8-3 and following

Iowa

Affidavit Procedure: $25,000 personal property

Simplified Probate: $100,000 total value of probate and nonprobate Iowa property

Statute: Iowa Code §§ 633.356, 635.1

Kansas

Affidavit Procedure: $40,000 personal property

Simplified Probate: No dollar limit on some estates if court and heirs agree

Statute: Kan. Stat. Ann. §§ 59-1507b, 59-3202 and following

Kentucky

Affidavit Procedure: No

Simplified Probate: By agreement of all beneficiaries; when spouse receives probate estate under $15,000 (intestate only, or where renunciation of will by spouse)

Statute: Ky. Rev. Stat. Ann. §§ 391.030, 395.455

Louisiana

This book is not applicable in the state of Louisiana.

Maine

Affidavit Procedure: $20,000 personal property

Simplified Probate: No fixed dollar limit

Statute: Me. Rev. Stat. Ann. tit. 18-A §§ 3-1201 and following; §§ 3-1203 and following

Maryland

Affidavit Procedure: No

Simplified Probate: Up to $50,000 of Maryland probate property; up to $100,000 if spouse is sole beneficiary

Statute: Md. Code Ann., [Est. and Trusts] §§ 5-601 and following

Massachusetts

Affidavit Procedure: No

Simplified Probate: $15,000 personal property, plus the value of a vehicle

Statute: Mass. Gen. Laws ch. 190B, § 1201-1204

Michigan

Affidavit Procedure: $15,000 personal property

Simplified Probate: $15,000; also if entire estate does not exceed homestead allowance, family allowance, exempt property, last illness and funeral costs

Statute: Mich. Comp. Laws §§ 700.3983, 700.3982, 700.3987

Minnesota

Affidavit Procedure: $50,000 personal property

Simplified Probate: Court can order if certain conditions met

Statute: Minn. Stat. Ann. §§ 524.3-1201, 524.3-1203

Mississippi

Affidavit Procedure: No, except that the inheritors of a bank savings account of $12,500 or less may obtain the funds by affidavit

Simplified Probate: $500

Statute: Miss. Code Ann. §§ 81-14-383, 91-7-147

Missouri

Affidavit Procedure: No

Simplified Probate: $40,000

Statute: Mo. Rev. Stat. § 473.097

Montana

Affidavit Procedure: $50,000 personal property

Simplified Probate: No fixed dollar limit

Statute: Mont. Code Ann. §§ 72-3-1101, 72-3-1103

Nebraska

Affidavit Procedure: $50,000 personal property; $30,000 real estate

Simplified Probate: If entire estate does not exceed homestead allowance, family allowance, exempt property, and last illness and funeral costs

Statute: Neb. Rev. Stat. §§ 30-24, 127, 129

Nevada

Affidavit Procedure: $20,000 personal property if no real estate owned in Nevada (available only to family members)

Simplified Probate: $200,000 with court approval
Statute: Nev. Rev. Stat. Ann. §§ 146.080, 145.040 and following, 146.070

New Hampshire

Affidavit Procedure: No
Simplified Probate: No dollar limit if surviving spouse (or if no spouse, an only child) is administrator and sole heir
Statute: N.H. Rev. Stat. Ann. § 553:32

New Jersey

Affidavit Procedure: No
Simplified Probate: No (unless there is no valid will, then up to $20,000 for a spouse or $10,000 if there is no spouse)
Statute: N.J. Stat. Ann. §§ 3B:10-3, 10-4

New Mexico

Affidavit Procedure: $50,000; also, if married couple owns principal residence worth $500,000 or less as community property and no other assets require probate
Simplified Probate: If entire estate does not exceed homestead allowance, family allowance, exempt property, and last illness and funeral costs
Statute: N.M. Stat. Ann. §§ 45-3-1201, 45-3-1203, 45-3-1205

New York

Affidavit Procedure: No
Simplified Probate: $30,000 personal property (plus certain types of exempt property, to specified dollar limits)
Statute: N.Y. Surr. Ct. Proc. Act Law § 1301

North Carolina

Affidavit Procedure: $20,000 personal property; $30,000 if intestate and spouse is sole beneficiary
Simplified Probate: Only if surviving spouse inherits everything
Statute: N.C. Gen. Stat. § 28A-25-1 and following

North Dakota

Affidavit Procedure: $50,000 personal property
Simplified Probate: If entire estate does not exceed homestead allowance, family allowance, exempt property, and last illness and funeral costs
Statute: N.D. Cent. Code §§ 30.1-23-01 and following, 30.1-23-03

Ohio

Affidavit Procedure: No
Simplified Probate: $35,000; $100,000 if spouse is sole beneficiary
Statute: Ohio Rev. Code Ann. § 2113.03

Oklahoma

Affidavit Procedure: $20,000
Simplified Probate: $200,000
Statute: Okla. Stat. Ann., tit. 58, § 245, 393

Oregon

Affidavit Procedure: No
Simplified Probate: $275,000; personal property up to $75,000, real estate up to $200,000
Statute: Or. Rev. Stat. Ann. §§ 114.515 and following

Pennsylvania

Affidavit Procedure: No

Simplified Probate: $50,000 personal property

Statute: 20 Pa. Cons. Stat. Ann. § 3102

Rhode Island

Affidavit Procedure: No

Simplified Probate: $15,000 of personal property if no real estate owned

Statute: R.I. Gen. Laws § 33-24-1

South Carolina

Affidavit Procedure: $25,000 personal property (but affidavit must be approved and signed by a judge)

Simplified Probate: $25,000 (not counting exempt property, last illness and funeral costs)

Statute: S.C. Code Ann. §§ 62-3-1201, 62-3-1203

South Dakota

Affidavit Procedure: $50,000 personal property

Simplified Probate: No limit

Statute: S.D. Codified Laws §§ 29A-3-1201 and following, 29A-3-301 and following

Tennessee

Affidavit Procedure: No

Simplified Probate: $25,000

Statute: Tenn. Code Ann. §§ 30-4-102 and following

Texas

Affidavit Procedure: $50,000 personal property if person dies intestate

Simplified Probate: No dollar limit if (1) value of property doesn't exceed what is needed to pay family allowance and certain creditors; or (2) either the will or all inheritors request "independent administration"

Statute: Tex. Est. Code, §§ 205.001-205.008, § 354.001, § 401.001

Utah

Affidavit Procedure: $100,000 personal property

Simplified Probate: If entire estate does not exceed homestead allowance, family allowance, exempt property, and last illness and funeral costs

Statute: Utah Code Ann. §§ 75-3-1201, 75-3-1203

Vermont

Affidavit Procedure: No

Simplified Probate: $10,000 personal property

Statute: Vt. Stat. Ann., tit. 14, § 1902

Virginia

Affidavit Procedure: $50,000 personal property; benefits, wages up to $15,000

Simplified Probate: No

Statute: Va. Code Ann. § 64.2-601, § 64.2-775

Washington

Affidavit Procedure: $100,000 personal property

Simplified Probate: Available to surviving spouse or domestic partner only if decedent left no will, the estate is community property, and decedent has no children or grandchildren from another relationship

Statute: Wash. Rev. Code Ann. §§ 11.62.010 and following; §§ 11.68.011 and following

West Virginia

Affidavit Procedure: No

Simplified Probate: $100,000; more under certain specified conditions

Statute: W.Va. Code § 44-3A-5

Wisconsin

Affidavit Procedure: $50,000 personal property

Simplified Probate: $50,000, and all to surviving spouse or child; also, an "informal" probate procedure that doesn't require a lawyer and has no fixed dollar limit

Statute: Wis. Stat. §§ 867.01, 867.03

Wyoming

Affidavit Procedure: $200,000

Simplified Probate: $200,000

Statute: Wyo. Stat. Ann. §§ 2-1-201, 2-1-205

California Exemptions From Normal Probate

California has two useful simplified probate procedures:

- **The "community property petition"** allowing all property left to a surviving spouse to be transferred by summary probate, and
- **An affidavit procedure** allowing personal property worth less than $150,000 to be transferred entirely outside of probate.

California also allows up to $20,000 worth of real estate to be transferred by filing an affidavit first with the probate court, then with the county recorder. Given the prices of California real estate, this procedure is rarely helpful.

The Community Property Petition

By using a community property petition, a surviving spouse can readily obtain the portion of the deceased spouse's property left to him or her. It makes no difference if it's jointly owned community property or the deceased's separately owned property. There's also no dollar limit either on the total amount of the estate or on the amount of the property that can be transferred to the surviving spouse by this method. Even if some of the deceased's share of the community property is left to others, the spouse can still obtain his or her portion of it, without the expense of probate.

The community property petition is a simple one-page, two-sided form that can be prepared by a surviving spouse who is entitled to property of a deceased spouse either from a will or by intestate succession if there was no will. The petition is filed with the local probate court, which sets a hearing date. Notice of the hearing must be given to certain people, including all beneficiaries named in the will. Then the hearing is held and the property ordered transferred to the surviving spouse unless someone contests the petition, which is very rare. Most surviving spouses should be able to handle the process without a lawyer. All the forms and instructions you need are in *How to Probate an Estate in California,* by Julia Nissley (Nolo).

The Affidavit for Personal Property

If a deceased left, by will or intestate, personal property and/or real estate worth less than $150,000 (net), the inheritors can obtain the personal property by filing a simple form, called an "Affidavit for Collection of Personal Property," with the people or organizations holding the deceased's property. In addition, the inheritors can also collect all of the following under the affidavit: all vehicles owned by the deceased, no matter how much they are worth, and up to $5,000 in back pay.

The purpose of the affidavit is to enable beneficiaries of a deceased person who left a small estate to obtain the cash and other assets they inherit immediately without a lot of red tape. The affidavit can be prepared by the inheritors who are entitled to the deceased's estate either by will or, if there's no will, by the laws of intestate inheritance. If there's more than one beneficiary under a will (or the intestacy laws if there's no will), all the beneficiaries must sign the affidavit. A copy of the affidavit is then presented to people or organizations holding the property left by the will; they must promptly release the assets to the beneficiaries. Forms and instructions are contained in *How to Probate an Estate in California,* by Julia Nissley (Nolo).

An affidavit doesn't have to be filed with any state agency. No court or other probate proceeding is required. There's no procedure to verify the inheritor's declaration that the deceased's net estate in California is worth less than $150,000. In this one instance, the law appears to go by the honor system.

EXAMPLE: Harry dies in Los Angeles. Under Harry's will, his sole beneficiary is his adult daughter Myra. Harry owned no real estate. His property is worth $165,000: $120,000 in savings; personal property worth $25,000, a car worth $15,000, and back wages owed Harry of $5,000. Even though Harry's estate, left by his will, exceeds $150,000, all of the property may be collected by Myra by affidavit. His bank CD and personal possessions are worth a total of $145,000, under the $150,000 limit. Separate exemptions allow his car and back wages to be claimed by affidavit.

Myra simply completes the affidavit and attaches one copy of the death certificate. She then gives them, plus her own ID, to Harry's bank; the holder of the personal property (in this case, Harry's landlord); the DMV; and the company that owes Harry the back vacation pay. The bank and the holder of Harry's personal property must release it to her promptly. The Department of Motor Vehicles will reregister the car in Myra's name, and the company will turn over Harry's unused vacation pay to her.

The affidavit must state, under oath, that the total value of the deceased's estate in

California is less than $150,000. However, as I've explained, certain items, such as vehicles, no matter how much they are worth, don't count toward the $150,000 limit.

Property in a living trust isn't counted toward the $150,000 limit. Thus, savvy Californians with good-sized estates can use other probate avoidance methods to pass their valuable items of property and rely on the affidavit procedure to avoid probate on the rest, which they leave by will.

EXAMPLE: Teresa has an estate consisting of a house in Los Angeles, with equity of $620,000; a summer cottage at Stinson Beach, with equity of $420,000; the furnishings of her two houses worth $80,000; a bank account of $60,000; life insurance with total proceeds of $300,000; and various heirlooms worth a total of $45,000. At her death, she wants her children to receive all her property, except for the heirlooms, which she intends to give to cousins and other relatives. Teresa doesn't think of herself as wealthy … but, in fact, her estate now amounts to $1,525,000. Rather than have all this property subject to regular probate she:

- transfers the houses and furnishings into a living trust, naming her children as beneficiaries
- creates a pay-on-death bank account for her savings, naming her children as beneficiaries, and
- assigns ownership of her life insurance policies outright to her beneficiaries, and gives up all ownership of the policies.

Now, only the heirlooms, worth less than the $150,000 limit, remain in Teresa's probate estate. She can distribute these by her will, and her inheritors can claim them simply and speedily by using an affidavit.

New York Exemptions From Normal Probate

New York law provides a simplified probate procedure for estates of personal property worth less than $30,000. Also, New York entirely exempts certain property of a deceased spouse that is set aside for the surviving spouse or the deceased's minor children if there is no spouse. The total amount of property that can be set aside for family use is $56,000. All property set aside for family use isn't counted as part of the $30,000 that can be exempted from probate. Thus, in theory, an estate totaling $86,000 could be eligible for New York's affidavit procedure if the maximum amount of exempt property was left to a surviving spouse or minor children.

Under the simplified probate procedure, the deceased's executor acts as a "voluntary administrator," preparing an affidavit listing the property and beneficiaries and filing it with the probate court (called "surrogate court") clerk. The executor then has authority to collect the deceased's personal property and distribute it to the beneficiaries according to the will or the intestacy laws.

The simplified probate procedure can be combined with other probate avoidance devices. Thus, if someone transfers big-ticket items like houses and stocks by living trust, he or she could then transfer small personal gifts with a total value less than $20,000 by his or her will, free from normal probate.

Texas Exemptions From Normal Probate

In Texas, regular probate is normally quite easy, though a lawyer is required. An uncontested estate can be heard by a judge within ten days of filing a petition for probate. Nevertheless, Texas also provides for two simplified probate procedures. The first, called "summary probate," is available regardless of the value of the estate if the value of all property does not exceed what is needed to pay the family allowance permitted by law and certain creditors. The second simplified procedure is called "independent administration." It is permitted if either the will or all the inheritors acting together specifically request it.

If using independent administration, the executor files an application to probate the will, exactly as in traditional probate. A hearing is then held on the validity of the will. If the will is proved valid, and it's shown that the estate has no outstanding debts or other problems, the court orders independent administration, dispensing with many of the tedious steps of normal probate. (The Texas statute is silent, however, on whether independent administration means reduced attorneys' fees, which means that it's up to your inheritors to negotiate.)

The court order admitting the will to probate authorizes transfer of the deceased's property to those entitled to it under the will. Furthermore, since the will has been proved in court, title to the property transferred in this way isn't open to challenge. However, independent administration does normally require an attorney, so the major drawback of normal probate is still involved and this option isn't, therefore, a fully satisfactory alternative to probate avoidance techniques.

Texas also has an affidavit procedure allowing personal property worth up to $50,000 to be transferred outside of probate, but the affidavit can be used only for people who die intestate, leaving no valid will. Thus, this affidavit procedure is of no use to people who plan their estates, which includes will writing.

Florida Exemptions From Normal Probate

Florida law provides two different types of simplified probate.

Summary Probate

Florida permits summary probate (called "summary administration") if both of the following are true:

- There's a will.
- The value of the entire estate subject to probate in Florida, less the value of property exempt from creditors, is less than $75,000.

Property exempt from creditors, under Florida law, includes:

- homestead property (basically, a house) exempted under the state constitution
- a "family allowance," specified by statute, for the support of the deceased's family, and
- certain property of a deceased person—household furniture, furnishings, and appliances (up to a net value of $10,000), cars, personal effects not disposed of by will (up to a net value of $1,000)—which can be claimed by the deceased's surviving spouse or minor children.

You can combine the summary administration procedure with other probate avoidance devices. For example, you could transfer all of your assets by living trust, leaving just $50,000 worth of personal property under your will. The property that passes under your will can be quickly transferred using summary administration.

Summary administration is also available in Florida if the deceased person has been dead for more than two years, regardless of the size of the estate.

No Probate Required

For certain very small estates, Florida doesn't require probate. These estates can consist only of personal property (not real estate). All the property must be exempt from creditors' claims except for any amount that is needed to pay funeral costs and two months' last illness expenses. After receiving a letter stating the facts above, the court will authorize the transfer of the property to the people who are entitled to it.

Estate Taxes

All U.S. citizens, and all others who own property in the United States, are currently subject to federal estate tax. All property you own, whatever the form of ownership and whether or not it goes through probate after your death, is subject to this tax.

Your estate is highly unlikely to be liable for payment of any federal estate tax because federal law exempts a large dollar amount of property from that tax. For 2014, the exemption is $5.34 million per person.

To find the most up-to-date information about the estate taxes, go to Nolo's website at www.nolo.com.

Federal Estate Tax Exemptions

Before worrying about federal estate taxes, obviously, you'll want to figure out whether you're likely to owe them. Almost all people won't, because their estates aren't large enough to be taxed. Several federal tax law exemptions and deductions allow you to leave substantial amounts of property free of estate taxes. The most important of these are described below.

The personal estate tax exemption. The personal exemption allows a set dollar amount of property to pass tax free, no matter who inherits it (I.R.C § 2010). For 2014, the exemption is $5.34 million.

Why this number? Because in 2012, Congress set the personal estate-tax exemption at $5 million, with an annual adjustment for inflation. $5.34 million is what the number worked out to for 2014. Each year the exempt amount will be increased

by whatever the amount of that inflation adjustment turns out to be. Technically, the adjustment could reduce the amount of the exemption if there is "negative inflation," but that seems rather unlikely.

The Internal Revenue Code (I.R.C.)

You'll see a number of references in this and other chapters to the "I.R.C.," which is the legal abbreviation for a set of tax laws known as the Internal Revenue Code. The Internal Revenue Code can be found in Title 26 of the United States Code (U.S.C.), the collection of all federal statutes. The IRS regulations (which determine how the codes should be enforced) can be found in Volume 26 of the *Code of Federal Regulations (CFR)*.

If your estate is worth more than the amount of the personal exemption for the year of your death—that is, if it is above the estate tax threshold—your estate will owe taxes unless other exemptions or deductions apply. The top estate tax rate is 40%.

If you have made taxable gifts during your life, the amount of the personal exemption will be reduced. Currently, you can give away property worth up to $14,000 per recipient in a calendar year free of gift tax. (See Chapter 16.)

Portability. The federal estate tax law contains another provision that can benefit wealthy couples. It's called "portability." With portability, if one spouse did not use up all his or her personal exemption, the remaining balance can be "ported" to the surviving spouse. This adds the unused portion to the surviving spouse's personal exemption.

CAUTION
Claiming Portability. For a surviving spouse to acquire, or claim, portability of an unused portion of a deceased spouse's estate tax exemption, that claim must be made on an estate tax return filed within nine months of the deceased spouse's death. The return must be timely filed even though no estate tax is payable by the deceased spouse's estate.

EXAMPLE: Gaston and Juliette had a shared estate worth $6 million. Gaston dies in 2014, leaving his $3 million to the couple's children. In doing so, Gaston has used up $3 million of his $5.34 million exemption. Juliette can port Gaston's unused $2.34 million, raising her exempt amount to $7.68 million (if she dies in 2014). But Gaston's estate must file a timely estate tax return, showing the amount of his unused exclusion and making an irrevocable election to use that amount for portability.

The requirement that a portability claim must be made on an estate tax return of the first spouse to die will likely cause many pointless returns to be filed with the IRS. For couples with any substantial estate, at the time of the first spouse's death, the value of the surviving spouse's estate at his or her death is unpredictable. So the prudent thing to do after the first

spouse dies would be to file an estate-tax return electing portability. Given that the exemption will be well over $5 million even without portability, most surviving spouses will never need to import the deceased spouse's unused portion of his or her exemption. But if a surviving spouse turned out to need portability, he or she couldn't get it if that earlier estate tax return hadn't been filed.

The federal estate-tax return is a lengthy, complicated document. Portability, as it is now, means that many of these costly-to-have-prepared returns will be filed with the IRS without ever serving any purpose.

The marital deduction. This deduction exempts from estate tax *all* property left to a surviving spouse. (I.R.C. § 2056(a).) The marital deduction is not allowed for property left to noncitizen spouses. But the personal estate tax exemption can be used for property left to noncitizen spouses.

Combining the marital deduction and portability. Wealthy couples can use both portability and the marital deduction to leave large amounts of money or property without estate tax on the death of either spouse.

EXAMPLE: Nancy and Todd have a shared estate worth $9 million. Todd dies in 2014, leaving his share, $4.5 million, to Nancy. The entire $4.5 million is exempt from estate tax because of the marital deduction. Nancy's estate is now worth $9 million, well above the $5.34 million personal exemption. However, Todd used up none of his $5.34 million exemption. So

Nancy ports his exemption and adds it to her own, making her total exemption $10.68 million. As a result, when she dies, no estate tax is owed on her $9 million estate.

The charitable deduction. The charitable deduction exempts all property left to a tax-exempt charity. (I.R.C. § 2055(a).)

In addition to these exemptions, several smaller exemptions are briefly mentioned in "Other Estate Tax Exemptions" below.

Estate Taxes on Property Outside the United States

If you own property or earn income in another country, your estate may well be subject to taxes in that country. But if you are also a U.S. citizen or resident, some or all of the property taxed by the other country may be taxed by the United States as well.

 SEE AN EXPERT
Get expert advice.
International estate tax planning requires a lawyer. If you own property or earn income in another country, you'll definitely need legal help with your planning.

The Big Picture: Estate and Gift Taxes

Before I get into the details of federal and state estate taxes, let's pull back and look at the underlying reasons for these taxes.

Whether or not to tax property transferred at death is a decision that every society with private property makes for itself. In the days of "survival of the fittest" capitalism in 19th-century America, there were no federal estate taxes. By contrast, in some European countries today, taxes take a very significant portion of larger estates. Currently, the United States is moving towards allowing more and more inherited wealth. Estimates vary, but for 2014, no more than ten thousand estates will be required to pay federal estate taxes.

Trying to reduce estate taxes to a minimum through estate planning is sometimes thought of as a form of lawyer's magic, by which taxes can be avoided completely no matter how large the estate. It's certainly true that there is a bit of gimmickry in some schemes of the very rich to avoid estate taxes. Indeed, avoiding or minimizing taxation at death has been criticized. Doubters maintain that it is a game for the rich, and that society would be better off if people couldn't pass immense sums from one generation to the next. Perhaps. Since I won't inherit big money, I'm not zealous to protect estates of billionaires. Still, I've noticed that even many progressives seem to prefer to leave whatever wealth they've acquired to family, friends, or worthy causes rather than turn it over to the government.

No Income Taxes on Inherited Property

Because quite a number of people worry about this, I want to state directly that someone who inherits property does not have to pay income taxes on the worth of the inherited property. There is one exception. A beneficiary who receives funds from a retirement plan with deferred income taxes, such as an IRA or a 401(k) plan, must pay income tax on the funds received. Also, after a person inherits property, any income subsequently received from the property is regular income and is subject to income tax.

Special rules for capital gains taxes on the sale of inherited property are discussed later in this chapter.

Until recently, federal estate taxes were an attempt to balance two conflicting principles: One, that everyone should be able to pass on property they've acquired; and the other, the idea that this is not a land of aristocracy—some of the wealth of the rich should be returned at death to the public for the general welfare. To achieve this balance, estate tax policy attempted to distinguish between property of the middle class, which is exempt, and property of the wealthy.

Under federal tax law, substantial gifts (currently more than $14,000 per year to any one person) are taxable to the giver. The gift tax rate is the same as the estate tax rate. This prevents wealthy people from giving away much or all of their estate shortly before death, and thus avoiding estate tax.

EXAMPLE: Marcus makes taxable gifts totaling $295,000 during his life. This amount is deducted from his personal estate tax exemption. When he dies in 2014, his net taxable estate is worth $5,500,000.

To determine the tax owed, first calculate the available exemption.

The personal exemption for 2014	$5,340,000
Subtract taxable gifts	– 295,000
Remaining exemption	$5,045,000

Then determine the taxable amount.

Taxable estate	$5,500,000
Subtract remaining exemption	– 5,045,000
Taxable amount	$ 455,000

Will Your Estate Have to Pay Taxes?

Whether or not your estate will owe federal estate tax depends on several factors: the size of your estate, who inherits it, and when you die.

Estimating Your Net Worth

You can't, of course, know what the value of your estate will be at your death. The best you can do is make a reasonable estimate of your current net worth (assets minus liabilities). This should be sufficient for estate tax planning purposes.

If you completed the property worksheets in Chapter 4, you should have a ballpark estimate of your current net worth. If you didn't complete the property worksheet, you'll need to make an estimate now, unless you know that what you own is well below the estate tax threshold. In that case, don't worry about estate taxes now. If you later strike it rich, that will be the time for you to learn about estate taxes and ways to reduce them.

Under federal estate tax law, most property is valued at its market value as of the date of the owner's death, less any debts on the property. However, a few types of property can be valued at less than their market value. Family farmland can be valued for its (continued) use as a farm, not at its highest possible market value. So can real estate used in a family business. So even if farmland would be worth more if sold to a developer to build an apartment complex or a shopping center, you don't have to use that higher value. (The specific tax rules on this are discussed in Chapter 28.)

Who Appraises Your Estate After You Die?

Having the value of your estate determined is the responsibility of the person you appoint to supervise your property. This is the successor trustee if the property is left by living trust or the executor if the property is left by will. If all property is left by joint tenancy, the surviving joint tenant has the responsibility to see whether an estate tax return must be filed or taxes paid.

The federal government isn't involved in appraising property in an estate. Obviously, though, the IRS can challenge and audit estate tax returns, just as it can audit income tax returns. In some states that impose estate taxes, official appraisals are done as part of the tax system. Most states, however, do not make governmental appraisals.

It may be difficult for an executor, a trustee, or a probate attorney to establish the market value of many items—works of art, closely held businesses, or stock in small corporations, for example. Saving receipts, bookkeeping records, and other documents stating the actual cost of items can be very useful and can save time and money later. Large estates that have many assets (appreciated real estate, art, interests in small businesses, to name but a few) can afford to hire an expert appraiser.

At your death, the amount in any individual retirement plan you own, such as an IRA, 401(k), or profit-sharing plan, is included in your taxable estate. This amount is not reduced by any income tax that a beneficiary must pay when he or she receives these funds.

Also, it may be hard to determine the value of some types of property, such as royalty rights or stock in a closely held corporation. Make your best guess—or pay for an expert's opinion.

Property Left to Your Spouse

As stated earlier, property that you leave to your spouse is not subject to federal gift or estate taxes, no matter how much the property is worth. This is called the "marital deduction."

> **EXAMPLE:** Pedro leaves his wife, Rebecca, $5,770,000. No estate tax is assessed.

Unmarried Couples Don't Qualify

There are no exemptions similar to the marital deduction for unmarried partners. Quite simply, the estate tax laws are written to encourage and reward marriage. Same-sex marriages performed in states that have legalized same-sex marriage receive the same benefits as marriages between a man and a woman.

 CAUTION
No marital deduction for property left to a noncitizen spouse. If your spouse is not a U.S. citizen, property you leave to her or him is not eligible for the marital deduction. The special estate tax rules that apply to noncitizen spouses are discussed below.

How the Marital Deduction Works

To stress the most important point about the marital deduction: It makes no difference how much money or property you give during life or pass at death to your spouse. Whether it's a $500,000 house, $3 million in emeralds, or a $500 million collection of Impressionist paintings, it's all exempt from estate tax. And the property's legal form makes no difference either; it can be community property, joint tenancy property, "quasi-community" property, or separate property.

You can use the marital deduction in addition to all other allowable estate tax deductions.

> **EXAMPLE:** Sue has an estate valued at $6.6 million. She leaves $1 million to her children and $5.6 million to her husband. All Sue's property is exempt from federal estate taxes—the $5.6 million because of the marital deduction and the $1 million because it is below the estate tax threshold.

The Marital Deduction Could Be a Tax Trap

The fact that no federal estate tax is assessed when property is left to the surviving spouse can mislead people into thinking that leaving everything to a spouse must be the best thing to do. It may not be.

If portability (a surviving spouse's option to use his or her deceased spouse's personal exemption) were eliminated from federal estate tax law, there could be tax drawbacks when one spouse leaves a large amount of money or property to the other spouse. Remember that portability was first made a part of federal estate tax law as of 2011. If Congress were to change its mind and repeal portability, then it would be undesirable for a spouse to use the marital deduction to leave everything to the surviving spouse if doing so would cause the surviving spouse's estate to exceed the personal exemption ($5.34 million for 2014).

It can be sensible for wealthy couples to prepare an estate plan that provides that maximum flexibility for dealing with estate taxes. The conventional estate planner's device for accomplishing this is called an AB disclaimer trust. (See Chapter 18 for a discussion of how these trusts work.)

> **EXAMPLE:** Barbara and Tim are an elderly married couple, each with an estate worth $7 million. Suppose Congress repeals portability for 2015 and thereafter. When Tim dies in 2015 leaving all of his property to Barbara, no tax is due because of the marital deduction. However, when Barbara dies later that year, her estate is now over $7 million, and her estate will owe tax on the amount that exceeds the personal exemption for that year. Barbara and Tim could have avoided that tax by using an AB disclaimer trust.

Special Rules for Noncitizen Spouses

No marital deduction is allowed for property one spouse leaves to the other if the surviving spouse is not a citizen of the United States. It doesn't matter that a noncitizen spouse was married to a U.S. citizen or is a legal resident of the United States. The surviving spouse must be a U.S. citizen to be eligible for the marital deduction.

In contrast, property a noncitizen spouse leaves to a citizen spouse is eligible for the marital deduction. Congress seems to have feared that noncitizen spouses would leave the United States after the death of their spouses, whisking away their wealth to foreign lands, so it would never be subject to U.S. tax. Presumably, Congress thought that citizen spouses will remain here.

Even without the marital deduction, a U.S. citizen can leave a noncitizen spouse a good deal of property free of estate tax. The personal estate tax exemption can be used for property left to anyone, including a noncitizen spouse. So property worth less than the estate tax threshold for the year of death can be left tax free to a noncitizen spouse.

EXAMPLE: Lucy leaves all her property to her husband Devi, a noncitizen. When she prepares her estate plan, her estate is worth $2.9 million—less than the current estate tax threshold. A few years later she unexpectedly inherits $3.3 million. She never revises her estate plan and dies in 2014. Her total estate is $6.2 million. The personal estate tax exemption is $5.34 million. Because Devi is not a citizen, the marital exemption does not apply and $860,000 of Lucy's estate is subject to tax.

There are two ways, however, that a spouse can give or leave property to a noncitizen spouse and obtain additional estate tax benefits. U.S. gift tax law provides that a citizen spouse can currently give the other, noncitizen spouse up to $145,000 per year free of gift tax. (I.R.C. § 2525(i) (2).) Thus, a citizen spouse with an estate of $5.9 million could give a noncitizen spouse $580,000 over four years. This would reduce the estate to under the estate tax threshold.

Further, all property left by one spouse to a noncitizen spouse in what's called a "Qualified Domestic Trust" (QDOT) is not subject to estate tax until the noncitizen spouse dies. (See Chapter 19.)

If a noncitizen spouse becomes a naturalized U.S. citizen before the deceased spouse's estate tax return must be filed (nine months after death), the surviving spouse is then entitled to the full marital deduction. For a prosperous couple residing in the United States, one of whom is not a U.S. citizen, obtaining the estate tax advantage of the marital deduction can be one good reason for becoming a U.S. citizen.

SEE AN EXPERT

Tax planning for noncitizen spouses. If you're married to a noncitizen and have an estate worth more than $5 million, you should see a lawyer to ensure that you comply with the special rules that affect noncitizen spouses. (See Chapter 29.)

Gifts to Charities

All gifts you make to tax-exempt charitable organizations are exempt from federal estate and gift taxes. It doesn't matter whether you make these gifts during your life or leave them at your death. If you plan to make large charitable gifts, be sure you've checked out whether the organizations are in fact tax exempt. The most common way an organization establishes that it's a tax-exempt charity is by obtaining a ruling from the IRS, under I.R.C. § 501(c)(3). (These organizations are referred to, in tax lingo, as "501(c)(3) corporations.") Many charitable institutions, particularly colleges and universities, provide extensive information about tax-exempt gift giving and offer a variety of gift plans.

Making substantial gifts to charities through trusts is discussed in Chapter 20.

Conservation Easements

If you own undeveloped land that has risen greatly in value and you would like the land to be preserved after your death, rather than, say, be developed for condos, consider creating a conservation easement. Your estate can obtain a sizeable tax break if you do so. Estate taxes on land with a conservation easement are cut by 40%. The maximum tax break here is $500,000. (26 U.S.C. § 2031.) With a conservation easement, limited agricultural and forestry land uses are allowed, but subdividing for development is prohibited. To be eligible for this easement, the land must be within 25 miles of a large metropolitan area, national park, or wilderness area, or ten miles from certain national forests.

Even if you don't create a conservation easement, the inheritors of the land can do so within nine months after your death and obtain the same estate tax benefits.

Other Estate Tax Exemptions

There are also federal estate tax deductions for:

- funeral expenses, which can range from minimal to many thousands of dollars
- estate expenses, such as probate fees; again, a wide range of possible expenses here, up to tens of thousands of dollars or even more, depending on the worth of the probate estate and state probate fee rules
- any claims against the estate, and
- a certain percentage of state estate tax paid and estate tax imposed by foreign countries on property the deceased owned there.

For most people, these exemptions are relatively minor. It's rarely necessary to estimate them to see whether or not your estate is likely to be liable for estate taxes. If you're close enough to the tax threshold so that these deductions may matter, you're close enough to consider estate tax planning.

Calculating and Paying Estate Taxes

The next section covers when an estate tax return must be filed, property valuation for estate tax purposes, how to calculate the amount of taxes your estate will owe, and when the taxes must be paid.

Filing a Federal Estate Tax Return

A tax return, IRS Form 706, must be filed for an estate with a gross value exceeding the amount of the personal exemption for the year of death. That's *gross,* not net. This means that, for purposes of deciding whether a return must be filed, you don't subtract the amount a deceased owed from what he owned. An estate tax return may have to be filed even though no taxes are actually due.

EXAMPLE: The gross value of Dan's estate is $5.9 million when he dies in 2014. The personal estate tax exemption for 2014 is $5.34 million. Because Dan's gross estate is worth more than the exempt amount, his executor must file an estate tax return. However, Dan's net estate turns out to be well under the estate tax threshold. It is worth $4.45 million, because of mortgages on his real estate investments. No tax is due.

If an estate tax return must be filed, it is due within nine months of the death of the deceased, but the IRS may grant extensions.

The executor of the deceased's will is legally responsible for filing an estate tax return, if one is due. If there is no will, but there is a living trust, the job falls to the successor trustee named in the trust.

In perhaps the most common situation, a person creates both a will and a living trust and names the same person to serve as executor and successor trustee. If the executor and successor trustee are not the same person, both must cooperate so the executor has sufficient financial information to determine whether an estate tax return must be filed and what the right figures are if a return is required.

SEE AN EXPERT

Obtaining and filing a return. If an executor must file a federal estate tax return, he or she will want to hire a tax expert to prepare Form 706. It is not an easy form to complete. *The*

Executor's Guide: Settling a Loved One's Estate or Trust, by Mary Randolph (Nolo), includes a thorough discussion of Form 706 and other federal tax forms an executor may be required to file.

You can obtain IRS tax forms in a number of ways. The easiest is to download forms and instructions for free from the IRS website, www.irs.gov. But you can also visit an IRS office, or call 800-829-1040 and enjoy a phone message offering more options than Life Savers has flavors.

Property Valuation

Under federal law, a deceased person's property can be valued either as of the date of death or six months afterwards (referred to in tax lingo as the "alternate valuation date"). This is an all-or-nothing proposition: Your executor cannot value some assets as of the date of death and others six months later. Which valuation date is best for your estate is a matter for your successor trustee and executor to decide with a lawyer, and perhaps a tax adviser as well.

EXAMPLE: Ellen dies on May 1, 2014. She owned real estate with a net worth of $5.8 million on that date. Six months after her death, her real estate is valued at $5.2 million. Her executor takes advantage of the alternate valuation date to value her real estate at the lower amount, so no estate tax must be paid.

There are special valuation rules for family farms or real estate used in a family business. See Chapter 28.

Calculating Federal Estate Taxes

There's no reason to try to calculate the precise amount of tax your estate will owe when you die. First, you don't know the year in which you'll die, so you can't know the amount of the personal estate tax exemption that will apply. Second, Congress could revise the estate tax law in the coming years. And finally, you can't know now exactly what your property will be worth at your death. However, if you want to understand how estate taxes actually work, read on.

Technically, the personal estate tax exemption works by use of a "unified" tax credit. The credit is called unified because the same rates apply to taxable lifetime gifts as to property left on death. The credit is the amount that would otherwise be due on the exempt amount for the year of death.

In practice, the unified tax credit means that if tax is owed, the rates start high. Estate taxes work with estate tax credits so that high rates will apply to any amount subject to estate tax.

> **EXAMPLE:** Esmerelda dies in 2014 with an estate of $6.6 million. The amount subject to tax is $1.26 million. The tax rate applied is 40%. The tax owed is $504,000.

More Information on Federal Estate Tax Laws

More detailed information about federal estate and gift taxes can be found in IRS Publication 950, *Introduction to Estate and Gift Taxes*. It's available free at many IRS offices or online at www.irs.gov.

You can also read the relevant federal tax statutes, if you dare to plunge into this morass of legalese. It is dense, even for tax professionals. Federal estate tax laws are found in the Internal Revenue Code, Title 26 of the United States Code, the official collection of all federal statutes.

Planning for Payment of Estate Tax

You have two approaches to consider when you're planning for payment of any estate taxes due after your death. The first is to specify, in your will or living trust, what assets are to be used to pay any taxes. Obviously, you'll need to make sure the assets you've named are worth enough to cover the tax bill. The second approach is to allow your executor or successor trustee to decide which assets should be used to pay estate taxes. You can also combine these approaches—specify certain assets and provide that if they don't cover all estate taxes, your successor trustee or executor can choose which other assets to use.

If your estate is over the estate tax threshold, it is unwise to be silent in your will and living trust about how any taxes should be paid. Without direction from you, the IRS will look to the law of the state where you lived (in legalese, your "domicile") to determine how taxes are paid. State laws vary significantly on this. And some states' laws are extensive and complex. Here, as in other aspects of estate planning, it's far better for you to make a decision than to let the matter rest with state law.

Reducing Federal Estate Taxes

What can you do to reduce federal estate taxes if you think your estate will be liable for them? Not as much as you might think, although for the very wealthy, high-priced experts do come up with ingenious, pushing-the-edge tax dodges. For the rest of us, aside from making use of the estate tax exemptions and deductions discussed above, there are only a few major ways you can lower estate taxes.

Give Away Property While You Live

While you're alive, you can give a certain amount of property each year free of estate and gift taxes. Currently, you can give property worth $14,000 or less per person per year. A couple can give $28,000 a year tax free to one person. Tax-exempt gift giving works well for people

who can afford it and can be particularly advantageous for those who have several children, grandchildren, or other objects of their affection. (See Chapter 16.)

Making gifts of portions of a family business or other business assets like stock options, can, in the right circumstances, significantly reduce or eliminate estate taxes. This use of gift giving is discussed in Chapter 28.

Create an Estate Tax–Saving Trust

You can use a number of different types of trusts to save on overall estate taxes, depending on your circumstances and desires. I discuss these trusts in detail in Chapters 18 through 23. If you individually, or you and your spouse together, have an estate exceeding the estate tax threshold, be sure to read those chapters carefully to determine whether you can use one or more of these trusts. You should make your final decision only after consulting an experienced estate planning lawyer.

The Federal Income Tax Basis of Inherited Property

Though it's not, strictly speaking, an estate tax matter, the question of how inherited property is valued, for the purpose of calculating gain or loss from subsequent sale, is closely related. It is a tax question, and it can apply to property you leave. Because this issue matters to so many people, I discuss it here.

Let's start with a definition. The word "basis" means the value assigned to property, from which taxable gain or loss on sale is determined. The concept of a property's basis is a tricky one, not made any easier by the fact that basis is not defined in the tax laws. When property is purchased, its basis is generally its cost. In fact, basis is often referred to as "cost basis." If you buy a painting for $5,000, for example, it has a basis equal to its cost—$5,000. If you sell the painting two months later for $16,000 (lucky you), your taxable profit is $11,000.

Sale price	$16,000
Basis	– 5,000
Gain	$11,000

The original cost basis can be adjusted up, for certain types of improvements to property, or down, for reasons like depreciation. If you make what's called a "capital improvement" to a house, such as putting in a new foundation, the cost of the improvement is added to the basis of the property. Capital improvements, very roughly, last more than a year.

EXAMPLE: Green Is Good, Inc., bought an old barn in which to design and make bicycles. The barn cost the company $270,000, so the company has a cost basis in it of $270,000. Over the next year, Green Is Good spent $230,000 for capital improvements to the barn, installing a new fire control system and a new roof.

Here's how the company determines the "adjusted basis":

Original cost	$270,000
Capital improvements	+ 230,000
Adjusted basis	$500,000

The company takes depreciation deductions for the barn on its income taxes of $30,000 over two years. The property's adjusted basis now becomes $470,000, since the deduction for depreciation lowers the adjusted basis of the property.

The barn is sold to T. Donald Bump (who plans to use the barn for a weekend getaway) for $600,000.

Green Is Good, Inc., determines its profit this way:

Sale price	$600,000
Basis	– 470,000
Profit	$130,000

T. Donald's cost basis in the barn is $600,000.

Now let's move to the tax basis of inherited property. Under federal tax law, the basis of inherited property is stepped up to its fair market value at the date of the decedent's death. Actually, this is a simplification of the rule, which is that the basis of inherited property is adjusted up or down to the market value as of the date of death. However, the assumption that prices of property rise over time is so ingrained in our economic life, whatever the short- or medium-term fluctuations, that the term commonly used is stepped-up basis. And, in practice, for property owned for any long period of time, the inheritor's basis—the net value of the property at death of the original owner—is normally higher than that of the original owner.

EXAMPLE: During the two years that T. Donald owned the barn until his death in 2014, he made no capital improvements to the barn. At the time of his death, when the barn was inherited by T. Donald Jr., it had appreciated in value to $800,000.

T. Donald Jr.'s basis in the barn is stepped up to:	$ 800,000
T. Donald Jr. sells the barn three months later for:	750,000
Basis	– 800,000
T. Donald Jr.'s loss:	($ 50,000)

The fact that the basis of property is stepped up at the owner's death to its fair market value means that it's almost always desirable to hold on to highly appreciated property until it can pass at death. That way, your inheritors obtain the advantage of the stepped-up basis rule. Thus, if T. Donald sold the barn a year before he died, when it was worth $780,000, he would have had to pay federal capital gains taxes (and possibly state taxes as well) on $180,000 ($780,000 sale price minus his $600,000 basis).

If T. Donald gave the barn to T. Donald Jr. during his lifetime, T. Donald Jr. would have had the same basis in the barn as T. Donald had—$600,000. Gifts made during life are not entitled to a stepped-up basis. Only transfers at death qualify for this desirable tax treatment.

Both Halves of Community Property Receive a Stepped-Up Basis

If you and your spouse own property in a community property state, both equal portions of that property will receive a stepped-up basis to current market value when one spouse dies. If a couple bought a community property home for $80,000 that is worth $700,000 when a spouse dies, each spouse's share is worth $350,000. The basis of each spouse's share, not merely the deceased spouse's share, is stepped up to that $350,000.

By contrast, in most all common law states, only the property owned by a deceased spouse receives a stepped-up basis. No property of a surviving spouse receives a stepped-up basis, even if that property was held in shared ownership with the deceased spouse.

State Inheritance and Estate Taxes

There are two types of state taxes to consider when making decisions about how to leave your property: inheritance taxes and estate taxes. This section introduces each type.

State Inheritance Taxes

At one time, many states imposed inheritance taxes, but now, just a few still do. The states listed below impose inheritance taxes on:

- all real estate owned in the state, no matter where the deceased person lived, and
- the personal property (everything but real estate) of residents of the state.

Inheritance taxes are imposed on the people who receive the property (the beneficiaries), rather than on the estate itself. Typically, beneficiaries are divided into different classes, such as "Class A: Husband or Wife," "Class B: Immediate Family," and "Class C: All Others." Each class receives different tax exemptions and is taxed at a different rate. Generally, the highest exemption and lowest rate goes to spouses, or "Class A."

States That Impose Inheritance Taxes		
Iowa	Maryland	New Jersey*
Kentucky	Nebraska	Pennsylvania
* called an estate tax, but functions as an inheritance tax		

If you live or own real estate in a state that imposes inheritance taxes, you may want to consider the impact of them. In many instances, the bite taken from an inheritance is annoying, but relatively minor. However, in some states, larger chunks can be taken, especially for property left to nonrelatives.

For example, Nebraska imposes a 15% inheritance tax rate on $25,000 left to a friend, but only 1% if it's left to your child. Many states impose no inheritance tax at all on property left to a surviving spouse. It's probably rare that someone would change the amount of property left to a beneficiary because of inheritance tax, but you should at least evaluate the issue if it applies.

RESOURCE
Learn more about your state's estate and inheritance taxes at www.nolo.com.

State Estate Taxes

Even if your state does not impose inheritance taxes, your estate may face a state tax bill. Many states have adopted an estate tax that is designed to replace revenue lost because of changes to the federal estate tax laws.

The details of these tax laws vary from state to state, but one important thing to keep in mind is that your estate may owe taxes to the state even if it is not large enough to owe federal estate tax. This could be true even if you use an AB disclaimer trust to reduce federal taxes. (See Chapter 18.) If you leave an amount of property that exceeds your state's estate tax exemption, your estate will owe state tax even if no federal tax is due.

States With Estate Taxes

The following states levy estate taxes.

State	2014 Exemption
Connecticut	$2 million
Delaware	$5.34 million
District of Columbia	$1 million
Hawaii	$5.34 million
Illinois	$4 million
Maine	$2 million
Maryland	$1 million
Massachusetts	$1 million
Minnesota	$1 million
New Jersey	$675,000
New York	$1 million
Oregon	$1 million
Rhode Island	$910,725
Tennessee	$2 million*
Vermont	$2.75 million
Washington	$2 million

*$5 million in 2015, repealed in 2016

EXAMPLE: Roy and Ann, residents of Massachusetts, have a combined estate of $3 million. When Roy dies in 2014, his share of the couple's property is $1.5 million. That amount goes to Ann. Roy's estate is well under the federal estate tax threshold of $5.34 million, so it owes no federal tax. However, Roy's estate will owe tax to Massachusetts, because the state imposes an estate tax on estates worth $1 million or more.

SEE AN EXPERT

Get more information about state estate taxes. If you live in a state that imposes an estate tax, there's little you can do to avoid it, beyond moving to another state with more favorable tax laws. (Though there's no saying that state won't change its laws, too.) For most estates, the state tax amount won't be onerous. But if you are prosperous and want to know whether your estate may face this type of tax, see a good lawyer with up-to-date information about this area of the law. (See Chapter 29.)

Your Residence for State Tax Purposes

States that impose estate or inheritance taxes on residents do so on everyone "domiciled in the state." "Domicile" is a legal term. It means the state where you have your permanent residence, where you intend to make your home. Generally, it's clear where your domicile is. It's the state where you live most of the time, work, own a home, and vote.

Sometimes, however, it's not so clear. If you have homes in different states, there may be no decisive evidence of which state is your domicile. For example, several states, eager for tax revenue, claimed that Howard Hughes was domiciled there. A less dramatic and more common example is a person who divides his time between

homes in two states. In some circumstances, it's quite possible that more than
one state would assert the person was
domiciled there.

EXAMPLE: Rita retired and moved from
New Jersey to North Carolina. However,
she returns often to New Jersey to visit
her children, keeps several bank and
brokerage accounts in New Jersey,
and never bothers to register to vote
in North Carolina. New Jersey might
claim, on her death, that Rita remained
domiciled there and never transferred
her domicile to North Carolina.

If you do divide your residence between
two or more states, be sure to make it clear
which state you are domiciled in. Normally,
this means being sure that you maintain
all your major personal business contacts
and vote in the state you claim as your
domicile. Obviously, if one state doesn't
have estate or inheritance taxes and the
other does, you might want to establish
your domicile in the no-tax state.

Gifts and Gift Taxes

We're used to thinking of gifts as a personal matter, not as an aspect of financial or estate planning. Up to a point, this is accurate; birthday or holiday presents don't normally have tax consequences. However, for a gift worth a substantial amount of money, the rules change. Currently, if you give more than $14,000 to one recipient in one year, the excess is subject to federal gift tax, unless the recipient is your spouse or another exemption applies.

Here we'll explore the federal gift tax rules and the major ways gifts can be used to save on or eliminate gift taxes.

Other Reasons to Make Gifts

This chapter focuses on the gift tax and making tax-exempt gifts, but I'm aware that many people, including those with estates over the estate tax threshold, are reluctant or unwilling to make big gifts simply to reduce their taxable estate. For them, the tax savings alone aren't worth the loss of the property given away. Making a large gift involves many factors, with tax consequences being only one, often a relatively small one. My focus on gift taxes and tax saving doesn't mean I'm suggesting that these matters should be central to your decisions regarding making substantial gifts. Still, even if your primary motive in making a substantial gift isn't to save on taxes, why not take full advantage of the gift tax rules?

The Federal Gift Tax: An Overview

Gift tax is assessed against the giver of a gift. The value of the gift, for gift tax purposes, is the net market value of the property at the date of the gift. Net market value means the market price, less any debts owed on the property.

The recipient of a gift is not liable for federal gift tax, unless the giver failed to pay any tax actually due. Only in that case will the IRS go after the recipient for gift taxes.

The Annual Exclusion

Federal law exempts from gift tax the first $14,000 you give to any person or noncharitable institution in a calendar year. Lawyers often call this "the annual exclusion." (I.R.C. § 2503(b).) The amount of the gift tax exclusion is indexed to the cost of living, rounded down to the closest thousand dollars. This means the cumulative increases in the cost of living must rise slightly more than 10% before the amount of the annual exclusion is increased to $15,000.

So, if you give someone $25,000, the first $14,000 of that gift is exempt from gift tax, while the remaining $11,000 is not. Married couples can combine their annual exclusions, which means that they can currently give away $28,000 of property tax free, per year, per recipient.

The annual exclusion can be important. You can use it repeatedly over a number of years to reduce the size of your estate.

Here are some examples of how the annual exclusion works:

- You give $8,000 to a cousin in one year: There are no federal gift tax consequences.
- You give $16,000 to the cousin in one year: $2,000 is subject to gift tax.
- You give $8,000 each to two cousins: None of the $16,000 is subject to gift tax.
- You give $7,000 each to two cousins, three years in a row: None of this $42,000 is subject to gift tax.

Spousal Gifts

All property one spouse gives to another is exempt from gift tax if both spouses are U.S. citizens—no matter how much the property is worth. However, if the receiving spouse is not a U.S. citizen, the rule changes. Only a set dollar amount per year can be given gift-tax free by a citizen spouse to a non-citizen spouse. For 2014, a citizen spouse can give $145,000 to a non-citizen spouse free of gift tax.

The Gift Tax Exemption

Aside from the annual gift tax exclusion, currently $14,000, there is a $5.34 million cumulative tax exemption for gifts. (Actually, it's a combined gift and estate tax exemption.) This means you can give away a total of $5.34 million during your lifetime without paying gift taxes.

If you make more than $5.34 million worth of taxable gifts in your lifetime, you will owe gift tax. All gifts you made that were exempt from tax because of the annual gift tax exclusion do not count towards this $5.34 million total.

Other Exemptions

The following gifts are completely exempt from federal gift tax:

- all property given to a tax-exempt charity (I.R.C. § 2522.), and
- gifts made to pay for someone's medical bills or school tuition (I.R.C. § 2503(e)).

This final exemption has a couple of twists. First, the money must be paid directly to the provider of the medical service or to the school. Gifts to pay for medical insurance, including payments to HMOs for amounts covering medical care, diagnosis, and treatment, are covered under this section. (I.R.C. § 213(d)(1)(D).) If you give the money to an ill person or a student, who then pays the bill, the gift is not tax exempt. Nor can you reimburse someone who has already paid a medical or tuition bill and have this be a tax-exempt gift. Second, you cannot pay for a student's other educational expenses, such as room and board, and have this treated as a tax-exempt gift.

You can combine different gift tax exemptions.

> **EXAMPLE:** Victor gives $14,000 outright to his son, $50,000 to his wife, and $20,000 to CARE (a tax-exempt charity), pays $17,000 for his grandson's tuition at college, and also

pays $21,000 for a daughter's medical bills. All these gifts are completely exempt from federal gift tax.

When Gift Taxes Are Paid

If the IRS assesses gift taxes against you, as giver of a gift, you do not pay the taxes until and unless your total taxable gifts exceed the amount of the personal gift tax exemption for the current year. Instead, any tax imposed on the gifts you make eats up some of your personal exemption and thus reduces the amount that can later pass tax free. So people with estates below the estate tax threshold don't have to worry about actually paying gift tax. However, you must file a federal gift tax return for any gift over the amount of the annual exclusion (to repeat it again, currently $14,000) to a person per year (IRS Forms 709 or 709-A). And if you have a substantial estate, having made taxable gifts may cut into what you can leave free of estate tax.

What Is a Gift?

Before exploring more about gifts and estate planning, let's be sure you know what a gift is, legally.

Foreign Gifts

Federal tax laws impose strict reporting and tax requirements on any U.S. citizen or legal resident who receives foreign gifts (any and all gifts made by a non-U.S. citizen) with a total value of more than $15,358 (in 2014) in one year. The amount increases annually to reflect the rate of inflation. Thus, if three residents of different countries each give you $5,000 within a year, you must report the full $15,000 received and pay tax. Note that the rules for receiving foreign gifts are very different from those governing domestic ones: With foreign gifts, it is the recipient, not the donor, who must report the gift and pay tax. A foreign gift does not include payments made directly to a school for tuition or to a medical facility for bills for the benefit of a U.S. person.

The rules governing foreign gifts are new and complicated. If you receive, or expect to receive, large foreign gifts, see a tax expert.

Some transactions simply can't, by law, count as taxable gifts. For instance, you can perform services—from dispensing medical treatment to repairing a trombone—freely, without being held by the IRS to have made a taxable gift of the market value of your services. Similarly, you can lend property to someone, even for an extended period of time, and there's no legal gift.

EXAMPLE: Grandpa Elijah has an old Rolls-Royce that he lets his grandson Jacob drive. Indeed, Elijah has basically turned the car over to Jacob, although Elijah still pays for the car insurance. There is no gift—and would not be even if Jacob paid for the insurance, since Elijah remains the car's legal owner.

The Giver's Intent

In common understanding, a gift is a voluntary transfer of property without receiving anything of value in exchange. (In legalese, anything of value is called "consideration.") In other words, a gift is a permanent transfer of property that isn't commercial in spirit.

From the point of view of the IRS, the crucial element in determining whether or not a gift is made is the giver's intent, which can be distinctly murky. For example, say you obtain a valuable painting from Frank. Did Frank intend to give you that painting or lend it to you? Or was he hoping to sell it to you and wanted you to have it for a while before he mentioned the price?

Because someone's intent may not be obvious (now or in the future), it is an excellent idea to give a gift with a written statement explaining that it's a gift, so that the status of the transaction is clear. If there is no clear written evidence, the IRS doesn't know when you transfer something for less than its market value whether you intend to make a gift or you're just a poor businessperson. So, it does the only

thing it can do—it looks at the "objective evidence" and demands gift tax if the transaction doesn't appear reasonable from a commercial (economic) point of view.

EXAMPLE: Linda paid $15,000 to her niece for an office lamp and deducted the $15,000 as an expense of her small business. If the IRS questions this transaction and contends it was really a gift, Linda must convince the IRS that this was a bona fide commercial transaction—for example, that the lamp was a valuable antique—not a gift disguised as a purchase.

Looking Deeper Into Gifts

For a fascinating discussion of the varied meanings of giving, read *The Gift: Imagination and the Erotic Life of Property*, by Lewis Hyde (Random House). The book brilliantly explores the spirit involved in giving and receiving a gift, from a Christmas present to creating a work of art, and how the giving spirit interacts with commercial culture.

The Recipient's Control Over the Gift

For a transaction to be a legal gift, the property must be delivered to and accepted by the recipient.

EXAMPLE: Matt puts $15,000 into a drawer for Nina. There's no legal gift until Nina removes the money.

The giver must release all control over the property. If the giver retains any interest in the gift property, there is no legal gift.

EXAMPLE: Sonya gives stocks she owns to her daughter, Misha, transferring the account into Misha's name. But Sonya continues to receive directly all of the dividends from the stocks. Legally, Sonya has not made a valid gift.

SEE AN EXPERT

Gifts of real estate can be tricky. Some parents want to give their house to a child and structure the gift so that no gift tax is assessed. For example, a parent may take a mortgage on the property, with payments of $14,000 a year, and then forgive each year's payment when it becomes due. The IRS has disallowed schemes like this on the grounds that no legitimate mortgage existed. If you want to make a gift of real estate free of gift tax, see a lawyer. (Chapter 29.)

A gift of real estate will be disallowed, for tax purposes, if the giver held onto some important right over the property—for example, the right to receive rents from a small apartment building. To avoid this problem, you must comply with all applicable IRS rules.

If you give a tangible item (such as cash, an heirloom, or pictures), the relinquishment of control necessary to establish a gift is usually easy to prove—the recipient gains unrestricted possession over the property. In other situations, the question of control may be more difficult to ascertain. For example, if a gift is contingent on a future event, that event must be determinable by some objective standard. "To Desiree, when she becomes 21," or "when she travels to Paris" is objective; "when she's happily married" is not.

Property you place in a revocable living trust isn't a gift because you retain full control over the property and can revoke the trust if you wish. The beneficiaries you name in the trust document have no current right to the trust property. Likewise, if you establish an irrevocable trust and retain the power to change who will benefit from it, even if you, yourself, are specifically excluded as a possible beneficiary, there's no gift.

EXAMPLE: Roger, a wealthy older man, puts money in an irrevocable trust for his grandniece Olivia, to be used for her eventual college and possible graduate school costs. He appoints a trustee and gives her authority to alter the purposes for which the trust money can be spent. Roger also retains the right to substitute a new trustee. Because Roger still has so much control over the trust property, there has been no gift for gift tax purposes.

Common Kinds of Gifts

Here are some types of transactions that are legal gifts:

- making an interest-free loan. Really? Yes. Federal law provides that an interest-free or artificially low-interest loan is a gift by the lender of the interest not charged. An "artificially low" interest rate is any rate below market interest rates when the loan is made. So, if you lend a friend $30,000 interest free, you are making a taxable gift of the interest you didn't charge. But because of the $14,000 annual gift tax exclusion discussed above, gifts of interest on most loans don't have gift tax consequences. For example, at a 5% simple interest rate, a single person can make an interest-free loan of $280,000 to a person without gift tax liability. A married couple could lend a person up to $560,000 interest free before the annual interest would exceed $28,000, the couple's combined annual gift tax exclusion.
- handing someone cash, a check, or any tangible item, with the intention of making a gift
- transferring title to real estate, stocks, or a motor vehicle into another's name, without receiving anything of value in exchange. Remember that if you reserve the right to receive any income from the property, such as rent or dividends, no valid gift is made.

- transferring property to an irrevocable trust you create to benefit another person. As mentioned above, the trust must have an objective standard of when the beneficiary will receive the property. An irrevocable trust means you can't change your mind and alter or terminate the trust once it is created. (By contrast, as we've mentioned, since a living trust is almost always revocable, naming someone as a beneficiary doesn't guarantee they will receive the property, so no gift is made.)
- irrevocably assigning a life insurance policy to another (see Chapter 12)
- forgiving a debt
- assigning a mortgage, court judgment, or other debt or loan owed you, without receiving fair compensation in return, and
- making a noncommercial transfer of your property into joint tenancy with another person (except for joint bank accounts. In that case, the rule is that a gift is made only when one depositor withdraws money deposited by the other).

SEE AN EXPERT

Partial gifts. Federal law authorizes "partial gifts." (I.R.C. § 2512(b).) These are gifts where you receive something of value back, but the gift is worth far more than what you received. Making a partial gift is a complex tax matter and you'll need to see a lawyer. (See Chapter 29.)

How the Federal Gift Tax Works

Before you can intelligently evaluate whether you want to use gifts as part of your estate plan, you need to thoroughly understand how the federal gift tax actually works. I touched on this above; now I present a more thorough treatment of this important subject.

Gift tax applies to all gifts made by U.S. citizens and residents and also to gifts of property by nonresident aliens if the gift property is physically located in the United States. The most obvious example is real estate in the United States.

Here are the basics.

Gift Tax Payment and Rates

As discussed, currently, if you give a gift worth more than $14,000, you must file a gift tax return (unless the gift is exempt from tax), and the IRS will assess a gift tax against you.

The IRS requires that the amount of the gift tax be used to reduce the amount of your personal estate tax exemption. You cannot choose to pay gift tax now and "save" all of your personal exemption for later use.

> **EXAMPLE:** Amber gives Beatrice an expensive car, worth $56,000; $14,000 is exempt from tax, so tax will be assessed on $42,000. Amber cannot simply pay the amount of the tax now and preserve the full amount of her personal estate tax exemption until her death. Rather, the IRS requires that she use up $42,000 of her personal exemption.

Gifts of Life Insurance Made Near Death

You can make almost any gift up to the moment you die without running afoul of IRS rules. However, a few types of gifts must be made at least three years before the giver's death, or the gifts are disallowed for estate tax purposes. A gift of a life insurance policy is the significant one in this category. If a life insurance policy is given away within three years of death, the IRS acts as if the gift were never made, and includes the full amount of the proceeds in the giver's taxable estate. (If you've already paid gift tax, that amount will be credited toward any estate tax due. I.R.C. § 2012(a).) This is for estate tax purposes only; it doesn't affect ownership of the policy, which remains with the recipient.

Disallowance of a gift of life insurance can result in a substantial increase in the size of the giver's taxable estate. The proceeds paid when the insured person dies are always worth much more than the value of the same policy given away before the insured dies. For example, a whole life policy that pays $300,000 at death might have a cash surrender value of only $50,000 two years or two days before the owner dies. (Gifts of life insurance are discussed in more detail below, and in Chapter 12.)

Gifts From a Living Trust and the Three-Year Rule

As trustee of your living trust, you can make gifts of living trust property directly from your trust at any time while you live. These gifts are not subject to the three-year rule. For a time, the IRS contended the three-year rule did apply here, but it never had much success in court. Finally, the Taxpayer Relief Act of 1997 explicitly provided that the three-year rule has no application to gifts made from a living trust. (I.R.C. § 2035(e).)

The Present Interest Rule

Under IRS rules, the annual gift tax exclusion applies only to gifts of what is called a "present interest." This means that the person or institution who receives the gift has the right to use it immediately. For the great majority of gifts, this is no problem. The receiver obtains full control when the gift is made. By contrast, gifts that someone can use only in the future, not when the gift was made, do not qualify for the annual exclusion. These are called gifts of a "future interest."

> **EXAMPLE:** Kim gives $10,000 outright to her friend Gayle and places another $10,000 in an irrevocable trust to benefit her friend Madeleine.

Madeleine, age 32, can use principal from the trust only when she turns 35. The gift to Gayle is a gift of a present interest, because Gayle gets the money now. The gift to the trust for Madeleine is a gift of a future interest, because she has no right to the money when Kim gives it. So gift tax is assessed against the $10,000 Kim gives to the trust.

Gifts to Minors and the Present Interest Rule

Gifts to minors can qualify for the annual exclusion, even though the minor isn't given (indeed, by law, cannot be given) full present access to or control of the gift property. Federal law (I.R.C. § 2503(c)) provides that in order to make a gift to a minor that qualifies for the annual exemption, three conditions must be met:

- The gift, and any income it produces, must be used or retained in trust or an UTMA account, for the minor's benefit.
- The remainder of the gift must go outright to the child when she or he reaches age 21. (The gift can go outright to the child when she or he is 18 or older, up to 21.)
- If the child dies before reaching the age to receive the gift outright, the remainder of the gift must be paid to his or her estate.

"Crummey" Trusts and the Present Interest Rule

To get around the present interest rule for gifts to adults or to children or grandchildren where the giver does not want the property turned over when the child becomes 21, lawyers invented a crafty device called a "Crummey" trust (so called because it was judicially approved in the case of *Crummey v. Commissioner,* 397 F.2d 82, 1968). For one of a number of reasons, a giver may not want a recipient to become the owner of a gift, but still wants to get the annual exclusion for the gift. One example is a gift to an irrevocable trust to pay for trust-owned life insurance on the giver's life. A gift to a trust is not generally a gift of a present interest. So, in order to obtain the annual exclusion, beneficiaries of the trust are given the right, for a limited time—as little as a few days—to accept (in legalese, to "withdraw") the gift. But they don't withdraw the gift, the period lapses, and the gift becomes owned by the trust. Because the beneficiaries had the legal right to take the gift, it now qualifies as a gift of a present interest and gets the $14,000 exclusion.

SEE AN EXPERT

Crummey trusts are tricky. If Crummey trusts seem fuzzy to you, don't feel alone. They are used only with more complicated estates where outright gifts are not desired. Crummey trusts must be created by a lawyer.

The Federal Gift Tax Return

You must file an IRS gift tax return when your regular income tax return is filed (normally, April 15) if you:

- have made nonexempt gifts over the amount of the annual exclusion to any person or organization during the previous taxable year, or
- have made gifts over the amount of the annual exclusion to a tax-exempt organization during the previous taxable year. No tax is assessed for such tax-exempt gifts, but the IRS still requires you to file a return. Who knows why?

The IRS does not require you to file a gift tax return for gifts between spouses (unless the recipient is not a U.S. citizen and the gift exceeds $145,000) or for gifts for educational or medical expenses to anyone, no matter how large the gift.

Using Gifts to Reduce Estate Taxes

For people with very large estates, making tax-exempt gifts while living, either to individuals or charities, can be a significant part of their estate plan.

Many people make substantial gifts primarily for personal reasons, but with the awareness that they're obtaining estate/gift tax benefits, as well. Using gifts that total up to $5.34 million, as well as annual exclusion gifts, to reduce the size of your estate when you die can be desirable if three things are true:

- Your estate may owe estate tax (see Chapter 15).
- The property you want to give has not greatly appreciated in value since you acquired it (if it has, it's better, for tax reasons, to transfer it at death; see "When Not to Give Property Away," below).
- You don't need all of your assets and income to live on.

Some Thoughts on Gift Giving and Taxes

Estate planners have developed a number of ways to use gifts to reduce, or even eliminate, estate tax for many people who would otherwise face a tax bill. Before plunging into this subject (game might be a better word), take stock of what you really feel about making gifts now. Will giving property to your children or grandchildren enhance their lives? Or are they not yet ready to handle or appreciate your generosity? For example, helping a 21-year-old get an education or the head of a new family buy a house may be a truly great gift. By contrast, you may not want your money spent by a young person on a two-week vacation in Las Vegas or an expensive car. (But then, doesn't every kid merit a convertible?)

This last concern, of course, requires an evaluation of how much money and property you think you'll need (or want) now and in the future, as well as what your resources are, including income from retirement plans, Social Security, savings, and investments. Some people, who may not want to use up any of their principal for gifts, may decide to use some of their income for gifts.

The Timing of Gifts

For wealthy people who engage in extensive tax-saving gift giving, the timing of making gifts can be important. To briefly summarize, if the cumulative gifts made are over the estate tax threshold, it's advantageous to make taxable gifts near the beginning of the tax year. Although the gift tax is the same no matter when the gift is made during the year, if you make a taxable gift in January, you do not have to pay the gift tax until April of the following year. In the meantime, the income from the gift goes to the recipient rather than increasing your taxable estate.

By contrast, charitable gifts are often given at the end of the tax year, so the giver can receive the income from the asset for most of the year, while obtaining the charitable tax deduction for that same year.

Using the Annual Exemption Repeatedly

Although the annual gift tax exclusion may not seem like an immense sum, it can often be used over time to achieve substantial estate tax savings. The key is using the exclusion as fully as possible. It's a simple matter of multiplication. If you use the $14,000 annual exclusion for gifts to one person for five years, you've given away five times as much ($70,000) tax free as you would if you gave the same $70,000 to the same person in one year and qualified for only one exemption. If you make $14,000 gifts to five recipients in one year, you've also given away $70,000 tax free. And if you make five $14,000 gifts to five people for five years, you've given away $350,000 tax free. (And since spouses can each make $14,000 gifts, giving as a couple multiplies your gift tax exemption by two.)

> **EXAMPLE:** Patti owns a successful small business, with an estimated net worth of $5 million. Her other assets are worth roughly $775,000. Patti intends to leave her business to her three children. To reduce the value of her eventual estate, she incorporates her business and starts giving her children stock. She can give each of her children stock worth $14,000 per year gift tax free—a yearly total of $42,000. For ten years, she gives each child $14,000 worth of stock, transferring a total of $420,000 tax free.

This example assumes the worth of the company remained the same for ten years and that the gift tax exclusion remained at $14,000, unlikely in the real world. In practice, Patti would have to review the worth of her company yearly, and check out the gift tax law from time to time.

Some Types of Repeated Gifts Could Land You in Tax Trouble

The IRS scrutinizes complex repeat-gift programs to catch those that cross the line from clever to forbidden. Usually, the IRS catches illegal gift-giving programs when it audits an estate tax return. It then disallows gift tax exemptions for previous gifts and hits the estate with a nasty tax bill for back gift taxes, interest, and penalties.

One area where you should tread very cautiously is making a gift that forgives a loan payment due to you. For example, some parents have made large loans to their children, intending to forgive repayments of $14,000 a year. The IRS, skeptical of these arrangements to start with, has set out rules you must follow if you want to prove that your transaction is a bona fide loan, not a gift in disguise. The bottom line seems to be that if you are meticulous about paperwork, this strategy can be successful.

The IRS starts with the presumption that a transfer between family members is a gift. You can get around that presumption by showing that you really expected repayment and intended to enforce the debt. In making that determination, the IRS considers whether or not:

- the borrower signed a promissory note
- you charged interest on the loan
- there was security (collateral) for the debt
- there was a fixed date that the loan was due to be repaid
- the borrower had the ability to repay
- you demanded repayment
- the borrower actually repaid some of the loan
- your records or those of the recipient indicate that the transfer was a loan, and
- the transaction was reported, for federal tax purposes, as a loan.

SEE AN EXPERT

Forgiving family debts. As you can see, there are a lot of hurdles to overcome if you want to legally forgive debts on a family loan. If you want to explore this further, see an expert attorney or accountant.

Giving Property That Is Likely to Appreciate

If you're prosperous and your estate will be subject to estate tax, it can make particularly good sense to give away property that you believe will appreciate substantially in the future, especially if it hasn't gone up in value much already. At first, this may seem a little complicated, but if you read what follows carefully, you'll see it really isn't.

Here is the basic idea. If property you own seems reasonably likely to go up in value substantially in the future, giving it away now not only excludes its present worth from your estate but also eliminates the value of its likely future appreciation from your estate.

EXAMPLE: Brook, in her 60s, recently purchased some vacant land for $161,000 cash. The property is located in an area she believes will be ripe for development in a few years. She intends to leave this land to her niece, Laura, when she dies. If she waits to transfer the property until her death, then the market value of the property at the time she dies will be included in her taxable estate. But if Brook gives the land to Laura soon after buying it in 2014, all of its appreciation in value, as well as its current worth, won't be included in Brook's taxable estate.

The gift will be subject to gift tax. $14,000 will be exempt from gift tax, but $147,000 won't be. Still, if Brook is right about the land increasing in value, the gift tax assessed will be far less than estate tax imposed on the appreciated property would be at Brook's death, for the obvious reason that the appreciated property will be worth more and, therefore, taxed at a higher rate.

By contrast, it usually doesn't make sense to give away property that has already gone up in value, especially if you may not live long. The reason is that the recipient of a gift will have the same tax basis in the property as the giver did (which is, very roughly, usually what the giver paid for the property). An inheritor, on the other hand, obtains a basis that is stepped up to the fair market value of the property at the time of death.

> **EXAMPLE:** Bill bought 1,000 shares of stock at $5 a share. It's now worth $30 a share and is still going up. If he gives it now to his daughter Betsy, her cost basis will be $5 per share. If he leaves it to Betsy upon his death, her stepped-up basis in the stock will probably be $30 a share or higher, depending on its market price when he dies.
>
> This difference will be vitally important when Betsy sells the stock. If its cost basis is $5 a share and she sells it for $30 a share, she will have to pay capital gains tax on the $25 per share profit. By contrast, if the basis is stepped up to $30 because the transfer is made at death, and she sells the stock at $30 a share, she won't owe any capital gains tax.

Gifts of Life Insurance

In some situations, making a gift of life insurance can substantially reduce or eliminate federal estate tax. In fact, from a gift tax standpoint, giving life insurance can often be the most advantageous way to transfer a large sum out of your estate, since the gift normally has a low value for gift tax purposes. But because gifts of insurance policies can be such a good tax deal for the giver, special rules apply. The most important one is that the gift must be made more than three years before you die to be effective for estate tax purposes.

Gifts of life insurance are discussed in Chapter 12. As I've discussed above, the value of the gift of an insurance policy is always much lower than the proceeds paid in the event of the insured's death.

Gifts of a Family Business

Gifts of minority interests in a family business can result in significant estate tax savings. Currently, sophisticated estate tax planners play some very fancy games here. See Chapter 28.

Gifts to Minors

You can make a gift to a minor (a child younger than 18) during your life, as well as leave property to a minor when you die. A minor cannot legally control any substantial amount of property in his or her own name. An adult must have that responsibility. If, while you are alive, you want to make a gift directly to a child, rather than to his or her parents or guardians, you have two choices:

- Give the money in a trust. If you, while living, make a gift to a minor using a properly drafted child's trust, you obtain the annual gift tax exclusion in the year the gift is made.

- Appoint a "custodian" for the gift, under your state's Uniform Transfers to Minors Act (UTMA) or Uniform Gifts to Minors Act (UGMA). (UTMA, UGMA, Let's Call the Whole Thing Off.) The UTMA applies in all states but South Carolina and Vermont, where the UGMA applies. The UGMA provides only a device for making gifts to minors while you live, not for leaving property to them when you die.

Using either act, you can, while you live, make a gift to a minor by naming an adult custodian for the gift property. (See Chapter 6.)

In most states, the custodianship must end when the child turns 18 or 21. Obviously, that satisfies the IRS age requirement that the minor must receive the gift outright by age 21. In Alaska, California, Nevada, Oregon, Pennsylvania, and Tennessee, however, for gifts you make to children during your life, you must be sure to provide that the recipient will receive the gift at some age between 18 to 21. These states' laws could be interpreted as extending the custodianship past age 21, if you don't provide otherwise.

Gifts to minors made while one is alive are often given primarily for personal reasons, not for gift tax savings. Your personal motives may override maximizing gift tax savings, or those motives may work harmoniously with gift tax rules.

EXAMPLE 1: Oksana, who is quite prosperous, wants to be certain her grandson Viktor and granddaughter Marya will have enough money to attend college. Viktor is 12 and Marya is ten. Oksana wants to make the gift now, so she can take pleasure in knowing that her grandchildren know their educational future is secure. She creates an educational child's trust for each, to last until the child is 30, naming their father as trustee. Oksana realizes that by doing this, she will not obtain the annual gift tax exclusion for any money she gives the trust, because, as I explained, federal tax law requires the child to receive the money outright by age 21 for the exclusion to apply. But Oksana wants adult supervision of the trust until the children are 30, because she doubts that any 21-year-old is likely to be able to handle large amounts of money responsibly. Her concern over this issue overrides any consideration of tax savings.

EXAMPLE 2: Biff decides to give an expensive thoroughbred horse worth $50,000 to his niece Brenda, age 16, who has loved horses since she was small. Biff makes the gift under his state's UTMA, which requires the horse to be legally turned over to Brenda when she becomes 21—which is fine with Biff. Biff names Brenda's mother, Josette, as custodian for the gift. They all know this is only technical, since Brenda will be, and wants to be, responsible for the horse.

Biff is not assessed gift tax on $14,000 of his gift. He is assessed gift tax on the remaining value of $36,000.

Making Taxable Gifts

If you are rich, it might be to your family's financial advantage to make taxable gifts. This is a high-end strategy; it only makes sense if you are someone who has already used up all of her or his gift tax exemption of $5.34 million for previous taxable gifts. Then, you'll have to pay gift tax when you make new gifts.

The basic idea is that by making the taxable gift and then paying the tax from your property while you live, you'll wind up paying less overall gift and estate tax than if you didn't make the gift. If you don't make the gift, that property plus the amount you would pay in gift tax is included in your taxable estate. Because of the graduated estate tax rates, the overall tax bite can be larger.

SEE AN EXPERT

To explore making taxable gifts, you'll need an expert. If making taxable gifts sounds confusing, that's only because it is. You need an expert to explore whether such a strategy is desirable for you. You'll probably have to crunch a lot of numbers, taking the following factors into consideration:

- the amount of money or property you can comfortably give away
- the gift tax on that gift
- the likely worth of your estate at death
- the estate tax exemption, and
- the possibilities of changes to the federal estate tax law.

Also, to prevent people from making taxable gifts as a deathbed tax ploy, the IRS includes any gift tax paid during the last three years of life in the decedent's taxable estate. (I.R.C. § 2053.) In other words, last-minute (or even last-year) gifts won't work to lower overall taxes.

For tips on finding and working with a lawyer, see Chapter 29.

When Not to Give Property Away: Tax Basis Rules

Much of this chapter has discussed why it is often advantageous, from an estate/gift tax point of view, to give away property before you die. But this isn't always the case. It's usually unwise to give away an asset (as opposed to leaving it at death) that has substantially appreciated in value since you purchased it, especially if you are older and likely to die before decades pass.

In order to understand why it is often better for the recipient to inherit appreciated property than to receive it during the giver's lifetime, you need to understand the tax concept of basis. While I've discussed this concept in Chapter 15, it's so important that here we focus on how this applies to gifts.

The tax basis of property is the value (dollar figure) from which the IRS determines gain or loss on a sale. When you purchase property, its basis is generally its cost. In fact, basis is often referred to as cost basis. If you make major (capital) improvements to property—for example, adding a deck to your house—the cost of the improvement is added to the basis of the property.

The recipient of a gift takes the same basis in the property as the giver had. This is called the "carryover" basis, in tax jargon.

> **EXAMPLE:** Lewella's basis in her house is $100,000 (net purchase price plus capital improvements). Lewella owns the house free and clear. The house now has a market value of $320,000. Lewella gives her house to Megan. Megan's (carryover) basis in the house is $100,000. If Megan then sells the house for $320,000, her taxable profit is $220,000 ($320,000 minus her basis of $100,000).

Remember, the value of a gift for gift tax purposes is its present net market value. Thus, for property that has increased in value since the giver acquired it, there are two different valuations. The lower original purchase price—the basis of the property for the gift recipient—and the higher current market value, the figure used for the giver's gift tax. In the above example, the IRS assesses Lewella's (the donor's) gift taxes on the $320,000 market value, but the basis to Megan (the recipient) is $100,000.

Different basis rules apply to inherited property. These inherited property basis rules are more advantageous to recipients.

The tax basis for property a person inherits is the fair market value at the date of the original owner's death. So if the value of the property has gone up since the owner acquired it, the tax basis is increased (in "taxese," stepped up) from the deceased's basis to the value of the property at death.

> **EXAMPLE:** If Lewella dies and leaves her house to Megan, Megan's basis in the house is increased to its market value at Lewella's death, which is $320,000.

This stepped-up basis rule means there are major capital gains tax savings for the recipient if an asset that has appreciated in value is transferred at death instead of given to that recipient while the giver is still alive.

> **EXAMPLE:** Edward owns a Redon pastel painting, which he bought as an astute art student for $20,000. Sixty years later, an appraiser informs him it's worth $1.3 million. If Edward were to sell the painting, his taxable gain would be $1.3 million less his basis of $20,000. If he gives the painting away and the recipient sells it, the tax situation is the same—only now it's the recipient who owes capital gains tax on the profit.

By contrast, if Edward dies and uses his living trust to leave the painting to the same recipient, this beneficiary's stepped-up basis in the painting is $1.3 million. If the beneficiary promptly sells the painting, there's no taxable gain.

Special Rules for Community Property

If you're married and own community property, another federal tax basis rule can be significant for any gift planning you consider. On the death of one spouse, the basis of each spouse's half of the community property is stepped up to the property's fair market value at the time of the spouse's death.

> **EXAMPLE:** Felicia and Max are residents of California, a community property state. They own a grand house in Malibu they bought decades ago for $100,000. The basis of each spouse's interest is $50,000, one half the purchase price. When Felicia dies in 2014, the market value of the house is $8 million. Because of the stepped-up basis rule for community property, the federal tax basis of each spouse's half interest in the house steps up to $4 million. If Max sells the house for $8 million shortly after Felicia's death, he will not owe any capital gains tax. The sale price equals the stepped-up basis of the house. In contrast, if the house had been sold before Felicia died, their

profit would have been $7.9 million. Under capital gains tax law, $500,000 of the amount would be exempt because the profit is from sale by a couple of a home. So capital gains tax would be assessed on $7.4 million.

Again, what all this means is that there may be a considerable federal tax advantage for inheritors if a couple retains, until one of them dies, community property that has substantially increased in value since they purchased it.

State Tax Basis Rules

Estate planning decisions are rarely affected by state tax basis rules. In general, the impact of state tax basis rules on gifts or inherited property is minor, because the tax rates involved are relatively low in those states that impose gift and estate taxes. If you want to explore your state's rules, you can either research that issue yourself (see Chapter 29) or consult an accountant or a tax attorney.

Using Gifts to Reduce Income Taxes

If you are prosperous and are willing to give income-producing property to someone in a lower tax bracket while you are still alive, you can achieve some overall income tax savings in addition to the possible federal estate and gift tax savings discussed earlier in this chapter.

With the current maximum income tax rate close to 40%, a gift to a person in a lower tax bracket, especially someone in the 15% bracket, will obviously result in less income tax being paid on income received from the property. Of course, you will not see the tax savings yourself, because you no longer own the property.

CAUTION

Be wary of giving property to children younger than 18. You might not obtain an income tax benefit for a gift to a child younger than age 18. The reason is that all income over $2,000 a year received by minors from any gift, is taxed, for federal income tax purposes, at the highest tax rate of their parents. This also applies to full-time students through age 23. See "Taxation of a Child's Income" in Chapter 6 for more information.

An Overview of Ongoing Trusts

An "ongoing" trust is a trust that is intended to operate as an independent legal entity for a long time, usually years or even decades, after the death of the person who establishes it (the grantor). Often, but not in all cases, an ongoing trust begins to operate as a separate legal entity only at the death of the grantor. An ongoing trust can be created in a will or in a living trust, or by a document making the trust operational while the trust grantor is alive. Once operational, an ongoing trust is irrevocable.

The two basic functions of ongoing trusts are to:

- save on estate taxes, and
- impose long-term controls on the management of trust property.

Some ongoing trusts serve both purposes, some only one.

Many people need only a simple probate avoidance living trust, not an ongoing trust. A living trust is not ongoing because it functions as a separate entity for only a brief time after the grantor's death. By the end of this chapter, you should have a pretty clear idea of whether or not you need some type of ongoing trust.

This chapter explores basic features common to all ongoing trusts. Other chapters delve into some specific types of ongoing trusts, including:

- AB disclaimer trusts, which may save on estate taxes (Chapter 18)
- other estate tax–saving marital trusts, including a "QTIP" trust to postpone payment of estate taxes (Chapter 19)
- charitable trusts (Chapter 20)

- other estate tax–saving trusts, including generation-skipping trusts, irrevocable life insurance trusts, and grantor-retained interest trusts (Chapter 21)
- combining ongoing estate tax–saving trusts (Chapter 23)
- trusts useful to people with children from a prior marriage (Chapter 24)
- trusts to impose controls over property (Chapter 25), and
- children's trusts or family pot trusts used to control property inherited by a minor or young adult (Chapter 6).

SEE AN EXPERT

Ongoing trusts and medical bills. Many people would like to include a "catastrophic illness" clause or provision in any ongoing trust they create, to prevent trust assets from being used to pay medical bills if a trust beneficiary suffers a catastrophic illness. Often, couples are particularly concerned with preserving their trust assets from claims by medical providers or government agencies. At the very least, the couple doesn't want both members' assets used to pay for one's catastrophic illness.

Unfortunately, no simple trust clause applicable in all states will achieve this result. A provision properly geared to current federal laws and regulations, your state's specific laws, and your situation may provide some protection. But such provisions rarely, if ever, consist of a single clause or paragraph; indeed, they may go on for pages and require sophisticated knowledge of all applicable laws and regulations. An expert lawyer must prepare such provisions. It's absolutely essential to be up to date here.

Trusts to Reduce Estate Taxes

One goal of some ongoing trusts is to save on estate taxes. Currently, most estates won't owe estate tax, but if you expect that yours will, there's good reason to want to cut the tax bill. Any federal estate taxes will take a substantial bite out of the property you leave behind. (See Chapter 15 for more about estate taxes.)

Any individual with an estate over the estate tax threshold should explore tax-saving trusts. If you are afraid that reading about tax-saving trusts will overwhelm you, don't give up. You don't need to master the complexities of actually preparing most of these types of trusts. This book contains no forms for preparing your own estate tax–saving trusts. Generally, these trusts are complex and technical and must be prepared by a lawyer.

I want to offer you sufficient information about major types of estate tax–saving trusts so you can decide whether it's worth your time and money to hire a lawyer to create one or more of them. Also, by reading the next six chapters, you should be able to tell whether a lawyer is providing helpful, accurate information and advice about estate tax–saving trusts or is primarily concerned with running up your bill.

Ongoing Trusts Used to Control Property

In addition to reducing estate taxes, ongoing trusts can also provide for the management and control of property you don't want to leave outright to someone. Property control trusts are particularly common when spouses have children from prior marriages. Often, each spouse wants to provide well for the other spouse. At the same time, each spouse doesn't want to leave everything outright to the other spouse, because each wants the bulk of his or her property to eventually go to his or her children. An ongoing trust can be used to achieve both these goals. (See Chapter 24.)

An ongoing trust to control property is also desirable or essential in other circumstances, including situations in which:

- You leave property to minors (or people who have been declared legally incompetent) who are not legally permitted to own substantial amounts of property outright.
- You believe the beneficiary can't handle money responsibly.
- The beneficiary has a disability and requires what's called a "special needs trust" to provide long-term support but not interfere with the beneficiary's eligibility for federal or state assistance.
- You decide you no longer want the burdens of managing your own property and want to turn that task over to someone else. For instance, someone who is old and ill may know that it's sensible to arrange for others to handle her finances. There are various methods to arrange for this, including preparing a durable

power of attorney for finances. (See Chapter 26.) Sometimes people prefer a trust, however, because it is a more traditional legal form and the trust property will avoid probate on the grantor's death.

Property control trusts for each of these situations are discussed in Chapter 25.

Ongoing Trusts and Avoiding Probate

Property left in ongoing trusts doesn't automatically avoid probate. Most ongoing trusts become operational only when the grantor dies. So, to avoid probate of property left in these trusts, ongoing trusts are usually incorporated as a part (a big part) of a living trust. By using a living trust, the property avoids probate after the person's death and goes straight into the now-operational ongoing trust.

> **EXAMPLE:** Pilar wants to establish an ongoing trust to manage the property she intends to leave to her kid brother, Juan, who is 20 years her junior. She wants to create an ongoing trust because Juan, age 28, has always squandered whatever money he's acquired and shows no signs of change. Within her revocable living trust, Pilar creates an ongoing trust in which the trustee she appoints controls how and when money is given to Juan from the trust. This trust will become operational only after Pilar dies.

Under the terms of the living trust, the property left to Juan will be transferred to the ongoing trust without probate.

As long as Pilar lives, the living trust, and the ongoing trust contained in the living trust, are revocable. When Pilar dies, the ongoing trust becomes irrevocable and cannot be changed by anyone, including Juan.

All of the ongoing trusts discussed in the next chapters can be made part of a living trust, except ongoing trusts that become operational before the grantor dies. To say this metaphorically, just because an ongoing trust and a probate avoidance living trust are technically different legal animals doesn't mean they can't drink at the same pond. I stress this here because it's important to understand you don't need to risk probate by creating an ongoing trust. I don't repeat this for each ongoing trust I discuss. These discussions are already complex enough.

What Ongoing Trusts Can't Do

Expert estate planning lawyers can sometimes come up with truly ingenious plans to fit a family's particular needs and save on estate taxes. But some lawyers and financial planners push the line of what's legally safe. It's up to you to decide how safe or aggressive you want to be. But before betting a big estate on the cutting-edge theories of any estate planner—

lawyer or not—it's wise to get a second, perhaps more conservative, opinion.

Those who believe trusts are truly lawyers' magic may seek or fall victim to what I call the "daydream" trust. In a daydream trust, the grantor wants to use an ongoing trust to:

- avoid all income and estate taxes
- shield the property from all creditors, and
- retain complete control over trust property or, at the very least, have full access to it in times of need.

It should come as no surprise that the daydream trust is just that—a fantasy. Tax rules do not allow people to escape legal responsibilities simply by use of a trust. You can't use a trust to escape responsibility for legal debts and obligations, including child support, alimony, court-ordered judgments, or any other legal debt.

Likewise, if you retain any control over your trust or benefit from it, the IRS will not let you use the trust to reduce your income taxes. It looks poorly on trusts designed to save big money on income and estate taxes, while at the same time giving the grantor great powers over trust assets.

When Ongoing Trusts Begin and End

Once an ongoing trust becomes operational, it is a legal entity separate from any person or organization. It is also, as I've stressed, irrevocable—which means you can't change the terms of the trust. Before the trust takes effect, however, you can revoke or change it at any time—you're not bound by its terms. Most people don't want an ongoing trust to become irrevocable while they are alive. Understandably, they don't want to be locked into giving away some of their property during their life.

When an Ongoing Trust Takes Effect

A trust becomes operational as soon as it is effective in the real world as a legally distinct entity. Most often this happens at the death of the trust creator. Once an ongoing trust becomes operational, the trustee must obtain a taxpayer ID number for the trust, keep accurate trust financial records, and file an annual federal trust income tax return and any required state trust tax returns.

> **EXAMPLE:** Alma, age 73, creates a living trust to avoid probate. As one component of this living trust, she creates an ongoing trust for her special needs daughter, with Alma's niece Maureen as trustee. Only when Alma dies does this ongoing trust for her daughter become operational and irrevocable. Then Maureen must handle the trust property and accompanying paperwork.

Occasionally, however, people want an ongoing trust to become operational and irrevocable during their lifetime. For example, charitable trusts are often set up this way. Such irrevocable trusts are operational as soon as the trust documents are signed and notarized. Trust property is promptly given to the charity, and the grantor retains certain rights to receive income from it. (See Chapter 20.)

There can be other reasons to make an ongoing trust operational during your lifetime, rather than at your death. For example, an irrevocable life insurance trust must be operational at least three years before the grantor's death to obtain estate tax savings. (See Chapter 21.)

How Long an Ongoing Trust Lasts

How long an ongoing trust lasts is defined in the trust document. While some trusts last for a set number of years, usually the end of the trust is triggered by a certain event. The trust may, for example, last until a surviving spouse dies; when that happens, trust property is distributed to the couple's children, and the trust ends. A trust for grandchildren may last until the youngest reaches age 30 or 35, or whatever age the grantor chooses, at which point the grandchildren receive all remaining trust property.

In most states, a legal rule called "the rule against perpetuities" requires a trust to have a set ending time or event. This rule prevents someone from tying up property for generations without that property ever being owned outright by anyone. For example, you can't leave property "first to my daughter, then equally to her children,

then equally to their grandchildren," and so on. Generally, society has decided that there should be a finite period during which the instructions of a deceased person can control the disposition of property. At some time, some person has to own the property outright and be free to sell it or give it away. Several states have liberalized their rule against perpetuities statutes. This matters to legal scholars, some of the very rich, and perhaps you, if for some unusual reason, you would like to set up a trust that lasts for several generations.

The intricacies of the rule against perpetuities have baffled law students for generations. For practical purposes, the rule means you can legally tie up property only for people who are alive when you die. That means you can leave trust property for your grown children to use during their lives and specify that, at their deaths, the property goes outright to their children. But if you try to impose controls on your nonexisting great-grandchildren's freedom to use or dispose of the property, you risk running afoul of the rule against perpetuities.

SEE AN EXPERT

Imposing controls for more than one generation. If you want to create controls on property for more than one generation, you'll definitely need an expert estate planning lawyer's advice to determine whether what you want is legally possible. See Chapter 29 for tips on finding and working with a lawyer.

The Trustee

The trustee of an ongoing trust has serious responsibilities, and choosing a reliable trustee is a crucial part of creating an ongoing trust.

The Trustee's Duties

For any type of ongoing trust, the trustee must manage the trust property prudently and comply with any specific management instructions in the trust document.

The trustee's powers are usually set out in detail (sometimes many pages of detail) in the trust document. For example, the trustee may be given the specific power to sell trust real estate or to buy or lease new real estate.

Terminology Note

When an ongoing trust is created as a component of a living trust, you are the original trustee. When you die, a person you've named as trustee for the ongoing trust manages it. Often, but not always, this person is the same as the successor trustee of your living trust. I refer to the person who manages an ongoing trust that becomes operational at your death simply as the "trustee."

General legal rules also govern the trustee. Legally, the trustee is a "fiduciary," which imposes the standard of highest good faith and scrupulous honesty when handling trust business, unless the trust document itself declares a lesser legal standard. For example, unless it's specifically authorized in the trust document, the trustee may not personally profit from any financial transaction involving the trust.

The trustee of an ongoing trust will most likely engage in various business or financial transactions on behalf of the trust. For instance, the trustee will probably deal with banks or other financial institutions. The trustee may well be involved in other trust financial matters, from leasing trust property to dealing with the IRS. The trustee may also have to make investment decisions or buy or sell trust property.

Sometimes, the trustee's actual financial responsibilities can be rather simple. For example, if the trust primarily consists of a valuable house, the trustee has to be sure the house is properly maintained and perhaps decide when to sell it. But often the trustee's work is more difficult. If much of the trust money is invested, the trustee must decide whether the investments are reasonable ones—neither absurdly cautious nor too risky. If the trust property includes a business or a complex investment portfolio, managing the property can be quite a task. For this reason, it's normally permissible for a trustee to hire financial or investment advisers and pay for their advice from trust assets.

The trustee of an ongoing trust must also distribute trust income (or principal) to the beneficiaries as the trust document directs or permits. Sometimes this, too, is far from simple. If the trust document allows the trustee some discretion in whether or not to distribute trust income or principal on behalf of a certain beneficiary, it may not be easy for the trustee to decide what to do.

The trustee of an ongoing trust that becomes operational at the grantor's death is responsible for handling all trust paperwork—for example, getting the taxpayer ID number from the IRS and keeping accurate trust financial records. Professional help can be used here if, in the trustee's judgment, it's necessary. The trustee is also responsible for filing the annual trust income tax return (IRS Form 1041). If any federal tax is owed, the trustee must pay it from trust funds. Finally, the trustee must handle any required state income tax return.

Eventually, when the trust ends, the trustee must distribute any remaining trust property to the final trust beneficiaries.

Because of these responsibilities, most trustees of ongoing trusts are paid. The trust document often allows the trustees to pay themselves "reasonable compensation" or a set amount per hour from trust property. Of course, you can expressly prohibit pay for your trustee, but it's not wise. Are you sure you can rely on a person to do the work required of a trustee without compensation? And even if someone would do it, do you really think it's fair? After all, the trustee will be spending time on work you created by establishing your ongoing trust.

Choosing the Trustee

Obviously, if you create an ongoing trust, you must give serious thought to who will serve as the trustee. The two most important criteria your trustee should meet are that you completely trust the person and that he or she wants to do the job.

The trustee should also have some financial common sense. You may decide, in fact, that you want your trustee to have considerable financial expertise. For instance, you may want a trustee who understands the difference between a balanced, fairly conservative investment portfolio—say, a mix of income-oriented stock and bond funds—and much riskier investment in someone's great idea for a new business or speculation in real estate.

If you can find all this in one person, fine, but remember—your trustee can always hire investment advisers. Someone you trust, and who is willing to do the job, can't be purchased.

Making this choice may also raise sensitive personal issues. For one thing, your trustee will have an ongoing relationship with the trust beneficiaries.

> **EXAMPLE:** Malik has three children from his former marriage. He wants to leave the income from his estate to his wife, Libby, during her life, and on her death, have his estate divided equally among his children. Who should be trustee of the ongoing trust he creates to achieve these goals?

Standards for Asset Management

Traditionally, unless a trust specified a different standard, a trustee was required to manage trust assets under what is called the "prudent person" rule. Essentially, this rule requires cautious investments and prohibits all but the most conservative of stock market transactions. More recently, the stock market boom of the 1990s led a number of states to adopt laws, called "prudent investor" rules, permitting trustees to play the stock market "prudently," unless the trust itself imposes a more restrictive standard. Beneficiaries of a long-term trust can, of course, benefit if a trustee invests trust property wisely, or luckily, in stocks. (As my wise brother put it, "It's easy to make money in a rising market.") But of course—and as we've seen—it's not obligatory that stock market prices rise. If the market falls drastically, or if the trustee doesn't pick winners, beneficiaries may wish more conservative investments had been chosen.

There's another serious potential problem here. Some irrevocable trusts leave income from trust property to a life beneficiary, often a spouse. There may be a lot less income if the trustee invests in stocks. Many stocks currently provide very little or no income (dividends); all the money is made if the stock price goes up and you sell. But a life beneficiary doesn't get any cash because a stock has increased in value, or even when the stock is sold for a profit. That profit goes to trust principal, not income.

One standard way to handle this issue is to allow the trustee discretion regarding standards for investment. Often, the surviving spouse is successor trustee. She or he will probably invest to obtain a decent return on trust principal. (See Chapter 18.)

SEE AN EXPERT

Trustee standard for property management. You may be concerned with what property management standard governs the trustee of your ongoing trust. Maybe you definitely do, or do not, want to allow investment or speculation in stocks. Or you may have concerns about balancing the interests of your spouse with your children regarding trust investments. (See Chapter 24.) If, for whatever reason, you want to define the property management standards that apply to your trustee, see an attorney to explore your alternatives and pin down the best standard for you.

Malik must carefully evaluate a number of factors:

- What is the relationship between Libby and his children?
- If Libby is the sole trustee, will she truly guard the trust principal for his children?
- If one of his children is the trustee, will that child be fair to Libby—or will he try to retain in the trust as much of the money as he can, regardless of what Libby needs?
- If Libby and one of Malik's children are cotrustees, can they get along?
- What will happen if they can't?

Different types of ongoing trusts raise different concerns about your choice of trustee. These issues are discussed in subsequent chapters, which cover various types of ongoing trusts.

Naming More Than One Trustee

Legally, you can name two, or even several, individuals to serve as cotrustees. But before you do, make sure you have a compelling reason. Having two or more people serve as trustees for a trust that may last a long time can lead to serious conflict or confusion.

If you decide to appoint cotrustees, you must decide how they will share authority—whether each can act separately for the trust or all must agree in writing to act for the trust. But even more importantly, you

must have complete confidence that all your trustees will get along. Do be cautious here. Sharing power and property can lead to unexpected results. If the cotrustees are prone to conflict, you may well create serious problems, and will be doing none of them a favor by having them share power.

If cotrustees can't agree, say, on how to manage trust property, the situation can get very messy. Your trustees could wind up in court. Not only would this probably waste trust money, but the end result might be much worse, and generate more animosity than if you had just picked one person to be trustee in the first place and let the chips fall where they may.

Trust Companies and Banks as Trustees

Would you and your beneficiaries be better served if a professional trustee (from a bank or private trust company) were named as a trustee? Generally, I believe not. Indeed, it's usually best to select a person you know and trust to serve as trustee. A trustee should have good money sense and be reasonably knowledgeable about the financial world, but in most cases does not need to be an expert.

Banks can be very impersonal, perhaps paying little attention to trusts worth less than (many) millions, or treating a beneficiary as a nuisance. In addition, they charge overall management fees and, often, additional fees for each tiny act, which can cost a bundle.

But if there is no person you trust who is willing to serve as trustee, and you want to create an ongoing trust, you'll have to select a financial institution as your trustee. Also, with certain complicated types of property, such as oil and gas interests, beneficiaries can benefit from professional management. Your best bet is probably to use a private trust company, a business that specializes in trust management. They tend to be smaller and less impersonal than banks, and more focused on trust management. If you're extremely cautious, you might even want to name another institution as an alternate trustee, just in case your first choice goes out of business or decides not to handle smaller trusts. But doing this means you have to make arrangements with two private trust companies—and this means extra work.

A possible compromise is to name cotrustees—an individual you trust and a financial institution. The hope is to get a measure of investment savvy but still have a real person in the mix. The reality may be less inviting. Many institutions won't accept a cotrustee arrangement. And whenever you appoint cotrustees, potential problems abound. Unless there's a financial institution you really feel comfortable with, a better bet is just to name an individual trustee, who can hire good financial advisers if needed.

Choosing a Successor Trustee

Since your ongoing trust will likely last a while, somewhere down the line your first choice may become unable to perform the job. So it's a good idea to give some thought to arranging for a successor trustee. You can simply name one or more successor trustees in your trust document. You can also authorize an acting trustee to name, in writing, additional successor trustees. The trustee would do this if—and only if—the trustee and any successor trustees you named are unable to serve. This should ensure that the position of trustee never becomes vacant. (If it did, there would have to be a court proceeding to name a new trustee.) Also, this ensures that any trustee will at least have been chosen by someone you trust.

> **EXAMPLE:** Shannon's living trust creates an ongoing trust for her two young grandchildren, to last until they reach age 35. She names the children's mother, Carolyn (her daughter), as the trustee and Carolyn's husband, Bill, as the successor trustee. She also includes in the trust document a provision allowing any trustee to name, in writing, additional successor trustees.
>
> Carolyn dies a few years after the trust becomes operational, and Bill becomes trustee. He writes a document naming his brother Al, then Al's wife, Jane, to serve as trustees if he can't. Before either child is 35, Bill is killed in a car crash. Al then becomes the trustee.

! CAUTION
An important and specific trustee power. One of the powers given to a trustee is the power to allocate income and principal of the trust. With an ongoing trust, you may want to include specifics about how you want the trustee to make these divisions. For instance, if you are an author and want your spouse to receive your royalties as trust income, the document must state this. The same is true for other property, such as reinvested dividends. If you don't spell out your intentions, state laws could defeat them. Various state laws define what is income and what is principal, in the absence of specific directions to the contrary. You could find your life beneficiary, most likely your spouse, unable to receive money you both thought was income.

Taxation of Ongoing Trusts

If an ongoing trust takes effect while you are alive, the property placed in the trust is a gift, subject to gift tax, unless the beneficiary is a tax-exempt charity. If the ongoing trust is created in a will or living trust and takes effect when you die, the property in the trust is part of your taxable estate; whether or not your estate will actually owe estate tax depends on its size, the year of death, and possibly other factors. In a few states, it is also subject to state estate tax.

From an income tax standpoint, it is rarely desirable to have an ongoing trust retain, for more than one year, income generated by trust property. Trust income tax rates are now higher than individual income tax rates. An ongoing trust is taxed on all income over $100 that it retains at the close of the tax year. If the trust distributes income earned in that year to a beneficiary, that income is taxed at the beneficiary's rate, not the trust's.

If a beneficiary's income tax rate will be lower than the trust's rate, the rule is simple: Trusts that retain income for more than one year pay more in income tax, and thus ultimately have less to distribute to the beneficiaries. So, in most cases, the trustee must feel that, for some non-income tax reason, it's vitally important that the trust accumulate income, assuming the trust authorizes it.

Current trust income tax rates begin at 15% for retained trust income and reach a top rate of 35% for retained trust income over $11,950.

Trust Income Tax Rates for 2013	
Retained Trust Income	**Income Tax Rate**
$0–$2,450	15%
$2,450–$5,700	$360 plus 25% of the amount over $2,400
$5,700–$8,750	$1,160 plus 28% of the amount over $5,600
$8,750–$11,950	$1,972 plus 33% of the amount over $8,500
Over $11,950	$3,011.50 plus 35% of the amount over $11,650

AB Disclaimer Trusts

An AB disclaimer trust may reduce or eliminate federal estate taxes for some high-wealth couples. It works by keeping the property of the first-to-die spouse out of the estate of the surviving spouse. Keeping each spouse's property separate makes the most of each spouse's personal estate tax exemption. However, because "portability" allows married couples to leave $10.68 million without incurring estate tax, most married couples will have no use for an AB disclaimer trust. That said, AB trusts may continue to be useful 1) for unmarried couples, who do not have the benefit of portability or 2) under the possibility that Congress could repeal portability for married couples.

Without Portability

An AB disclaimer trust will be most useful to wealthy couples who cannot take advantage of portability. Unmarried couples fall into this category, as could married couples if Congress were to repeal portability.

As described in Chapter 15, portability allows a surviving spouse to use his or her deceased spouse's unused personal exemption. Without portability, it would be important for each member of a wealthy couple to use up most, or all, of his or her estate tax exemption, which an AB disclaimer trust is designed to do.

EXAMPLE: Suppose Congress repeals portability. Brenda and her husband, Henry, each have an estate worth $3.5 million. Brenda dies in 2014 when the estate tax exemption is $5.34 million. If she leaves her property directly to Henry, his estate will be $7 million, which is over the estate tax threshold. So when Henry dies, his estate will owe tax. However, if Brenda leaves her property through an AB disclaimer trust, instead of directly to Henry, her personal estate tax exemption will apply, and there will be no estate tax due at her death or at Henry's death because each estate will remain under the $5.34 million exemption. After Brenda's death, Henry will receive income from the trust and will also be able to use trust property, such as their house.

With portability, Brenda and Henry would have no need for an AB disclaimer trust. With portability, when Henry dies his estate could use all of Brenda's personal exemption (which went unused because of the marital exemption)—allowing him to leave up to $10.68 million without owing estate tax.

If Henry and Brenda weren't married, the AB trust would have also saved on estate taxes, because it would keep Brenda's property out of Henry's estate, keeping the estate under the amount of his personal exemption.

AB Trusts Defined

An "AB trust" is a lawyers' term for a trust that eventually splits into two basic components, Trust A and Trust B. Typically, each spouse creates an AB trust—each with the potential to create a Trust A and Trust B. But only one Trust A ever becomes operational, that of the deceased spouse. And only one Trust B ever becomes operational, that of the surviving spouse.

The surviving spouse is the "life beneficiary" of Trust A. The surviving spouse can be given the rights to all income from Trust A property, to use of that trust's property, and to invade (spend) trust principal for basic needs, like health care. But legally, the surviving spouse never owns the property in Trust A. When the surviving spouse dies, the property in Trust A goes to the final beneficiaries that the deceased spouse named in the trust document. The surviving spouse cannot name beneficiaries for Trust A.

The property in Trust A is part of the deceased spouse's estate and eligible for that spouse's estate tax exemption.

> **EXAMPLE:** Cecilia and Lew have been married for over 20 years. Cecilia has a daughter, Maria, from an earlier marriage. Cecilia and Lew create an AB trust. Cecilia dies. Her trust property goes into Trust A. Lew's property goes into a revocable Trust B. Lew is the life beneficiary of Trust A and can use Trust A property until his death. Maria is the final beneficiary of Trust A, so

when Lew dies, any remaining Trust A property will go to her.

Cecilia's estate is worth $3 million. All of the trust property is eligible for her personal estate tax exemption. For estate tax purposes, none of her estate is combined with Lew's.

How AB Disclaimer Trusts Work

An AB *disclaimer* trust is a type of AB trust that gives the surviving spouse flexibility to either take or "disclaim" the deceased spouse's property, depending on the current state of the estate tax law.

It allows a surviving spouse to determine what amount (if any) of the deceased spouse's trust property to inherit outright, and what amount, if any, should go to an ongoing Trust A.

Disclaimers in Estate Planning

A "disclaimer" allows a beneficiary to decide whether to accept all or part of a property left to him or her. Anyone has a legal right to disclaim any gift property; no one can be compelled to accept an inheritance. The use of disclaimers in estate planning is discussed in depth in Chapter 22.

Here's how it works: In the trust document, each spouse leaves at least the bulk of his or her trust property to the other. Each spouse further specifies that any property disclaimed by the surviving spouse should go into Trust A. When the first spouse dies, the survivor assesses the overall financial situation, the amount of the estate tax exemption for the year of death, and the survivor's financial needs. Then the survivor decides how much of the deceased spouse's property to accept, and how much to disclaim. Any disclaimed property goes into the Trust A. During his or her lifetime, the surviving spouse will usually receive any income from Trust A and will be able to use the property in that trust, but he or she will never own Trust A property.

EXAMPLE 1: Wendy and Victor have a co-owned estate worth $9 million. They prepare an AB disclaimer trust. Wendy dies in 2014, leaving her $4.5 million estate to Victor. The estate tax exemption for 2014 is $5.34 million, with "portability." Victor decides he wants to receive all of Wendy's money outright. So he does not disclaim any of her property. His estate is now worth $9 million, under the combined portable exemption of $10.64 million.

EXAMPLE 2: The exact same example, except that Wendy dies in December 2015, when it's becoming clear that Congress will likely repeal portability for 2016 and thereafter. If Victor inherits Wendy's $4.5 million, his total estate of $9 million will be over the estate tax threshold. So Victor decides to disclaim all of Wendy's trust property. That property goes into Wendy's Trust A, and receives her estate tax exemption. So both Victor's and Wendy's estates are under $5.34 million and Victor will be able to use the property in Trust A during his lifetime.

EXAMPLE 3: Ben and Jamulla get married. Each has been married before. Ben has an estate worth $2 million, while Jamulla's is worth $4 million. They prepare a AB disclaimer trust. Jamulla dies in 2014, when the estate tax exemption is $5.34 million. However, Ben decides to disclaim none of Jamulla's property, because he wants to obtain the $4 million outright. If Jamulla had children from her first marriage and they were the final beneficiaries of Trust A, they may not be excited about Ben's decision.

An AB disclaimer trust is a form of insurance that would be beneficial for married couples if the federal estate tax law changes, particularly if portability is eliminated. If there's no financial benefit to using a disclaimer, the surviving spouse will not use it. But if using a disclaimer can achieve substantial overall tax savings, the surviving spouse will have the option to disclaim. The key is that the surviving spouse is not locked into anything. He or she can disclaim nothing, all, or somewhere in between, depending on the circumstances at the time.

The Tax Basis of AB Trust Property Inherited by Final Beneficiaries

Final beneficiaries receive the property in an AB disclaimer trust after the life beneficiary (the surviving spouse) dies. The tax basis of that property for the final beneficiaries is its net market worth (its stepped-up basis) on the *date of death of the trust creator* (the first spouse to die), not the date of death of the life beneficiary. (Income tax basis is defined and explained in detail in Chapter 15.) The point of an AB disclaimer trust is to prevent a life beneficiary from having legal ownership of trust property so that the property is not included in his or her estate. And because the life beneficiary never has ownership of the property, the property is not entitled to a stepped-up basis at his or her death.

IRS Restrictions

All AB disclaimer trusts must comply with applicable IRS regulations. If yours doesn't, any possible estate tax savings you're after will be lost.

The trustee cannot be given complete freedom to spend trust principal for the life beneficiary. If the trustee has such unlimited rights, the IRS will regard the life beneficiary as the legal owner of the trust property and impose estate tax on it when the life beneficiary dies.

The IRS does, however, allow the trustee to spend (invade) the trust principal for the life beneficiary's "health, education, support, and maintenance ... in accord with his or her accustomed standard of living." (IRS Regulation 320.2041-1(c)(2).) Spending trust principal for these purposes is allowed because, according to the IRS, the need for these expenditures can be judged against an "ascertainable standard."

> **EXAMPLE:** Arlo leaves his property in an AB disclaimer trust with his wife, Sirpa, as the life beneficiary. Sirpa is the trustee and she has the right to invade trust principal for her health care, education, support, and maintenance. As trustee, she may sell trust property, invest it, or exchange it. For instance, if the trust includes a home, she could ordinarily sell it and buy a retirement condo with the proceeds.

By contrast, if the trust document says that trust assets can be spent for, say, the "comfort" or "well-being" of the life beneficiary, the IRS considers this an "unascertainable" standard. In that case, the trust assets will be regarded as legally owned by the life beneficiary and included in her taxable estate, even if no trust money was in fact ever spent for these purposes.

You don't have to give the trustee the full powers to spend principal that the law allows. In some situations, particularly second or subsequent marriages, one or both spouses may not want to give a surviving spouse the right to spend trust principal for support, and may even want to further restrict use of trust property. Normally, this is because a spouse wants to be sure trust property remains intact for his or her own children or other final beneficiaries. Indeed, you can forbid spending any of the trust principal at all. (See Chapter 24.)

Is an AB Disclaimer Trust Right for You?

AB disclaimer trusts aren't for everyone. You must be quite prosperous before you need to even consider one. Even if you are wealthy, before deciding to use one, consider the following issues.

Size of Your Estate

In my opinion, if you and your spouse or partner have a combined estate worth more than $5 million, and you plan to leave all or the bulk to each other, you should investigate using an AB disclaimer trust.

Your Intended Beneficiaries

If you don't want to leave the bulk of your property for use of your surviving spouse, but want instead to leave substantial amounts of property directly to other beneficiaries, an AB disclaimer trust won't accomplish your goals.

Duty to File Trust Tax Returns

If Trust A becomes operational because the surviving spouse disclaims some of the deceased spouse's property, the trustee of Trust A must obtain a taxpayer ID number and file an annual trust income tax return for that trust. This usually isn't a big deal, but like any tax return, it requires some work.

Complicated Record Keeping

Likewise, the surviving spouse must keep two sets of books and records, one for his or her own property, and one for the disclaimed property in Trust A.

Potential Family Strife

An AB disclaimer trust works best when all involved—both spouses and all final beneficiaries—understand and agree on the purposes of the trust. Usually these goals are to possibly save on overall estate tax and to give the surviving spouse the maximum allowable rights to use trust income, and principal if necessary. Without this agreement among the spouses and final beneficiaries, serious conflicts may develop. This can be particularly true when there are children from a prior marriage.

If there is any potential for conflict between the surviving spouse and the final beneficiaries of the trust, an AB disclaimer trust may well provoke or aggravate it. After all, in theory at least, there is an inherent conflict of interest between the life estate beneficiary and the final beneficiaries. The final beneficiaries may want all the trust principal conserved, no matter what the surviving spouse needs. On the other hand, the surviving spouse may want or need to use up most or even all of the trust principal for health care, education, or maintenance.

Another conflict can arise if the surviving spouse becomes ill and can no longer serve as trustee. If a child who stands to eventually receive trust assets takes over as successor trustee, it's possible the child might be more concerned with preserving principal than with a parent's medical or other needs. I've heard of such situations, where it seemed to other family members and friends that a child disregarded his parent's basic needs to protect the trust principal for him- or herself.

Conflicts can also occur if the final beneficiaries believe the surviving spouse, as trustee, is not managing the trust property well—for example, by investing in very speculative stocks or risky real estate deals. If this situation arises, there can be real trouble, possibly even a lawsuit.

An AB disclaimer trust is less likely to create strife down the road if:

- Family members trust each other, are reasonably close, and are able to work out any conflicts that might arise.
- The final beneficiaries understand that taking the trouble to create an AB disclaimer trust is a generous act; after all, the trust is designed to benefit the children, not the people who create the trust. The final beneficiaries could receive much more of the couple's estate than they would have if the spouses had left property outright to the other.

- The trust document itself is as clear as possible as to your intentions, leaving little or no room for interpretation.

Final Beneficiaries in Second Marriages

Couples in second or subsequent marriages may want to name different final beneficiaries for each spouse's property. Often, each spouse wants children from a prior marriage as final beneficiaries. Fortunately, each spouse creates his or her own separate AB disclaimer trust, so each has the right to choose the final beneficiaries for his or her trust property. (This issue is discussed further in Chapter 24.)

Unmarried Couples

An unmarried couple can achieve the same possible estate tax savings with an AB disclaimer trust as can a married couple. Of course, the marital deduction is not available for unmarried couples. Any amount one of you owns in excess of your personal exemption will be subject to tax when you die.

Single People

A single person, not a member of a couple, normally has no need for an AB disclaimer trust. But if for some reason he or she decides to use one, it certainly can be used. There is no legal requirement that an AB disclaimer trust be used only by a couple.

Choosing Trustees for an AB Disclaimer Trust

Normally, an AB disclaimer trust is combined with a shared living trust. (See Chapter 17.) That way, when one spouse dies, property first avoids probate. Then the surviving spouse decides about disclaiming. When you create an AB disclaimer trust, you'll need to choose trustees for the initial trust and for the trusts that go into operation when the first spouse dies.

Most couples want the surviving spouse to serve as the trustee of Trust A, which becomes operational if the surviving spouse disclaims any of the deceased spouse's property. To do that, the trust document simply makes both spouses trustees of the AB disclaimer trust. Because Trust A cannot become operational until one spouse dies, only the surviving spouse will actually serve as trustee.

> **EXAMPLE:** Mark and Vera have three grown children and a combined estate worth approximately $7.6 million. In their AB disclaimer trust document both spouses are named as trustees of the trust. Mark dies first. Vera becomes sole trustee, and it is her responsibility to decide whether to disclaim, and if so for how much. If she does disclaim to Trust A, she will be trustee of that trust.

Living trust documents normally name a successor trustee for Trust A, as well as Trust B, to take over management of the trust property if the surviving spouse becomes incapacitated. You may also want to name an alternate successor trustee. If you don't want your surviving spouse to be trustee of your Trust A, you can name someone else. For example, your spouse may be unwell, not sensible about financial affairs, or simply uninterested.

If you wish, you can name more than one person to serve as successor cotrustees. For example, you might want to name your two adult children, or your spouse and one adult child, as cotrustees. When selecting the successor and alternate successor trustees for an AB disclaimer trust, ask yourself several questions about your choices:

- Does the person want to serve?
- Is the person capable of handling the trustee's duties?
- Would trust management duties create an undue burden on that person?
- Will the trustee be paid?
- Do you completely trust the person to manage the property as you wish?

Do You Need a Lawyer to Create an AB Disclaimer Trust?

You may wonder whether or not it's wise to prepare an AB disclaimer trust yourself, without the aid of an attorney. If you and your spouse have a combined estate worth roughly $5 million or less, you may decide to explore going it alone. Couples in this situation can find forms and complete instructions for preparing an AB disclaimer

Naming an AB Disclaimer Trust as the Beneficiary of Your Retirement Accounts

With any retirement program, you name one or more beneficiaries to receive whatever remains in the account (if anything) at your death. If you may have substantial assets in a retirement account, in particular an IRA, is it wise to name your AB disclaimer trust as a beneficiary of that IRA?

First of all, what happens if the surviving spouse does not want to disclaim the retirement account? You need to name your spouse as the initial beneficiary, and the AB disclaimer trust as alternate beneficiary, so that it receives the retirement account money only if the surviving spouse disclaims it.

Next, if an AB disclaimer trust is the beneficiary of an IRA, the required minimum distributions are substantially accelerated compared to the time allowed for distribution if the surviving spouse is the beneficiary. Longer distribution times are generally desirable for IRA payouts, because they result in lower income tax payments. On the other hand, if there are substantial funds left in an IRA when the owner dies, those funds may be needed to make sure that the decedent's estate uses all, or nearly all, of the applicable estate tax exemption.

IRAs, 401(k)s & Other Retirement Plans: Taking Your Money Out, by Twila Slesnick and John C. Suttle (Nolo) provides a thorough explanation of rules governing withdrawals of retirement funds by named beneficiaries after the plan creator dies. It includes an explanation of what happens if a trust is the beneficiary.

> **CAUTION**
> **You might need to complete additional paperwork to validly name your AB trust as beneficiary of your retirement plan.** For example:
> - Federal law requires that all funds in a 401(k) or 403(b) plan be left outright to a surviving spouse, unless that spouse has given a written waiver of that right.
> - Retirement accounts purchased with community property are co-owned equally by both spouses. If you want all funds in such an account to go to your Trust A, you need a written agreement called a "declaration of gift" from your spouse.

If you're thinking about using a retirement account as a significant source of funds for an AB trust, keep in mind that individual retirement plans (except Roth IRAs) are "wasting accounts." Once you reach age 70½, you must withdraw a certain percentage of the account each year. So, if you live well beyond 70, you may withdraw most or even all the funds in the account before your death. Still, you may understandably be concerned about what happens to your retirement account money if you die prematurely or if, for any reason, your account contains significant funds at your death.

trust in the book *Make Your Own Living Trust*, by Denis Clifford (Nolo). The AB trust provided in that book is designed for couples who want to allow the surviving spouse the maximum legal rights over the trust property, while still gaining the estate tax–saving advantages of this type of trust.

You should consult a lawyer and should not attempt to write a trust yourself if:

- You and your spouse or partner expect to have a combined estate exceeding twice the estate tax threshold. Consult a good estate planning lawyer to explore more sophisticated options to reduce estate tax.

- You want to impose limits on the rights of the surviving spouse to use trust property. This includes many couples in second or subsequent marriages, who want to be sure the bulk of their property is preserved for children from prior marriages.

- You need a more complicated type of ongoing trust, such as a special needs trust for a child with a disability or a spendthrift trust for a child who can't properly manage money.

- You want to review all your estate planning options with an experienced attorney.

Other Estate Tax–Saving Marital Trusts

Federal estate tax laws treat the married and unmarried differently. This chapter covers tax-saving trusts available only to those who are legally married in the eyes of the federal government. You can skip this chapter if you are not married.

To save on estate tax, married couples can take advantage of several kinds of trusts other than the AB trust discussed in Chapter 18. This chapter covers the most popular and useful kinds, including:

QTIP Trusts. A QTIP trust allows a married person to name the surviving spouse as the life beneficiary of trust property. When the second spouse dies, the property passes to final beneficiaries named by the first spouse. In federal tax jargon, this type of trust is called a qualified terminable interest property trust. Usually, this obtuse moniker is shortened to "QTIP." So far, a QTIP trust sounds just like an AB disclaimer trust, right? What's different for QTIPs is that, when the first spouse dies, all the property in the trust is exempt from estate tax, no matter how much it's worth. This is because under IRS rules, property in the QTIP trust qualifies for the unlimited marital deduction.

However, property remaining in the QTIP trust when the second spouse dies is included in that spouse's estate for estate tax purposes. So taxes are postponed, not eliminated. The principal reasons for using a QTIP are to avoid paying any estate tax when the first spouse dies, which makes more money available to the survivor and, perhaps more importantly, to retain control over who finally gets the property. This can be a significant concern in second or subsequent marriages.

QTIPs are most often used if each spouse has an estate substantially exceeding the estate tax threshold. If each spouse has an estate roughly worth the personal exemption amount, then that married couple will generally need only an AB disclaimer trust. However, in second or subsequent marriages, even when an estate is under the estate tax threshold, some people choose a QTIP trust. This is because the trust can provide income and limited support for a current spouse and preserve the remaining assets for children of a former marriage. Some estate plans consist of just a QTIP trust for all of a person's assets.

QDOT Trusts. If you're married to a noncitizen and have an estate worth more than the estate tax threshold that you want to leave to your spouse, consider a QDOT trust. This trust lets you defer estate tax until the death of the second spouse. Property left in any other manner to a noncitizen spouse does not qualify for the unlimited marital deduction, so any amount over the estate tax threshold is taxed.

Marital Deduction Trusts. These types of trusts have been largely replaced by QTIP trusts. A marital deduction trust provides the estate tax postponement of a QTIP, but unlike a QTIP, permits the surviving spouse to name the final beneficiaries, make gifts of principal, and accumulate income.

QTIP Trusts

The four basic purposes of a QTIP trust are to:

- Postpone estate tax on the estate of the first spouse to die until the second spouse dies.
- Leave money and property for the use (but not outright ownership) of the surviving spouse.
- Name final beneficiaries to receive the trust property at the death of the surviving spouse. (These beneficiaries are often children or grandchildren, including those from a prior marriage.)
- Allow for some after-death (lawyers call it "postmortem") flexibility. As I discuss below, your executor (the person in charge of carrying out the terms of your will) can evaluate the estate tax situation and choose whether or not a QTIP you've created should actually become operational.

SEE AN EXPERT
Find a knowledgeable lawyer.
To prepare a QTIP trust, you need an expert estate planning lawyer. Many complex issues can arise when actually preparing the trust, and mistakes can cost a bundle in estate taxes. The IRS regularly refuses to grant trusts QTIP status because they didn't conform to all applicable federal regulations. If that happens, estate tax isn't postponed, and the major benefit of a QTIP is wasted. (For tips on finding a good lawyer, see Chapter 29.)

How QTIP Trusts Work

As noted above, a QTIP trust is similar in many aspects to an AB disclaimer trust. In each case, a spouse is the grantor—that is, the person who creates the trust. Each spouse can create a separate QTIP trust for his or her property, whether it's separately owned property, half of shared property, or both. With all QTIPs and AB disclaimer trusts, the surviving spouse is the life beneficiary. The original grantor gets to name the final trust beneficiaries—normally, his or her children—to receive his or her trust property when the surviving spouse dies.

The big difference between these two types of trusts is that with a QTIP, no federal estate tax is assessed against trust property when the first spouse dies—no matter how much that property is worth.

You can use an AB disclaimer trust and a QTIP trust together. Indeed, using these two trusts for each spouse is the foundation of the estate plans of some wealthier people. When the first spouse dies, property worth up to the amount of the personal exemption for that year is placed in an AB disclaimer trust. The AB disclaimer trust allows the surviving spouse to take full advantage of the deceased's personal exemption, so no estate tax will be due on the amount in that trust. The deceased spouse's remaining property goes into the QTIP trust, which is exempt from estate tax until the death of the second spouse.

EXAMPLE: Juliette, in her second marriage, has three children from her first marriage and an estate worth $8 million. She prepares an AB disclaimer trust, leaving to that trust the maximum amount of the estate tax exemption in the year of her death. She also prepares a QTIP trust for her remaining property. Her husband is the life beneficiary; her children are the final beneficiaries.

She dies in 2014. The estate tax exemption is $5.34 million, so that amount is placed in the AB trust. The remaining $2.66 million is placed in the QTIP trust.

Long-Term Tax Consequences of QTIP Trusts

It's vital to understand that estate tax on QTIP trust property is not eliminated. When the second spouse dies, tax must be paid on all property in that spouse's estate. Under current tax law, this includes the full net worth of all property in the QTIP, valued as of the date of the surviving spouse's death.

EXAMPLE: Sheila leaves property worth $4 million in a QTIP, with Atah, her husband, as life beneficiary. No tax is due at her death in 2014. Atah has an estate of $3 million of his own, so his total estate, which now includes the property in the QTIP, is worth $7 million. When Atah dies, some of his estate will be subject to estate tax,

unless the estate tax exemption has risen to $7 million or more for the year of his death (or he has managed to lose a couple of million before his death).

QTIPs at a Glance

- A QTIP trust creates a life estate for the surviving spouse, who is entitled to:
  - use trust assets, such as a residence, for his or her lifetime
  - receive trust income regularly, and
  - spend trust principal to the extent allowed by the trust document.
- In the trust document, the grantor names final beneficiaries, who will inherit the QTIP trust assets when the surviving spouse dies.
- No estate tax is assessed when the grantor dies.
- When the surviving spouse dies, the full net value of the property in the QTIP (as of that date) is included in his or her taxable estate.
- The QTIP assets do not go through probate after the death of the surviving spouse.

If the property in the QTIP trust increases in value during the surviving spouse's life, that increase is subject to estate tax when that spouse dies. Again, this is not true for property in an AB trust. With an AB trust, the value of the trust property for tax purposes is determined only once, at the date of death of the grantor spouse.

> **EXAMPLE:** Ivan creates a QTIP trust with property that is worth $3 million when he dies. By the time his wife, Olga, dies five years later, the value of the trust property has risen to $7 million. This total $7 million is included in Olga's taxable estate.

Who Can Benefit From a QTIP Trust

QTIPs are popular with some wealthier couples who decide that postponing tax payment until the second spouse dies is worth any possible eventual tax cost. They strongly do not want to have any of their estate eaten up by tax when the first spouse dies, even if more taxes are paid in the long run. Moreover, it's far from clear, usually, that it will cost more in the long run. With a QTIP, a surviving spouse who outlives the other by a significant period of time—say a few years or more—will receive income from all the deceased spouse's property, without having had any taken out to pay estate tax. The money the surviving spouse receives from the trust property may exceed any additional tax paid on that spouse's death.

Use a QTIP instead of leaving property outright to the surviving spouse if one spouse or both prefers the control a QTIP provides—the power of the original grantor to name the final beneficiaries for the trust. A unique advantage of a QTIP trust is that

it allows you to have the trust property treated, tax wise, as if the surviving spouse inherited it outright using the marital deduction, and simultaneously allows you to impose controls over this property and specify who eventually inherits your share.

Finally, because each member of a couple can create separate AB disclaimer trusts and QTIPs, neither spouse must sacrifice his or her personal estate tax exemption. Rather, the usual plan, as we've said, is for each spouse to create a AB disclaimer trust to use his or her personal estate tax exemption, and a QTIP trust to postpone payment of estate tax on any additional property.

QTIPs are commonly used when one spouse in a second marriage is older and more affluent than the other. Typically, the wealthy spouse wants to provide adequate financial resources during the other spouse's life, but also wants the trust property to go to kids from an earlier marriage after the surviving spouse's death. An AB disclaimer trust alone won't work well here, because it depends on each spouse owning a significant part of the couple's property (as is usually the case in long-term marriages). But a QTIP does the job nicely. A full 100% of the wealthier spouse's property is available for the surviving spouse's use as life beneficiary, because no estate tax is levied when the first spouse dies.

> **EXAMPLE:** Sam, who is in his late 70s, has assets worth $6 million when he marries Angela, his second wife. She

has very little property of her own. If Sam dies before Angela does, he wants to be sure she is provided for, but he also wants to ensure that his children from his previous marriage are the final beneficiaries of his property.

Sam feels that to continue in their affluent lifestyle, Angela may need all the income his $6 million could provide. Sam does not want to leave Angela money outright (which he could do, tax free, using the marital deduction) because he wants to preserve his property, to the extent possible, for his children.

So Sam creates a QTIP trust, containing all of his assets, that will become effective at his death. Angela is the life beneficiary. Sam designates his children as the trust's final beneficiaries, to receive all that's left when Angela dies. No tax will be due at Sam's death (if Angela is still alive) because all property in a QTIP trust takes advantage of the unlimited marital deduction. Income from the trust property will go to Angela for her life. Also, if he chooses, Sam can specify that trust principal can be used for Angela's "support, education, health, or maintenance" in any amount. Or, at the other extreme, he can greatly restrict invasion of the principal, to ensure that it's conserved for his children.

If you are in a second or subsequent marriage, you may be concerned with balancing the interests and needs of your current spouse and your children from a former marriage. (See Chapter 24.) Exactly how these needs sort out depends on the situation; there is more than one good way to use a QTIP trust in estate plans.

EXAMPLE: Sol is married to Rosalie and has two children from a previous marriage. His estate is worth $6 million. He creates a QTIP trust of $3 million to take effect at his death. All of the income from the trust will be paid to Rosalie for her lifetime, and at her death the assets of the trust will go to his children.

Sol also leaves $1.5 million outright to each child. No estate tax will be due on this $3 million because of Sol's personal estate tax exemption.

Thanks to the marital deduction, no tax is due on the other $3 million in the QTIP trust. At Rosalie's death, the trust principal—the amount as of the date of her death—will be counted as part of her taxable estate.

The Surviving Spouse's Rights

The surviving spouse must receive the sole right to all income from property in the QTIP trust. Also, the surviving spouse must have the right to require that the trustee sell non-income-producing property and invest the sale proceeds in income-producing assets. If the spouse doesn't have these rights, the IRS will rule that the QTIP property doesn't qualify for the marital deduction.

The Right to Receive All Trust Income

The surviving spouse must receive all of the income from an operational QTIP trust. There are no exceptions to this rule. The trustee (who is usually the surviving spouse) must distribute all income periodically (at least annually) to the spouse, and cannot accumulate income in the trust. If the surviving spouse becomes incapacitated, the trustee must spend the income for the spouse's benefit.

As long as the surviving spouse lives, the trustee of a QTIP trust cannot spend any of the principal or income from the trust for the benefit of anyone else. In general, this rule protects both the surviving spouse, who receives a continuing income, and the final beneficiaries, who are to later receive the trust principal.

But occasionally it can be troublesome. For example, suppose the surviving spouse remarries or earns a very large amount of money and no longer really needs the trust income. The spouse might want to end the trust and have its principal distributed to the final beneficiaries. Can't be done. A QTIP trust cannot end until the second spouse dies.

Or suppose that one of the final beneficiaries really needs some money from the trust, and the surviving spouse wants to give it. Officially, the trust's income, as well as the principal, cannot be spent directly on anyone else during the surviving spouse's lifetime. For example, if the surviving spouse wants to help out, she must do so indirectly. Since all trust income is hers to do with as she wishes, once she receives some income, she can give it to the needy final beneficiary. But this is a legal gift, subject to gift taxes. Also, she won't be able to channel any of the principal to the final beneficiary.

EXAMPLE: Alice creates a QTIP trust to become operational at her death, with the income going to her husband, Mark. He has no rights to spend trust principal. At Mark's death, the assets of the trust will pass to her five children from two previous marriages.

Mark has a substantial estate himself, and several years after Alice dies, he remarries a very wealthy woman. But the income from the trust must continue to go to him. Meanwhile, Alice's oldest son, Edward, has business trouble and desperately needs money to keep afloat. Because the trustee cannot use any of the principal of the QTIP trust for the son's benefit, even though Mark wants this, the business fails. This is hardly what Alice would have wanted. (Of course, Mark can give the income from the trust to the son, after he receives it, but he cannot touch trust principal.)

SEE AN EXPERT
Defining income and principal.
When any beneficiary, such as a spouse, will serve as trustee, make sure that your trust document spells out what is income for the trust and what will be principal. If you don't, state law will do

it for you and may defeat your intentions. For instance, in some states, dividends that have automatically been reinvested will be treated as principal. The spouse may need those dividends for living expenses. Discuss this with your lawyer.

The Right to Demand That Trust Property Produce Income

You can put any kind of property into a QTIP—a house, furniture, money, stock, even a business—but, as mentioned, the surviving spouse has the right to demand that any non-income-producing property be converted into a form of property that does produce income. So if the trust includes a safe deposit box full of gold coins or a collection of valuable antique chairs, the surviving spouse can demand they be sold and the profits invested in income-producing property.

> **EXAMPLE:** Gretchen creates a QTIP trust and names her husband, Lloyd, as the life beneficiary. The trust assets consist of stocks, bonds, a residence, and a vacation home. After Gretchen's death, Lloyd decides that the income is not enough for him to live on in the manner he's used to. Using his authority as trustee, he sells the vacation home and invests the proceeds in property that yields income, such as bonds.

Powers That May Be Given to the Surviving Spouse

Now let's look at the powers a grantor is allowed by the IRS to include in a QTIP, but that are not mandatory.

The Power to Spend Trust Principal

As discussed, a surviving spouse must receive all the income from property in a QTIP trust. There is no flexibility here. But when it comes to permitting the spouse to spend (invade) principal, it's a different story—you have great flexibility.

Because the surviving spouse is considered, for estate tax purposes, the owner of all property in the QTIP, he or she can be given the right to invade trust principal for his or her benefit for any reason and for any amount he or she wants. (This is another way in which a QTIP trust differs from an AB disclaimer trust.) However, it's unusual to grant such broad power to spend trust principal. After all, this, in effect, leaves the property outright to the surviving spouse. If that's what you want, just do it directly, and no estate tax will be imposed at your death because of the marital deduction. Most QTIP trust grantors want to impose some restrictions on the surviving spouse to protect the principal for the final beneficiaries.

Sometimes, the surviving spouse is given no right to spend trust principal, period. In other situations, the right to invade principal is defined very specifically and narrowly, such as for emergency health care only. Or the trust document may limit the right to spend trust principal to the IRS "objective need" standard, allowing invasion only when necessary for the surviving spouse's "education, health, support, or maintenance." (IRS Reg. 20.2041-1(c)(2).)

If the surviving spouse has the right to spend trust principal, there's an inherent risk of conflict between the spouse and the final beneficiaries, so the trust document creating the trust should be very specific about the spouse's rights. The last thing you want is a fight over what assets can and cannot be used or what standard the spouse must meet to justify spending principal.

The surviving spouse frequently serves as trustee of a QTIP trust. If, however, broad invasion powers are granted, you may want to name a disinterested party as trustee or cotrustee, to avoid or at least reduce the chances of hostility and conflict between the beneficiaries.

The 5 and 5 Power

The 5 and 5 power is a distinct right that allows the spouse to get $5,000 or 5% of the trust principal, whichever is greater, each year. There are no restrictions on how the surviving spouse can spend this money.

The surviving spouse does not have to use this 5 and 5 right in any given year. But if it is not used in a particular year, that year's right is lost. In other words, the right does not accumulate from year to year.

EXAMPLE: Isabelle is the trustee and life beneficiary of a QTIP trust established by her late husband. The trust document includes a 5 and 5 power. If she doesn't exercise this right this year, she cannot take an extra 5% or $5,000 out of the trust principal next year.

The 5 and 5 power is not currently used much by sophisticated estate planners; it is usually better to use more controlled methods of allowing the surviving spouse access to the trust principal. (This is discussed in Chapter 18.)

The Power to Distribute Trust Property Among Beneficiaries

One of the most important features of a QTIP trust is the power of the original grantor to control who gets the trust assets when the surviving spouse dies. Often, a grantor specifies that the assets go to his or her children. But a trusted spouse who survives many years after the other spouse's death may be in a far better position to know just which individuals in a group of final beneficiaries designated by the grantor need more than others, or which ones don't really need an inheritance at all. With a QTIP trust, the grantor can choose the group of possible final beneficiaries, but let the surviving spouse decide how much each one actually inherits. The surviving spouse formally makes this decision in his or her living trust or will. In legal terms, this is called giving the spouse "a limited power of appointment" over the assets in the trust.

EXAMPLE: Sara is married to Emmanuel, nine years younger than she is. Sara fully trusts Emmanuel and is confident he loves her family. Sara has two children, Alison and Lori, from a prior marriage. When Sara prepares her QTIP, Alison has two young children (and wants more) and Lori is single. Sara wants to provide for her own children but also leave direct gifts to her grandchildren.

She specifies that her children and grandchildren will be the final beneficiaries of her QTIP trust. She provides that each daughter will receive 30% of the trust property, and that the remaining 40% shall be divided among all her grandchildren when final distribution of the trust assets is made. She doesn't want to specify the precise divisions now because there may be (she hopes) additional grandchildren. And if Emmanuel survives her by a considerable time, she believes he will be in a far better position to decide how much money should be given to each grandchild. So she gives Emmanuel authority to make the decision regarding actual distribution to the grandchildren.

Allowing the spouse to make such a decision can produce a fair and just distribution—one that may not have been foreseeable when the trust was created. One child may have completely dedicated himself to the family business, another may have special needs, and yet another child may have amassed such wealth that he or she needs less than the others. However, granting this power to the spouse is not very common in QTIPs. Most grantors want absolute control over who the final beneficiaries are. But if you have complete confidence in your spouse's judgment, granting this power can be sensible, especially when some desired beneficiaries are very young (or even unborn) when the trust is prepared.

The QTIP Election

A unique aspect of QTIPs is that the executor you name in your will must elect, on your federal estate tax return, to place property you left in a QTIP into that trust. Your executor has the final say here. You cannot require that he or she elect QTIP tax treatment for your property. If your executor doesn't properly make the QTIP election, no valid QTIP trust exists, period.

The QTIP election itself amounts to listing the property that is to go into the trust. Seems simple, but it has surely been done wrong. In one case, an executor hurriedly filed an estate tax return, forgot to mark the box and then sought IRS permission to file an amended return electing a QTIP. Nope, said the IRS, which sometimes seems to take special delight in denying proposed QTIP trusts eligibility for the marital deduction.

Deciding how and whether to make the QTIP election can be difficult. The executor has several choices:

- not to elect the QTIP

- elect that all property the deceased left in the (possible) QTIP trust actually be treated as QTIP property, or
- elect to have only a portion of the trust property treated as a QTIP—for example, the executor can elect to have 60% of the trust property treated as a QTIP and 40% not. That 40% may then be subject to estate tax at the first death.

These options make possible a great deal of strategic after-death tax planning. Key tax decisions can be made in light of current circumstances rather than being frozen years before. But in some family situations, it can require the wisdom of Solomon (not to mention high-quality tax advice) to decide which election option to take.

For larger estates, this QTIP election is sometimes used to equalize the value of each spouse's estate. For example, sometimes it makes estate tax sense to choose not to elect a QTIP and allow the deceased spouse's possible QTIP trust property to be included in the taxable estate. If electing the QTIP would result in the surviving spouse's estate being much larger than that of the first spouse to die, higher overall estate tax would be paid. So, in such a case, after the first spouse's death, the executor might elect to go ahead and pay any estate tax assessed against that deceased spouse's property, because the tax rate is lower on this amount of property than it would be if this property were combined, for estate tax purposes, with the surviving spouse's.

This means the surviving spouse must accept tax payments now in exchange for overall tax savings later. Usually, the surviving spouse is the executor and is in charge of making this decision. But if the surviving spouse isn't the executor, and the two disagree, there can be a real power struggle.

Another option is for the executor to elect to have only a percentage of the deceased spouse's property receive QTIP treatment. This is called a partial QTIP election. This, too, can be used to lower overall estate tax. Any percentage of the trust property not elected for QTIP treatment usually remains in the trust for the surviving spouse's benefit, but it does not receive QTIP estate tax treatment. Estate tax is paid on the portion not elected. In this case, two separate financial records must be kept—one for the trust property that is QTIP property and another for property that is not.

SEE AN EXPERT
Directing QTIP property to someone other than the surviving spouse. If you want to direct in your will or living trust that any unelected QTIP property goes to someone other than the surviving spouse, you'll need to consult an expert estate planning lawyer. The law in this area is complicated and unclear.

A number of issues can contribute to the decision your executor makes regarding the QTIP election. One factor is simply that circumstances may have changed (indeed, they always do, according to the Buddha and Heraclitus) since you prepared the QTIP trust. Your original estate plan may not be the most financially desirable one after your death.

Making a partial QTIP election has significant drawbacks, however. An executor can make a partial QTIP election only in terms of a percentage or fraction of the total property originally left for the QTIP. For example, a trustee can elect to have 40%, or 63%, or one third of the total property originally left for the QTIP actually qualify for QTIP tax treatment. What the executor can't do is name specific assets to be included in or excluded from the QTIP. The IRS simply doesn't allow that kind of maneuvering. The executor can of course decide what assets he or she wants to exclude, figure out the percentage and then take out those assets to make up the excluded amount, but it must be reported as a fractional percentage, not as specific items of property.

The real-world consequences of a partial QTIP election can be difficult. For example, there can be much paperwork if two thirds of your house is owned by a QTIP trust and one third owned by another trust. Also, it can complicate matters like real estate tax or refinancing. Because of the complexities, many sophisticated estate planners do not usually recommend partial QTIP elections.

Summary: IRS Requirements for a Valid QTIP Trust

In order to qualify as a valid QTIP trust under federal law (I.R.C. § 2056(b)(7)), the trust document must specify all of the following:

- All income from the trust must be distributed to the surviving spouse at least annually.
- The spouse can demand that the trust property be converted to income-producing property.
- No one, not even the surviving spouse, may spend principal for the benefit of anybody but the spouse.
- The executor of the deceased spouse's estate must elect, on the deceased's federal estate tax return, to have the trust treated as a QTIP.

The Reverse QTIP Election

A "reverse QTIP election" is a special legal procedure designed to avoid losing the personal exemption because of another tax imposed on gifts and bequests that skip generations. (See Chapter 21.) Without a reverse QTIP election, as long as estate tax exists, all assets that are left by a grandparent to a grandchild (skipping the middle generation) or in other generation-skipping plans are subject to an extra tax, called the generation-skipping transfer tax or GSTT.

Sometimes a QTIP trust leaves the trust principal, at the death of the surviving spouse, to the grantor's grandchildren or other beneficiaries more than one generation away. When this happens, the law considers the surviving spouse (the life beneficiary) the one transferring the property for GSTT purposes. This means that an inheritance worth up to the amount of the surviving spouse's GSTT exemption can go to the grandchildren GSTT free. However, when the first spouse's executor makes a reverse QTIP election, the first spouse who died is legally the person who makes the eventual transfer to the grandchildren. This preserves that first spouse's GSTT exemption and allows the second spouse to transfer another amount to grandchildren free of the GSTT.

This reverse QTIP election relates only to generation-skipping trusts and the generation-skipping transfer tax. It is an entirely separate matter from the basic QTIP election, where the executor decides whether or not to use a QTIP, and if so, how much property to actually place in the QTIP trust.

Planning for a QTIP

You must plan for and create a QTIP trust document before you die. No one has any authority to create one for you, and obtain its estate tax–postponing advantages, after you die.

A vital decision you must make is who will be the trustee, or trustees, of your QTIP trust. The trustee usually is your surviving spouse, but a grown child or someone else entirely can serve. Above all, choose the person you trust the most— and, of course, one who is willing to take the job.

If you plan to choose your spouse, ask yourself these questions: Do you fully trust your spouse to protect the trust principal, your final beneficiaries' inheritance? Do your final beneficiaries feel the same way? If either answer is "no," or you're not positive, perhaps a child should serve as cotrustee. Or, if you believe one of your children (and not your spouse) has the wisdom to best balance the needs of the surviving spouse against the final beneficiaries' rights to their eventual inheritance, you may want to name the child as sole trustee.

Obviously, there's no one-size-fits-all answer when it comes to choosing the trustee. A good lawyer may be able to help, by focusing your attention on your personal situation, but the final decision is definitely yours. (Choosing a trustee is discussed in Chapter 17.)

Remember also that the executor of your will has the authority to decide whether or not property in the trust should actually receive QTIP treatment. So it's common to have your QTIP trustee be the same person as your executor.

By law, you cannot deny the executor the power to decide whether or not to elect QTIP tax treatment for property you include in your QTIP trust, so it's obviously vital that you have an executor you trust completely to make the best judgment in light of the interests of all trust beneficiaries—life beneficiary and final beneficiary.

Trusts for Noncitizen Spouses: QDOTs

If you are married to someone who is not a citizen of the United States, property you leave to that spouse is not entitled to the unlimited marital deduction. In plain English, as long as estate tax exists, you cannot leave your noncitizen spouse an unlimited amount of money free of federal estate tax. The rule applies even if the noncitizen spouse is a legal resident of this country. Congress wanted to prevent noncitizen spouses from inheriting large amounts of money and then leaving the country with no U.S. estate tax ever being collected.

What can you do if you want to leave a large estate to a noncitizen spouse? First, it may make excellent sense to have the noncitizen spouse become a U.S. citizen. Usually this is possible, given some time. If, for whatever reason, a spouse doesn't obtain U.S. citizenship, there is one very important estate tax exemption that can be used by a citizen spouse for property left to a noncitizen spouse.

The personal estate tax exemption is available to each spouse, no matter who inherits the property. So a citizen can

leave her noncitizen spouse property worth up to the amount of her personal tax exemption in the year of death free of federal estate tax. Any amount over that is subject to estate tax.

However, property of any worth left to a noncitizen spouse in what's called a "qualified domestic trust" (QDOT) is allowed the marital deduction. (I.R.C. § 2056(A).) The federal estate tax that would otherwise be assessed on property in a QDOT is deferred until the noncitizen spouse dies. QDOTs are used only by spouses with an estate exceeding the estate tax threshold, because only these estates must pay federal estate tax.

 SEE AN EXPERT

The rules governing QDOTs, estate tax, and noncitizen spouses are complicated. The United States has estate tax treaties with some countries that allow you to choose between the provisions of the treaty or the provisions discussed here. If you're married to a noncitizen and have an estate worth more than the estate tax threshold, you must get expert help with your estate plan.

Strict federal laws govern QDOT trusts. For example, if any trust principal is distributed to the noncitizen spouse during his or her life, estate tax is assessed on the amount distributed. So, if the trust pays $150,000 from principal for a spouse's new boat, that amount is immediately subject to estate tax. There is a special exemption from estate tax for QDOT principal distributions to the noncitizen surviving spouse in cases of "hardship." The IRS defines hardship as an immediate need relating to health, maintenance, education, or support that cannot be met with other reasonable means.

For instance, if $150,000 were paid to the spouse from the QDOT for medical care (instead of a boat), the full amount would be exempt from estate tax if no other reasonable means of paying for this care were available. This is decided on a case-by-case basis. It's pretty awful to have the IRS so intimately involved in your daily living, but QDOTs can lead to such a situation.

Income the noncitizen spouse receives from the QDOT trust is taxable as regular income. Of course, this is true for any person, whether a U.S. citizen or not, for income received from any ongoing trust.

Gifts to Noncitizen Spouses

Under a special gift tax regulation, a citizen spouse can currently give up to $145,000 per year (adjusted annually for inflation), free of gift tax, to a noncitizen spouse while both are living. (IRS Reg. 2523(i)(2).) By contrast, if both spouses were citizens of the United States, they could give any amount to each other free of gift tax. (See Chapter 16.) While the annual $145,000 exemption for gifts to noncitizen spouses is more limited than for gifts to citizen spouses, it is still a substantial amount. A U.S. citizen with an estate that's likely to owe estate tax should consider making large annual gifts to the noncitizen spouse.

When the surviving noncitizen spouse dies, the QDOT trust assets are subject to estate tax. The tax is based on the value of the assets in the trust when the noncitizen spouse dies. Any increase in value in the trust property during the life of the surviving spouse is subject to estate tax on that spouse's death, unlike property in an AB trust.

A valid QDOT trust must meet all of the requirements of any trust that qualifies for the marital deduction, including:

- The surviving spouse must be entitled to receive all income from the trust.
- The QDOT trust must be "elected" by the executor of the grantor's estate on the estate tax return.

In addition, the QDOT must also meet the following special requirements:

- At least one of the trustees of the trust must be either a U.S. citizen or a U.S. corporation. Thus, the surviving spouse cannot be the sole trustee.
- The trust must comply with applicable IRS regulations. These regulations impose special security requirements (such as posting a bond or providing a letter of credit when the trustee is an individual) on QDOTs in excess of $2 million.

EXAMPLE: Juan, a U.S. citizen, has an estate worth $6 million. He is married to Maria, who is a legal resident of the United States but not a citizen. Juan's estate plan includes an outright bequest to Maria of the amount that is exempt from federal estate tax because of Juan's personal exemption. The remaining assets will go into a QDOT trust for Maria's benefit during her life and will be distributed at her death to their children. Juan appoints his brother Ricardo, who is a U.S. citizen, to serve as cotrustee with Maria of the QDOT trust. (Juan could also use a U.S. bank or another institution as a cotrustee.)

Juan dies in 2014. $5 million of his estate goes directly to Maria. The other $1 million goes to the QDOT. His executor makes the election for the QDOT trust on Juan's federal estate tax return. No estate tax is due because of the personal tax exemption and the QDOT trust. Maria will receive all of the income from the trust for her life and may receive necessary principal for her support. If she receives principal, it will be subject to estate tax upon distribution. At Maria's death, the assets remaining in the trust will be taxed.

The QDOT rules have one opening that is an incentive to a noncitizen spouse to become a U.S. citizen. If the spouse becomes a citizen before the deceased spouse's estate tax return is filed (generally, nine months after the death) or before any distribution of principal is made to the noncitizen spouse, property in the trust will receive the full marital deduction, and assets may be invaded during the spouse's lifetime without paying estate tax. The trust is no longer a QDOT, and the remaining assets will be subject to tax only when the surviving spouse dies.

A unique and extremely helpful aspect of a QDOT trust is that it doesn't necessarily have to be created before the grantor's death. If someone who is married to a noncitizen prepared a trust before the federal QDOT law went into effect in 1988, or just didn't know about the law, the surviving noncitizen spouse can request of the IRS that the estate plan be "reformed" to meet the guidelines of a QDOT trust. For example, if a citizen simply left all property outright to a noncitizen spouse, the spouse can request the creation of a QDOT trust and obtain an estate tax deferment for the property.

Marital Deduction Trusts

Before 1981, when the IRS authorized the use of QTIP trusts, a marital deduction trust (I.R.C. § 2056(b)(5)) was the mainstay of estate plans for many couples. These trusts are similar to QTIP trusts in that taxes on trust property can be postponed until the death of the surviving spouse, and the surviving spouse is the life beneficiary of the trust. Before QTIP trusts, they were the only way to obtain the full marital deduction and retain control of the property during the life of the surviving spouse. In the past, these trusts were especially used to manage business affairs of the husband when the wife had no knowledge or interest in them.

Today, the QTIP trust has replaced these other trusts in popularity, but marital deduction trusts may still be useful in situations where one of their special features is desired.

You may want to create a marital deduction trust if:

- You want your spouse to be able to give away trust principal to someone else (such as a child) during your spouse's lifetime.
- You want your spouse to choose who will inherit trust property after his or her death.
- You want the trust to hold property that is not income producing. In one type of trust, the spouse cannot demand that the property be sold to produce income, as can the spouse under a QTIP trust.
- The trust will hold property such as a business and will need to reinvest the income, rather than pay it regularly to the surviving spouse.

SEE AN EXPERT

Get help with a marital deduction trust. Marital deduction trusts are quite technical and must comply with applicable tax law and IRS rules. These trusts must be drafted by experts experienced with this type of trust.

Like a QTIP, one spouse creates a trust, naming the other spouse the life beneficiary. Trust property qualifies for the marital deduction, so no estate tax on property in the trust is paid when the first spouse dies. The trust property that remains when the second spouse dies is included in the taxable estate of that spouse.

There are two types of marital deduction trusts. Let's look at each.

Power of Appointment Trusts

A "power of appointment" trust names the spouse as the lifetime beneficiary. As in a QTIP trust, the spouse is entitled to receive trust income and can require that trust property be converted to income-producing property. But with this type of trust, you must also give your surviving spouse either the right to invade the trust principal for any reason or to name the beneficiaries that will receive the trust property at your spouse's death or during his or her life. This is called a power of appointment. (See also Chapter 25.) This is in direct contrast to a QTIP trust, where you can, and normally do, limit the right to invade principal and you name the final beneficiaries.

The flexibility of invading principal and giving gifts of principal can be very attractive. When you prepare your trust, it may not be at all clear whether your surviving spouse will need access to the trust principal. Perhaps one or more of the final beneficiaries will genuinely need some of the trust principal while the surviving spouse is alive. One way to handle these uncertainties is to create a power of appointment trust and give the spouse power to make gifts of principal.

> **EXAMPLE:** Peter drafts a power of appointment trust for his wife, Lisa. Lisa will receive all income from the

trust and can choose who will inherit the assets at her death. During her life, Lisa is authorized to give trust principal to each of their two children.

After Peter dies, Lisa is quite well off from other sources, but one of their children loses his job, and he and his family are threatened with eviction from their recently purchased home. Lisa decides to distribute $120,000 of trust principal to the child, bailing him out of this crisis.

This gift is a taxable event for estate tax purposes. Since the trust property will be part of Lisa's taxable estate, she will use part of her personal estate/ gift tax exemption by making this distribution.

The spouse doesn't have to have both an unlimited power to invade principal and a power to name beneficiaries. Just one of the powers, such as the power to choose who inherits trust property, is all that is required.

If you give your spouse the right to name final beneficiaries of the trust property, you can then limit any powers to invade principal. For instance, the document could name only certain people (such as the children) who could receive principal. Or, you can choose not to grant the power to invade principal to anyone, including the spouse.

The surviving spouse does not have to use the powers granted by the trust document. For example, you can designate the final beneficiaries, and if your spouse does nothing to change them, the property will pass to those you have chosen.

Estate Trusts

An "estate" trust is a special type of marital deduction trust requiring that when the surviving spouse dies, all remaining trust principal must go into his or her estate. This means that the surviving spouse gets to choose the final beneficiaries, by will or within a living trust. Also, the estate trust property will go through probate on the death of the surviving spouse. What makes this trust special is that the trust property can be, and remain, nonincome producing. In all of the other trusts that defer taxes because of the marital deduction (including QTIP trusts), this is not possible.

EXAMPLE: Suzanne's property holdings include several acres of woodland and a small house by a river. Suzanne grew up spending much happy time on this land (and in the river) and she wants to be sure the land is preserved for her children. As it is now, the land is not income producing, and the house has no electricity and only rudimentary plumbing. Suzanne doesn't want the property improved or sold, so she leaves the land in a marital deduction estate trust. Specific directions in the trust document state that the land may not be sold while the trust lasts.

The other feature of this type of trust is that when the trust property does produce income, it does not have to be paid out to the spouse. At the trustee's option, the income can be accumulated, increasing the amount of the trust principal. If this occurs, income is taxed at the trust's higher tax rate. Sometimes, this disadvantage may well be offset by allowing for business growth or other investment purposes.

EXAMPLE: Arturo owns a large auto repair business with his brother, Sol. He leaves his share in an estate trust with his wife, Gilda, as life beneficiary. No tax is due because of the marital deduction. Sol will serve as trustee and manage the firm, reinvest income, and guide the business growth. Gilda directs by her will that at her death, the trust property will go to their children.

Charitable Trusts

I f you want to make a gift, especially a substantial one, to a charity, using a charitable trust may allow you to do it in a way that gives you significant tax benefits. As you'll see, there are several charitable trusts to choose from, and all can offer real financial advantages.

Besides offering estate and income tax advantages, estate planners see charitable trusts as a good tool for both being generous and ensuring retirement income.

That said, if your basic estate planning goals are to pass on your property to family or friends, leave a few minor charitable gifts, and pay less estate tax, then a charitable trust is probably not for you. The income tax and estate tax breaks charitable trusts can offer probably won't make up for the amount of property that must be given to a charity instead of to your family.

An Overview of Charitable Trusts

There are two basic types of charitable trusts, each with its own obtuse name:

- charitable remainder trusts, including popular pooled charitable trusts (I.R.C. § 664), and
- charitable lead trusts (IRC §§ 664 and 671).

These trusts have certain features in common:

They can become operational while you are alive. To gain the maximum tax advantages, most people create charitable trusts during their life, in their highest income-producing years. A basic purpose of these charitable trusts is not simply to make a gift to a charity, but also to provide some income (or other benefits), often later on in life, to you or to someone else you choose.

They are irrevocable. Once you create a charitable trust and it becomes operational, it is irrevocable. You cannot change your mind and regain legal control of the property you have given to the trust.

Only tax-exempt charities are eligible. In order to obtain the tax benefits, you must make your gift to a charity that is approved by the IRS. Normally, this means a charity that has gained tax-exempt status under Section 501(c)(3) of the Internal Revenue Code. The IRS maintains a long list of acceptable public charities, which include educational institutions, research organizations, and well-known organizations like United Way or CARE. Usually, the easiest way to determine whether the charity you want to make a gift to is an approved organization is to check with the IRS. IRS Publication 526, *Charitable Contributions,* explains how you can check on approved charities. You can also call the IRS at 800-829-1040 to ask whether a particular organization is tax exempt.

You get an income tax break. The value of the charitable gift is deductible from your income tax.

Let's take a quick look at the two kinds of trusts. Then, later in the chapter, we'll look at them in more detail.

The Basics of Charitable Remainder Trusts

With a charitable remainder trust, you give property to an irrevocable trust and name an income beneficiary and a final beneficiary. The final beneficiary is always the charity.

The income beneficiary can be (and often is) yourself, but it can be your spouse, mate, child, or anyone else. There can be more than one income beneficiary. This person (or persons) receives a set payment from the trust or a set percentage of the worth of trust property for the term defined in the trust. For example, the income beneficiary might receive 7% of the value of the trust per year, or a fixed sum of $8,000 per year. However, you cannot give the income beneficiary the right to receive all trust income, except in certain situations if the income beneficiary is your spouse.

You state, in the trust document, how long the income beneficiary will receive income from the trust property. This payment period can be a set number of years, or until the income beneficiary dies. At most, the income beneficiaries can have only the right to receive trust income during their lives. They never legally own the trust property, and it can never be included in their taxable estates.

The charity itself is usually the trustee of the trust property. As trustee, the charity is responsible for making proper payments to the income beneficiary. Usually, the charity converts any non-income-producing property, such as raw land or artwork, into income-producing property.

Money received by the income beneficiary may be subject to gift tax. If an income beneficiary is anyone other than you or your spouse, the payments from the trust are considered a taxable gift from you to that person. Currently, if more than $14,000 in income is received per year, you will be assessed gift tax on the excess and will have to file a federal gift tax return. (See Chapter 16 for more information about gift taxes.)

Establishing a charitable trust can give your inheritors an estate tax break. When the trust assets become solely owned by the charity—that is, when the income beneficiary's interest ends—they are no longer part of your taxable estate.

The Basics of Charitable Lead Trusts

With a charitable lead trust, the charity receives income from the trust property for a set period of time. Then the trust property goes back to you or someone else you named to receive it. In other words, the process is the reverse of that used with charitable remainder trusts.

Selecting a Trustee for a Charitable Trust

You can serve as trustee of your own charitable trust, or you can choose someone else. Most people choose the charity itself to serve as trustee. In fact, most large public charities insist on serving as trustee. They want to manage all gifts made to them, including yours. Large charities have experienced investment staff, and many people prefer to turn management and investment of trust property over to them.

Know Your Charity

Many people make gifts to charities they know well, whether from publicity or personal experience. If you don't know the charity, investigate it thoroughly, including its history, annual financial reports, and current management.

You can check out particular charities on the Internet. For example, www.guidestar. org offers analyses of hundreds of thousands of charitable organizations. Also, www.bbb. org/us/charity provides lots of information to help you evaluate charities, including a booklet published by the Better Business Bureau called *The Wise Giving Guide*.

A larger charity can also offer you other services. It may assist you in preparing the trust document, and it may administer the trust free of any charge for the trustee's services. And while you probably can't impose investment decisions over the charity serving as trustee, you can direct where you want the trust property to go after the income beneficiary's interest ends. For instance, if the trust will benefit a school, you could probably require that

the property be used only for scholarship purposes in a certain field or to enhance the library's facilities and holdings.

Matters can be different if you're making a gift to a smaller, less-established charity. Its cause may be noble, and its staff dedicated, but that's far from a guarantee of investment experience and sophistication. So with a small or new charity, you may decide that it's wisest to name yourself as trustee, to better manage your property. But check to be sure the charity will allow it; even some small charities insist on serving as trustee of a charitable trust, or that you use an investment firm of their choice.

Before you agree to let the charity serve as trustee, do the following two things.

Work with a lawyer knowledgeable in charitable trusts. An experienced lawyer can help you clarify what your income requirements are and what risk you might incur if the charity is trustee. You need to know whether the charity has a good investment record—one that will protect your income interest. The lawyer should also be able to suggest other possible trustees, aside from yourself—perhaps a corporate trustee, like a private trust company.

Investigate the charity's management style and investment staff. If the charity is the trustee, you can't control what the trust assets are invested in, so it's vital that you have confidence in the charity's investment personnel. Who in the charity will actually be doing the trustee work? Does that person seem open and easy to talk to? Do you feel confidence in his or her judgment and sympathies? How sophisticated is the potential trustee—and his or her staff—in money and investment management?

Don't choose the charity to be the trustee unless you are confident that the people who will actually manage your trust and its property will protect the income beneficiary's interests. Any trustee, including a charitable organization, has a "fiduciary duty" to do what's best for all the trust beneficiaries. But you want to rely on real people you actually trust, not abstract legal rules.

Naming a Backup Charity

To protect the income tax savings of a charitable trust, consider naming another tax-exempt charity as a backup beneficiary, or provide in the trust document that the trustee can choose another charity if this need arises. In the unlikely event that the chosen charity becomes defunct or loses its IRS tax-exempt standing, this ensures that there can be no (retroactive) loss of any income tax deduction. It also ensures that the charitable gift will never be subject to estate tax, because there will always be a valid, tax-exempt charity entitled to receive the trust property when the income beneficiary's term ends.

The Income Tax Deduction

You may get substantial income tax advantages by creating a charitable trust.

That's because over time, you can deduct the full value of the gift to the charity from your income tax. The fact that a charitable remainder trust makes payments to you or some other beneficiary for many years doesn't change this basic rule.

Where things get tricky, though, is in determining the actual value of the gift to the charity for income tax deduction purposes. The value of your gift to charity is not simply the value of the property when you give it to the trust. With a charitable remainder trust, the IRS deducts from this value the estimated value of the payments the income beneficiary has a right to receive from the trust property.

Things are reversed in a charitable lead trust. The income tax deduction is the estimated value of the income the charity will receive.

Once the IRS determines the worth of a gift to a charitable trust, you are entitled to deduct 100% of this amount. But this deduction cannot be taken in a single year. Rather, you can deduct a certain percentage of the amount in the year the gift is made, and deduct the rest over the next five years.

The amount of the first year's deduction depends on how the IRS classifies the charity and on your annual income. The most you can possibly deduct is 50% of your adjusted gross income for the first year, if your gift is cash. If instead of cash, your gift is appreciated property, such as appreciated securities, the maximum amount deductible from your income tax in the first year is 30% of the value of the gift.

EXAMPLE: Christopher creates a charitable remainder trust, with a cash gift, and the charity CARE as the final beneficiary. He names himself as the income beneficiary. The IRS will determine the worth of his gift, for income tax purposes, by subtracting the value of his retained interest in the income from the trust principal. If the value of the gift is less than 50% of his income for the year, he may deduct the entire gift that year.

If, instead, Christopher had given appreciated securities to the trust, he would have been able to deduct only up to 30% of the amount of his income on that year's tax return. In either case, he can deduct the rest of his gift over the next five years. And in either situation, the deductions save substantially on income taxes.

Replacing the Donated Money for Your Inheritors

If you want to donate large sums to charity but are afraid that your inheritors might need the money, you are in luck if you are in good health. Many people take the money saved by the income tax deduction and purchase life insurance to cover the money "lost" by the gift to the charity. You can then remove the life insurance from your estate for estate tax purposes.

Determining the Value of a Gift to a Charitable Remainder Trust

If you make an outright gift to charity, the income tax deduction permitted by the IRS is the gift's value at the time you make it. For example, if you write a $100,000 check to the Audubon Society, you're entitled to a $100,000 income tax deduction.

By contrast, if you make a gift to a charitable remainder trust while you are alive, determining the amount of your tax deduction is more complicated. The IRS determines the value of the charitable trust gift from tables that estimate your life expectancy (or that of whoever is the income beneficiary), current interest rates, and what the charity is expected to receive—that is, how much principal will be left—when the income beneficiary's interest ends. The more the charity is expected to get, the bigger the tax deduction; the larger the expected return to the income beneficiary, the lower the deduction.

EXAMPLE: Zola, who is 80 years old, creates a charitable remainder trust. She gives $800,000 in trust to her favorite charity, Save the Children, and retains the right to receive income equal to 6% of the trust principal annually for her life. After her death, the charity will receive all remaining trust property outright.

Curt, who is 40 years old, creates the same kind of trust, with the same amount of property and the same retained income rights. Under IRS rules, the value of Zola's gift to the charity is worth substantially more than Curt's, which means she can take a larger tax deduction. The reason is that Curt, who is just 40, will (under life expectancy tables) live much longer than 80-year-old Zola, so the trust will pay out much more money to Curt than Zola.

Because IRS calculations are influenced by prevailing interest rates, the precise worth of a gift to a charitable remainder trust depends on when the gift is made. Many large, experienced charities have professional staff members who will figure out your actual tax deduction for you. Otherwise, to determine the actual amount, you need to see an expert who has the most current IRS tables. You could dig up the tables yourself, but figuring out how to use them, interweaving estimated interest rates, your life expectancy, and the value of the charity's interest is definitely not easy; indeed, for the uninitiated, it's close to impossible.

Giving Appreciated Property to a Charitable Trust

One of the most useful features of a charitable trust is that it provides a method to turn highly appreciated assets into cash without paying any capital gains tax up front. If you donate a non-income-producing asset to a charitable trust, the charity can convert it into an income-producing

one. Though a charity isn't legally required to do so, it surely will if the asset—say an appreciated house or painting—isn't producing any, or much, current income. And whatever the profit from such a sale, no capital gains tax is assessed; charities are simply not liable for capital gains tax.

Here's how it works: You donate an appreciated asset to the charity, using a charitable remainder trust. The charity sells it for its current market value. The charity retains all the money received, without any subtraction for capital gains tax. As the grantor, you benefit in two ways. First, you get a tax deduction based on the sale price (the current value) of the asset. Second, the income you receive from the trust property will be based on this amount—which will obviously be higher than if capital gains tax had to be paid out of the sale's profits.

EXAMPLE: Toni owns stock currently worth $600,000, which she paid $20,000 for 20 years ago. She creates a charitable remainder trust, naming the Red Cross as the beneficiary. She funds her charitable trust with the stock. The Red Cross sells the stock for $600,000 and invests the money in a safe mutual fund. No taxes are paid. Toni, as the income beneficiary, will receive income from this $600,000 for her life.

Technically, there is a capital gain (profit) of $580,000 on the stock sale—that is, the sale price less Toni's original $20,000 purchase price. Had Toni sold the stock herself, she would have had to pay the capital gains tax.

Toni's trust document specifies that her annual income from the charitable trust will be 3% of the value of the trust property (currently $600,000). The IRS calculation of Toni's income tax deduction will also start from a gift worth $600,000.

Capital gains tax may enter the picture when you begin receiving income payments from the charity. Part of your payments will be considered a return of capital—that is, a return of a portion of your gift—and part will be taxed as capital gains. But any tax owed will be spread over a long period of time. Large charities will send you a year-end statement breaking down what, if anything, is taxable and how.

A Closer Look at Charitable Remainder Trusts

There are different types of charitable remainder trusts. Each one offers different advantages and drawbacks. The four main types are:

- **Annuity trusts.** These pay the income beneficiary a fixed amount each year.
- **Unitrusts.** These pay the income beneficiary an amount equal to a percentage of the trust assets each year.
- **Charitable gift annuities.** These are similar to annuity trusts but less complicated. The charity sets the amount of income that you receive.
- **Pooled income trusts.** These let you contribute to an existing charitable trust and receive income for a set time.

Charitable Remainder Annuity Trusts

This type of trust provides a fixed dollar amount of income every year (an annuity) to the trust's income beneficiary, regardless of the value of the trust assets. When creating the trust document, you name the income beneficiary—often yourself—and the term of the annuity period—often your lifetime. You also state the precise dollar amount of annual income that the life beneficiary must receive throughout this period.

Once you have established the set yearly payment, and the trust is operational, you can't change that figure. For instance, if you create a trust worth $250,000 and specify that the charity pay you $13,000 a year for the rest of your life, you can't subsequently say, "Oops, I forgot about inflation. How about $18,000 a year?"

You can, theoretically, make the payments as high as 50% of the value of the trust. However, the law requires that the charity must actually receive at least 10% of the original gift at the end of the term. If the payment is set too high, it would require spending principal, possibly using up much of the gift before the payment term is over. Obviously, this defeats your desire to make a gift to the charity. And there are practical limits. First, the higher the set payments, the lower your income tax deduction. Second, a charity is unlikely to accept a gift, particularly if it must serve as trustee, where it is likely, or even possible, that much of the trust property will be consumed before the charity gets anything. The IRS requires that the minimum payment from the trust must be at least 5% of the initial fair market value of the trust assets. (IRS Reg. 1.664-2(a)(2).)

The advantage of this type of trust is that if the trust somehow has lower-than-expected income—for example, during a period when interest rates are extremely low—the income beneficiary still receives the same annual income. The trustee must invade the trust principal, if necessary, to make the payments. This can't be done with other types of charitable remainder trusts.

If you create a charitable remainder annuity trust, you don't obtain a hedge against inflation. Payments from an annuity trust remain the same, even if there's significant inflation or the trust assets significantly increase in value.

You cannot give additional assets to a charitable remainder annuity trust after it's operational. (IRS Reg. 1.664-2(b).) Once the trust is created and funded, that's it. Of course, you could create a new, second trust, and many people do, but this is a fair amount of bother, especially with subsequent record keeping. So you should carefully decide, before creating a charitable remainder annuity trust, how much money you want to put in it and how large an annuity you want.

There are income tax advantages to using an annuity trust. The same property contributed to an annuity trust has a higher value for income tax deduction purposes than if placed in a charitable remainder

unitrust. If you are not concerned about inflation and wish to reduce your estate tax and income tax, an annuity trust is often a better choice than a unitrust.

Charitable Remainder Annuity Trusts at a Glance

- You create and fund the trust, with appreciated assets if possible.
- You take an income tax deduction, the amount of which is calculated according to IRS rules.
- The trustee (usually, the charity) converts all trust property into income-producing assets. No capital gains tax is due on the sale profits.
- The trustee pays a set amount to the income beneficiary for the annuity period.
- At the end of the annuity period, trust assets go outright to the charity. The value of these assets is not subject to federal estate tax.

Charitable Remainder Unitrusts

With this popular form of a charitable remainder trust, the trustee pays income each year from the trust to an income beneficiary—again, usually the grantor. But instead of a fixed amount, the income beneficiary gets a percentage of the current value of the trust property. For example, the trust document could specify that the income beneficiary receives 5% of the value of the trust assets yearly. Each year, the trust assets must be reappraised to obtain a current worth figure. If the value of the trust assets increases because of wise investment decisions by the trustee (or simple good luck), the payments received by the income beneficiary also increase. It is in the charity's interest to have the principal grow as much as possible so it will receive more at the end of the term.

Similarly, because the income beneficiary receives a fixed percentage, not a flat dollar amount, if inflation pushes up the dollar value of the assets, the payments to the income beneficiary go up accordingly. So a charitable remainder unitrust can serve as a hedge against inflation, in contrast to an annuity trust, where payments remain fixed no matter how rampant inflation becomes.

The payment to the trust income beneficiary must, under IRS rules, be at least 5% of the value of the trust assets each year and not over 50%. But here again, practical considerations, such as the grantor's desire to make a gift to charity, and the charity's willingness to accept and manage the trust property, mandate that the percentage be reasonable. It cannot be so excessive that it consumes all the trust property during the income beneficiary's period of payment. The IRS requires that a minimum gift of 10% of the original assets go to the charity.

In certain situations, the trust document can direct that the income beneficiary be given all the income from the trust:

- if the spouse of the grantor is the income beneficiary, or
- if the trust property is the grantor's residence or family farm.

If you create a charitable remainder unitrust, you can transfer more property to the trust later, if the power to make additional gifts was expressly included in the original trust document. (IRS Reg. 1664-3(b).)

Here's an example of how a charitable remainder unitrust can provide income tax relief, reduce estate tax, and provide other benefits.

EXAMPLE: Felix, age 60, earns a very comfortable salary and owns assets worth $5 million. Much of his property consists of his home and stock that he bought years ago. The stock has appreciated substantially in value; it cost $600,000 and is now worth $1.6 million. It currently pays little in dividends.

If Felix sells the stock and buys income-producing assets, he'll be obligated to pay capital gains tax on his profit from the sale. Setting up a charitable remainder unitrust offers one way to avoid this tax and guarantee income later, when Felix retires. Felix establishes a charitable remainder trust with himself as the income beneficiary for life and his alma mater, his state's university, as the final beneficiary. Felix funds the trust with the stock.

For income tax purposes, his donation to the charity is the full market value of the stock, less the IRS deduction based on his retained interest, age, and current interest rates.

The $1 million profit on the sale of the stock is not taxed. The trustee reinvests the entire $1.6 million into investments that pay well. The trust document requires income to be paid to Felix at 6% of the trust value annually for life. This figure will be $96,000 the first year; it will change each year as (or if) the value of trust assets changes. Obviously, if the value of the investment increases, Felix will receive more money. And equally obviously, it's desirable that the charity make wise investments to increase the odds that the trust principal will increase.

So far, Felix has avoided paying capital gains tax while turning an asset that paid little income into one that pays him much more. His income tax deduction will be almost $400,000, more than enough to buy life insurance to replace the gift amount for his inheritors, if he is healthy. He can then remove those proceeds from his taxable estate.

But there is even more good news. Felix has also reduced his estate to a level where much less estate tax may be due at his death. Felix has given money to the school for its eventual use instead of giving it to Uncle Sam. And he has a guaranteed income for life.

If Felix lives for 15 years while receiving income from this trust, the trust should pay him at least $96,000 x 15, or $1,440,000. If the trustee invests the original $1.6 million wisely, that principal amount should also increase significantly in 20 years. If the principal increases, Felix will receive more than $96,000 a year.

Charitable Remainder Unitrusts at a Glance

- You create and fund the trust, with appreciated assets if possible.
- You take the income tax deduction.
- The trustee (usually, the charity) converts all assets into income-producing assets. No capital gains tax is due on any profits from the sales.
- The value of the trust property is redetermined annually.
- The trustee pays a percentage of the revalued trust assets to the income beneficiary annually.
- At the income beneficiary's death, trust assets go outright to the charity. The value of these assets is not subject to estate tax.

Charitable Gift Annuities

Charitable gift annuities are becoming increasingly popular, especially with educational institutions. They are nothing more than charitable remainder trusts with a different name.

Charitable gift annuities are very simple trusts. You contact the charity, say your alma mater, and inform them of your intentions to make a donation in the form of a charitable gift annuity. Their staff, with great enthusiasm, will furnish you with the information you need and forms to fill out. You and the charity sign a contract setting out the terms of your donation, including the amount and duration of the payments made to the income beneficiaries you have named, usually you and your spouse. The charity handles everything, including setting the percentage it will pay to the beneficiaries. All you have to do is to transfer the assets to the charity, usually appreciated stock.

This type of arrangement works well for those who are less wealthy, but still wish to make a contribution. Some charities will set up an annuity with as little as a $5,000 gift. They figure your tax deduction for you and you just sit back and receive your income payments. With the tax savings and income payments combined, you will probably recoup the donated amount within several years.

Charitable gift annuities also set a minimum age for those wishing to donate; for most organizations, it's 50 to 65. That suits most people who are interested in annuities, who are approaching retirement and looking for regular income.

If you want to make a gift but are younger, you can defer the payment of benefits until the required age. You'll still get a tax deduction for your charitable gift now, and if your donation grows (as it's invested by the charity) you won't owe tax on the increase in value.

RESOURCE
Learn more on Nolo.com. Nolo provides a more in depth look at charitable gift annuities at www.nolo.com/legal-encyclopedia/charitable-gift-annuities.html.

Charitable Gift Annuities at a Glance

- You donate assets to the charity, often appreciated stock.
- You take an income tax deduction for the present value of the gift less the income you will receive.
- The charity pays you an amount of money each year; this amount is determined in the initial contract.
- At your death, the assets you donated belong to the charity.

Pooled Income Trusts

A popular type of charitable remainder trust is a pooled income trust, which allows people of more modest means to take advantage of charitable income tax deductions, donate to their favorite charity, and receive an income for a set period. You don't set up your own pooled income trust;

the charity does it. You simply donate to the charity. It pools your donation with other money it's been given and manages all the money in one big trust.

Not every charity offers pooled income trusts, but most large ones do. Many universities and museums have established them for their loyal supporters. If a pooled fund is available, the charity will surely be delighted to discuss it with you, and help set up the paperwork.

Pooled income trusts operate very much like mutual funds. You contribute money, bonds, or stocks to the charity. (Highly appreciated stock is desirable because, as we've discussed, the charity can sell it for its present market value and pay no capital gains tax.) The charity pools a number of individuals' donations, invests the money, and pays interest to the donors according to its earnings. You can specify that your earnings be retained until you reach a certain age, such as retirement age of 65 or 70, with payments to start then. The charity receives what remains of your gift after your death. If invested wisely, chances are the charity's share will have appreciated in value significantly by then.

You cannot give tangible property—from real estate to jewelry—to a pooled trust. It's not permitted under federal law. This is not true for other types of charitable trusts.

In a pooled charitable trust, the charity is always the trustee—you have no option here. If you don't think that a charity will manage your gift well, its pooled income charitable trust is simply not for you.

Pooled income trusts can be attractive for many reasons. The charity does all of the work of setting up the trust and managing the assets. Also, unlike other charitable remainder trusts, you can easily add amounts to the trust after the initial contribution. So if you don't have a large portfolio or cash to donate at one time, you can still build a nice retirement income and at the same time benefit a good cause, by donating smaller amounts over the years.

A deduction from your income tax is allowed every time you make a donation. The amount of the deduction is figured by using the IRS tables to value the charity's remainder interest.

> **EXAMPLE:** Yuki is a businesswoman in her 40s with a salary of $80,000 a year. She is not married and has no children. She wants to support her favorite museum and also plan for her retirement. Yuki contributes $10,000 to a charitable pooled fund managed by the museum and takes her income tax deduction, the exact amount of which is determined by the IRS tables. A year later she does the same thing.
>
> She keeps this up for 20 years, adding more in high-income years and less in years when she has unexpected expenses. By age 65, when she needs the income, her pooled shares, having been well managed by the fund, are worth around $400,000. She will receive whatever income this amount generates.

Yuki has accomplished both of her goals—giving a substantial amount to charity and providing a retirement fund for herself.

!

CAUTION

Carefully check out pooled charitable trusts. The pool must meet strict federal requirements in order for your contributions to be tax deductible. (I.R.C. §§ 170(f)(2)(A) and 642(c)(5).) The rules dictate who can serve as trustee and how contributions are combined and invested. If you are dealing with a "brand name" charitable pool, you should be safe. If not, and your own investigations have not reassured you that the charitable pooled trust you're considering fully complies with federal law (and this may not be easy to determine), you may want to take all the information you can gather about the trust to a good tax adviser.

Charitable Pooled Income Trusts at a Glance

- You contribute assets to a charity that has established a pooled trust.
- You take an income tax deduction.
- The charity combines your assets with other contributions in a fund.
- The fund pays income to you, based on the fund's income on all pooled gifts.
- You can make additional gifts. If so, you take further income tax deductions.
- The fund keeps paying you for life, based on your total contributions.
- At your death, the assets you contributed go outright to the charity.

A Closer Look at Charitable Lead Trusts

A charitable lead trust works in reverse fashion from any form of charitable remainder trust. In a charitable lead trust, the charity initially receives a set amount of income from the trust for a set period, usually a number of years. If the charity's income from the trust property drops below the set level, the charity can invade the trust principal to pay itself the set amount. At the end of the period, the trust principal goes to the final beneficiaries named by the grantor. Usually, the final beneficiaries are the grantor's surviving spouse or children.

There are two basic types of charitable lead trusts:

- **Unitrusts.** Here, a set percentage of the trust's net worth is paid to the charity for a period of years. The actual amount paid can vary over the years, as the trust assets are reappraised each year.
- **Annuity trusts.** With these trusts, the grantor provides that a set dollar amount is to be paid to the charity each year.

Charitable lead trusts do not offer all the tax advantages of charitable remainder trusts, but they do offer some of the same income tax advantages. For instance, if you donate appreciated property to a charitable lead trust and the charity sells it, no capital gains tax is assessed. Also, tax law allows you an income tax deduction of the amount that the charity is expected to receive, based on IRS tables.

Charitable lead trusts that become operational while the grantor lives are rarely used, because they involve a significant income tax drawback: Income from the trust paid to the charity (during the set payment period) is taxed to the grantor, because the assets will revert back to him or her or his or her inheritors later. So the grantor must pay income tax on income the charity, not he or she, receives. This can effectively cancel out the original tax deduction—not a highly desirable state of affairs. Still, these types of trusts are used occasionally, mainly by the very wealthy. They can make sense if you have highly appreciated assets that you want ultimately to remain in the family, not be given to charity.

> **EXAMPLE:** Clark, a wealthy industrialist in his early 50s, wants to take advantage of every tax break he can find. He and his wife have many assets that will let them continue to live very well when they retire.
>
> With the help of his lawyer, Clark creates a charitable lead trust, funded with real estate that he long ago paid $100,000 for and which is now worth $2 million. He chooses as the income beneficiary a research institute for the cure of Parkinson's disease and sets the income payments to the institute at 8% of the trust assets a year. At Clark's death, the trust assets are to go to his children.
>
> The trustee sells the real estate and invests the proceeds in mutual funds. Clark avoids a large capital gains tax that would have been assessed if he

personally sold the property, and the charity isn't taxed on the sale. Clark takes an immediate income tax deduction of the charity's projected income from these assets, based on the IRS tables that consider his life expectancy and interest rates. He knows he will have to pay tax on the income the charity obtains from these assets, but he hopes the gain he's achieved from avoiding capital gains tax will cancel out this drawback.

> Even more important to him, Clark is able to leave the trust property to his children. Also, he feels satisfaction that he has contributed to the possible cure of a horrible disease.
>
> It's impossible to say exactly how much income tax Clark will pay on what the trust earns during his life, because it depends on how long he lives and on income tax rates. Let's say Clark lives for 25 more years. If the trust earns 8% a year, that's $80,000. At current top rates, income tax the first year would be $24,800, although the rate does decrease for the very wealthy over the next few years.

SEE AN EXPERT
Naming a child's trust as the final beneficiary of a charitable lead trust. When children or young adults are the final beneficiaries of a charitable lead trust, it can be a good idea to create a child's trust to receive the trust principal, in case the children are not old enough or responsible enough to handle the

money when the charitable term ends. If children are the final beneficiaries, one child may need more money than the others, so a family pot trust may be advisable.

When the final beneficiaries don't need their inheritance right away, a charitable lead trust created upon the death of the grantor can occasionally be useful. It can let you save on estate tax, give to charity, and still (eventually) benefit your family or other beneficiaries. If a charitable lead trust becomes operational on the grantor's death, any negative income tax consequence to the grantor is avoided. The grantor won't be earning any more income. (Death solves that concern.) The purpose of the trust becomes the reduction of estate tax. The value of the charity's income interest for the period of years is not included in the taxable estate.

EXAMPLE: Rachel directs in her living trust that upon her death, a charitable lead trust of $4 million be established for a period of 15 years. During those years, income payments will go annually to her favorite charity. At the end of the period, the remainder will go to her niece. The charity's interest in the trust is calculated using the IRS tables. This amount is deducted from the taxable value of Rachel's estate and could save the estate a bundle.

Charitable Lead Trusts at a Glance

- You create and fund the trust, with appreciated assets if possible.
- You take an income tax deduction.
- The trustee converts all trust property into income-producing assets.
- Income goes to the charity for the set period.
- You pay income tax on trust income paid to the charity.
- At the end of the set period, all trust property, including appreciation, goes to the beneficiaries you chose.
- At your death, the amount the charity received is removed from your estate for estate tax purposes.

Types of Charitable Trusts: A Comparison				
	Charitable Remainder Annuity Trust or Gift Annuity	**Charitable Remainder Trust**	**Pooled Income Trust**	**Charitable Lead Trust**
Primary goals	Income tax and estate tax savings; fixed income for life	Income tax and estate tax savings; hedge against inflation	Income tax and estate tax savings; income (possible for retirement)	Income tax and estate tax savings (though they can cause significant tax disadvantages); preservation of trust assets for final beneficiaries
Property you can transfer to trust	Money or tangible property	Money or tangible property	Money and stocks	Money or tangible property
Transfer additional property later?	No	Yes	Yes	Yes, if permitted in original trust document
Income tax deduction available to you	Larger than with unitrust, because IRS values the charity's share higher	Smaller than with annuity trust, because IRS values the charity's share as less	Yes	The value of charity's income interest for set period
Trustee	Anyone you choose, including yourself or the charity	Anyone you choose, including yourself or the charity	The charity only	Anyone you choose, including yourself or the charity
Income beneficiary	You or anyone else you name	You or anyone else you name	You or anyone else you name	The charity
Final beneficiary	The charity	The charity	The charity	You or beneficiaries you name
Income paid to income beneficiary	Fixed dollar amount each year, even if trust principal must be used	Fixed percentage of trust assets each year	Interest earned from donors' contribution to the pool	Fixed dollar amount or percentage of trust assets, whichever you specify in trust document

Other Estate Tax–Saving Trusts

ndividuals or couples with very large estates can use various types of trusts to save on estate taxes. For this chapter's purposes, "very large" means that even if a couple uses an AB disclaimer trust, one or both of their estates will be well over the estate tax threshold. The tax-saving trusts described in this chapter can be used by anyone, whether married, unmarried, or single.

These trusts, however, are complicated. You'll need a lawyer to prepare the trust documents.

Generation-Skipping Trusts

People who want to leave substantial property to their grandchildren may find themselves confronting an unexpected obstacle—the "generation-skipping transfer tax" (GSTT). This tax applies to property worth more than the GSTT exemption that you leave to third-generation beneficiaries, such as your grandkids. One way to both reduce overall estate tax and escape the GSTT is to use a carefully funded generation-skipping transfer trust, called, appropriately, a GSTT trust.

The GSTT exemption is the same as the personal estate tax exemption, $5.34 million (in 2014). This amount is the combined exemption for both a generation-skipping trust and the personal estate tax exemption. The total amount allowed for both the estate tax exemption and the GSTT exemptions is the same—the dollar limit of the exemption for the year of death. There is, however, one exception. If a deceased spouse did not use all of her or his estate tax exemption, the remaining amount can be "ported" to the surviving spouse. In that case, when the surviving spouse dies, the total amount that can be transferred free of estate tax and GSTT is the exempt amount for the year of that spouse's death, plus the amount "ported" from the deceased spouse.

A GSTT trust provides income to one generation of beneficiaries (called the middle or second generation) and then leaves the trust property outright to the next, or third, generation. One of the income beneficiaries—such as a child— usually serves as trustee. The main benefit of a generation-skipping trust is that the trust property avoids estate tax when the second generation dies, because that generation never owns that property outright. In addition, if the trust property is worth less than the GSTT exemption amount (discussed below), the property avoids the GSTT when the third generation receives it. In the right situation, these trusts can save a family a bundle on overall taxes.

> **EXAMPLE:** Alex, a grandparent, establishes a generation-skipping trust of $3 million to take effect at his death. His children, the middle generation, receive the income generated by the trust property while they are alive. They're called the income beneficiaries. When Alex's children die, the trust principal is not part of their taxable estate. The entire amount is turned over to his grandchildren, who are termed the final beneficiaries.

There are no estate tax savings when the person from the older generation dies. All property in the generation-skipping trust is subject to estate tax at that point.

Use of a generation-skipping trust is not limited to your direct descendants. It can be used anytime you have beneficiaries in two subsequent generations and, of course, a sizable amount of money you're willing to tie up for a generation.

> **EXAMPLE:** Monroe, who has a lot of money, decides to leave $2 million to his niece and her three children in a generation-skipping trust. His niece, the middle generation, receives trust income for her life. When she dies, the trust ends and the property is distributed equally among her three children (the third generation). No estate tax is assessed at her death, because she didn't legally own the trust property.

This tax break is limited to the amount of the current GSTT exemption. Any property placed in the trust that exceeds the GSTT exemption in the year of the grantor's death is subject to a hefty generation-skipping transfer tax. The GSTT rate is the highest rate on the federal estate tax scale at the time the tax is applied, when the middle generation dies. (The GSTT is defined in I.R.C. § 2611.)

The GSTT exemption is $5.34 million in 2014. Members of a couple can each transfer their personal GSTT exemption amount free of GSTT. However, the GSTT exemption is not automatically available. To claim it, your executor must file for the exemption using federal estate tax forms. If your executor does not make this filing, you will lose all the benefits of the exemption.

This is complicated stuff. It is important to remember that we are talking about two different taxes here, but with one single exemption. There are not two separate exemptions. For example, let's say in 2014 you have an estate of $7 million. You decide to leave $4 million in a generation-skipping trust, and the remaining $3 million outright to your children. Here are the estate tax consequences:

Personal/GST exemption for 2014	$5,340,000
Less exemption for generation-skipping trust	-$4,000,000
Amount of remaining exemption	$1,340,000
Value of remaining property subject to estate tax	$3,000,000
Amount subject to estate tax	$1,660,000

The value of the property in the generation-skipping trust will not be subject to estate tax when the middle generation dies.

SEE AN EXPERT
Getting help. As you can see, GSTT trusts are very tricky. I provide only an overview of the subject. If you think a generation-skipping trust may be desirable, you absolutely need an expert in the field.

Fussy actuarial rules apply if you create a GSTT trust to benefit your "nonlineal" descendants—that is, anyone except children, grandchildren, and so on—to determine which generation they are in. Basically, the rules provide that a "generation" occurs every 25 years, except the "child" generation starts when a beneficiary is over 12½ years younger than the grantor.

> **EXAMPLE:** Shanto leaves money in a trust that will pay income for life to his friend Lolly, who is 15 years younger than he is. At her death, the principal will go to Lolly's children. This is a generation-skipping trust, and Lolly will be considered a member of the "child" category.

Is a Generation-Skipping Trust for You?

You must have a substantial estate—usually at least several million dollars (individually) before a generation-skipping trust could make sense. With a generation-skipping trust, the middle generation can have the right to receive all trust income, but only restricted rights to spend principal.

Will Your Spouse Need Your Property?

Trusts paying income to children and then leaving assets to grandchildren are desirable only if your spouse is already fully provided for—from his or her own property, other property you leave for his or her benefit, or both. Your spouse could also receive income from the trust, and

have a limited right to invade principal, but if spousal need is a real concern, a GSTT is probably not what you need.

One Way the Rich Stayed Rich

Before the adoption of the generation-skipping transfer tax, when Congress put a limit on the right to pass money to one's grandchildren free of estate tax in the middle generation, people with many, many millions (even billions) of dollars would leave the bulk, or perhaps all, of their property in generation-skipping trusts. Estate taxes were, of course, due when the trust grantor died, but no taxes at all would be assessed when the middle generation died. These types of trusts enabled the very wealthy to escape all estate tax in every other generation. And the income from a trust of many millions normally proved quite sufficient for the middle generation to live an affluent lifestyle. (Couldn't you survive adequately on the income from, say, $200 million?) Since Congress created the GSTT in the 1980s, there is no tax advantage in creating a generation-skipping trust worth more than the GSTT exemption.

Will Your Children Need Your Property?

If you establish a generation-skipping trust, your children (the second generation) will not have outright ownership of any of the trust property (principal). They can serve as trustees and receive trust income. And, if expressly allowed by the trust document, they can spend trust principal if deemed necessary by the trustee for their "health, education, support, or maintenance."

What this amounts to is that, for most people, a generation-skipping trust makes sense only if you're sure your children (the middle generation) will be financially comfortable without unrestricted access to the assets in the trust.

Dynasty Trusts

A "dynasty" trust is intended to last for several generations, or perhaps forever. Basically, it's a generation-skipping trust but instead of lasting two generations, it goes on and on. It achieves this by using successive life estate trusts. As long as the trust creator has lineal descendants, there will always be a new life estate beneficiary (or more than one) when the previous one(s) die.

Dynasty trusts can be established only in states (about twenty of them) that have abolished "the rule against perpetuities." This ancient rule was intended to abolish "dead-hand" control over property and it essentially limited trust duration to two generations. I think it's a good rule. Long-term dead-hand control over property seems both undesirable and egotistical. However, if you live in a state where dynasty trusts have become legal and have several million to spare and the desire to set up control that could last for centuries, discuss this type of trust with an attorney.

Creating Two Generation-Skipping Trusts

Each member of a couple (married or not) can transfer the exemption amount in a generation-skipping trust free of GSTT. Thus, a wealthy couple can create two generation-skipping trusts for their children and grandchildren, placing quite a lot of money in the trusts.

In second or subsequent marriages, each spouse may want to create a generation-skipping trust for her or his own children from a prior marriage, and for their children's children.

How the GSTT Works

Any gift of trust property to a beneficiary two generations down, no matter how it is made, is subject to the GSTT.

When the GSTT Is Assessed

The GSTT, if applicable, is assessed when the final beneficiaries of a generation-skipping trust receive their property. Usually, this happens only after the middle generation dies.

In tax lingo, this event is called a "taxable termination." Two other types of transfers are also subject to the GSTT.

A "direct skip" is an outright gift to someone two (or more) generations down. For instance, if you leave $7 million outright to a grandchild, only the GSTT exemption amount of that gift avoids the GSTT. The rest is taxed at the highest estate tax rate. Also, the entire $7 million is included in your taxable estate, and so is subject to estate tax at your death. So the property is taxed twice.

Sometimes, a generation-skipping trust directs or permits payment to a beneficiary two generations removed from the grantor, while the middle generation is still alive. This is a "taxable distribution" and any such payments will be taxed under the GSTT if the amount in the trust originally exceeded the personal exemption amount.

How the GSTT Is Assessed

Whether or not a generation-skipping trust is subject to the GSTT is determined when the grantor dies—that is, when the trust becomes operational. If the amount in the trust at the time the grantor dies is less than the exempt amount, then all property in the trust is exempt from the GSTT tax. The tax will not apply when the trust assets are eventually distributed to the grandchildren, even if the worth of the trust assets has increased significantly by that time.

> **EXAMPLE:** Frank is a widower with two children and four grandchildren. His total estate is worth $9 million. He sets up a generation-skipping trust of $5 million to take effect at his death. This $5 million is included in Frank's taxable estate when he dies in 2014.
>
> The trust will pay the income to his children for their lifetimes. When they die, the principal goes to the

grandchildren. When the children die, the property in the trust is worth $3.5 million. No GSTT is assessed, because the amount in the trust when Frank died did not exceed his estate tax exemption.

Options With Generation-Skipping Trusts

You have some flexibility when you set up a generation-skipping trust. Sometimes, trust income is made available to the grandchildren—for example, for their education—while their parents (the middle, income generation) are still alive.

In addition, other estate planning devices can be useful in combination with a generation-skipping trust. Most common is use of an AB disclaimer trust. (See Chapter 18.) Sometimes, a generation-skipping trust is combined with leaving property outright to a surviving spouse or through a QTIP trust.

Securing the GSTT Exemption

The GSTT exemption must be claimed by submitting the proper forms to the IRS. Simply establishing the trust is not enough to obtain the tax break for the middle generation. Upon the death of the creator of the GSTT trust, the estate representative must obtain and file the required documents.

Irrevocable Life Insurance Trusts

After your death, all the insurance proceeds from a policy you owned are included in your taxable estate. (See Chapter 12.) If the payout is large, it may push the value of your estate over the federal estate tax threshold. So finding a way to remove life insurance proceeds from your taxable estate can save your inheritors a bundle in estate tax.

One way to remove life insurance proceeds from your estate is to use an irrevocable life insurance trust. This trust is a legal entity you create that becomes operational while you are alive. The trust becomes the owner of life insurance you previously owned as an individual or of any new policy purchased in the trust's name. Because the policy is owned by this legally independent trust, you are not the legal owner of the insurance proceeds, which, therefore, are not included in your taxable estate. Normally, the beneficiaries of the policy remain the same as they were before you set up the trust.

Irrevocable life insurance trusts aren't for everyone who faces estate tax. Indeed, simply giving the policy to someone you trust is normally a better approach. Life insurance trusts are for those who don't want the risks involved in giving their policy outright to another person. For instance, when the beneficiary of the life insurance isn't yet mature enough to be trusted with ownership, an irrevocable life insurance trust can be very desirable.

 SEE AN EXPERT

Get help. If you want to create or explore using a life insurance trust, see an experienced lawyer before you trundle off to your insurance company. In addition to the complexities of any irrevocable trust, there are potential problems unique to a life insurance trust.

IRS Requirements

Strict IRS requirements govern irrevocable life insurance trusts. To gain the estate tax savings this type of trust can offer, you must conform to these rules.

The Trust Must Be Irrevocable

The life insurance trust must be absolutely irrevocable. If you retain any right to revoke or amend the trust, or affect the insurance policy in any way—such as by naming a new beneficiary—the IRS will consider you to be the legal owner of the policy. That means the proceeds will be included in your taxable estate.

You Cannot Be the Trustee

Remember that the purpose of this trust is to remove the life insurance from your estate. You cannot control the trust, so you cannot be trustee. If you try to retain any rights that a trustee must have, the IRS will say you still own the policy.

Your spouse can be trustee, but you must be careful with this arrangement. You'll need expert legal help to make sure that your spouse is not given certain powers or too much power that might make your spouse the legal owner of the policy. You want to keep the proceeds out of both of your estates, not just your own.

You can name your grown child, another relative, a friend, or even an institution to serve as trustee. No matter whom you choose, you'll have more control over the trustee than you would over someone to whom you gave an insurance policy outright, because you create the trust document that establishes the trustee's powers.

> **EXAMPLE:** Pilar is the divorced mother of two children, in their 20s, whom she has named as beneficiaries of her universal life insurance policy. It will pay $500,000 at her death. In addition to the insurance policy, Pilar has an estate of $5 million. She wants to remove the proceeds of the policy from her estate.
>
> But Pilar has a problem. Although she loves her kids dearly, neither child is sensible with money, and she doesn't trust them enough to give her policy to them outright. She fears they might fail to make the premium payments, or possibly even cash in the policy in a time of financial desperation. She wants to be sure the policy is kept in force until her death, so that all the proceeds—far more than the cash-in value of the policy—will be distributed to her children on her death.
>
> Pilar decides to create an irrevocable life insurance trust for the policy and to name her sister, Julianna, the person she's closest to, as the trustee.
>
> Even aside from the crucial fact that Pilar trusts Julianna, there's no real reason for Pilar to worry about Julianna cashing in the policy. If Julianna did that, she wouldn't receive the cash surrender value herself; the trust, not Julianna, owns the property. The cash-in money would remain in the trust until Pilar's death.

The Trust Must Exist for at Least Three Years Before Your Death

You must establish the operational trust at least three years before your death. If the trust has not functioned for at least three years when you die, the trust is disregarded for estate tax purposes, and the insurance proceeds are included in your taxable estate.

This three-year rule is crucial. It means that if you want to establish an irrevocable life insurance trust, you should do so promptly. Clearly, it would be unfortunate to create an irrevocable life insurance trust and die before the end of the three-year period, negating all estate tax savings the trust offered.

The reason for this three-year rule is that the estate tax savings offered by an irrevocable life insurance trust (or any transfer of life insurance ownership) can be so substantial that the IRS wants to prohibit last-minute transfers of life insurance, in anticipation of death. Three years seem like a pretty long "last minute," but lengthy or not, the rule exists. If you want to create an irrevocable life insurance trust, do it soon. You gain no benefits from waiting.

Paying Insurance Policy Premiums

One major concern when creating an irrevocable life insurance trust is how future premium payments to the insurance company will be made. The IRS has ruled that payment of premiums alone does not constitute an "incident of ownership" of a life insurance trust. So, the person who sets up the trust should be able to continue to make the payments. However, check to make sure that this remains acceptable to the IRS (rulings can change) before choosing this payment option.

At least two other payment options are available to you. First, you can give money to the beneficiaries each year so that they can make the payments themselves. Of course, you'll have to trust the beneficiaries to spend that cash on policy premiums. Second, you can include what are called Crummey trust provisions (so named because someone named Crummey was the first to have this type of trust validated) in your irrevocable life insurance trust.

Here's how Crummey trust provisions work: The trust document provides that each year, each trust beneficiary has the right to receive up to the maximum that can be given to a beneficiary, per year, free of gift tax from the trust property (currently $14,000). Usually, the beneficiaries have a deadline, say January 15, to claim their money for the year.

Each year, you give up to the maximum amount per person to the trust. Now things get tricky. Each year the beneficiaries decline to accept this money. By doing this, the gift is converted from a "future interest" (not eligible for the annual gift tax exemption) into a gift of a "present interest"—which means it qualifies for this exemption. The trustee uses this declined money to pay that year's insurance premium. Any balance left over after the year's premiums have been paid is saved in the trust for future premium payments.

You should be aware that the IRS has made no secret of its distaste for Crummey trust provisions. So far, the Crummey method has remained legal, but the IRS may well find a new avenue of attack in the future. If the Crummey provision fails down the line, the gifts to the beneficiaries will be taxable, and not subject to the annual exclusion. Even so, gifts for the amount of a premium are small when compared to the eventual proceeds.

If neither of these methods provides enough cash to pay the yearly insurance premium, or if you consider the Crummey provisions too complicated and risky, what can you, the grantor, do? Perhaps you could purchase a single-premium policy, so there's no worry about future payments. Another approach is simply to give money to the trust and be assessed gift tax on it.

When Circumstances Change

Sometimes tricky personal concerns arise when preparing or living with an irrevocable life insurance trust. For example:

- What happens if you get married, divorced, or have a child after setting up an irrevocable trust? Legally, it's up to the trustee to decide who the beneficiaries of the policy should be. Of course, a trustee who cares for you will probably revise the insurance beneficiaries as you want. For example, the trustee could add your new child as a beneficiary.

- Suppose you get divorced, and your ex-spouse is one of the beneficiaries of the life insurance policy and also of Crummey trust provisions you created to pay the premiums? Here's where matters can get very touchy. If the trustee simply removes the ex-spouse as a beneficiary of the policy, the ex-spouse could claim the trustee was really acting under your control. This could cause the entire trust to fail for estate tax purposes.

With personal complexities like these, you must see a lawyer.

Grantor-Retained Interest Trusts: GRATs, GRUTs, and GRITs

Names to the contrary, this section is not about lifting weights or Southern cooking. Rather, it covers three types of irrevocable estate tax–saving trusts with the common feature that you keep either income from trust property or use of that property for a period of years. Then the trust ends and the property goes to the final beneficiaries you've named. These trusts can let you make a gift to people you love, save on gift

taxes, and save again on estate taxes—a good deal.

These types of trusts are called:
- grantor-retained annuity trusts (GRATs)
- grantor-retained unitrusts (GRUTs), and
- grantor-retained income trusts (GRITs).

These trusts are for people who have enough wealth to feel comfortable giving away a substantial hunk of property. If you believe you'll want or need full control over all your property until you die, they are not for you.

Overview of GRATs, GRUTs, and GRITs

GRATs, GRUTs, and GRITs vary in some important aspects—such as how payment to the grantor is determined—but all have much in common. Here is how these trusts work to save on gift and estate tax.

You start by placing property in one of these trusts. You can be, and usually are, the initial trustee of your trust. You also retain some interest in that property for a set period. The retained interest can be income generated from the trust property, or the right to use that property—such as living in a trust-owned house. You name final beneficiaries, who will receive the trust property when this period ends or at your death, whichever comes first.

Once established, the trust is irrevocable—you can't change your mind and take back any property from the trust. No matter how much you may subsequently need that property, it can never again be yours outright.

For gift tax purposes, the value of the gift you make to the trust is determined when the trust is established. This value never changes. You hope that while you have a retained interest in the trust property, the value of that property will increase significantly. If you outlive the trust period and the property is turned over to the final beneficiaries before your death, this increase in value will never be subject to gift tax or estate tax. The only taxes ever assessed on the transaction are the gift taxes when the property is first placed in the trust. And because you no longer own the property at your death, the entire amount is excluded from your taxable estate.

Because you have retained an interest in the property—such as receiving income from the trust—the value of the gift, for gift tax purposes, is reduced; it is less than the property's market value. The gift tax is assessed on the value of the gift to the final beneficiaries, according to complex IRS tables.

The annual gift tax exclusion is not available, because the gift is not one for present use by any beneficiary but rather for use in the future. However, when you make your gift to the irrevocable trust, no gift tax must actually be paid, unless you have already used up your gift tax exemption by making previous taxable gifts.

As you'll see, the trick here is for you to survive the trust period (set by you in the trust document), so that the trust property is turned over to the final beneficiaries during your lifetime. If you do, the remaining value of the trust property will not be counted in your taxable estate. If you don't, the trust assets, complete with all appreciation in value, are included in your taxable estate. You gain nothing, estate tax wise, and the money and time spent drafting the trust and administering it will have been wasted.

Both married and single folks can use a grantor-retained interest trust. Because estate tax breaks for single people are few and far between, a grantor-retained interest trust can be an attractive tax avoidance technique for a wealthy single person.

Here's a rough example to show you how these trusts work.

> **EXAMPLE:** Phyllis, age 65, creates a GRIT. She funds it with her house, worth $4.4 million, and retains the right to live in the house for 15 years. She names her son as the final beneficiary. The value of the gift (her house) to the trust is determined when she creates the trust. Her right to live in the house for 15 years is her income value, what it would cost someone to occupy the premises for that period. This is subtracted from the $4.4 million gift for tax purposes.
>
> Phyllis survives the 15-year period she set. When she becomes 80, the house, now worth $5.5 million, is legally turned over to her son. Because gift tax was assessed on the $4.4 million value of the house at the time the trust was created minus her retained interest, Phyllis has avoided paying gift tax on more than $160,000. Moreover, she has removed the house from her taxable

estate, for the obvious reason that she's no longer the owner of it.

As you've probably already suspected, this trust sounds so terrific that it must have risks. When she turns 80, Phyllis will no longer own her house. If her son doesn't charge her rent, the IRS will consider him to have made a gift of the rent to his mother. The son may have to file a gift tax return. (See Chapter 16.) Worse, her son could decide to sell the house, leaving Phyllis out on the street. Plus, as discussed above, if Phyllis does not survive the time period she set in the trust document, the whole gamble collapses, and nothing is achieved, tax wise.

Grantor-Retained Annuity Trusts (GRATs)

A GRAT provides a grantor with a fixed annual payout from the trust.

How GRATs Work

To establish a GRAT, you transfer some valuable asset, from cash to real estate to stocks to any property with significant value, to the trust. Under the terms of the trust document, the trustee (usually yourself) dips into the trust assets and pays you an annual fixed sum (an annuity) for a set term of years. At the end of this term, the remaining trust assets go to the final beneficiary, perhaps your child, as the trust document directs. (I.R.C. § 2702.)

The benefit of a GRAT results from the fact that the IRS values the gift to the final beneficiaries only when the trust is established, not when the remaining trust property is later distributed, as long as you outlive the trust period. Your retained interest greatly reduces the value of the gift for gift tax purposes, even though the final beneficiary will normally receive (at a minimum) the full amount given.

The IRS tables used to determine the gift tax value of a gift to a GRAT are nearly impenetrable to all but real experts. They take into account the term period, life expectancy, and the interest rates when the GRAT is created. Rather than bore and quite possibly confuse you with a detailed explanation of how valuation works, let's simply say that it is one big reason you must see an expert if you want to set up one of these trusts.

> **EXAMPLE:** Hattie, a 60-year-old widow, has assets worth $3 million. She sets up a GRAT with $1 million. The trust will last for 15 years and will pay Hattie $40,000 a year during the term. At the end of the term, or when Hattie dies, whichever happens first, the remaining trust assets will go equally to her three children. The value of the gift to the trust for gift tax purposes is set by an IRS formula that first subtracts Hattie's annuity interest ($40,000 x 15 years, or $600,000) and then considers Hattie's life expectancy and the amount in the trust ($1 million).
>
> After subtracting the $600,000 value of Hattie's retained interest, the gift is initially worth $400,000. But now the

IRS tables take into account Hattie's life expectancy and the interest rates when the trust is created. As a result, the value of the gift for gift tax purposes will be less than $400,000.

GRATs at a Glance

- You create and fund the trust, establishing the dollar amount of the annuity you will receive each year for the set period.
- The value of the gift, for gift tax purposes, is determined when you fund the trust.
- The trustee pays you an annuity each year.
- When the annuity term ends, trust assets go to the final beneficiary.

The more benefit you retain from the trust property, the less the property is worth for gift tax purposes. It follows then that the younger you are, and the longer the term during which you will benefit from the gift, the lower the taxable value of the gift. Likewise, the higher the annuity payments to you, the lower the taxable value of the gift.

EXAMPLE: Sudata funds a GRAT with $1 million, retaining an annuity of $40,000 annually. But this GRAT is for a period of only ten years, rather than 15.

Her total benefit is $40,000 x 10, or $400,000, rather than $600,000 for a 15-year period. The gift tax value of the gift to the final beneficiary is close to $600,000. (As discussed, the exact

figure will be different, because of the IRS calculation tables.) That means a lower gift tax assessment.

If the value of the gift to the final beneficiaries exceeds the amount of the current estate tax exemption, you will have to pay gift tax when the trust is funded.

EXAMPLE: In 2014, Max places $7 million in a GRAT and reserves a $60,000 annuity for himself for ten years. This results in a total benefit to him of $600,000 and a gift (to the final beneficiary) worth roughly $6.4 million. (Again, the IRS tables must be used to determine the precise taxable value of the gift.) Because the value of the gift exceeds the $5.34 million gift tax exemption for 2014, Max will have to pay gift tax on roughly $1 million.

Increasing the Tax Savings From a GRAT

A GRAT is an irrevocable trust, which means that usually it functions as a separate taxable entity. However, it can be constructed in such a way that all income and capital gain from the trust are taxed to you, the grantor. This is called making the GRAT a "grantor trust." This way, more money is eventually given to the final beneficiaries.

EXAMPLE: Theo funds a ten-year GRAT with a stock portfolio. Language in the trust document makes it a grantor trust. During the ten-year period, income from the trust is taxed to him and not to the trust. Also, during the trust term, as trustee, he sells part of the stock and makes a hefty profit. But Theo, not the trust, personally pays the capital gains tax due. This allows the trust assets to grow in value, and at the same time, further reduces Theo's estate.

Grantor-Retained Unitrusts (GRUTs)

A grantor-retained unitrust, or GRUT, is very similar to a GRAT, with one important difference: The income payment to you (the grantor) is not a fixed amount annually. Instead, the amount is equal to a percentage of the value of the trust assets for that particular year.

Each year, the new current value of the trust assets must be determined. Assuming a decent economy, in a well-managed trust, the worth of the assets should gradually increase over the years. In that case, the annual payments you receive would also get larger.

If the percentage payment is larger than the trust's earnings—for example, you're entitled to 8% of the trust's net worth but the trust property earned only 5% this year—the rest comes out of the principal. Any trust income above the percentage set for you is added to the trust assets.

Just as with a GRAT, the gift tax value of the gift to the final beneficiary is established when the trust is created. The taxable value of a GRUT gift, for gift tax purposes, is determined by a complex IRS formula. The formula considers how much

you can expect to receive over the set period, your age and life expectancy, and how long the trust is supposed to last. The older you are, the more valuable the gift; the longer the term of the trust, the lower the gift value.

GRUTs at a Glance

- You create and fund the trust, establishing the percentage return you will get each year for however many years you want the trust to last.
- The value of the gift, for gift tax purposes, is determined when you fund the trust.
- The trustee pays you the established percentage of assets each year.
- Trust assets are appraised annually.
- When the term ends, the trust is terminated. Trust assets go to the final beneficiary.

Because your annual payment is based on the value of the trust property, a GRUT can give you some hedge against inflation. For example, say you have $1 million in a GRUT and get 7% of the value of the trust assets per year. If suddenly there's 20% annual inflation, the dollar value of the trust assets will, presumably, also increase by roughly 20%, to $1.2 million. Obviously, 7% of $1.2 million is a higher number than 7% of $1 million. But all you are really doing is keeping up with inflation. In real dollar terms, you receive the same amount, although you receive more (inflated) dollars.

No such hedge against inflation is available to grantors of a GRAT. They receive a set dollar amount every year, period.

> **EXAMPLE:** Ravi, aged 60, has an estate worth $2.5 million. He puts $300,000 into a GRUT that will last for ten years. Then the trust assets go to his friend Monica. The trust specifies that during each year of the ten-year period, Ravi will receive 8% of the trust's net worth.
>
> The first year, the trust pays out $24,000 to Ravi—8% of $300,000. If Ravi survives the ten-year period, Monica will likely receive more than $300,000, and surely far more than the value the IRS assigned the gift when the trust was created. In addition, Ravi will have removed the $300,000 from his taxable estate.

Drawbacks of GRATs and GRUTs

The potential benefits of a GRUT or GRAT are rarely worth the risks involved unless you are quite wealthy. If you have $10 million, putting $2 million in a GRUT or GRAT makes more sense than putting $500,000 in one if you have $2 million. Also, an expert must set up the trust, which is complicated and expensive.

Whether or not the drawbacks are likely to affect you depends on your family and tax situation. You should be aware of these drawbacks and evaluate how they could affect you and your beneficiaries before you create one of these trusts.

You Lose Control Over Trust Assets

As already stressed, once a GRAT or GRUT is established and operational, you lose legal ownership of the trust property. You can't later on turn around and decide that the income you receive from the trust isn't enough and insist on higher payments. Nor can you get the trust assets returned to you personally. Further, you cannot add to, or subtract from, the trust principal. Under IRS rules, the amount put in the trust must stay there, period. Practically speaking, this means that if you or someone in your family suffers a financial disaster, the trust property isn't available to help out.

Further, if you do survive the trust term, you lose all benefit from the trust assets because they go to the final beneficiary at the end of the set term. Suppose you live for another ten years after the trust ends. You may well have become accustomed to the payments from the trust—or worse, may need them for expenses, such as medical costs. But anything you receive from the trust property (after the trust ends) will have to be a gift to you from the final beneficiaries—if they choose to make it.

Estate Tax Savings Are Not Guaranteed

Usually the biggest concern when deciding whether to use a GRAT or GRUT is the possibility that you won't outlive the period you've set to receive income from the trust. If you die before the trust period ends, all the trust property is legally part of your estate. All your possible estate tax savings are lost.

If you are married, you can plan to defer taxes in such circumstances by having the trust assets go to your spouse. All property left to your spouse (if he or she is a U.S. citizen) can pass estate tax free under the marital deduction. If the surviving spouse is young and healthy, that spouse can make or revise his or her own estate plan to try to soften the estate tax blow when he or she dies.

But if the surviving spouse is elderly or in poor health and may not live long, or if you are single, your untimely death and the resulting addition of the trust property to your estate could mean higher estate taxes. In hindsight, another form of estate plan, such as a program of direct gift giving, would have been preferable.

Grantor-Retained Income Trusts (GRITs)

If you set up a GRIT, you receive all income from the trust assets for a set period. The assets go to the final beneficiary when you die or the term ends. GRITs were enormously popular before 1990. In that year, Congress took away any tax savings if the trust assets eventually benefit your family. "Family" includes your spouse, lineal descendants, ancestors, siblings, and spouses of any of these family members.

The law left one exception. The one remaining form of GRIT that can save on taxes and be used for family members is

called a "qualified residence GRIT," more commonly known as a "qualified personal residence trust."

Qualified Personal Residence Trusts

A qualified personal residence trust (QPRT) is funded with only your personal residence and nothing else. (I.R.C. § 2702.) This personal residence may be either your primary residence or a vacation home. You can do this for both, but you will need two separate trusts, one for each house. If the vacation home is sometimes rented by others, to qualify for a QPRT, you must actually use the home each year for the greater of 14 days or 10% of the time it is rented. So, if it is rented for 180 days a year, you must personally use it for at least 18 days, 10% of 180 days.

Here's how the QPRT works. You put your residence into a trust for a set period, usually about ten years. Your retained "income interest" during the term is the right to occupy the residence. When the term of the trust ends, the property goes to the final beneficiary you named in the original trust document.

Again, in order to obtain your goal, the trick is to outlive the term of the trust. If you don't survive the term, the full current value of the house is included in your taxable estate and your attempt at a reduced value gift fails.

If you set up a QPRT, you are usually the trustee. The trust document gives you full control over management of the house—it's almost like retaining actual

Low Interest Rates Can Reduce the Appeal of a QPRT

With a Qualified Personal Residence Trust (QPRT), you give away your house, but not until some set future date. The delay of the gift reduces the gift's value. Under IRS rules, the amount of the reduction is called the "reasonable rate of return" (for the time you occupy the house). This "reasonable rate," which is called the "7520" rate (named after a section of the Internal Revenue Code) is published every month by the IRS. Currently, the 7520 rate is at historically low levels. This is not good for a QPRT, because the lower the reasonable rate, the higher the value of the gift for federal gift tax purposes. This means more gift tax is assessed than if the rate were higher.

If you give a house worth $2 million to a qualified personal residence trust, and your kids have to wait ten years to get it, the value of the gift is reduced by the reasonable rate of return, the 7520 rate. If the 7520 rate is 3.5 %,

your taxable gift would be valued at more than $1,200,000. But if the reasonable rate were 7%, your gift would be valued at $850,000.

Confusing as this may be, it may not be the end of the story. If the value of your home rises rapidly, in a few years there would be a substantially higher net value of the house on which to calculate the reasonable rate of return. So it might turn out to have been wiser to put your house in a QPRT, now, at a 3.5% reasonable rate, than a few years later, even if the reasonable rate had risen to 7%.

> **SEE AN EXPERT**
> **Get help from an expert.** If you've read this, you've surely learned that establishing a QPRT is a tricky business. Talk to an expert to evaluate whether or not a QPRT makes sense for you.

home ownership. Among other things, this means that you can still take an income tax deduction for mortgage interest and real estate taxes on the house.

When carefully drafted, the trust document creating your QPRT can allow you to make additional payments to the trust for mortgage payments, taxes, insurance, and improvements. The document should also

give you freedom to sell the property and reinvest the proceeds in another home.

Possibly more importantly, you can retain the right, under IRS rules, to sell a principal residence and reinvest sale proceeds of $250,000 without capital gains tax. You may be able to take the proceeds and convert the QPRT into a GRAT.

Reversionary Interests in a QPRT

One of the major reasons for the popularity of QPRTs is that the grantor can retain certain "reversionary interests." Many estate planners suggest that wealthy couples include a specific type of reversionary interest clause in a QPRT. This clause directs that if one spouse dies before the end of the term, the house is to be returned to the spouse's estate and given to the surviving spouse, so the unlimited estate tax marital deduction can be used.

> **EXAMPLE:** Celeste puts her summer cottage in a QPRT that will last 15 years; at the end of that period, the cottage will go to her daughter, Anna. But Celeste keeps a reversionary interest in the cottage so that, if she dies during the term of the trust, the cottage reverts to her estate instead of going to her daughter. This would result in the property actually passing to Celeste's husband, so no estate tax will have to be paid if Celeste dies during the term.

In the past, you could structure a QPRT so that you had the right to purchase back the property from the trust before the term ended. Because the IRS viewed you as the property's owner until the trust period ended, you had no taxable gain or loss on this purchase. This technique was widely used to give the final beneficiaries a cost basis in the residence of current market value. The IRS, however, was extremely critical of this procedure, and now prohibits the sale of the residence back to the grantor or the grantor's spouse. (See Prop. Treas. Reg. 25.2702-5.)

SEE AN EXPERT

You will need expert help to draft a QPRT. If you think a QPRT is right for you, see an experienced and knowledgeable attorney who keeps up to date with trust and tax laws.

QPRTs at a Glance

- You create the trust and fund it with your house. You retain the right to live in the house or to sell it and buy a new one.
- The value of the gift for gift tax purposes is determined when you transfer the house to the trust. It is reduced by your retained interest of living in the house.
- When the term ends, the trust is terminated and the final beneficiary receives the trust assets.

Drawbacks of QPRTs

As with all grantor-retained interest trusts, the flip side of the potentially big tax advantages of a QPRT are potentially big disadvantages. The drawbacks are essentially the same as for a GRAT or GRUT, covered above. One drawback unique to a QPRT is that at the end of the trust period, you no longer own your home. If you want to stay, you will owe fair rent to the final beneficiaries. For the wealthy, paying rent is often just another good way to pass on money to their children without gift tax and also to reduce their estate and, consequently, its tax. But for people with less money, it could surely be at least a burden, if not a grave risk.

Regular GRITs

You establish a "regular" GRIT by giving property of any kind, such as stock, money, or land, and retaining the right to the income from the property for a set term. Congress eliminated the advantages of regular GRITs for direct family members, but not for other beneficiaries. In fact, nieces, nephews, and cousins, as well as friends, can still be final beneficiaries for GRITs funded with property other than a personal residence. This is one strategy unmarried couples can use—and indeed, benefit from—because they are not legally "family."

In a regular GRIT, you receive all of the income from the trust property for a set term. The gift tax value of the gift consists of what the final beneficiary is expected to receive at the end of the set term. As with all of the other grantor-retained interest trusts, the IRS values the property for gift tax purposes when the trust is established, and does not revalue it again when the property is distributed to the final beneficiaries. Your income interest is subtracted from the total worth of the property to determine the value of the gift. The IRS tables used for this calculation take into account current interest rates, your age, and the length of the term.

Remember King Lear

In a perfect world, a parent might create a QPRT for the benefit of a child or grandchild, who will lovingly allow the parent to continue to reside in the house until death. The child or grandchild would then, at the death of the parent, move in or sell the house.

Sadly, this is not always what happens. (Surprise—there's need and even greed in some families.) When several children are the final beneficiaries, they may decide to sell the property as soon as they become its legal owners. If they need the money and don't care what happens to the parent (the grantor), that parent could find him- or herself losing a place to live.

Even if the parent is wealthy and could afford another house, a QPRT might make it easier for a well-meaning child to pack a parent off to a nursing home. After all, the child could rationalize, it's not even the parent's house anymore.

Making another trust the final beneficiary of a QPRT can sometimes alleviate these potential problems, if you select a trustee who'll treat you honorably. Still, the trustee has a legal obligation to the final beneficiaries to produce the most income possible from the trust, which might necessitate selling the house. And if you can't trust your own kids, how can you be confident a separate trustee will be more reliable?

The actual gift is usually substantially discounted for gift tax purposes.

> **EXAMPLE:** Joseph creates a ten-year GRIT for the benefit of his longtime companion, Al. He funds it with a stock portfolio worth $1 million. Because he will receive all of the income for ten years, the gift to Al in the GRIT is valued at much less than what Al will receive. For estate and gift tax purposes, the gift retains its original gift tax value no matter what the stock is worth ten years later, when Al becomes the owner (assuming Joseph is still alive). If Joseph doesn't survive the term, the full value of the trust assets as of the date of his death will be included in his taxable estate, just as if he had done nothing.

Regular GRITs at a Glance

- You create and fund the trust, specifying how long it is to last. The trust beneficiary must not be a "family member."
- The value of the gift for gift tax purposes is determined when you fund the trust.
- The trustee pays you all income annually.
- When the term ends, the trust is terminated, and trust assets go to the final beneficiary.

As with the other trusts discussed above, the shorter the term, the larger the taxable gift to the final beneficiary. But if you are in good health, and especially if you are single, regular GRITS still offer an attractive method of giving gifts, reducing the size of an estate and saving on taxes at the same time.

Questions to Ask About a Grantor-Retained Interest Trust

If a GRAT, GRUT, QPRT, or GRIT sounds appealing, you need to sit down with an estate planning expert and carefully assess your situation. An expert should compare using any of these trusts with other possible estate planning alternatives. At the end, make sure you can answer these questions:

- How do the tax savings from this type of trust compare with simply giving the gift directly (with any gift tax assessed), or making the gift over a period of years, using the annual gift tax exclusion repeatedly and allowing the beneficiary to invest the money you give?
- What are the likely savings overall, taking into consideration possible capital gains tax paid by the final beneficiary if he or she sells the trust property?
- Given your age, health, and financial situation, and your feelings about money and security, can you risk parting with these assets irrevocably?
- Are you confident that your present feelings about whom you name as your final beneficiaries will remain the same for years?
- Is it better to create a grantor-retained interest trust and pay gift tax now (if

necessary) on the gift property? Or is it wiser to hang on to the property and let your estate pay any estate tax due on this property after your death?

- Is a grantor-retained interest trust really desirable? Consider your overall financial picture and the possible alternatives, including:
  - the personal estate tax exemption
  - a program of tax-exempt gifts over a number of years
  - using an AB disclaimer trust so both spouses' personal estate tax exemptions are used
  - QTIP trusts
  - charitable trusts, or
  - life insurance policies owned by others on your life.

Answering these questions, and other personal ones that will surely come up, is time-consuming and requires a high level of expertise in estate planning. And remember that regulations concerning these discounted gifts change frequently, particularly the IRS interest tables. If your expert can't address all of your questions or thinks that you should leave all these decisions up to him or her, quickly find another expert who is willing to listen to you and work with you, on your terms.

Disclaimers: After-Death Estate Tax Planning

t may sound strange, but after you die, one or more of your beneficiaries may decline part or all of the property you left them. Refusing to take an inheritance is called "disclaiming" it. A beneficiary has the legal right under federal law (I.R.C. § 2518) to disclaim or refuse all, or any part, of a gift. If a beneficiary disclaims property, it goes to the person you specified in your trust or will to receive it if the primary beneficiary cannot or does not take it. In other words, the person who winds up with the gift is the alternate beneficiary for that gift, or, if you didn't name an alternate beneficiary, your residuary beneficiary.

You may wonder why anyone in our materially oriented society would be so unworldly as to refuse even some of an inheritance. It's not because the people who disclaim are noble or saintly. (They may be, but that's not what disclaimers are about.) The most common reason people disclaim gifts is to lighten their individual or their family's overall estate tax burden. Also, some people simply want property they could inherit to go instead to needier relations, without having to give it to them and being subject to gift tax. Disclaimers can also be used with an AB disclaimer trust, as explained in Chapter 18. Disclaimers can be an important tool for any substantial estate.

Advantages of Disclaimers

Disclaimers can be an effective way for a beneficiary who already has plenty of property to pass a gift along to another person (usually a family member) who has less. Also, disclaimers can be used to save on estate and gift taxes.

EXAMPLE: Roger, an elderly widower, has an estate worth $540,000. He leaves it equally to his two children, George and Carlotta, and provides that if one of them cannot or does not take his or her half, it will go to the other. When Roger dies, his middle-aged children are in very different financial shape. Carlotta is a prosperous clothing designer, with an estate of roughly $3 million. Her husband has a similar-sized estate. George hasn't fared well financially. His real estate business (his latest enterprise) was marginal from its beginning five years ago, and it has been in a serious slump over the past year. George has almost no savings or other assets and a child with special educational needs.

Carlotta and George are close. Carlotta decides to disclaim her half of her father's estate so the entire $540,000 goes to George. Carlotta disclaimed the gift not to save on estate tax, but because she felt George needed it and she didn't.

Estate and Gift Tax Savings

Once an estate reaches a certain size ($5.34 million in 2014), estate tax kicks in—and the tax is hefty. (See Chapter 15.) And no matter what happens with the estate tax laws, disclaimers will always be important for many who need or want to shift assets to a different heir after someone's death.

Disclaimers reduce estate and gift taxes because, under federal tax law, any property disclaimed by a beneficiary is never legally owned by that person. That means it cannot be included in that beneficiary's taxable estate at death. In addition, no gift tax is assessed against the person who disclaims a gift (in effect, giving it to someone else), again because the person never owned it.

While estate tax still exists, disclaimers can be particularly useful when a primary beneficiary already has a large estate and receiving the gift could add significantly to his or her eventual tax bill. If the alternate beneficiary has much less wealth, then overall estate tax is reduced.

> **EXAMPLE:** Barton dies in 2014 and leaves his estate of $1 million to his sister Elizabeth. She is in her late 70s and already has an estate worth $5 million. The alternate beneficiaries for Barton's estate are Elizabeth's two children, both in their 30s, with very little property.
>
> If Elizabeth accepted the gift, her estate would total $6 million, over the estate tax threshold. If Elizabeth instead disclaims the gift, it will be divided between her two children, and no estate tax will be due at her death.

Clearly, disclaiming property can result in substantial estate tax advantages. It is solely up to the beneficiary to decide whether or not to disclaim a gift. A beneficiary who is insecure, needy, or even a tad greedy may choose not to disclaim property, even though disclaiming might be the wisest choice in light of "objective" personal need and overall estate tax consequences. But after all, the gift was left to that beneficiary. Disclaiming may make sense from the entire family's point of view, but it's hard to see it as a moral obligation.

Fine-Tuning Gifts

Disclaimers can allow beneficiaries to make adjustments regarding who gets what, no matter how much an estate is worth. This can be done to equalize beneficiaries' financial positions. The power to disclaim can also help beneficiaries avoid problems of owning something together, having to come up with the money to buy out co-owners, or having to sell property that one of them loves.

> **EXAMPLE:** Tony, a bachelor, leaves his entire estate to his two nephews, Phil and Angelo, in equal shares. Each is the alternate beneficiary for the other's gift.
>
> Among the assets at Tony's death is an ocean beachfront vacation home. Phil, with a sizable estate of his own, doesn't care about the ocean and spends his summers in the mountains. Angelo, on the other hand, is not as well-off financially and has vacationed every summer of his life at the beach cottage. Phil disclaims his one-half interest in the beach property, keeping

it out of his already large estate (and paying no gift tax whatever) when it then goes to Angelo.

Disclaimers can also be used when a person wants the property to go to the next in line for the gift.

EXAMPLE: Babette leaves her house to her three children, in equal shares. Her living trust provides that the alternate beneficiaries for each child's share are his or her children. When Babette dies, all three of her children are quite well off. Two intend to accept their share of the house. One child, Fritz, disclaims his share because he decides it's wiser to let it pass to his children, who are in their early 20s and starting their careers (or, at least, starting to earn money). Fritz knows his children will find much security in the financial nest egg his disclaimer provides for each.

If Babette had specified that the alternate beneficiaries for the house were her other children, Fritz would not have disclaimed his share. He would not have wanted that share divided between his brother and sister, bringing no benefit to his children.

Adjusting for Unforeseen Circumstances

Disclaimers can also be valuable under pressing circumstances. For instance, a person may be overgenerous or overoptimistic regarding his finances when he prepares his estate plan, and his financial situation at death may turn out to be worse than he anticipated. Beneficiaries can use disclaimers to achieve fair results—results the person would surely have wanted if he'd known how his finances would turn out.

EXAMPLE: Sven, who's doing well in business, prepares a living trust that leaves $300,000 each to his three children and the rest of his estate to his spouse. Later, after some business setbacks and an extended illness, his wealth has dwindled. When Sven dies, there will be almost nothing left for his widow after the $900,000 is given to his children. The children generously disclaim their inheritance so the money will go to their mother for her support.

This sounds good—indeed, ideal—but there is, of course, an obvious risk if a disclaimer is needed for this purpose. A child or any beneficiary may be unwilling to give up an inheritance, no matter what hardship that creates for someone else, even a parent. It would have been wiser for Sven to rewrite his living trust after his business reversals, simply leaving all his property to his wife.

IRS Rules for Disclaimers

Federal law requires that a beneficiary's disclaimer must be "qualified." This means that it must meet certain rules set out in I.R.C. § 2518. If these rules aren't met, the person disclaiming will not avoid legal ownership of the property for estate or gift tax purposes, and the major purpose of the disclaimer will be lost. The IRS requirements are:

- The disclaimer must be in writing.
- A disclaimer by an adult must be completed within nine months of the death of the person leaving the property.
- A minor who has been left property must disclaim within nine months after reaching age 21.
- The person who disclaims property may not accept any benefit from the property before disclaiming it. (A limited exception exists for a surviving spouse).
- The person refusing the property may not direct where it then goes. The deceased person's will or trust document determines who receives the disclaimed property.

Putting the Disclaimer in Writing

A beneficiary who wants to disclaim inherited property—for whatever reason and whatever the type of property—is responsible for putting the disclaimer in writing. The beneficiary must deliver the written disclaimer to the person who is in control of the property at that time. This is usually the successor trustee of a living trust or the executor of a will.

EXAMPLE: In her living trust, Carla leaves a money market account to her son, Francisco, and another of roughly equal value to her daughter, Eva. The trust provides that if either child dies before Carla does, the money goes to the other. She names Francisco as successor trustee of her trust.

At Carla's death, Eva is financially comfortable, but Francisco is struggling. Eva is also aware of the fact that her mother spent a large amount on her college and graduate education, while Francisco chose not to go to college. She wishes to disclaim, so he can receive the money directly from Eva's estate without it being a taxable gift from her.

As successor trustee, Francisco is bound by law to follow the directions in his mother's trust. If Eva calls him up and tells him to take her money, he can't legally do it. He needs the written disclaimer so he can follow the trust instructions and satisfy IRS regulations. Only when armed with the signed disclaimer from Eva will he have the power to change his mother's primary instructions and take the money himself. (See "Including Disclaimers in Your Estate Plan," below, covering complexities that can arise when a trustee of a living trust disclaims trust property or receives it by disclaimer.)

The Nine-Month Deadline

IRS rules require that a disclaimer by adults must be made within nine months of the death of the original giver—that is, the trust grantor or will writer.

SEE AN EXPERT

Disclaimers by minors. A minor can disclaim a gift within nine months of becoming age 21. This raises some odd questions: Who manages the property until the minor turns 21? What can be done with it? Who may benefit from the property during this time? The answers depend on state law. It's a very complicated legal matter. If you are the parent or guardian of a minor who has been left property and think it's possible the minor would want to disclaim that property at age 21, seek some good professional advice.

The nine-month period is designed to allow enough time for survivors to begin getting back on their feet emotionally and to get the information they need to make wise financial decisions.

EXAMPLE: Makoto dies suddenly in 2014, leaving a wife, Hanako, in her 60s, and two adult children. His living trust leaves everything to Hanako or, if she doesn't survive him, to the children. Makoto's elder son, Keiji, who is executor of the will, sees immediately that Makoto's estate is worth about $3 million. Hanako has substantial assets of her own. When Keiji hires a lawyer, the lawyer advises that Hanako disclaim some of the property for tax purposes. But no one in the family wants to think about these issues shortly after Makoto's death.

The nine-month period gives the attorney time to draft a tax savings plan and explain it to the family. Also, the family has a chance to look at the situation and assess who needs what, and when.

In the end, Hanako decides to disclaim a substantial portion of Makoto's property. But it's not only possible estate-tax savings that motivate Hanako. She believes her children need this money now, when they are working hard and trying to raise their own children. With the disclaimer, they get it, with no taxable gift having been made by Hanako.

No Personal Benefit

A beneficiary who wants to disclaim property cannot use or accept any benefit from the property. Also, a beneficiary who will receive any benefit from the property after the disclaimer cannot disclaim the property. For example, a beneficiary cannot disclaim property that then goes into a trust that pays, or even could pay, the beneficiary any income. For instance, if you were to disclaim a gift that goes into a family pot trust with 15 potential beneficiaries, including you, the disclaimer is not valid. The property still goes to the next beneficiary in line, but the transaction is considered, legally, a simple gift, and you may be assessed gift tax if the property is valuable enough.

Including Disclaimers in Your Estate Plan

You might help your inheritors by directly incorporating your wishes concerning disclaimed gifts into your estate plan.

Planning for Disclaimers

Even though disclaimers are expressly authorized by federal law, incorporating a specific disclaimer provision in your living trust or will can create a helpful guide for your beneficiaries. A clause permitting beneficiaries to disclaim gifts you leave tells them that you know about disclaimers and personally authorize them. A beneficiary who wants to make a disclaimer doesn't have to worry about going against your desires. Also, not all beneficiaries (or successor trustees or executors) know about disclaimers, so specifically authorizing them can be a good means of alerting your beneficiaries that they exist.

You can also specify who is to receive property that one of your beneficiaries disclaims. This would be desirable only if you don't want a disclaimed gift to go the alternate beneficiary. This might be the case if the alternate beneficiary is likely to be in the same financial position as the primary beneficiary, as can be the case with husband and wife.

EXAMPLE: Chang, a widower, leaves his $500,000 estate to his son Tai, with Tai's wife, Claudia, as the alternate beneficiary. But Chang also provides in his living trust document that should Tai disclaim any property, it then goes to Chang's favorite nephew. When Chang dies, Tai's and Claudia's assets are quite large; neither needs the inheritance. By contrast, the nephew, who is just starting out in business, really needs the money. Tai disclaims the gift, and the $500,000 goes directly to the nephew.

Because Tai never owns the property, his own estate is not increased for estate tax purposes. Nor has he made a taxable gift by disclaiming the gift and letting it go to Chang's nephew.

If Tai had accepted the gift, he could remove it from his estate by subsequently giving it to the nephew. But this would mean Tai would be assessed gift tax for that gift.

Problems With Trustees Directing Disclaimed Property

The law does not allow a person who disclaims property to determine who will receive it instead. This can present problems for trustees when the disclaimed property is held in trust.

Many trusts do not allow the trustee to determine who receives any trust income or property. The beneficiaries and their shares are all specified in the trust document. But if a beneficiary is considering disclaiming property that will then go into a trust, and the beneficiary is a trustee that has any powers at all over the trust assets, expert advice is needed. For instance, a power to distribute trust principal if a child needs it could raise a red flag for the IRS. Even a power by the trustee to allocate income and principal might cause a disclaimer to fail.

Someone who both serves as the successor trustee of a living trust and inherits trust property may run into complications disclaiming property. The basic rule is that if you have any authority to direct where any of the disclaimed property will go, you can't disclaim it. For gift and estate tax purposes, it will be considered your own property and a gift from you to the person who receives it. To avoid this problem, you must either resign as trustee or decline the authority to direct distribution of trust property.

> **EXAMPLE:** Tsultrim and her husband, Yeshe, each create a living trust, providing that on a spouse's death, $1 million of that spouse's property goes directly into a trust for their children. Any remaining property goes outright to the surviving spouse. The surviving spouse will serve as trustee of the children's trust and have broad trustee powers, including the authority to distribute trust principal and income to the children if they need it.
>
> Yeshe dies first. The couple's estate turns out to be larger than expected, so it would be desirable, from the overall estate tax viewpoint, for Tsultrim to disclaim the property Yeshe left to her

and let it go into the children's trust. Estate taxes would be lower in the long run if some tax were paid on part of Yeshe's property at his death.

> But as long as she serves as trustee of the trust for the children, Tsultrim can't disclaim any of the property Yeshe left her. That's because, as trustee, she has the authority to direct the distribution of property to the trust beneficiaries. To have a valid disclaimer, she will have to also disclaim this authority or resign as trustee altogether. Otherwise, every distribution to a child would be considered a gift from her and taxed accordingly.

If you anticipate that a disclaimer may make sense, you can include a brief letter or note in the envelope with your will or living trust alerting the executor or successor trustee to the law about disclaimers so they can make intelligent choices about their powers and get help from a tax adviser if necessary. In fact, you may want to suggest that the executor or successor trustee make no distributions whatsoever until all concerned have consulted a tax expert.

When you're preparing a living trust, be sure to discuss disclaimer possibilities with an estate planning expert, and be sure the trust document is drafted so that potential problems are eliminated to the extent possible. For example, if your successor trustee would have to resign to make her disclaimer valid, it's vitally important that you name the right alternate successor trustee.

Combining Estate Tax–Saving Trusts

I f you have a really large estate, you may want to use more than one tax-saving trust in your estate plan. There are no legal rules or even fixed customs regarding how to combine trusts. This chapter can give you a sense of the possibilities offered. Your individual situation and desires will determine what combination, if any, is right for you.

SEE AN EXPERT

Combining estate tax–saving trusts requires a lawyer. Combining estate tax–saving trusts involves sophisticated, technical legal work. So it should come as no surprise that you must hire a lawyer to do the work. Indeed, to understand precisely how different options could work for you, you'll need to carefully discuss your situation with a lawyer. Your legal bill will probably be substantial. But then, you must have considerable wealth before it's worth combining different trusts, and doing so can (presumably) save you and your inheritors a bundle. A good lawyer's cost is probably well worth it.

Combining Two Estate Tax–Saving Trusts

One or both members of a couple, especially in second or subsequent marriages, may want to combine an AB disclaimer trust with a QTIP trust. The spouse who creates the trusts names the other as life beneficiary of both trusts. Each trust's final beneficiaries, also named by the spouse who creates the trusts, receive that trust property when the life

beneficiary dies. If the spouse who created the trusts survives the other, all his or her property goes, via the trusts, directly to the final beneficiaries.

By combining these two trusts, you can achieve several desirable goals:

- You make use of your personal estate tax exemption with the AB disclaimer trust.
- If your spouse survives you, all of your property over the amount of the personal exemption in the year of your death is placed in the QTIP trust and qualifies for the unlimited marital deduction. No federal estate tax is paid on your death.
- Your surviving spouse, as life beneficiary, has restricted rights to spend principal of Trust A, which conserves trust assets for the final beneficiaries. Restrictions are also normally imposed on the rights of the surviving spouse to spend principal of the QTIP trust. Under IRS rules, the surviving spouse must be given unrestricted rights to all trust income generated from assets in the QTIP trust.
- You determine who will ultimately receive all property in your AB and QTIP trusts after your surviving spouse dies.

EXAMPLE 1: Malcolm, age 61, has been married to Sadie, age 47, for four years. He has three children from a former marriage. Sadie has some assets of her own, consisting of savings worth $225,000. Malcolm, on the other hand, owns his house and various investments worth a total of $8 million. He also owns a life insurance policy that will pay $200,000 to Sadie at his death.

Although his children seem to accept Sadie, Malcolm senses uneasiness among them about whether they'll actually receive the inheritance they've been expecting from him. What might happen if Sadie survives Malcolm by 20 or 30 years: A remarriage? A sudden urge to seek thrills and bet fortunes at the racetrack?

Wanting to take care of everybody, and also to avoid hard feelings, Malcolm creates the following plan. (See Chapter 24 for a fuller discussion of using AB trusts with second marriages.)

If Sadie survives him, upon his death, his property will be divided into an AB trust, which will contain property worth the amount of the personal exemption at the year of his death, and a QTIP trust for the rest of his property. Sadie is the life beneficiary of both trusts, to receive all trust income. She has no rights to spend either trust principal. When Sadie dies, the property in both trusts will go to Malcolm's three children in equal shares.

Malcolm names Sadie and his daughter Hilda, the most levelheaded of his children and the one who gets along with Sadie the best, to be co-trustees of both trusts.

EXAMPLE 2: Carla has assets worth $7 million; her husband Peter's property totals $200,000. Carla is 73, Peter is 66. Carla has two children by a previous marriage. She wants to be sure her estate will avoid estate tax no matter when she dies. She also wants both to preserve her estate for her children and to help Peter to live a comfortable life, if he survives her.

Carla creates an AB trust and a QTIP trust. Peter is the life beneficiary of both trusts, and her children are the final beneficiaries. Carla dies in 2014, when the personal estate tax exemption is $5.34 million. That amount of her property is placed in the AB trust. The other $1.66 million goes into the QTIP trust.

The property in the AB trust is tax free under the personal exemption. The amount in the QTIP is tax free under the marital deduction.

Combining a Charitable Trust With Other Estate Tax–Saving Trusts

If you want to leave some of your property to causes you care deeply about, you may be eligible for some tax breaks. For example, gifts made to tax-exempt charities through a charitable trust are exempt from estate tax. The other potential benefits of using a charitable trust are that you take an income tax deduction on the worth of the

Leaving All Property Over the Exempt Amount Outright to the Surviving Spouse

Many couples, particularly in first marriages, have no need for a QTIP trust. Commonly, these couples share ownership of most or all of their property and want the same people, usually their children, to eventually inherit their property. These couples have no desire for the primary purpose of a QTIP trust, which is to guarantee that a spouse controls final disposition of her or his property. Rather, a spouse simply leaves all property over the exempt amount outright to the other spouse, trusting that spouse will do what's best for everyone.

> **EXAMPLE:** Miles and Suno, in their early 50s, have been married over 25 years. They have two children and substantial assets (all co-owned) worth over $6 million. Their estate plan consists of preparing an AB disclaimer trust and a direction that any property above the exempt amount be left outright to the surviving spouse.
>
> While both Miles and Suno want their children to eventually inherit their property, neither wants or feels the need to impose on the other the restrictions of a QTIP trust. If one spouse dies prematurely, the other may survive for decades. Why limit this spouse's right over the deceased spouse's property?

property you give to charity and you also avoid paying capital gains tax if the charity sells the assets you gave it after they've appreciated.

Unless you are extremely wealthy or don't want to leave anything to family or friends, you may understandably be reluctant to give or leave significant assets to a charity. Fortunately, you can make a charitable gift, but do it in such a way that the value of the property donated is replaced in your estate. That way your other beneficiaries receive almost as much as they would have without the charitable trust.

How can you make this magic happen? In the right circumstances, by creating both a charitable trust and an irrevocable life insurance trust. You buy a policy payable to your noncharity beneficiaries, and transfer that policy to the trust. The proceeds of the life insurance policy will be roughly equal to the amount your individual beneficiaries would have inherited from you if you hadn't made the charitable gift. And because you've established the life insurance trust, the proceeds from the policy won't be included in your taxable estate.

Here's a summary of how you might use a life insurance trust to replace money "lost" to individual beneficiaries because of a charitable gift:

1. You make a gift to charity through a charitable trust.
2. You create the life insurance trust. You fund it, for the purpose of making premium payments, with the income

tax savings you obtained by making the charitable gift. This means there is no significant actual cost to you to create and fund the trust. You choose a life insurance policy that will pay out, at your death, more or less the same amount that you gave the charity.

3. You include Crummey provisions in your life insurance trust document. These clauses allow gifts you make to the trust to qualify for the annual gift tax exclusion. Otherwise, if you gave money directly to the trust, it wouldn't qualify for the exclusion.

4. Your gift money remains in the insurance trust until the trustee spends it on insurance premiums. The net effect is that you have indirectly paid the insurance proceeds. (You can get in trouble with the IRS if you pay them directly.)

EXAMPLE: Aldo has four children and assets worth $6 million. He funds a charitable trust with land currently worth $700,000. He bought the land for $300,000. The charity sells the land and buys stock that will provide payments to him for life. The charity will take what remains of the trust assets at his death.

When he creates the trust, Aldo obtains a significant income tax deduction. Also, by giving the land to charity, he avoids capital gains tax on the increase in value of $400,000 when the land is sold and converted to income-producing assets. And by removing $700,000 from his estate, he saves on estate tax, lowering his taxable estate to $5.3 million.

The property Aldo has given to charity would have gone to his children. But if he had kept the property, it might have been subject to estate tax, depending on the year of his death. If he chooses, he can give the payments made to him from the charity directly to the children as gifts.

Aldo creates an irrevocable life insurance trust. He buys and transfers to the trust a life insurance policy for $700,000—very roughly, the amount "lost" to his children because of his charitable gift. Each year, Aldo gives the trustee the amount of the premiums, which his children may withdraw. They refuse these "gifts" and the trustee pays the premiums.

If you are in reasonably good health (and especially if you're young), replacing the donated assets by life insurance is usually the preferred choice. If you are elderly, in poor health, or not insurable for any reason, you can try other replacement methods.

EXAMPLE: After Aldo establishes his charitable trust, he discovers that he is ill and that insurance on his life would be too costly, if available at all. He still sets up an irrevocable trust for his children and donates money to it. The money he donates to the trust is subject to gift tax, but the trustee purchases assets he and Aldo hope will greatly appreciate in value. Depending on the expertise of the trustee and some luck, the money each child would have received but for the charitable gift may eventually be recouped.

Combining Three Different Estate Tax–Saving Trusts

For larger estates, you may even want to make use of several different estate tax–saving trusts. For instance, you could combine an AB disclaimer trust for property worth up to the exempt amount at death with a generation-skipping trust and a charitable trust.

> **EXAMPLE:** Guillermo and Maria, a couple in their late 70s, have assets worth $16 million, owned equally. They want to leave their property to their children and grandchildren and to some friends and charities.
>
> Guillermo and Maria each prepare living trusts, leaving specific gifts to identified friends. Then they create an AB disclaimer trust and transfer the bulk of their property to that trust. Using the AB trust, each spouse:
> - sets up a charitable trust, leaving $900,000 to named charities, and
> - sets up four generation-skipping trusts, one for each of their

grandchildren (each trust is funded with $500,000).

> The rest of each spouse's trust property is left to the surviving spouse, with the right to disclaim. All disclaimed property goes to Trust A of the deceased spouse.
>
> Guillermo dies in 2014. His specific gifts are transferred to the named beneficiaries and $900,000 goes to the charity in trust. Maria disclaims $2 million of his property, which goes to the four generation-skipping trusts. All Guillermo's remaining property goes to Maria.

Using Ongoing Trusts and Gift Giving to Reduce Estate Tax

Ongoing trusts can be combined in a number of ways to reduce estate tax for the wealthy. You can leave gifts to your spouse, children, grandchildren, and to charities, all by using different trusts. Here's an example of combining a generation-skipping trust, a charitable remainder unitrust, an irrevocable life insurance trust, an AB trust, and a QTIP trust, all in one estate plan.

> **EXAMPLE:** Doris is 65 and married to Ted, her second husband. She has two children from her first marriage, both of whom are financially comfortable, and six grandchildren. Doris's estate

is worth $7 million; Ted has a much smaller estate of $160,000.

If she dies first, Doris wants Ted to continue to live in the prosperous style they've enjoyed, but she also wants most of her assets to go eventually to her children and grandchildren. She also wishes to contribute a sizable portion of her estate to charity. First, she sets up a charitable remainder unitrust of $1 million. Ted and Doris will receive income from the trust annually. Next, she takes an income tax deduction based on the value of her gift to the charitable trust. Using the money saved on income tax, she purchases life insurance and funds an irrevocable life insurance trust. The beneficiaries of the life insurance are her children; they will receive an amount roughly equal to the amount she gave to charity. Proceeds from the life insurance trust will not be included in her estate for estate tax purposes.

Doris also establishes an AB trust, with Ted as the life beneficiary. When Ted dies, this trust's assets will be shared by her children.

Next, she establishes a generation-skipping trust of $1 million, with income paid to her children during their lives. This trust may be subject to federal estate tax when Doris dies, but not when the middle generation (her children) dies. When they die, this trust's assets will be distributed to the grandchildren tax free.

Any remaining property in Doris's estate will go into a QTIP trust, with all income going to Ted for life, and the assets to her children at his death. The trustee, one of Doris's children, can use the principal of this trust for Ted's medical care or basic support if the trustee decides it is needed.

Finally, Doris also adopts a plan of giving gifts from her present income while she's alive, to keep her estate from increasing and eventually resulting in more estate tax. She gives $14,000 annually, gift tax free, to each of her two children, their spouses, and the six grandchildren. This is a total of ten people, so $140,000 a year is given away tax free.

Property Control Trusts for Second or Subsequent Marriages

In many second or subsequent marriages, one or both spouses may feel truly conflicted about estate planning. On one hand, a surviving spouse may well need use of, or income from, the deceased spouse's property, or may even need to spend some of that property to live as comfortably as before. On the other hand, if a spouse has children from a former marriage, he or she may want to be sure that the bulk of his or her property eventually goes to those children. A spouse may not want the other spouse to wind up with complete legal control of his or her property. A surviving spouse who controls the property of the deceased spouse could decide to leave the deceased spouse's children nothing. These kinds of concerns—which can be dicey at the best of times—become even more complicated if your current spouse and children from a former marriage don't get along.

Unmarried Couples

This chapter talks in terms of subsequent marriages and surviving spouses because most people who do this type of estate planning are married. But the principles apply equally to unmarried couples with children from previous relationships.

This chapter discusses basic estate planning options for couples in second or subsequent marriages. (From here on, I use the shorthand "second marriage" to refer to any marriage after the first, whether it's the second or the seventh.) The focus is on trusts, particularly what I call a "marital property control trust." This type of trust imposes controls over your property after your death, so that the surviving spouse has some use of it, or income from it, but never owns it outright. The property goes to your children (or other beneficiaries you've chosen) when the surviving spouse dies. By placing restrictions on the surviving spouse's rights to trust property, you can feel confident that most or all of the trust principal will remain intact for your children. Marital property control trusts are, of course, no guarantee that family conflicts and tensions will be eliminated or even reduced. But they can achieve at least some control over your assets and give you the comfort that you've done your best to provide for your spouse and your children.

This chapter focuses exclusively on concerns of spouses in second marriages, because for many people, this is a central concern of their estate planning. But trusts imposing property controls can be useful in many situations, not just those involving second marriages. (See Chapter 25.)

 RESOURCE

Learn more about estate planning for second marriages. For a thorough exploration of all significant estate planning concerns that can arise in second or subsequent marriages, see *Estate Planning for Blended Families*, by Richard E. Barnes (Nolo).

Evaluating Your Situation

Tolstoy began *Anna Karenina* with the famous sentence, "Happy families are all alike; every unhappy family is unhappy in its own way." Whether families involving second marriages are happy or not, each is certainly unique in its own way. With a "blended" (or not so blended) family, you have to make a realistic appraisal of your unique situation to do sensible estate planning. Here are some factors to consider:

Your financial status. You'll need to take into account the value of property you and your spouse each own separately, and the value you own together.

The relationship between you and your spouse. Here, you'll need to think carefully about your needs and expectations and those of your spouse. For example, do either of you depend on an income from or property of the other? Is one of you significantly younger? Is one or both of you in bad health? What expectations do you each have regarding inheriting the other's property and what do you each want to do with the property you own?

Do you have a prenuptial agreement? A "prenup," as a prenuptial or premarital agreement is commonly called, is a legally binding agreement made before marriage that covers property rights—what's his, what's hers, what's theirs—during the marriage and after it ends, whether by divorce or the death of one spouse. (A "postnup" is a similar type of agreement that's made after marriage, though it may be subject to more restrictions than a prenup.) Prenups can override most state marital property laws. However, in many states, you can waive spousal inheritance protections only if you comply with detailed requirements at the time you write and sign your contract. (In addition, you can't use a prenup to waive rights to child support and, in some states, you can't give up the right to alimony. Of course, these issues usually come up during a divorce, not while making an estate plan.)

CAUTION
If you have made a prenup or a postnup. Marital property agreements can affect or even control a spouse's inheritance rights and ability to leave property. If you have a prenup or postnup, be sure that your estate planning documents—your will, any trusts, and all beneficiary designations—are consistent with the terms of your marital contract.

RESOURCE
If you want to learn about prenups. This potentially touchy subject is sensitively and thoroughly explored in *Prenuptial Agreements: How to Write a Fair & Lasting Contract*, by Katherine E. Stoner and Shae Irving (Nolo).

Do you know (and agree on) who owns what? Property ownership can become complex in blended families, especially over time. There can be his property, her property, and our property. And the "our" can be all owned equally, or some equally and some not, or all unequally. If there are any complexities in your property ownership, it's wise to prepare a written marital property agreement setting out who owns what, and signed by both spouses.

Legal constraints controlling how you can leave your property. Various circumstances may restrict what you can do with your property at death. For instance, if you have a prenuptial agreement, you can't unilaterally change it when planning your estate. Your spouse must consent to any changes you want to make to that agreement.

Similarly, if you have a 401(k) or 403(b) plan, by federal law your spouse must receive all funds in the account when you die, unless your spouse waives that right in writing.

Also, in common law states, your spouse has a legal right to inherit a certain portion of your property (usually one third to one half), no matter what you want. (See Chapter 3.) In most states, this right can be waived.

What are your relationships with your children? Just as you must consider the needs and expectations of your spouse, you must think about your relationship with each of your kids. For example, how do you feel about leaving property to your children, particularly if you have children from your present marriage as well as from a former partnership? What do you think your children need or deserve? Do you want to leave each of them an equal amount of property?

What if you become incapacitated? If you're in a second marriage, you should decide what you want done if you become unable to handle your own medical and financial affairs. Chapter 26 discusses the specific documents you can prepare to appoint someone and give that person legal authority to make decisions for you if you can't make them for yourself. Emotions run high in this area, especially in blended families, so reduce the possibility of uncertainty, confusion, or conflict by creating a clear, binding statement of who can act for you and under what limits.

And the final problem, how do you reconcile all these concerns in your estate plan? You must decide how to apportion and balance the property you leave to your spouse with property you leave to your children, as well as any other beneficiaries you want to name.

There are a number of legal devices you can use to carry out your desires. You can simply leave some property outright to your spouse and other property outright to your children. But often the pie doesn't seem quite big enough for that. A spouse may want to leave property for the use of a surviving spouse for life, then to children from former marriages. The most commonly used device to accomplish this is an AB "marital property control trust," discussed below. Other devices that can be used or adapted for second-marriage estate planning include making gifts while living (see Chapter 16), using a QTIP trust (see Chapter 19), and making gifts of minority interests in family businesses (discussed in Chapter 28).

How a Marital Property Control Trust Works

While an AB marital property control trust is in some ways similar to an AB disclaimer trust (discussed in Chapter 18), there are also crucial differences. Both types of trust allow a spouse to leave his or her trust property:

- to the surviving spouse, using a "life estate"; and
- to those named by the deceased spouse to be the final trust beneficiaries, who will receive the property after the surviving spouse dies.

As the life-estate beneficiary, the surviving spouse never acquires legal ownership of the deceased spouse's trust property. The surviving spouse has no right to determine who will be the final beneficiaries of that property; that has already been irrevocably decided by the deceased spouse. Instead, the terms of the trust determine the surviving spouse's right to use the property during his or her lifetime. He or she is normally given the right to income from trust property and the right to use trust property, such as living in a house owned by the trust. The surviving spouse may also be given the rights to "invade" (use) trust principal for basic needs, such as health care costs.

The difference between the AB marital property control trust and the AB disclaimer trust lies in the extent of the surviving spouse's right to use trust property. With an AB disclaimer trust that is intended only to save on estate tax,

the surviving spouse is usually granted the maximum rights to use or spend trust property allowed under IRS rules. In contrast, an AB marital property control trust imposes more extensive restrictions on the rights of the surviving spouse to protect the trust principal so that it remains intact (or at least close to intact) for the final beneficiaries.

EXAMPLE: Lisi and Greg got married in their late 30s. Lisi had a child from a prior marriage; Greg had two children from his prior marriages. Lisi and Greg then had a child together, Dory. Lisi and Greg are now in their early 50s, and decide it's time to prepare their estate plan.

Lisi owns separate property worth $700,000, and Greg owns separate property worth $410,000. Together they own a house that cost $320,000, and is now worth $510,000. Each contributed half the down payment for the house, and they share mortgage payments equally. Also, they own other shared assets worth a total of $375,000.

Each spouse creates a marital property control trust. The other spouse, as life beneficiary, has these rights in the trust property:

- to remain in the house for life
- to receive the income from any trust property, and
- to spend trust principal only for medical costs that can't be paid for from other resources.

Each spouse names the final beneficiaries for his or her trust. Lisi decides that her final beneficiaries are Dory and her daughter from her prior marriage, who will share her trust's principal 50/50. Greg, who is not close to his children from his prior marriage, names them and Dory as his final beneficiaries. Dory will receive 70% of his trust property and the other two children will equally share the remaining 30%.

Because the purpose of an AB marital control trust is to preserve assets for your final beneficiaries, it's immaterial whether or not those assets will be subject to estate tax. You may want to create this type of trust even if your estate is well under the estate tax threshold.

EXAMPLE: Benny and Belle marry when they are in their late 50s. Benny has two children, ages 26 and 24, one each from two prior marriages. Belle has one child, age 19, from her prior marriage. Benny has an estate worth roughly $425,000; Belle's is worth $623,000. Neither estate is at all near the estate tax threshold.

Because neither spouse has enough property to be securely self-sufficient if the other dies first, each creates an AB marital property control trust, allowing the other spouse income for life from the trust but absolutely no right to invade trust principal. This way, they've each ensured that their estate will remain intact, to be received

by their child or children after the surviving spouse dies.

How to Set Up an AB Property Control Trust

Usually, a marital property control trust is combined with a living trust to avoid probate. In that case, the marital property control trust remains revocable, as a component of the living trust, as long as you live and are mentally competent. After your death, your living trust property is transferred to your marital property control trust without probate proceedings. At that point, your marital property control trust becomes irrevocable.

SEE AN EXPERT

Getting help. Because of the complexities involved in setting up this type of trust, you'll need to work with a good lawyer. See Chapter 29 for tips on how to find one.

Restricting the Surviving Spouse's Rights Over Trust Property

You may impose a wide variety of restrictions on your surviving spouse's rights over the property in your AB marital property control trust. For instance, the surviving spouse may be given the right to receive income from the trust, but no right whatsoever to spend trust principal. Or you can name someone other than the surviving spouse to be the trustee of the trust. This obviously keeps one source of real-world power from the surviving spouse. If someone else is the trustee, there's presumably less chance that the surviving spouse will get more than the trust document allows.

EXAMPLE: Leticia, in her 70s, marries Ben, also in his 70s. Leticia has been married twice before and has one grown child from each marriage, a daughter, Lindsay, and a son, Kevin. Her estate consists of her condo, worth $595,000 (all equity), and savings of $1.6 million. Ben owns much less, about $40,000 in savings and stocks. He also receives a modest pension plus Social Security.

Leticia wants her property to eventually go to her two children equally—but if she predeceases Ben, she doesn't want him thrown out on the street. She places her house and savings in a marital property control trust. She appoints Lindsay as trustee.

The trust document gives Ben the right to remain in the house, with all its current furnishings, for his life. If he leaves it for more than four consecutive months, whether to move to some tropical paradise or to a nursing home, the house and furnishings can be sold or rented if the trustee decides that's desirable. Thus, Leticia leaves it up to Lindsay to decide what should happen to the house if Ben vacates

it for more than four months. Leticia doesn't want to require that the house be turned over to her children in these circumstances. She just wants to protect her children, and not have the house empty or rented out by Ben. Leticia fully trusts Lindsay to make a wise decision if this matter comes up.

Ben is also to receive $15,000 per year from the income generated by the money in the trust. If the trust's annual income is lower than $15,000, Ben receives that lesser amount. If the income exceeds $15,000, Ben can be given any portion of the additional income if Lindsay, the trustee, determines he needs it for basic needs, such as health care or everyday expenses.

Each marital property control trust involves the unique circumstances of the couple and final beneficiaries involved. There are no set rules dictating what's right. You must try to foresee the future needs of your spouse and balance those needs with your desire to protect most, if not all, of the principal for your children or other final beneficiaries.

Here are some examples of the controls that can be placed on the surviving spouse's right to trust property:

- Someone other than the survivor can be named as trustee.
- The survivor can live in a house owned (or partially owned) by the trust, but has no right to sell it.

- The survivor can live in a house and can sell it, but only for the purpose of buying another residence, and then only with the approval of all trust beneficiaries.
- The survivor can live in a house but cannot sell it or rent it. And if the survivor moves into a nursing facility and remains there for more than a set time, the house must be turned over to the trust's final beneficiaries.
- The survivor (who is not the trustee) will be paid trust income only as the trustee determines is necessary for medical care or other basic needs.
- The survivor may drive a valuable car owned by the trust, but can sell it only with consent of at least one final beneficiary.
- The survivor must follow specific directions set out in the trust document, down to how he can use many items of trust property and care for valuable items such as antiques.
- If the surviving spouse remarries, the trust ends and the trust property goes to the final beneficiaries.

If your spouse and children don't get along, you may need to face the possibility that you will not be able to create a trust that will make all of them happy. In this case, you simply have to arrive at a resolution that seems the most wise and fair to you.

EXAMPLE: Dottie and Sam have been living together for six years. Dottie is in her 50s and is the sole owner of a prospering women's clothing company. She owns, free and clear, a house worth $290,000, which she bought over 25 years ago. Her business is worth perhaps $1.5 million. (It's usually fairly hard to determine the market value of a small business, because often there is no actual market for it.) Her other assets total $130,000, so her total estate is worth $1.92 million. Sam owns property worth $200,000 and receives a small Social Security allotment.

Dottie has no children. Eventually, she wants her property to go to her niece, Betsy, who works with her in her business. Sam wants his property to go to his two children.

Dottie decides that Sam might need income beyond his Social Security income and whatever his $200,000 may generate, to continue to live in the comfortable style they've enjoyed together. Also, she wants to keep her business intact—most of all, so that Betsy can eventually inherit it, but also so it can produce income for Sam. So Dottie creates an AB marital property control trust, with Sam as the life beneficiary. She names Betsy as trustee, because Betsy will manage the business owned by the trust. Sam is entitled to:

- live in their house for the duration of his life
- sell it and buy another place, if Betsy consents, and

- receive 25% of any profits from the clothing company (leaving the rest for the business to expand or maintain itself), and any income from other assets in the trust; when Sam dies, all the trust property goes to Betsy.

Sam also creates an AB marital property control trust that allows Dottie the income from his assets for her life but prohibits her from spending principal. When Dottie dies, Sam's property will be divided between his children.

Sam's children do not get along well with Dottie, so he's reluctant to appoint one of his children as trustee of his trust. He feels confident that Dottie would not abuse the position of trustee. So he names her to be trustee, with the provision that she must give both children copies of the trust's annual income tax return so they can see that the principal is not being spent.

The Role of the Trustee

Obviously, choosing the right trustee for a marital property control trust is vital. The trustee will have authority to manage the trust property and to make authorized payments to the surviving spouse. (The trustee often has considerable discretion regarding how to manage and invest trust property.) Further, the trustee may have some enforcement—or at least checking-up—responsibilities, to be sure that the

surviving spouse's use of trust property complies with trust requirements. These duties can require diplomacy or tough decision making.

Heading Off Family Conflict

Choosing the trustee can be a difficult task, requiring some serious thought. If your current spouse and your children are on good terms or, better yet, really trust each other, you may not face much of a problem. Still, even when the nicest of people are involved, you should understand that there's an inherent potential for conflict between the surviving spouse and the final beneficiaries. The surviving spouse may want or believe she or he needs to spend trust property, including principal. The final beneficiaries clearly have an interest in preserving as much of the trust principal as possible. As you may have observed, even usually kind people can at times act in self-interested, and even mean-spirited, ways.

Whatever rules and restrictions you place over the surviving spouse's rights to trust property, it will be the trustee who must enforce them. So it's best if both you and all the beneficiaries have complete confidence in this trustee. If your surviving spouse or one of your children fits that bill, you're fortunate. But certainly it's not unheard of that children from a prior marriage don't really trust one's current spouse sufficiently to want him or her to be sole successor trustee. Similarly, the spouse will not want his or her rights—including, perhaps, such basic rights as where he or she can live—to be supervised by a child with whom he or she has a hostile relationship.

If you find yourself facing this situation, it will be no surprise that there's no magic solution that will please everyone. The best you can do is think long and hard about who is most likely to be fair to all involved, and to be seen by all as such. If your spouse and children trust another family member—a sister, perhaps—choosing her to serve as trustee, assuming she's willing, may be the best solution. If the potential for conflict and mistrust between the surviving spouse and the final beneficiaries is severe, you may need to look for a more unconventional solution.

> **EXAMPLE:** Alberto is married to Miranda. Alberto also has a son, Francesco, age 23, from a prior marriage. To put it bluntly, Francesco and Miranda can't stand each other. What's worse, Alberto thinks neither of them is a particularly good money manager. Alberto discusses the trustee issue with Miranda and Francesco (separately) and they all agree that a trusted friend, Benito, should serve as trustee. Francesco has known Benito for many years, likes him, and is relieved that Benito, not Miranda, will be the trustee. Because Benito is Alberto's age and may predecease Miranda, Alberto puts a provision in his trust that allows Benito to appoint another trustee if he can't do the job.

Benito promptly names his wife, Carla, to step in if necessary.

Another possibility is simply to name whomever you feel will be most fair, even if that person is your spouse or a child mistrusted by others involved, and let the chips (and sparks) fall as they may.

Naming Cotrustees

It's rarely a good idea to name cotrustees for an AB marital property control trust. You may hope to reduce potential conflict by naming your spouse and one of your children to serve as cotrustees, but if they don't get along, it could make matters worse. The result could be a case of trustee gridlock, where each person's vote cancels out the other. Even a simple matter like payment of trust income could lead to a court battle, if the trustees don't agree what "income" is. And if your spouse and your child or children get along, why bother with cotrustees?

Instead, consider requiring that the trustee provide annual trust income tax returns to all trust beneficiaries, or even copies of all monthly trust bank account statements. This allows nontrustee beneficiaries to check up on the trust without risking cotrustee power struggles.

Naming a Financial Institution as Trustee

If you can't find any family member or friend you think would be a suitable trustee, you have a serious problem. Your last resort is to name a financial institution, such as a private trust company, to serve as trustee. As discussed, there can be real drawbacks to this. (See "Trust Companies and Banks as Trustees" in Chapter 17.)

Many financial institutions will not handle trusts with property worth less than $250,000 or even $500,000. This eliminates many marital property control trusts altogether. Also, financial institutions usually charge hefty fees for serving as trustees. Finally, these institutions can be quite bureaucratic and impersonal, especially when handling trusts that seem like small potatoes to them. So if you must name one as trustee, try to establish a personal relationship with someone you can trust in the institution first.

Savings on Estate Taxes

For couples in second marriages with combined estates exceeding the estate tax threshold, an AB marital property control trust can be used for dual purposes: both to impose controls over the surviving spouse's rights to trust property and to save on overall estate taxes.

EXAMPLE: Khosro and Maheen, a couple in their late 70s, have a shared estate worth $7 million, with each owning half. Their home and personal belongings are valued at $400,000, and savings and stocks total $3.6 million. Khosro has a child from his previous marriage and Maheen has two from

hers. They have no children from their marriage.

Each spouse creates an AB marital property control trust for all of his or her property. The trust documents provide that trust income will go to the surviving spouse, who also will have use of the home. The principal will be maintained for their respective children. The surviving spouse is not given the right to spend trust principal, even for health needs. The surviving spouse will receive income from the deceased spouse's share of their stocks and savings. Khosro and Maheen both feel that when combined with the surviving spouse's own assets, plus Social Security and retirement benefits, this amount of income will be sufficient.

Khosro and Maheen are also pleased because each will make use of their personal estate tax exemptions. Whatever year the first spouse dies, estate taxes will at least be reduced, if not eliminated.

There is nothing particularly tricky about using a marital property control trust to achieve estate tax savings. Basically, you— or, more accurately, your lawyer—prepares the trust document, imposing whatever controls you want over the surviving spouse's rights to trust property. The trust property is subject to estate tax when you die. If your estate is under the amount of the personal exemption for the year of death, all the trust property is exempt from tax. And because that property is never legally owned by your surviving spouse, it will not be subject to tax when he or she dies.

Other Approaches

What do you do if you are considering using an AB marital property control trust both for control and tax savings, and anticipate conflict between beneficiaries? Begin by realizing that there are no fixed rules here. You really do have to come up with your own individual solutions. For instance, instead of a marital control trust, you could buy an annuity or insurance policy with the proceeds going to the survivor and leave all other property to the children. Or, you could leave your children a hefty chunk outright, then leave the rest in trust with your spouse as the life beneficiary and grant him, as trustee, fairly generous powers to spend trust principal. The principal may never be touched, but even if it is gobbled up, at least the children have already gotten something.

Working With a Lawyer

If you decide you want an AB marital property control trust, you'll need to have the trust document prepared by a good estate planning lawyer. There are too many options and possibilities for you to safely prepare one yourself. Also, there are no reliable self-help materials available. A good estate planning lawyer will have experience with other people in second

or subsequent marriages and may be able to offer helpful suggestions for resolving your particular problems. She or he can also draft trust language that clearly and unambiguously expresses what you want. With this type of trust, it's especially important to avoid any potentially unclear phrases in the trust document. You don't want to leave any opening for beneficiaries to fight over what you intended.

Although you will need a lawyer, you can still do much of the essential work yourself. (See Chapter 29.) After all, it's best not to wander into a lawyer's office and start discussing your situation at $300 or more per hour. Try to work out a tentative plan before your first visit.

The principal issues with a marital property control trust are practical, human ones: working out what's fair (as best you can) and deciding who will be most able to carry out your decisions as successor trustee of your trust. These concerns may be easy to state but, in real life, they can be quite difficult to resolve. The best advice I can give is to be candid with yourself. Try to face family and domestic realities, even if they're not all rosy and romantic. Once you've carefully thought about your situation, needs, and desires, write down your specific concerns and what, if any, special problems you anticipate. This should mean less time spent with a lawyer, thus reducing your fee—which likely will still be enough to make you blink.

Trusts and Other Devices for Imposing Controls Over Property

n a number of situations, the right estate plan includes the use of an ongoing, irrevocable trust that imposes controls over beneficiaries' rights to trust property. One such situation—married people who want to ensure that their property eventually goes to their children from prior marriages—is discussed in Chapter 24.

I call the types of trusts discussed here "property control trusts." Here are some of the circumstances in which you might want to consider using one:

- One of your beneficiaries is a minor. (Children's trusts are discussed in Chapter 6.)
- A beneficiary is a young adult who is not yet mature enough to manage significant sums of money or property. (Also discussed in Chapter 6.)
- You want to leave money for a child's education.
- A beneficiary has a disability and will probably always need help managing property. These are called "special needs trusts." You can use one of these trusts to leave property to a beneficiary while also preserving his or her eligibility for government benefits.
- You believe a beneficiary is improvident with money, and want someone else to always be in charge of the trust funds. These are called "spendthrift trusts."
- You want the trustee to decide how to distribute trust income or principal among several beneficiaries. These are call "sprinkling trusts." (For minor children, this type of trust is called a "family pot trust." See Chapter 6.)
- You want to authorize someone else to decide who will receive your property after you die. This is called a "power of appointment." While it's not technically a trust, it is used for property control purposes, and so I discuss it here.

A property control trust is a complex legal animal. You are trying to impose limits on what can happen with trust property in the future. But since the future cannot be foreseen, you're struggling with what is, at best, very difficult: how to create a trust document that will last for a long time and achieve what you want. Rather than worrying about coming up with a detailed plan now, you may decide to allow the trustee broad powers to decide how to use the trust property for a named group of beneficiaries.

Still, in spite of inherent uncertainties, the property control trusts discussed here have been effective over the years for many, many people. Generally, using one of these trusts is far more desirable than not doing anything to handle a difficult beneficiary situation.

Most of the property control trusts discussed here become operational only after your death. In some circumstances, however, a trust can become operational when it's initially created.

> **SEE AN EXPERT**
>
> **Property control trusts require a lawyer.** Most of the property control trusts discussed in this chapter must be prepared by a knowledgeable estate planning attorney. Usually, these trusts involve many uncertainties, and they can tie up property for decades. Drafting such a trust is not easy and cannot safely be done without legal help.
>
> Nolo does provide a resource to help you prepare a property control trust for a special needs child, discussed below.

Educational Trusts

A relatively common type of property control trust is one created to help beneficiaries pay for college or other schooling. These trusts are rarely set up by children's parents—most parents just pay educational costs directly, out of their own pockets. Commonly, grandparents or other older relatives who want to help young relations use these trusts.

Creating an educational property control trust often involves resolving many rather difficult issues including:

When the trust becomes operational. If the beneficiaries are very young and you are unlikely to live until a child begins college, this is not a serious problem. You can arrange for the trust to become operational at your death. But if the children are older, near or at college age, you may want the trust to become operational now, while you live.

If you create the trust now, there can be significant gift tax consequences. However,

Congress seems to be moving toward exempting educational expenses from taxes. Hopefully, someday, all gifts that pay for educational expenses will be exempted, including those placed in trust.

Also, if you want one of these trusts to become operational while you're alive, you must decide whether you will be the initial trustee and who will continue to serve after your death.

> ### New Alternatives to Educational Trusts
>
> You may now place funds in tax-advantaged educational accounts to pay tuition and other school-related costs for young people, without the bother of a separate educational trust. See Chapter 6 for more information about these accounts.

How a beneficiary qualifies for benefits. There are many questions you'll need to ask yourself when deciding how trust money will be distributed to beneficiaries. For example, what education levels must a child reach to get payments from the trust? If, say, you decide that your grandchild must attend college full time to receive payments, what constitutes "full time"? What qualifies as a college? Your grandchild may discover another way to learn—for instance, apprenticing with a metal sculptor. Would the trustee have authority to approve the payment of trust benefits? What about graduate school?

If there's more than one (potential) trust beneficiary, other issues arise. For example, if one grandchild attends Columbia Medical School, while the other grandchild goes to a low-tuition community college, their expenses will vary greatly. Can unequal payments be made to different beneficiaries? Lawyers call a trust where a trustee can pay different amounts of principal or income to different beneficiaries based on their needs a "pot" or "sprinkling" trust—all the dough is in one pot. By contrast, if you want each child to have the same amount of money, you could direct that this be done or set up a separate trust for each child.

Adding new beneficiaries. You'll want to consider what happens if new, potential beneficiaries are born after you die. For instance, if you're creating a trust for all your grandchildren, do you want the trustee to be able to make payments to any future grandchildren born after your death? If you do, accomplishing this is largely a matter of proper legal drafting of the trust document, by an expert lawyer.

What happens if no beneficiaries attend college? You should decide what happens to the trust money if none of the beneficiaries go to school. For example, can the trust income be used for grandchildren's "emergencies"? What kinds? What else might you want to do with the trust principal if it's not all spent on educational costs?

When the trust ends. You must decide when the trust will end. Often this happens when the youngest child reaches a certain age. You'll also need to think about what happens to any money left in the trust when it ends. You can set out a plan—such as outright distribution of the funds—or leave this up to the trustee.

If you think you want to create an educational trust, first try to tentatively resolve these questions and any others you think of. Write out your basic thoughts and resolutions of the issues. Then see an experienced estate planning attorney to have your trust prepared.

> **EXAMPLE:** Rada has two nephews, one who wants to be a doctor and another who lives his life for music. He sets up an educational trust that will pay all college and graduate expenses for both children, including room and board. He also specifies that education includes private music lessons, instruments, and supplies to further the career of his musical nephew. He names his brother, the father of the boys, as trustee. He gives the trustee discretion to decide what other expenses are educational. When the youngest nephew turns 40, the trust ends and any remaining amount is divided between them and distributed outright.

Trusts for People With Special Needs

Parents or others who care about someone with serious physical or mental problems can face difficult estate planning questions. Understandably, they want to provide for their loved one to the extent possible, for as long as that person lives. If that person cannot be expected to manage property, the property must be left in a property control trust, usually called a "special needs trust." The trust document must be carefully drafted, so that the trustee has enough flexibility to deal with the beneficiary's medical or other special needs.

There's another important concern here. A child or other loved one with a disability often requires long-term assistance from government programs. Money and property left directly to people with disabilities may disqualify them from receiving government help. By creating a special needs trust, parents or others can provide for a person with disabilities without risking loss of government benefits, including health care payments. The key to this kind of trust is that the beneficiary is not named as trustee and has no legal control over trust assets. Instead, the trust maker chooses a trusted person to serve as trustee. Because the person with special needs never owns the trust assets, they do not count when determining eligibility for benefits.

RESOURCE

You can make your own special needs trust. *Special Needs Trusts: Protect Your Child's Financial Future*, by Stephen Elias and Kevin Urbatsch (Nolo) provides clear explanations, instructions, and forms, so you can create a special needs trust for your child (or someone else's) without jeopardizing public benefits.

Choosing the Trustee

A primary concern with a special needs trust is making sure you select a trustee, and successor trustee, who will be willing and able to do the job. The trustee must be attentive to the beneficiary's situation, discerning what is needed and providing for those needs to the extent possible. The trustee will need to be in close contact with the person with special needs, so it is essential that the two get along. And finally, the trustee should have the savvy to deal with various institutions, including banks, doctors, hospitals, and government agencies.

If there is no person you trust to be trustee, consider joining a "pooled trust" for people with special needs. These are trusts run by nonprofits who administer, as trustee, each child's trust in that pool.

How a Special Needs Trust Works

The trustee of a special needs trust can spend trust income or principal for a wide variety of the beneficiary's needs that are not covered by federal or state benefits. Government benefits—most notably Supplemental Security Income (SSI) and Medicaid—may be reduced if the trustee gives the beneficiary cash or pays for the beneficiary's food or shelter. This means that the trustee must make payments for the beneficiary, rather than to him.

SSI is administered by the Social Security Administration (SSA). To remain eligible for benefits, the beneficiary cannot have cash resources, which include bank accounts, stocks and bonds, and real estate (other than a home) worth more than $2,000. However, under SSA guidelines, the property in a special needs trust doesn't affect eligibility for Social Security assistance as long as the beneficiary cannot:

- control the amount or frequency of trust payments, or
- revoke the trust and use the property.

In other words, the beneficiary must have no rights to demand and receive money from the trust, either income or principal. Nor can the beneficiary simply revoke the trust and obtain the trust principal. All power over the trust principal, including payment of income or principal to the beneficiary, must be given to the trustee.

Local SSA offices have wide latitude in interpreting these guidelines. For example, some SSA offices may require that the trust document show that the trust creator didn't "intend" the trust property to be used as the primary source of aid or income for the disadvantaged person. Happily, a well-drafted special needs trust can avoid these problems.

SEE AN EXPERT

If you go to a lawyer for a special needs trust. Because the government rules here are complex and can change suddenly, a distinct legal subspecialty has developed: lawyers who prepare special needs trusts. The truth is that you really need not only an estate planning expert, but also someone who is knowledgeable in drafting special needs trusts. (See Chapter 29 for a discussion of how to find the right lawyer for you.) Don't rely on a general practice lawyer, most of whom are not nearly knowledgeable enough to properly prepare this type of trust.

Spendthrift Trusts

A spendthrift trust is designed to minimize an unreliable beneficiary's ability to squander trust principal. The "spendthrift" beneficiary may be someone who simply has no head for money and could easily waste trust principal if controls weren't placed on his or her right to get at it. This type of trust is also used when a beneficiary might squander trust principal on drugs, alcohol, gambling, or some other compulsive behavior. Creating a spendthrift trust is an attempt to balance concern for the beneficiary with a realistic appraisal of his or her more wasteful or destructive impulses.

Spendthrift may sound like a harsh epithet to apply to a loved one, but sitting down to work out a good estate plan demands facing facts, even painful ones. If you want to help someone who is financially irresponsible, a spendthrift trust can be a very sound idea.

With a spendthrift trust, the beneficiary is never the trustee. The trustee can spend trust money for the beneficiary's needs or make payments directly to the beneficiary, as the trust document directs or permits. The beneficiary has no right to spend trust principal. Nor does he or she have the legal right to pledge trust principal, or future income expected from the trust, as security for a loan.

EXAMPLE: Pierre wants to leave money to his son, Maurice, a charming fellow who's always spent money as if he were a millionaire. (He's not.) So Pierre creates an ongoing spendthrift trust for the benefit of Maurice, to take effect after Pierre dies. The trust will be managed by Pierre's prudent, bourgeois brother Jean-Paul, who will dole out trust income to Maurice on the first of each month. If Jean-Paul predeceases Maurice, first Jean-Paul's wife, Anne-Marie (also quite prudent), and next, their son Charles (a chip off the old block) will serve as trustee.

Under the terms of the trust, Maurice cannot obtain the trust principal or pledge his expected trust income to obtain credit. The trust will end when Maurice becomes 50, by which point Pierre hopes he'll have learned financial prudence. If not, Pierre simply accepts the risk that he'll waste the trust principal at that age.

At the extreme, a spendthrift clause can give the trustee power to cut off benefits, temporarily or even permanently, to a beneficiary who becomes uncontrollably self-destructive. Income withheld could be accumulated in the trust or paid to another beneficiary named in the trust document.

Giving the trustee this power, however, is rarely, if ever, wise. It imposes a troubling burden on the trustee, who must decide what behavior by the unreliable beneficiary is so bad that income should be withheld. Even if certain offending behaviors are spelled out in the trust document, it's the trustee who must actually determine whether the beneficiary's behavior justifies withholding income payments. How is the trustee to make this determination? Must he or she play detective, or hire a professional to spy on the beneficiary?

Perhaps the most that you can wisely do is to describe, in the trust document, specific, objective acts which, if undertaken by the beneficiary, would allow the trustee to withhold income payments. For example, the trust document could provide that if the beneficiary were convicted of certain types of drug offenses, payments could be withheld. But even here, is this really the wisest course? Even if the beneficiary were in prison (where access to drugs should be greatly reduced), wouldn't receiving income payments from the trust be a help? Having some personal cash could ease a prisoner's life in many ways, from purchasing canteen food to affording good legal representation.

A less draconian method is for you to direct the trustee to continue to make payments for the benefit of a beneficiary who's become obviously self-destructive (such as paying his or her rent, food bills, or other basic needs) but withhold direct payments to that beneficiary. This still imposes on the trustee the burden of evaluating the beneficiary's behavior, with all the difficulties that involves. But sometimes imposing such a burden is necessary, particularly when the beneficiary's behavior could become (or already is) truly dangerous.

In other situations, you may decide that the trustee must make regular (monthly or quarterly) payments to the beneficiary, regardless of the beneficiary's behavior. These payments can be defined in the trust document as all of the trust income, a set amount, or a percentage. If you choose this option, you must accept the risk that the beneficiary won't spend the money wisely. No trust can prevent a beneficiary from squandering money once it's in his or her pocket.

The rigidity of some spendthrift trusts can be a problem down the road. What happens if the beneficiary needs more money than the monthly payment allowed? Does the trustee have the power to spend trust principal if the beneficiary becomes ill and lacks funds to pay medical bills? Or suppose the beneficiary sees the error of his or her wasteful ways and decides to settle down and go to dental school. Can the trustee use the principal to pay the beneficiary's tuition? You may decide to allow the trustee to spend trust principal for the beneficiary, either for specific needs or as the trustee determines is desirable.

Sprinkling Trusts

Perhaps the most flexible property control trust of all is termed a "sprinkling" or "discretionary" trust. Under either lingo, this type of trust gives the trustee authority to "sprinkle" both the income and principal of the trust between named beneficiaries.

(Sometimes this is called allowing sprinkling powers.)

A sprinkling trust differs from other trusts, including all other trusts designed to control property, in that you don't specify what property each beneficiary gets, or when. Rather, you leave money in the trust and name the group of possible beneficiaries. The trustee determines which of these beneficiaries will receive payments from trust income or principal, and how much. You can specify when the trust should end and what happens to any money left in the trust, or you can leave these matters to the trustee.

In the trust document, however, you can give the trustee rules to follow. For instance, the trustee could be allowed to spend trust principal only for a beneficiary's educational or medical needs. Or a trustee might have the power to pay out only trust income, not principal. Or he or she could have the power to give no more than 20% of the trust principal to any one beneficiary in any one year.

Usually, the trust document provides that if the trustee decides it's best, income may be accumulated in the trust instead of being handed out to any beneficiaries. However, the income tax rate applied to retained trust income may well be higher than the rate applied to trust income received by beneficiaries. (See Chapter 17.) So it's unlikely that a trustee would decide to retain trust income beyond one tax year and thus effectively cost the beneficiaries money in higher taxes.

By law, you must name an independent ("disinterested") trustee—that is, a trustee who has no financial interest in how the trust money is distributed and is dispassionate enough to hand out money as it's genuinely needed. Thus, a surviving spouse normally should not serve as trustee of a sprinkling trust.

Adding Sprinkling Powers to an AB Trust

If you create an AB trust, you may want to give your trustee the power to use trust income or assets for the final beneficiaries, probably your children. A sprinkling AB trust can be appropriate for a couple with a large estate, when the surviving spouse has plenty of assets and may not need or want regular income payments.

Creating "sprinkling powers" in an AB trust can help you take care of possible needs of other beneficiaries, such as your children, during the surviving spouse's life. At an extreme, for example, if a wealthy surviving spouse marries someone even wealthier, the trustee can choose not to pay anything at all to that spouse, but to spend (or save) all the trust income and assets for the children or other named beneficiaries.

More commonly, one child may need more money for education or support than another. When the beneficiaries are young, a sprinkling trust allows great flexibility over the years and makes the assets available when necessary.

Other Uses of Sprinkling Trust Provisions

Sprinkling trust provisions can be used in a wide variety of property control trusts. For example, if you want to leave property for minor children or young adults, you may create a "family pot trust." This is a kind of sprinkling trust where you choose to let the trustee decide, according to the actual needs and circumstances of the children, how much money to pay to each child. (See Chapter 6.)

Similarly, a grandparent may create a sprinkling trust for grandchildren or, for that matter, for adult children. Indeed, sprinkling trust provisions can work well in any situation where a number of beneficiaries may need payments from the trust for a long period of time, and you have complete confidence in the trustee.

Choosing an Independent Trustee

No matter the type of sprinkling trust, a key to making one work well is to appoint a disinterested, independent trustee—someone you trust completely. Because a sprinkling trust is intended to operate over a lengthy period, you also need to select at least one successor trustee, and often an alternate successor trustee, with similar care.

An "independent" trustee means a trustee who cannot benefit from the trust—that is, is not a beneficiary of any kind. Even someone who is named as an alternate beneficiary (or fourth alternate, for that matter) cannot serve. If the trustee has a financial interest in the trust, the IRS may consider him or her to be the legal owner of all the trust property and include it in his or her taxable estate when he or she dies, which is definitely not what you want.

The surviving spouse cannot be the trustee of a sprinkling AB trust. As the life beneficiary, the surviving spouse obviously has an interest in trust payments. Indeed, normally, the surviving spouse receives all trust income during his or her life. But creating a sprinkling trust means there are other possibilities. Allowing the surviving spouse to be the trustee in this situation means the IRS will regard him or her as the legal owner of all trust property. That property will be included in his or her taxable estate when he or she dies, defeating the purpose of an AB trust.

You need a trustee who, although he or she has no financial interest in how the trust money is distributed, is personally interested in the welfare of the beneficiaries and will remain alert to their financial needs. A sprinkling trust, by its very nature, can create conflict among the beneficiaries. After all, they may all think they need money—and a lot of it—from the trust, so the trustee may have some serious personal, as well as financial, issues to handle. If you can't find a legally independent but emotionally involved person, and someone you fully trust, who'll do the job, a sprinkling trust isn't for you.

Trusts to Manage Your Own Property

If you tire of coping with your property and financial affairs, you can arrange for someone else to manage them. One method is for you to put your property in a trust, to be managed by a trustee for your benefit. The trustee would have the authority to spend any amount of trust income or principal for you. You can define as carefully as you like in the trust document what standard of living you expect. (Of course, there must be sufficient assets in the trust to pay for that standard of living.)

Unlike the other trusts discussed in this chapter, there's no need to make this type of trust irrevocable. Indeed, there are real drawbacks if you do so. The trustee would have to obtain a trust taxpayer ID, maintain trust financial records, and file an annual trust income tax return. None of this would benefit you. And, obviously, if you changed your mind, you would have no legal power to end the trust and regain control of the trust assets.

If the trust is revocable, you should make yourself one of the trustees. If you don't, under IRS regulations, the tax requirements applied to irrevocable trusts will apply to your revocable trust as well. One simple way to avoid this problem is for you to name yourself and some other person as cotrustees, and provide in the trust document that either trustee may act for the trust. The other person, as cotrustee, in reality becomes the sole manager of the trust property. But as long as you remain one of the official trustees, no tax reporting obligations are imposed on the trust.

You can also use other devices to allow another person to manage your property for you. One method is to give another person authority, using a document called a "durable power of attorney for finances," to manage your property. It's always a good idea to create a durable power of attorney for finances as part of your estate plan. (See Chapter 26.)

If you have transferred property to a living trust, there is no need to create any other device to handle that trust property in case you become incapacitated. A standard clause in a well-drafted living trust authorizes your successor trustee to take over management of your trust property, if necessary, for your benefit as long as you live. If this happens, the living trust remains revocable, in case you regain the ability to manage your affairs.

Powers of Appointment

A "power of appointment" is simply the power to determine how someone's assets are distributed after his or her death.

EXAMPLE 1: In her living trust, Anita authorizes her husband, Frederico, to distribute all her property among her children as he wishes, if he outlives her. If he doesn't outlive her, Anita grants the same authority to her brother, Marcello.

EXAMPLE 2: Malcolm, a widower, has two children: Veronica, age 24, and Jamal, age 22. Jamal has a serious drug problem. Malcolm certainly doesn't want to leave any property outright to Jamal if he's still using drugs when Malcolm dies. On the other hand, Malcolm hopes Jamal will see the light and cease using drugs, so he surely doesn't want to cut Jamal out irrevocably. So in his living trust he creates a power of appointment in his best friend, Ted. Ted will decide, after Malcolm's death, if Jamal can be given property outright because he has been clear from drugs for a specified period of time. (Of course, determining this may not be easy.) If Ted decides Jamal still suffers from drug addiction, then the property left for Jamal will go into a trust for him, managed by Ted.

There can be a number of wise reasons to use a power of appointment. One reason is that you are unsure, when you prepare your estate plan, exactly who you want your beneficiaries to be. You don't want to create a sprinkling trust, because the trustee normally has the power to distribute trust money only among beneficiaries named in the trust document. If you trust someone—a spouse, brother, or friend—completely, it may make sense to postpone the choice of beneficiaries, and what property beneficiaries will receive, until later.

EXAMPLE: Jason and Beverly, an elderly couple, have a substantial estate. They leave large specific gifts to family and some friends. Each also intends to leave one third of his or her estate to benefit minority grade school students. Rather than selecting the beneficiaries for this education gift, each provides that their daughter Celia has a power of appointment to distribute the property to whatever organizations she decides will best carry out her parents' goals.

Kinds of Powers of Appointment

There are two kinds of powers of appointment: "general" and "special" (also called "limited"). A general power of appointment can have adverse estate tax consequences, while a limited power of appointment does not.

With a general power of appointment, you name a person to distribute your property to the beneficiaries he or she chooses—including him- or herself. You can define a set time period for this decision to be made, or leave it open.

Authorizing a general power of appointment is rarely a good idea. Under IRS rules, the person who has a general power of appointment will have the full value of the property subject to that power included in his or her taxable estate at his or her death. This is true even if he or she never gives any property to him- or herself, had no intention of doing so, and in fact gave it all to someone else. The practical effect is

that as long as estate tax exists, this property is subject to estate tax twice—once when you die and once when the person to whom you gave the power of appointment dies.

EXAMPLE: In his living trust, Martin gives his wife Helen a general power of appointment over property worth $800,000. Martin's total estate is worth $6 million, so it is subject to federal estate tax. Helen's estate is worth $2 million, aside from the property subject to the general power of appointment. Shortly after Martin's death in 2014, Helen gives the entire $800,000 to their three children. Nevertheless, when Helen dies, that $800,000 is included in her taxable estate because she had the power to give all this money to herself if she had chosen to. So the $800,000 has been included in two taxable estates, which is clearly undesirable.

By contrast, a special or limited power of appointment is restricted as you see fit. Most importantly, the person who has the power cannot give the property to her- or himself, use it to pay her or his creditors, or leave it in her or his estate. This eliminates the double estate tax problem of a general power of appointment.

Typically, if you give someone a limited power of appointment, you specify which people (beneficiaries) the holder of the power can give property to. For instance, the person appointed can be given only the right to divide property among your four children. Or, as another example, you might direct the person to give at least 15% of your property to each of the children, with the remaining 40% to be distributed among them as the person with the special power of appointment determines.

EXAMPLE: Woody sets up an AB trust, leaving the income from the trust to his wife, Janet, and the principal to their three children upon Janet's death. He includes a limited power of appointment authorizing Janet to direct how the trust assets will pass to the children, if she so chooses. Janet lives for 20 years after Woody's death and receives the income from the trust. During that time, Sarah, one of the children, gives birth to a child with severe disabilities. The other children are all financially well-off and don't, in Janet's opinion, need money from the trust.

Janet considers what Woody would want if he were alive and could make the decision. Then, in her will, she exercises her limited power of appointment, by leaving 75% of the trust property outright to Sarah, with the understanding that Sarah will use the money primarily for her child with special needs. The other 25% of the trust property is divided between their other two children.

SEE AN EXPERT

Watch out when using limited powers of appointment and disclaimers. With a limited power of appointment, problems can arise if the person given the power also wants to use a disclaimer at the grantor's death. If one disclaims (refuses) property that then goes into a trust, the one disclaiming cannot then direct where the disclaimed property eventually goes. So disclaiming is inconsistent with having any power of appointment, even a limited one. (See Chapter 22.) Discuss this with your estate planning lawyer if you think this problem might come up.

Limited Power of Appointment in QTIP Trusts

Limited powers of appointment are also occasionally included in QTIP trusts. As discussed in Chapter 19, a QTIP trust is basically a device to defer estate tax until the death of a surviving spouse, while allowing the first spouse to die to name the final beneficiaries for his or her estate.

When a surviving spouse is given a limited power of appointment over QTIP trust property, the surviving spouse simply has some control over the final distribution of the assets in the QTIP trust, within the limits the grantor imposed. The grantor can choose the final group of beneficiaries, such as his or her children, and allow a spouse to determine the amounts received by each one. The grantor, then, still controls who the final beneficiaries are—just not how much each receives.

EXAMPLE: Gert leaves $2 million in a QTIP trust with the income going to her much younger husband, Raphael, for his life. She gives him a limited power of appointment to choose at his death how much each of her four children by a previous marriage will receive of what is left. Raphael may benefit for many years from the trust, and he may adjust the final outcome according to the children's needs. But if he remarries (and Gert expects, or suspects, that he might), the trust terms prevent him from shifting these assets to his new bride or to anyone else.

Combining Property Control Trusts With Estate Tax–Saving Trusts

Sometimes one or more property control trusts are combined with one or more tax-saving trusts as the central part of the overall estate plan.

EXAMPLE: Parnell, in his 60s, has an estate worth $5 million. He recently married Moira, who has little property of her own. He has two children from his prior marriage—a daughter, Maeve, who he worries cannot handle money, and a son, Padraic, who has severe disabilities. Parnell wants to leave some property for Padraic's needs, while also ensuring, as best he can, that Padraic will remain eligible for the government medical and rehabilitation services he now receives. Parnell also wants to provide for Moira if she outlives him and leave some property on her death to Padraic and Maeve.

After working with an expert lawyer, Parnell decides to create three trusts:

- A special needs trust for Padraic, to be funded with the amount of the personal estate tax exemption in the year of Parnell's death.
- A QTIP trust for the remainder of his property, to provide income for Moira and postpone estate tax on the balance of his estate. Maeve and Padraic are the final beneficiaries of this trust and will share the trust property equally when Moira dies. Parnell specifies that Padraic's share of this property will be added to his special needs trust.
- A spendthrift trust for the property Maeve will eventually receive from the QTIP trust when Moira dies.

Parnell still has many matters he must resolve. For example, who should be trustee of the QTIP trust? Can Moira invade the trust principal? Who is the trustee of the spendthrift trust? How long will it last? Can the trustee decide that Maeve has become financially responsible and turn the trust principal over to her? With Padraic, Parnell faces the problems involved in creating any special needs trust.

Parnell also has to decide what he'll tell his family members about his estate plan. Moira surely needs to know about the QTIP, but how much does he want to tell his children? If he's not on good terms with Maeve, maybe he doesn't want to tell her about the spendthrift trust. But letting her discover this only after he dies could be very hurtful. Parnell decides he will write Maeve a letter, explaining his estate plan, and why he's decided it's best to leave her property in a spendthrift trust. Parnell knows Maeve has a fierce temper. He hopes that by writing her, he'll lessen the chance of a screaming fight between the two of them, Parnell being no saint himself. But if Maeve has some time to reflect on Parnell's plan, perhaps they can discuss it later, without rancor. Parnell also informs Padraic that he's created a special needs trust to try to protect him over the years.

Incapacity: Making Medical and Financial Decisions

We tend to think of estate planning as something we do now to arrange for handling important matters when we die. This definition has the advantage of being concise, but it's a bit too simple. As we grow older, many of us face the stern reality that before we die we may not be mentally or physically competent for some period of time, perhaps an extended period. A thorough estate plan must consider this possibility.

This chapter discusses how you can best ensure that your rights, dignity, and wishes will be protected if you ever become incapable of making or communicating decisions regarding medical treatment. It also covers how you can name someone to handle your finances if you can't manage them yourself.

If your health deteriorates and you become unable to make financial or medical decisions, another adult must have legal authority to make these for you.

There are two ways you can deal with this possibility.

Do nothing. If you don't make any arrangements in advance and you become incapacitated, a judge will appoint someone (called a conservator, guardian, custodian, or curator, depending on the state) to make decisions for you. Court proceedings for incapacitated people are almost always undesirable, unless there's no other option. These proceedings are costly, time-consuming, and expose to public concern what most people prefer to keep private.

If you suffer a medical emergency and become incapacitated, and you haven't prepared documents covering your medical care, that care will be determined according to hospital protocol or a doctor's decisions made after discussion with your immediate family members. You may get care that is very different from what you would have wanted.

With finances, people sometimes simply ignore the requirement of court proceedings—for example, a son might sign his ill father's name to the father's retirement check. Unfortunately, there's an unpleasant legal term for this act: forgery. Ignoring the law isn't wise, and it's often not practical either. Over an extended period of time, it's almost impossible to adequately manage another's affairs this way.

Create legal documents controlling how your affairs should be handled if you become incapacitated. Using medical directives, you can provide binding instructions concerning use of life-sustaining medical technology and other types of treatment; you can also appoint someone to enforce your wishes and make any other medical decisions for you that you can't make yourself. And with a durable power of attorney for finances, you can authorize someone to manage your financial affairs, and specify any limits or directions as to how your property should be handled.

RESOURCE
Planning for long-term care. When planning for incapacity, you should also consider the possibility that you may need long-term

health care, either at home or in a nursing facility. These matters are discussed in detail in *Long-Term Care: How to Plan & Pay for It*, by Joseph Matthews (Nolo).

Medical Decisions

The increasing use of life-sustaining medical technology over the last decades has raised fears in many that our lives may be artificially prolonged against our wishes. The right to die with dignity, and without the tremendous agony and expense for both patient and family caused by artificially prolonging lives, has been addressed and confirmed by the U.S. Supreme Court, the federal government, and the legislatures in every state.

This individual right can also provide protection in a situation where doctors might wish to provide a patient with less extensive care than he or she would like. For example, a doctor may be unwilling to try experimental treatments or maintain long-term treatments on a patient who the doctor feels has slim chances of recovering (or, worse, couldn't pay the bill).

The United States Supreme Court has held that every individual has the constitutional right to control his or her own medical treatment. The Court also stated that medical personnel must follow "clear and convincing evidence" of a person's wishes—even if those wishes are directly opposed by the patient's family. (*Cruzan v. Director, Missouri Dept. of Health*, 497 U.S. 261 (1990).)

The Importance of Putting Your Wishes in Writing

In recognition of the legal right to control one's own medical treatment, every state authorizes individuals to create simple documents stating their wishes concerning medical care. The directions expressed in the documents will be followed if you are no longer capable of communicating to medical personnel your choices regarding life-prolonging and other medical care.

It is important to note that many of these documents take effect only if you are diagnosed with a terminal condition or are in a permanent coma. Your documents do not come into play if you are able to communicate your wishes in any way or are only temporarily unconscious, as with general anesthesia.

Writing down your medical care instructions can help alleviate your fears, whether they're about receiving unwanted medical treatment or having desired medical treatment withheld. It can also help relieve family members from having to make agonizing decisions about what kind of treatment you would want. This can be particularly important when family members have different ideas about what care you should receive. Also, doctors and hospitals have their own rules and beliefs about what is proper medical treatment, and even if your family knows your wishes and tries to assert them, medical personnel are not necessarily bound to follow them without a valid health care document.

Types of Medical Care Documents

There are two basic documents that allow you to direct your medical care, both grouped under the broad label "health care directives." You need to prepare both. First, you need a "declaration," a written statement that you make directly to medical personnel that spells out the medical care you do or do not wish to receive if you become incapacitated. (A declaration can go by various names, including medical directive, advance health care directive, or directive to physicians. It may also be called a "living will," but it bears no relation to a conventional will that you use to leave property at death.) A declaration functions as a contract with your treating doctors, who must either honor your wishes for medical care, or transfer you to other doctors or a facility that will honor them.

Second, you'll want what's often called a "durable power of attorney for health care," also known as designation of health care surrogate or patient advocate designation in a few states. In this document, you appoint someone you trust to be your "attorney-in-fact" (sometimes called your "agent" or "health care proxy") to see that your doctors and health care providers give you the kind of medical care you wish to receive. In most states, you can also give your attorney-in-fact broader authority to make decisions about your medical care—excluding, of course, matters you covered in your declaration.

An increasing number of states combine both documents into a single form.

If Your State Forms Are Not Detailed Enough

When it comes to medical care documents, there are many differences in the forms and formats used by different states. Some state laws say that a specific form must be followed for a declaration to be valid. However, since the Supreme Court ruled in the *Cruzan* case that every individual has a constitutional right to direct his or her own medical care, the most important thing to keep in mind is that your directions should be clear and in writing.

If you feel strongly about a particular kind of care—even if your state law or the form you get does not address it—include your specific thoughts about it in your document. If you are using a state form that does not adequately address your concerns, write them in on the form with the additional request that your wishes be respected and followed.

What You Can Cover in Your Medical Care Documents

As mentioned above, your health care declaration is the place to write out what you do and do not want in terms of medical care if you become unable to speak for yourself. You don't need to become a medical expert to complete your documents, but it will help you to become familiar with the kinds of medical treatments that are commonly administered

Planning for Incapacity: Vocabulary

Several terms used in this chapter sound similar but have distinct meanings. Here's a chart to help you keep them straight.

Term	Also Called	What It Means
Health Care Declaration	• Living will • Directive to physicians • Health care directive • Medical directive	A legal document in which you state your wishes about life support and other kinds of medical treatments. The document takes effect if you can't communicate your own health care wishes.
Durable Power of Attorney for Health Care	• Medical power of attorney • Power of attorney for health care • Designation of surrogate • Patient advocate designation	A legal document in which you give another person permission to make medical decisions for you if you are unable to make those decisions yourself.
Advance Health Care Directive		A legal document that includes both a health care declaration and a durable power of attorney for health care. It is currently used in more than one-third of the states.
Health Care Agent	• Attorney-in-fact for health care • Patient advocate • Health care proxy • Surrogate • Health care representative	The person you name in your durable power of attorney for health care to make medical decisions for you if you cannot make them yourself.
Durable Power of Attorney for Finances		A legal document in which you give another person authority to manage your financial affairs if you become incapacitated.
Attorney-in-Fact for Finances	• Agent for finances	The person you name in your durable power of attorney for finances to make financial decisions for you if you cannot make them yourself.
Springing Power of Attorney		A durable power of attorney that takes effect only when and if you become incapacitated.

to patients who are seriously ill. These include:

- blood and blood products
- cardiopulmonary resuscitation (CPR)
- diagnostic tests
- dialysis
- drugs
- respirators, and
- surgery.

In addition to the treatments listed above, you may want to give some thought to the issues of pain medication, food, and water. The laws of most states assume that people want relief from pain and discomfort and specifically exclude pain-relieving procedures from definitions of life-prolonging treatments that may be withheld. Some states also exclude food and water (commonly called nutrition and hydration) from their definitions of life-prolonging treatments. But there is some controversy about whether providing food and water or drugs to make a person comfortable, also have the effect of prolonging life.

If you feel adamant about not having your life prolonged, you may choose to direct that all food, water, and pain relief be withheld, even if your treating doctor thinks those procedures are necessary. Again, under the U.S. Constitution, you are allowed to impose these instructions even if your state's law is restrictive, and your doctors are bound to follow your instructions or transfer you to another provider who will. You should be sure to name an attorney-in-fact to oversee your wishes, so that there will be someone available to lobby on your behalf.

On the other hand, you may feel concerned about how much pain or discomfort you'll experience during a final illness. In this case, you may prefer to have your life prolonged rather than face the possibility that discomfort or pain will go untreated. Obviously, it's an extremely personal choice. You're free to leave the instructions that feel right for you.

To make an informed decision about which procedures you do and do not want, as well as others that might pertain to your particular medical condition, it may be a good idea to discuss your medical care document with your physician. He or she can explain medical procedures more fully and can discuss the options with you. You will also find out whether your doctor has any medical or moral objections to following your wishes. If your physician does not agree to follow your wishes, consider finding a doctor who will.

Even when you have specified your wishes in medical care documents regarding life-prolonging medical treatment and comfort care, certain decisions may still be difficult to resolve:

- when, exactly, to administer or withhold certain medical treatments
- whether or not to provide, withhold, or continue antibiotic or pain medication, and
- whether to pursue complex, painful, and expensive surgeries that may serve to prolong life but cannot reverse the medical condition.

To deal with situations like these, your durable power of attorney for health care allows you to appoint someone who understands your wishes and can be trusted to make these decisions in accordance with your wishes and in your best interest. To provide some guidance, your power of attorney may authorize the appointed person to:

- give, withhold, or withdraw consent to medical or surgical procedures
- consent to appropriate care for the end of life, including pain relief
- make decisions about any issues you have not covered in your declaration
- hire and fire medical personnel
- visit you in the hospital or other facility even when other visiting is restricted
- have access to medical records and other personal information, and
- get any required court authorization to obtain or withhold medical treatment if, for any reason, a hospital or doctor does not honor your written instructions.

You can also use your durable power of attorney to provide any other specific instructions you have for your attorney-in-fact.

EXAMPLE: Sara is seriously ill, faces major surgery, and knows that, at a minimum, she will be unable to make all her own medical decisions. She prepares a durable power of attorney for health care, delegating to her sister, Kerry, the authority to make health care decisions for her. To make sure that her own wishes are complied with, she inserts several restrictions regarding Kerry's power. Specifically,

Sara wants to be sure she is operated on by Dr. June Lee at Mattan Hospital. So, in defining her attorney-in-fact's authority, she includes the following clause:

"My attorney-in-fact shall comply with my stated desire that all surgery performed on me be done at Mattan Hospital, 134 Ridge Road, Linda Vista, California, by Dr. June Lee, unless Dr. Lee is unable to perform such surgery."

When Your Health Care Directives Take Effect

Your health care directive takes effect when you no longer have the ability, or capacity, to make your own health care decisions. Essentially, lacking capacity means that:

- you can't understand the nature and consequences of the health care choices that are available to you, and
- you are unable to communicate your own wishes for care, either orally, in writing, or through gestures.

Practically speaking, this means that if you are so ill or injured that you cannot express your health care wishes in any way, your directive will spring immediately into effect. Usually, this happens only if you are diagnosed as close to death from a terminal condition or if you are permanently comatose. If there is any question about your ability to understand your treatment choices and communicate clearly, your doctor (with the input of your health care proxy or close relatives) will decide whether it is time for your health care directive to become operative.

In some states, it is possible to give your health care proxy the authority to manage your health care immediately. If your state allows this option, you may prefer to make an immediately effective directive for any of several reasons, including:

- Allowing your proxy to put your document into effect quickly, without first having a doctor confirm that you are incapacitated. This may be particularly important if you are not under the care of a doctor with whom you have an established, trusting relationship.
- Keeping control in the hands of your proxy. You may feel that your proxy, not a doctor, is the best person to decide that you can no longer direct your own medical care.
- Asking your proxy to step in early and make decisions for you even if you still have the capacity to make your own choices. You may want this if illness, exhaustion, or other circumstances leave you feeling that you'd like someone you trust to deal with your doctors and make treatment decisions for you.

Making an immediately effective document will not give your proxy the authority to override what you want in terms of treatment; you will always be able to dictate your own medical care if you have the ability to do so. And even when you are no longer capable of making your own decisions, your proxy must always act in your best interests and try diligently to follow any health care wishes you've expressed in your health care directive or otherwise.

Finally, to ensure that your document takes effect and your wishes are followed if your need for care arises unexpectedly, you should place copies of your health care documents with several people, including your regular doctor, your health care proxy, and at least one other trusted relative or friend.

Choosing an Attorney-in-Fact or a Proxy

There are a number of things to consider when choosing your health care attorney-in-fact or proxy. Most important, of course, is to choose someone that you trust to do the job right, if it becomes necessary. And a very difficult and painful job it may be. Your attorney-in-fact may be faced with confusing medical choices and opinions, under grave circumstances. Certainly no simple guide exists telling attorneys-in-fact how to handle what real life may throw at them or how to cope with the emotions that can arise when trying to act in the best interests of an incapacitated and possibly dying loved one. The truth is that even carefully prepared health care documents may only offer vague guidelines when it comes to the reality of a specific illness. Choosing an attorney-in-fact is a serious matter, requiring serious discussion with the person you choose. This is not a choice to be made without serious reflection.

Here are a few other things you should think about. Appoint someone who:

- is likely to be present when decisions need to be made—most often, this means someone who lives nearby or who is willing to travel and spend time at your side during your hospitalization
- would not easily be swayed or bullied by doctors or family members who disagree with your wishes, and
- is capable of understanding your medical condition and any proposed life-prolonging measures.

It is also a good idea to appoint a backup or replacement attorney-in-fact in case your first choice is unable or unwilling to serve. Make it clear, however, that the second person is only an alternate. It is not wise to appoint coproxies: Having two people make decisions would only complicate the process.

CAUTION

Do not appoint your doctor or another health care provider as attorney-in-fact. Although your doctor is an important person for your proxy to consult concerning health care decisions, you should not appoint your doctor as your attorney-in-fact or proxy. The laws in most states specifically forbid treating physicians and other health care providers from acting in this role—to avoid the appearance that they may have their own interests at heart that prevent them from acting according to your wishes.

Where to Get Medical Care Forms

Some states require residents to use specific forms designed for those states. In any case, it's always a good idea to use your state's form, because doctors and hospitals will be familiar with it.

You do not need to consult a lawyer to prepare your state's medical care forms. The forms are usually simple and can be obtained, free or for a nominal fee, from a number of sources, including:

- local senior centers
- local hospitals (ask to speak with the patient representative; by law, any hospital that receives federal funds must provide patients with appropriate forms for directing health care)
- your regular physician
- your state's medical association
- The National Hospice and Palliative Care Organization (provides free health care directive forms for every state); you can order your state's forms by calling 800-658-8898 or you can download forms from the website at www.nhpco.org, and
- *Quicken WillMaker Plus* (software from Nolo); it contains forms for all states except Louisiana, and thorough instructions to help you complete them.

For general information, search for "End of Life" on AARP's website, www.aarp.org.

Finalizing Your Medical Care Documents

After completing the documents directing your medical care, there are just a few steps you must take to make them valid and binding.

Signing your documents. Every state law requires that you sign your documents— or direct another person to sign them for you—as a way of verifying that you understand them and that they contain your true wishes. If you are physically unable to sign them yourself, you can direct another person to sign them for you.

You must sign your documents, or have them signed for you, in the presence of witnesses or a notary public—sometimes both. (This depends on your state's law.) The purpose of this additional formality is so that at least one other person can attest that you were of sound mind and of legal age (at least 18) when you made the documents.

CAUTION

Keep documents up to date. The laws on medical care forms can change, so a particular form, which was the right one in your state several years ago, may by now have been replaced by a different, usually more complete form. In most states, documents you completed while an old law was in effect remain valid. Nevertheless, you should review your health care documents every few years, to be sure that your documents reflect your present wishes and that you have the form with which doctors and other health care providers are most comfortable.

RESOURCE

Learn your state's requirements. You can learn your state's finalization requirements for health care documents in the Living Wills & Medical Powers of Attorney section of Nolo.com. Go to www.nolo.com/legal-encyclopedia/living-wills.

Making and distributing copies. After you complete your health care documents, you should keep the originals where your attorney-in-fact can easily find them if the need arises. Ideally, however, you should also make an effort to make your wishes for your future health care widely known. Give copies of your documents to:

- your attorney-in-fact
- any physician with whom you now consult regularly
- the office of the hospital or other care facility in which you are likely to receive treatment
- the patient representative of your HMO or insurance plan
- close relatives, particularly immediate family members—spouse, grown children, siblings
- trusted friends, and
- your clergy or lawyer, particularly if you are in regular contact with a member of the clergy or a lawyer but you do not have a family member who lives nearby.

Keeping Track of Copies

Keep the original of your medical directive in an easily accessible place in your home, where your attorney-in-fact can quickly locate it.

You should also keep a list of all the people and places that have copies of your medical directive. Then, if you change the terms of the directive, you will be able to retrieve each of the copies or have them destroyed.

Changing Your Mind— And Documents

You can change any type of medical care document as long as you are of sound mind. Therefore, neither your decisions about health care nor your appointment of an attorney-in-fact are final decisions. Anytime you wish to change the terms or attorney-in-fact, however, you must prepare a new document and finalize it properly— according to the formalities that must be followed in your state. You should also

Health Care Documents and HIPAA

If you've recently visited a doctor, you know there's a law requiring patients to sign forms regarding medical privacy and the release of medical information. This federal law is called "HIPAA," the Health Insurance Portability and Accountability Act. Some lawyers have argued, or worried, that HIPAA requirements apply to your agent's powers under your health care directive, and that you must prepare special HIPAA release forms to give your agent the authority to take over your health care decisions for you. Fortunately, this is not the case. Your health care power of attorney authorizes the person you name as your agent to obtain the medical information necessary to put your document into effect and carry out your wishes. As stated by the California Medical Association:

"CMA has received calls from physicians and other caregivers who have heard rumors

that existing Advance Health Care Directives are invalidated by HIPAA's privacy rule, and that patients need to fill out new HIPAA-compliant ones. This is simply not true .... Nothing in the privacy rule regulations changes the way in which an individual grants another person power of attorney for health care decisions. The U.S. Department of Health and Human Services has confirmed on its website that state law regarding health care powers of attorney continues to apply."

Some states have begun to add HIPAA authorizations to their health care power of attorney documents, but doing so actually goes beyond what the law requires. You needn't be concerned about HIPAA. What's vital is that you prepare your health care documents and select the right person to enforce your medical instructions and make other health care decisions for you if necessary.

make sure that all copies of the document you made earlier are destroyed.

Review your medical care documents occasionally to make sure they still accurately reflect your wishes for your medical care. Advances in technology or changes in health care attitudes are two of the kinds of changes that may cause you to revise your view about the kind of medical care you want.

In addition, you should consider making new documents if:

- you move to another state, or
- the attorney-in-fact or proxy you named to supervise your wishes becomes unable to do so.

In an Emergency: DNR Orders and POLST Forms

In addition to the health care documents discussed in this chapter, some people may want to make a Do Not Resuscitate, or DNR, order. Some states are also supplementing or replacing DNR orders with a similar form, often known as a POLST form.

DNR Orders

A DNR order tells emergency medical personnel that you do not wish to be administered cardiopulmonary resuscitation (CPR). DNR orders are used both in hospitals and in situations where a person might require emergency care outside of the hospital. In some states, DNR orders go by a different name, such as "Comfort One." In other states, if you are using the document

outside of a hospital or other health care facility, the document may be simply called a "DNR form" or "DNR directive." Here, we use "DNR order" because that is the most common name for the document.

You may want to consider a DNR order if you:

- have a terminal illness
- are at significant risk for cardiac or respiratory arrest, or
- have strong feelings against the use of CPR under any circumstances.

In most states, any adult may secure a DNR order.

Because emergency response teams must act quickly in a medical crisis, they often do not have the time to determine whether you have a valid health care directive explaining treatments you want provided or withheld. If they do not know your wishes, they must provide you with all possible lifesaving measures. But if emergency care providers see that you have a valid DNR order—which is often made apparent by an easily identifiable bracelet, anklet, or necklace—they will not administer CPR.

If you ask to have CPR withheld, you will not be given:

- chest compression
- electric shock treatments to the chest
- tubes placed in the airway to assist breathing
- artificial ventilation, or
- cardiac drugs.

If you want a DNR order, or if you would like to find out more about DNR orders, talk with a doctor. In most states, a doctor's signature is required to make the DNR valid—he or she will often need to obtain and complete the necessary paperwork. If the doctor does not have the form or other information you need, call the Health Department for your state and ask to speak with someone in the Division of Emergency Medical Services.

POLST Forms

Many states are starting to use a form that is similar to a DNR order, but differs in a few important ways. The form is most often called Physician's Orders for Life Sustaining Treatment (POLST), though some states use other terms, such as Clinician's Orders for Life Sustaining Treatment (COLST) or Medical Orders for Scope of Treatment (MOST). A POLST form may be used in addition to—or instead of—a DNR order.

A POLST is often prepared to ensure that different health care facilities and service providers (including EMS personnel) understand a patient's wishes. In most states, a POLST form is printed on bright paper so it will easily stand out in a patient's medical records. To be valid, the form must be signed by a doctor or other approved health care professional.

Unlike a DNR order, a POLST form includes directions about lifesustaining measures—such as intubation, antibiotic use and feeding tubes—in addition to CPR. The POLST form helps to ensure that medical providers will understand your wishes at a glance, but it is not a substitute for a thorough and properly prepared Advance Directive.

When you enter a hospital, hospice, or other health care facility, a member of the staff may ask whether you want to complete a POLST form. If not, you can ask for one.

RESOURCE

Learn more. To learn more about POLST forms, including information about POLST forms in your state, go to the POLST section of Nolo.com at www. nolo.com/legal-encyclopedia/physicians-orders-life-sustaining-treatment.

Letting People Know About Your Wishes

If you obtain a DNR order or make a POLST form, discuss your decision with your family or other caretaker. If you are keeping a DNR form at home, be sure that your loved ones or caretakers know where it is. Even if you are wearing identification, such as a bracelet or necklace, keep your form in an obvious place. You might consider keeping it by your bedside, on the front of your refrigerator, in your wallet, or in your suitcase if you are traveling. If your form is not apparent and immediately available, or if it has been altered in any way, CPR will most likely be performed.

Financial Decisions

A durable power of attorney for finances allows you to name someone you trust (called your attorney-in-fact) to handle your finances if you can't. Every state recognizes this type of document. If you become unable to manage your finances and you haven't prepared a durable power of attorney, your spouse, closest relatives, or companion will have to ask a court for authority over at least some of your financial affairs. This procedure— called a conservatorship or guardianship proceeding—can be time-consuming and expensive. (See "Guardianships and Conservatorships," below.) In contrast, preparing a durable power of attorney is simple and inexpensive—and if you do become incapacitated, the document will likely appear as a minor miracle to those closest to you.

Granting Authority to Your Attorney-in-Fact

Any power of attorney arrangement depends upon trust and understanding between you and the person you appoint to handle your affairs. You can help make this relationship work by putting specific instructions in your document regarding financial actions you do and do not wish the attorney-in-fact to take. Your attorney-in-fact has only the financial authority you grant him or her in the document. Normally, an attorney-in-fact has authority to handle all regular financial matters,

such as depositing checks and paying bills. Beyond the basics of routine financial maintenance, it's up to you to decide what you want to authorize.

While you may want to define and limit your attorney-in-fact's authority in some matters, you obviously can't foresee every financial concern that might arise. So it's vital that you choose someone you trust, and who has sound financial judgment, to be your attorney-in-fact. While this doesn't have to be the same person as your attorney-in-fact for health care, it's sensible to name the same person for both roles unless you strongly believe someone else should handle your money. If you do name different people for these two jobs, be sure they can work well together.

In your document, you can specify whether or not you want your attorney-in-fact to be paid for taking care of your finances. (An attorney-in-fact is always entitled to reimbursement from your assets for any expenses he or she incurs on your behalf, but you may decide to authorize additional compensation.) In many family situations, the attorney-in-fact is not paid if the duties won't be complicated or burdensome. If your property and finances are extensive, however, and your attorney-in-fact will need to devote significant time and energy to managing them, it seems fair that you provide compensation for the work. Most importantly, discuss and resolve this issue with your proposed attorney-in-fact before you finalize your document.

The Attorney-in-Fact's Duties

Commonly, people give an attorney-in-fact broad power over their finances. But you can give your attorney-in-fact as much or as little power as you wish. You may want to give your attorney-in-fact authority to do some or all of the following:

- use your assets to pay your everyday expenses and those of your family
- buy, sell, maintain, pay taxes on, and mortgage real estate and other property
- collect benefits from Social Security, Medicare, or other government programs or civil or military service
- invest your money in stocks, bonds, and mutual funds
- handle transactions with banks and other financial institutions
- buy and sell insurance policies and annuities for you
- file and pay your taxes
- operate your small business
- claim or disclaim property you inherit or are otherwise entitled to
- represent you in court or hire someone to represent you, and
- manage your retirement accounts.

Whatever powers you give the attorney-in-fact, he or she must act in your best interests, keep accurate records, keep your property separate from his or hers (unless you specify otherwise in the power of attorney document), and avoid conflicts of interest.

As with health care directives, you can change the attorney-in-fact or any other provision of your durable power of attorney for finances any time, as long as you are of sound mind.

SEE AN EXPERT

Powers of attorney and Medicare. If you're concerned about protecting your assets from the reach of a nursing facility or from Medicare, see an attorney who specializes in asset preservation. Federal law prohibits transferring assets within three years of applying for Medicare, so an expert attorney is a must.

When Your Durable Power of Attorney for Finances Takes Effect

There are two kinds of durable powers of attorney for finances: those that take effect immediately, and those that don't become effective unless a doctor (or two, if you wish) certifies that you are incapacitated. Which to choose depends, in part, on when you want your attorney-in-fact to begin handling tasks for you.

If you want someone to take over some or all of your financial tasks now, you should make your document effective as soon as you sign it. Then, your attorney-in-fact can begin helping you with your finances right away—and can continue to do so if you later become incapacitated.

On the other hand, you may feel strongly that your attorney-in-fact should not take over unless and until you are incapacitated.

In this case, you have two options. If you trust your attorney-in-fact to use his or her authority only when it's absolutely necessary, you can go ahead and make your durable power of attorney effective immediately. Legally, your attorney-in-fact will then have the authority to act on your behalf—but, according to your wishes, won't do so unless he or she decides that you can't handle your affairs yourself.

If you're uncomfortable making a document that's effective immediately, you can make what's known as a "springing" power of attorney. It doesn't take effect until a physician examines you and declares, in writing, that you can't manage your finances.

There are some real inconveniences involved in creating a springing power of attorney. First, your attorney-in-fact will have to go through the potentially time-consuming and complicated process of getting the doctors' statements.

This may be made even more difficult by HIPAA. Unlike health care documents, it's unclear whether or not HIPAA rules apply to durable powers of attorney for finances. Without a valid HIPAA release, a doctor might refuse to prepare a statement for your agent that confirms your incapacity.

Second, though it's not too likely, some people and institutions may be reluctant to accept a springing power of attorney, even after your attorney-in fact has obtained the necessary doctors' statements and your document is perfectly legal. A bank, for example, might question whether you have, in fact, become incapacitated. These

hassles could delay your attorney-in-fact and disrupt the handling of your finances.

If you truly trust your attorney-in-fact (and you should), you may find that it makes more sense to create a document that's effective immediately and then make clear to your attorney-in-fact when he or she should take action under the document. Ultimately, of course, the decision is yours—and you should choose the option that feels most comfortable to you.

SEE AN EXPERT

See a lawyer for a springing durable power of attorney for finances. If you truly aren't comfortable granting someone immediate authority over your finances, you should see a knowledgeable lawyer to make sure you obtain a properly drafted springing document. The lawyer can make sure that your document includes all the necessary legal language, including a valid HIPAA release.

Finalizing Your Durable Power of Attorney for Finances

After you've completed your durable power of attorney for finances, you must observe certain formalities to make it legal. But these requirements aren't difficult to meet.

You must sign your durable power of attorney in the presence of a notary public for your state. In some states, notarization is required by law to make the durable power of attorney valid. But even where law doesn't require it, custom does. A durable power of attorney that is not notarized may not be accepted by people your attorney-in-fact needs to deal with. A handful of states also require you to sign your document in front of witnesses. Witnesses must be mentally competent adults, and your attorney-in-fact may not be a witness. Some states impose additional witness requirements as well and a few require your attorney-in-fact to sign the power of attorney or a separate consent form before taking action under the document.

Finally, if your document grants power over real estate, you must put a copy of your document on file in the land records office of any counties where you own real estate. This process is called "recording," or "registration" in some states. (You don't have to record your document until it takes effect. This means that if you make a springing power of attorney, your attorney-in-fact can record the document later, if you ever become incapacitated.) In just two states, North Carolina and South Carolina, you must record your durable power of attorney for it to be durable—that is, for it to remain in effect if you become incapacitated.

 RESOURCE

How to find the forms you need. You can use *Quicken WillMaker Plus* (software from Nolo) to prepare a durable power of attorney for finances that is valid in your state.

What to Do With the Signed Document

If your power of attorney is effective immediately, give the original signed and notarized document to the attorney-in-fact. He or she will need it as proof of authority to act on your behalf.

If the durable power of attorney won't become effective unless you become incapacitated (a springing durable power of attorney), keep the notarized, signed original yourself. Store it in a safe, convenient place that the attorney-in-fact can reach quickly, if necessary. Your attorney-in-fact will need the original document to carry out your wishes.

You may also wish to give copies of your durable power of attorney to the people and institutions your attorney-in-fact will need to deal with—banks or government offices, for example. If the document is already in their records, it may eliminate hassles for your attorney-in-fact later. If you're making a springing durable power of attorney, however, it may seem premature to contact people and institutions about a document that may never go into effect. It's up to you.

Durable Powers of Attorney for Finances and Living Trusts

Many living trusts provide that the successor trustee is to manage the trust property if the grantor becomes incapacitated. Even if you use a durable power of attorney to appoint someone (your attorney-in-fact) to handle your property if you become incapacitated, property in your living trust still remains subject to your successor trustee, not the attorney-in-fact. This division is typically only one of terminology, not substance, because most people appoint the same person to handle both jobs.

Some people who plan to transfer all of their property under a living trust ask why they need to bother with a durable power of attorney for finances at all. The reason is that you're likely to receive income, even if you become incapacitated, from pensions, Social Security, and other sources, and you will need a durable power of attorney for finances to handle this money, maintain your personal bank account, pay bills, and so on.

Guardianships and Conservatorships

If you are concerned about a person who is already incapacitated and unable to make decisions, most of the advice in this chapter will not apply to you. At that point, the person can no longer create valid legal documents or delegate responsibility for decisions to others. If the person made no durable powers of attorney or living trust, financial institutions, government agencies, health care providers, and bureaucrats of every variety may either refuse to take action regarding the person's affairs, or take action with little regard for the person's wishes.

In this situation, you'll probably have to go to court to ask a judge to appoint you or another relative or friend to act on the person's behalf. There are procedures in every state to do this. Some states have only one legal category, usually called guardianship; others have a second category that is often limited to financial matters and is called conservatorship.

In general guardianship proceedings, the legal question is whether or not a person has become "incompetent"—that is, unable to handle his or her own affairs. In many states, this requires that medical evidence of incompetence be presented to the court. In more limited proceedings to establish only a financial conservatorship (see below), the court can act if it finds that the person is unable to handle financial affairs even though he's not completely legally incompetent.

When appointing a guardian or conservator, a judge follows certain preferences established by state law. Most states give preference to the incompetent person's spouse, adult children, adult siblings, or other blood relatives. (In a few states, a judge may give highest priority to a registered domestic partner.) Judges have some flexibility in choosing the guardian; the judge may use his or her discretion to pick the best person for the job. Without strong evidence of what the incapacitated person would have wanted, however, it is unlikely that a nonrelative would ever be appointed over a relative who wants the position. Because of this, guardianship or conservatorship proceedings can cause great heartache if an estranged relative is chosen as conservator over the person's partner or close friend.

In conservatorship or guardianship proceedings, a person has a right to appear in court with an attorney and to consent or object to all proposed authority. In many states, if the person does not have an attorney, the court may appoint one. Similarly, any change in the conservator or guardian's authority requires an additional court order to which the person can consent or object. The conservator or guardian is accountable to the court and will be held responsible for any mismanagement of the person's property.

In some states, it is possible to handle conservatorship proceedings without the assistance of a lawyer if no one challenges the need for the conservatorship and its scope. More complicated guardianship procedures, however, do require the assistance of a lawyer, particularly if anyone, including the person alleged to be incompetent, does not agree that the guardianship is needed or thinks that the person seeking to be guardian is not the right person for the job.

Financial Conservatorship or Guardianship

A conservator or guardian can be appointed by a court solely to protect a person's property—savings, real estate, investments, or other assets. He or she can also conduct daily financial affairs, such as paying bills, or arrange for services when the person is unable to do so. This type of limited management assistance is appropriate when the person is still capable of caring for himself or herself personally, but because of disorientation or disability is unable to responsibly carry out financial tasks. In this situation, the conservator or guardian does not have power over the person's personal conduct, but has authority over financial or other affairs as the court orders.

An advantage of a limited conservatorship or guardianship is that it leaves the person free to make many important decisions independently: where to live, with whom to associate, what medical care to receive. Nonetheless, it is still a court process in which a judge makes a ruling, occasionally against the person's will, that gives another person authority over a part of his or her life. It is, therefore, a procedure to be used only if voluntary procedures such as making a durable power of attorney are no longer possible.

Full Guardianship

Full guardianship is an extreme measure that severely restricts the legal rights of a person based on a court's finding of incompetence. It reduces that person's legal status to that of a minor, with no control over her or his own money or property, decisions about medical care, or institutionalization. A person under full guardianship loses even the right to vote.

If a person retains some degree of orientation and capability, a legal finding by a court that he or she is incompetent can be emotionally devastating and, in fact, self-fulfilling. The person deemed legally incompetent may well give up the will to care for himself or herself and become much less competent than before. Obviously, seeking a full guardianship is a very serious step, to be taken when a person's mental condition leaves no other choice.

Body and Organ Donation, Funerals, and Burials

People facing the grief and reality that someone they love has died face other immediate problems: disposing of the body and arranging the ceremonies desired to mark the death. It's hard to even talk directly about a body once life has left it; the word "corpse" sounds unfeeling, and "cadaver" is worse. Statutes often refer to a dead body as "the remains," a word technically accurate and almost as disturbing. Perhaps it's because many of us don't like to contemplate death that the language we have invented for it can be awkward. But, however it is described, the reality is the same: a body must, somehow, be removed from the place of death and disposed of. And if desired, commemorative ceremonies need to be carried out.

Most people die in hospitals or nursing homes. These institutions want a dead body removed quickly. So it's nearly inevitable, if no planning has been done, for family or friends to turn to "professionals"— funeral homes. Often they do it without reflection or much knowledge of what the traditional funeral establishment offers or what it charges for its services. This passive approach often means family and friends pay far too much for a funeral they don't even like—and worst of all, for funeral goods and services that don't suit the person who has died.

Grief, guilt, sorrow, religious conviction, doubt, or whatever survivors are feeling often leave them distraught and confused. In these circumstances, expenses can seem trivial. However, I believe it's no slight to the deceased, or to the feelings of those who survive, to suggest that nothing is gained by needless costs. Funerals can be expensive. According to the National Funeral Directors Association, the average cost of a conventional U.S. funeral is more than $7,000. It's one of the most expensive items the average American family ever purchases. To many, including this author, this is a huge and unnecessary cost to comply with the biblical injunction: "Remember, man, thou art dust and to dust thou shall return."

Making Your Own Choices

More and more people are reflecting on what they want to happen to their bodies when they die. They are making choices that have emotional meaning for them and save their families needless expense.

Broadly viewed, there are four choices available (I don't cover some of the more esoteric options, such as cryonics/body freezing).

Donating the entire body to a medical school. This must be arranged beforehand. If you do this, the school uses the body for studies after which the body is usually cremated, and the remains buried or scattered. However, family members or friends can request that the body be returned when the study is complete— usually within a year or so. Even if a person opts for whole body donation, that donation may be refused at death for any of a number of reasons, requiring survivors to make other plans.

Donating specific body organs to an organ bank. If you donate organs, the rest of the body is normally returned to those responsible for cremation or burial, which means that someone still must arrange for its disposal.

Arranging a traditional funeral service conducted by a commercial funeral home. This includes cremation or body burial.

Arranging a simple funeral service, without embalming of the body. You can do this independently or with the help of a funeral or memorial society.

Planning for the immediate, practical aspects of your death is essential to make sure your wishes are carried out. To take one example, if you wish to donate body parts or organs, it's almost essential to authorize it, in writing, before your death. Similarly, if you want a nontraditional funeral, such as cremation with your ashes scattered over the sea, it may not happen unless you arrange the details yourself. (Each state has rules governing how and where ashes may be scattered, though it's legal in every state to scatter or bury ashes on private property as long as you have the landowner's permission.) Even for a traditional commercial funeral, planning is desirable. Costs for death goods and services vary widely—for example, caskets are commonly marked up from five to ten times their wholesale costs. So, comparison shopping can often result in big savings.

In my view, there's really no good reason to plan how to save money on probate fees or estate taxes and then toss a chunk of it away on an overpriced funeral. Equally important, there's no reason to dread thinking about what kind of death notice and ceremonial service will be fitting, if you want them. Once you've decided what is appropriate, you need to convey your intention to others, preferably in a written declaration. This kind of planning can achieve much more than saving money. It provides survivors with essential guidance and offers you peace of mind that you've made arrangements to your liking.

Leaving Written Instructions

You should put your wishes regarding the disposition of your body in writing. Under most states' laws, written burial instructions left by a deceased person are binding, assuming, of course, the instructions don't violate state laws on body disposition. Even where laws do not specifically require that a deceased person's instructions be followed, they almost always are. You can also ensure that your wishes are followed by joining a local funeral or memorial society.

It's best to prepare typed or printed burial instructions in a distinct document, separate from your will or other estate planning papers. Keep the instructions in a safe and readily accessible place, known to whomever will have the responsibility for implementing them. Or simpler yet, give a copy to the person you've chosen to be responsible for carrying out your desires. If you've joined a funeral society or chosen a mortuary, make sure it has a copy of your wishes.

If you don't leave legally binding written instructions, your next of kin (the closest family relation) will have legal control over the disposition of your body. This can pose insoluble problems if a friend or partner knows you wanted a specific type of disposition that the next of kin opposes. Without legally binding written instructions, the friend or partner is powerless to prevent the next of kin from controlling the disposition.

RESOURCE
More help with final arrangements.
Nolo offers two excellent resources to help you decide on final arrangements—from burial or cremation to memorial ceremonies—and leave instructions for loved ones. Nolo's *Quicken WillMaker Plus* software helps you prepare a final arrangements letter that makes your wishes clear. Or, if you prefer to use a workbook, *Get It Together: Organize Your Records So Your Family Won't Have To*, by Melanie Cullen and Shae Irving, provides a complete system to help you organize all your important paperwork and personal information, including instructions for final arrangements to your survivors.

About Death Certificates

Whenever a person dies, a physician must complete a death certificate shortly after the death and file it with the appropriate governmental agency, often a local registrar of health. Those responsible for winding up a deceased person's affairs will need certified copies of the death certificate to transfer certain types of property to inheritors. For example, to collect money from a pay-on-death bank account or to end a joint tenancy of real estate, the inheritors need a certified copy of the death certificate. To wind up a probate avoidance living trust, the successor trustee will often need several copies of the death certificate. For information about obtaining copies of a death certificate, see Chapter 31.

Donating Your Body or Organs

If you want to leave your body, or parts of it, for medical research or instruction, you have two choices:

- you can leave your entire body to medical science, usually a medical school, or
- you can donate certain body organs or tissues to transplant facilities.

You cannot do both. Medical schools generally won't accept a body from which any part has been removed, except sometimes for eye transplants.

The procedure for donating a body to a medical school is simple. Contact the school, see if it accepts bodies for instruction and study, and if so, what legalities and forms it requires. Medical facilities are legally prohibited from paying for bodies, but many will absorb the cost of transporting a body—at least within certain distance of the institution.

Many, but not all, medical schools won't accept bodies that are too old or too diseased, or if death occurred during surgery. So it's important to have a backup plan if you're thinking about body donation.

The other option, donating body organs, is also a generous and useful act. There is a great need for many types of organ donations. Heart transplants get the most publicity, but many more organs, tissues, and bones can and are being transplanted, including middle ear, eyes, liver, lungs, pancreas, kidneys, skin tissue, bone and cartilage, pituitary glands, and even hip or knee joints. A gift of a vital organ is one of the most precious and loving acts one can make. I know this well, as I have a friend who was saved from blindness by a cornea transplant.

To authorize organ donation, it's a good idea to obtain a donor card and carry it with you at all times. In most states, you can use your driver's license for this purpose; the motor vehicles department will give you a card to carry and perhaps a sticker to place on the front of your license. In addition, your health care directive is often a good place to state your wishes regarding organ donation. An increasing number of states are providing a place on their official forms for such instructions. Also, after your death, your immediate family can consent to donating your organs—unless you've left instructions to the contrary.

Time is truly of the essence for the successful removal of donated body parts, so if you want to have organs removed on death you should make arrangements beforehand and discuss your intentions with family and friends. Most people put off making these arrangements, no matter how intensely they may want to donate their organs. With donation of body parts, procrastination may result in your intentions being frustrated because they cannot be carried out fast enough.

Death Notices

When someone dies, one of the first things that most families do is notify others. For close friends and relatives, phone calls normally work. But what about notifying the many other people whose lives have been touched by the deceased, such as former neighbors, golf partners, sailing or bowling friends, retired business associates, and other friends? Doing this promptly is important, as many of these people will wish to attend one or more of the events that usually occur very soon after death, such as a wake, lying-in, funeral, or memorial ceremony. And other people will wish to communicate with the family and extend their sympathy.

In many communities, notification is handled by a local newspaper, with either a death notice or an obituary. It is also becoming increasingly popular to publish death notices online using sites like www. legacy.com.

Most newspapers have a relationship with an online provider, so that when you submit your death notice to the newspaper, you also have the option of creating an online version of the notice.

Death notices generally must be paid for and consist of small print listings of the date of death, names of survivors, and location of any services.

An obituary is a news item, usually prepared by the staff of the newspaper. It runs in standard type, contains a small headline—for example, "Former Local School Principal Dies"—and is free. In small towns, many local newspapers prepare obituaries for a large percentage of people who die, giving more space to those who were locally prominent. In large metropolitan papers, however, very few people's deaths are sufficiently newsworthy to qualify for obituaries, and even fairly prominent people have their deaths recorded in the paid death notices, if at all.

Death notices must be promptly published. This can raise a real problem for survivors. Just when they are beset by difficult emotions and serious practical problems, someone has to collect and publish the details of the dead person's life. Common problems involve remembering or locating dates, parents' full names, details of key events, correct spellings for clubs and other affiliations, to mention just a few.

One solution to this problem is to prepare your own death notice. This might sound a bit macabre, but it will probably only take you a little while, and those who are later spared the task will surely be appreciative. Just look at existing examples in the publication in which you want your notice to appear and follow the general form it uses to write one out.

What about writing your own obituary? With many local newspapers, you can help write the news story about your death in advance. The paper will have a form on which you can list all relevant biographical information, including your education and employment history, civic responsibilities, names of children, and so on. If this form is filled out in advance, it can be given to the paper immediately after death and will be used to write the news story. In addition to completing this form, you may want to actually try your hand at writing your own obituary, leaving blank your date of death. Does this sound weird? Well, yes, a little, but remember, if you don't do it, someone you love may have to deal with a reporter precisely when there will be far more pressing practical and emotional concerns occasioned by your death. To get an idea of what an obituary should look like, read a few in your local paper or online. In my experience, if a family submits a well-written, factual obituary immediately after a person's death, a local newspaper is likely to use a good part of it, or at least echo its major themes.

Services and Ceremonies Following a Death

Many people wish to have input about the ceremonies held after their deaths. You may have a favorite church, synagogue, or temple where you would like the service held, or a particular priest, pastor, rabbi, or monk to conduct it. You may know how you want the service to be conducted. Of course, in many religious and spiritual communities, the broad outlines of rituals that accompany a death are well established. Usually, however, when it comes to the particular prayers to be read and songs to be sung, there's room for personal choice. If the service won't be held by a religious institution, individual input becomes more urgent. It's sad to attend, as I have, funerals of good friends held in a commercial funeral home where not one personal word was said.

If you have specific ideas about ceremonies you want held after your death, the best way to make sure your wishes will be carried out is to put them in writing. Simply include a brief statement as part of your final instructions.

Funerals

For funerals, you have two basic options: Use a commercial funeral home or make arrangements in advance through a nonprofit funeral or memorial society.

Commercial Funerals

The traditional American funeral, as provided by a commercial funeral home or mortuary, normally includes the following:

- The funeral director takes care of the paperwork required for death and burial certificates.
- The funeral home removes the body from the place of death and embalms it.
- The embalmed body is shown at an open casket ceremony, or there is a closed casket. Many funeral parlors have their own chapels and encourage all services to be held there, rather than in churches.

Funerals are always products of culture. Our own culture, which studiously avoids contemplating death, is also made nervous by trying to decide what type of funeral is appropriate. At times in the past, expensive funerals and burials were scorned as ostentatious and wasteful, and the norm was a simple, dignified, and inexpensive service. In other times, as in 17th-century England, expensive funerals and grand tombs were in vogue for those with status and wealth.

There is no single American cultural tradition concerning funerals and burials. Most Americans do hold ceremonies when a person dies, of course, and many ethnic and religious traditions are deeply ingrained, such as the Jewish custom of burial within 24 hours, the Buddhist practice of sitting with the body for several days, or the Irish wake. But, generally speaking, for those not close to their ethnic roots, a significant cultural vacuum exists. It should come as no surprise that this vacuum was filled by business.

Before the Civil War, burials in America were most often simple affairs—a religious ceremony, a plain pine box, and quick burial. Undertakers did not exist until roughly the 1860s; originally they practiced some other trade, often carpentry. During the Civil War, bodies of dead soldiers were embalmed so they could be shipped home for burial. Next, undertakers emerged as a distinct trade; they later evolved into funeral directors and began to proclaim themselves professionals. The plain pine box was transformed into a luxurious coffin. Funerals became theater, and their cost rose accordingly. Embalming the dead body and showing the embalmed remains became standard funeral parlor practice—a practice that obviously adds substantially to the cost of burial, and one not used (and, indeed, regarded as barbaric) in most other countries. The funeral industry also developed a rationalization for embalming. It claimed that viewing the embalmed body is useful for the living, because seeing a lifelike body enables the viewers to cope with their grief. The term they invented for this is "grief therapy." Some funeral homes also offer "after care" help to a widow or widower, sometimes including support groups and professional therapists.

As many people sense, there's something odd, as well as expensive, about traditional American funerals. This shift in attitude was originally sparked by Jessica Mitford's book *The American Way of Death* (Simon & Schuster), a pioneering examination of commercial American culture in one of its more rapacious and grotesque areas. Written with wit and grace, Mitford's book (now over five decades old, but still influential) raised many questions about American funeral customs. As a result of her book and the efforts of many others, many beneficial legal changes have occurred.

Legal reform has aided the growth of funeral and memorial societies, which, in turn, have introduced real price competition into the commercial funeral business. Now some commercial funeral homes have begun to advertise less expensive funerals. So, if you do want to patronize a traditional funeral parlor, shop around for the best prices on costs and services. Mortuaries are legally required to give those who ask a detailed price list of their goods and services.

RESOURCE
Learn your state's rules about funerals, cremation, and embalming. Some states have rules about how a body can or must be treated after death. You can learn your state's rules in the Getting Your Affairs in Order section of Nolo.com at www.nolo.com/legal-encyclopedia/affairs-in-order.

Embalming

One great expense of a traditional funeral is embalming the body. Generally, state law doesn't require embalming unless the body will be transported by common carrier, such as a commercial plane, or county health officials order embalming as a protection against the spread of contagious disease (a very rare event). There are those who claim that embalming is a necessary health measure, but there's little evidence to support this. If a body must be preserved for a short time, refrigeration is at least as reliable, and far cheaper.

In embalming, preservative and disinfectant fluid is injected into the arterial system and body cavities, replacing blood. Embalmed bodies aren't preserved for eternity, though medical science can do this for exceptional reasons (keeping Lenin's body on display, for example). Generally, an embalmed body begins to decompose rapidly within a few weeks.

By embalming the body, a funeral parlor can preserve it sufficiently to allow open-casket viewing of the body at a funeral service, a popular practice with some Americans. How one feels about this is, of course, a private matter. The important point is to realize that open-casket viewing—and embalming—are far from inevitable practices. The choice is up to survivors or to you, if you make plans for your own burial.

Costs

The major factor in the total cost of a funeral—and the item most grossly marked up—is the price of the casket. Not surprisingly, funeral directors generally urge as expensive a casket as possible.

Anyone who's ever been casket shopping can tell you it's a bit like visiting a car dealership. There's always a larger, fancier model available, with more expensive options. The question all too often becomes not how much a casket costs, but how much you are willing to pay. In most facilities, rental caskets are available for those who wish to be cremated or who choose not to purchase a casket.

The cost of a traditional funeral can easily add up to many thousands of dollars. In addition to the casket, there's normally a charge for each extra, and there are a lot of possible extras, including flowers, special burial clothing, additional limousines, clergyman's honorarium, music, and cards. Also, watch out for fraudulent fees, such as "handling" charges or AIDS body handling costs.

Flowers have become traditional at American funerals. A significant percentage of all flowers sold by commercial florists in America are sold for funerals. Not surprisingly, the florist industry resists any attempt to cut back on the practice of sending flowers to funerals. Some people prefer that money that would have been spent on flowers be given to a particular charity. Sometimes funeral notices or announcements state "Please omit flowers." Whether flowers are a beautiful and moving statement or an unnecessary expense is a choice each person can make; again, the point is to realize that there's a choice.

Finally, transporting a body from a distant place of death, or to a distant burial place, is particularly expensive. If you must arrange for the return of a body from a distant place of death, consult a customer service representative of the airlines to make sure you get the most affordable rates.

Funeral Societies

Funeral societies are private, nonprofit organizations, open to any who wish to join. They are devoted to the concept of simple, dignified burial services for a reasonable cost. There's usually a small fee for joining. Members are entitled to the burial programs offered through the society. Funeral societies don't generally employ their own morticians, or own their own cemeteries; rather, they have contracts of varying types with cooperating local mortuaries and crematoriums. The societies make a price list of goods and services available, and members choose the mortuary and service they would like. After a death, the society ensures that only the services selected are performed and billed for.

Specific policies, funeral costs, and options vary somewhat from organization to organization, but the basics are common to all. Dignified, simple funerals can be arranged for hundreds of dollars, not thousands. Members are concerned not only with reducing the excessive costs, but at least equally with what they believe are the excesses and lack of spiritual values inherent in many commercial funerals. As the literature of the funeral societies notes, in the traditional funeral, the emphasis is on the dead body—lying in an open

casket, embalmed, often painted, rouged, or otherwise altered cosmetically in the belief that the embalmer's skills will make a more lifelike body, and that viewing a lifelike dead body is a sign of respect or affection.

Funeral societies want new members and readily provide information on their programs, services, and membership rules, as well as the names of all cooperating mortuaries. If you move, there's a good chance you can transfer your membership to another society; there are funeral societies in most urban areas of the United States.

There are hundreds of funeral societies throughout the United States. To locate one near you, check the phone book or contact:

Funeral Consumers Alliance
33 Patchen Road
South Burlington, VT 05403
802-865-8300
www.funerals.org

Cremation

Cremation means the burning of the body. Cremation is common in many parts of the world and is now used for roughly half the deaths in the United States. It's opposed by certain religions, such as Muslims and Greek and Jewish Orthodox creeds. Catholics used to require the permission of their local bishop to be cremated, but the Catholic Church no longer bans cremation outright.

Be careful if you make a direct arrangement with a profit-making cremation organization. Some have been known to rip off customers, charging "handling," "transportation," or "disposal" fees. Regular fees commonly are $1,000 or more for a "basic" cremation, plus possible additional charges of $350 to $700 for scattering the ashes, and $1,500 to $20,000 for putting the ashes in an (attractive) container.

Despite the risk of excessive costs, it is possible to arrange for a sensibly priced cremation. By law in many states, a crematory cannot require that a casket (rather than a bag) be used in cremation. This makes sense, as it seems particularly needless to pay for an expensive wood casket that is almost immediately burned. Cheaper wood caskets are often used, by custom, if no contrary directions are given.

Whether and how ashes can be scattered depends on state law. Scatterings were rare a few generations ago, but there has been a marked increase in their number as the number of cremations has grown. Cremated remains can be removed from the place of cremation or inurnment and disposed of by scattering by the person with the legal right to control the remains. Once again, leaving specific instructions regarding your wishes is a sound idea. A permit may be required for scattering in some locations. However, as noted earlier, in all states it's legal to scatter or bury cremated remains on private land, as long as the landowner approves. The crematory or mortuary involved should be able to handle any necessary paperwork involved in scattering or burying ashes.

RESOURCE
Learn your state's rules about funerals, cremation, and embalming. Some states have rules about how a body can or must be treated after death. You can learn your state's rules in the Getting Your Affairs in Order section of Nolo.com at www.nolo.com/legal-encyclopedia/affairs-in-order.

Burials

A body must be disposed of in a lawful way. Unless it's cremated and the ashes scattered or kept in an urn or in a licensed columbarium (a building in which urns and ashes may be kept), it must be buried somewhere. Often this means the remains must be buried in a cemetery (graveyard, if you prefer the more descriptive word).

In this country, there's a wide variety of cemeteries, including profit-making ones, large mutually owned ones, church burial grounds, small co-ops, municipal ones, and national cemeteries, in which most veterans and their spouses are entitled to a free burial.

Most American cemeteries, however, are private businesses. You have to buy your way in. Private cemeteries are normally separate businesses from funeral homes, although they often have working relationships with one another. Sometimes, though, they compete, and some cemeteries sell caskets. Usually, the fact that private cemeteries are separate means only that there's one more transaction to arrange—buying a burial plot. This

You Can Go Green

Burial and cremation can be hard on the environment. Embalming chemicals, metal caskets, concrete burial vaults, and cremation emissions take a surprising toll.

It's not difficult to make green arrangements that use biodegradable materials and avoid toxins. Some choices are remarkably simple—and most are significantly less expensive:

- **No embalming.** Embalming fluid contains toxic chemicals—including up to three gallons of formaldehyde. Embalming is rarely required by law or to carry out final wishes.
- **Eco-coffin or biodegradable urn.** You can use a simple wood casket, cardboard box, or fabric shroud for burial. There are many options for biodegradable coffins and urns (for ashes that will be buried), including homemade ones.
- **Home funeral.** While it's more work, your loved ones may find a home funeral to be more satisfying. Most states permit home funerals, but Connecticut, Indiana, Louisiana, Nebraska, and New York require the involvement of a funeral director.
- **No in-ground vault.** Vaults are concrete containers that are placed in the ground to surround a casket. They aren't required by law, but many cemeteries demand them to make landscape maintenance easier. Look for a cemetery that doesn't require a vault or find out whether you can legally refuse one.
- **Green cemeteries.** The Green Burial Council has developed a certification process for cemeteries that want to go green. Learn more and locate green facilities at www.greenburialcouncil.org.
- **Cremation conservation.** Cremation uses fewer resources than burial, but it's not entirely clean. If you have amalgam fillings—fillings that contain mercury—in your teeth, you can ask that they be removed before cremation.

purchase can often be arranged through a funeral society or a funeral home. If there's a specific cemetery you desire, you should be sure the funeral home or society can arrange for that particular purchase. Also, you might save money if you select your own cemetery, as prices can vary significantly.

Probably the best known private graveyard in the world is Forest Lawn Cemetery in Los Angeles. Evelyn Waugh's justly famous satire of Forest Lawn, *The Loved One,* hasn't diminished the success of this cemetery. Many people still choose (or their relatives choose) to be buried in its "splendor." Depending on how much splendor is desired, this can be quite expensive indeed.

Cemetery costs, like everything else, are going up. The minimum cost includes:

- the plot
- the coffin enclosure, which normally consists of a vault or grave liner of concrete and steel. Cemetery owners sometimes say vaults are required to prevent the land bordering the grave from eventually collapsing. Although this danger is often nonexistent or exaggerated, yearly vault sales have recently been estimated to amount to nearly one-half billion dollars. Many vaults are bought through a funeral director, although they are usually cheaper if bought from a cemetery.
- opening and closing the grave, and
- upkeep.

Many cemeteries sell "perpetual care," which they claim means that the grave will be attended "for eternity." This sounds pretty grandiose until you realize that graves don't require much care—what this really means is that the grass will be cut. And even this task doesn't amount to much in many modern urban cemeteries, which have eliminated the use of headstones, substituting plaques that are planted flush to the ground, so as not to interfere with the power mower.

If you haven't got enough to worry about, you could worry about what will happen when we run out of cemetery land. It'll take a while, surely, although one expert suggests that in only 500 years, at the present rate of graveyard growth, all the land in the United States would be graveyards.

Finally, if there's to be a headstone or plaque, why not create your own epitaph? It's your last opportunity for self-expression.

Among my favorite epitaphs are:

Cast a cold eye, on life, on death. Horseman, pass by! —Yeats

and the classic:

On the whole, I'd rather be in Philadelphia.—W.C. Fields

RESOURCE

More information about making your own final arrangements. How to arrange for a funeral or burial yourself, with organizational help, is discussed in *Quicken WillMaker Plus* (software from Nolo). You may also want to read the highly regarded book, *Caring for the Dead: Your Final Act of Love*, by Lisa Carlson (Upper Access Books).

Family Business Estate Planning

If you own an interest in a small business, whether as a sole proprietor, partner, shareholder in a closely held corporation, or member of a limited liability company, estate planning can get complicated fast. If a substantial part of your estate is a profit-making business of significant value, you'll need to look into three broad areas:

- operation of the business after your death
- estate tax concerns, and
- avoiding probate.

Estate planning for the small business owner requires the assistance of an attorney experienced in the field. This chapter gives you only a broad-brush introduction to the major concerns.

Operation of the Business

The death of the sole or part owner of a small business is likely to seriously disrupt that business. If no planning has been done, the disruption can be catastrophic, sometimes resulting in the failure of the enterprise. You need to have a sound succession plan. Who will take over the business? Will family members run it? (Roughly 80% of all U.S. businesses are family owned. The second generation takes over about 30% of these businesses, but only 10% of the third generation continues on.) If someone else will run the business, how will family members or other inheritors be paid for your interest?

Keeping Ownership in the Family

Obviously, to keep business ownership in the family, one or more family members must be willing and able to run the business. If they are, and you're the sole owner of your business, your main concerns are probably about dealing fairly with all your close family members. (See "Treating Family Members Fairly," below.)

If you share ownership of a business, you must consider the rights of the other owners, even if there are capable family members who want to inherit your share. Commonly, a partnership agreement, corporate bylaws, a shareholders' agreement, or the operating agreement of a limited liability company (LLC) controls the disposition of a deceased owner's interest in the business. You need to create a business estate plan that is in harmony with the documents that restrict your options.

Agreements between co-owners of a business normally cover the right of the surviving owners to buy the deceased owner's interest. One standard provision gives the surviving owners a "right of first refusal," allowing them to buy the interest for the price offered by an outside would-be purchaser. If there is no outside offer, another provision may provide a method for determining the value of the deceased owner's interest in the business. A related issue here is whether the surviving owners must buy out the deceased owners' share, or simply have the option to do so.

The agreement should also state how buyout payments will be made. Often the agreement allows the surviving owners to pay for a deceased owner's share over months or years. Particularly if the business is a corporation, determining the most desirable payout process can involve sophisticated tax planning.

Arranging to buy out a deceased owner's share necessarily involves practical financial problems. Will the business really have the money to make the payments? What happens if it doesn't? If the surviving owners aren't required to buy out a deceased owner's share, what happens if they decide not to? The inheritors can try to sell that share, but, if it's a minority share they may not find an outside buyer. Then what?

In the absence of an owners' agreement, the rights of the surviving owners are determined by the laws of the state where the business is located. It is not sensible to rely on these laws, since they are highly unlikely to fit the needs of you or your family. It's much better to work out an agreement beforehand.

RESOURCE

For information on how to draft a business agreement to cover sale and valuation issues, see these Nolo books:

- *Business Buyout Agreements: Plan Now for Retirement, Death, Divorce or Owner Disagreements,* by Bethany Laurence and Anthony Mancuso
- *Form a Partnership: The Complete Legal Guide,* by Denis Clifford and Ralph Warner

- *Your Limited Liability Company: An Operating Manual,* by Anthony Mancuso, and
- *Incorporate Your Business: A Legal Guide to Forming a Corporation in Your State,* by Anthony Mancuso.

Treating Family Members Fairly

If you have more than one child, and some will run the business and some won't, you may have to resolve some difficult fairness issues. Do you want to leave all your children roughly the same amount? If so, what's the best way to leave the business and your other assets so that all your children are treated equally? If you don't want to leave equal shares, do you want to explain your decision to your children, in your estate planning documents or elsewhere? There certainly aren't any rules here; you have to figure out what works best for you and your family.

> **EXAMPLE:** Dante and Grace own a thriving construction business. This corporation is roughly 80% of their net worth. They have five children. After Dante and Grace die, two of the children, Steve and Patricia, will take over the business. The other three aren't interested in working in it. How can Dante and Grace achieve their goal of leaving each of their children an inheritance of roughly the same value?
>
> One possibility is to leave the business to Steve and Patricia, and divide the remaining 20% of the estate among the

other three children. The difference would be made up by the proceeds of life insurance. But the cost of life insurance turns out to be prohibitive. So Dante and Grace consider leaving the business (and the rest of their estate) equally to all five children. Only Steve and Patricia will have any voting or management powers in the business. Of course, this leaves the other three children without control over the bulk of their inheritance. Also, what if Steve and Patricia can't agree about management decisions? They've had some nasty fights in the past.

Dante and Grace strongly believe it's in all the children's best interests to keep the business going. The best hope for this is to have Steve and Patricia run it. So Dante and Grace decide to leave equal shares to all five, with only Steve and Patricia having management powers in the business. The other children will share equally in all profits from the business, including any profits made from an eventual sale of the business.

Dante and Grace amend the corporation bylaws to require that if Steve and Patricia have a dispute they can't resolve themselves, they must try mediation and, if that fails, compulsory arbitration. Dante and Grace aren't thrilled with their plan, but feel it's the best they can do. They will talk with each child to explain why they've made their decision, and how they'd like the business to work.

Other complicated issues can arise if several children will be—or already are—involved in running the business. How do you determine who will have key leadership roles in the business? How do you structure your estate plan so that your wishes will be carried out? Do all the children involved understand and accept your plan? If one or more don't, how can you best diminish the potential for conflict? All sorts of worries can come up when planning for a family business and more than one child. But remember, you can't control all of the "what ifs." Once you're gone, your estate planning can, at best, impose limited control over what happens to your family business. You need faith that the children you selected to manage your business will do a good and fair job.

Sales to Outsiders

What happens if no family member wants to carry on your business? Or there's no one you believe is capable of running it? If it's a sole proprietorship, it must be sold. If it's a shared ownership business but no co-owners are willing or able to buy your share, your inheritors would likely seek to find an outside buyer for their interest. In any case, how can you try to maximize your children's inheritance?

It's rarely desirable to simply close down or sell a business as soon as its owner dies, unless it's a one-person service business. Even if your beneficiaries do not want to participate in running the business over the long term, you'll want them to have some flexibility in the timing of the sale—which means the business must be capable of continuing in a profitable fashion for a while. One way to achieve at least short-term continuity is for key employees, the owner, and the future owners to agree in writing that these employees will stay around and continue to run the business for a period of time after the owner's death, perhaps in exchange for some portion of the eventual sale proceeds. Another way to accomplish this is to incorporate the business and make the key employees officers of the corporation and minority stockholders, perhaps through a stock option plan. Of course, the officers can still quit at any time, but they are less likely to do so if they have an ownership interest in the business.

Reducing Estate Taxes

Family business owners often dread estate taxes. Will these taxes eat up the business? Will it have to be sold to raise cash to pay the estate taxes? What can be done to lower them? Happily, there are a number of legal methods owners can use to reduce or avoid estate taxes on a family business.

First of all, remember that no estate taxes will be assessed unless the net value of the deceased owner's portion of the business, combined with his or her other assets, is over the estate tax exemption (which is over $5 million). If a sole proprietor owns a business worth $2 million and has other assets worth $1 million, no estate tax will

be assessed. If two people equally share ownership of a business worth $6 million, and each has $1 million in other assets, each has an estate of $4 million, so there will be no estate tax.

Forming a Business to Save on Taxes

Even if you're not now a small business owner, you may wonder whether you should create a business simply to take advantage of special tax breaks applicable to family businesses. Would, say, a "family limited partnership" save your inheritors money? Be careful here. Simply labeling your assets a "family business" does not make them so in the eyes of the IRS.

There must be significant and legitimate nontax reasons for creating the family limited partnership, and the partnership must be operated as a business. This means that profits must be distributed (roughly) according to legal ownership. If the person who creates the limited partnership continues to treat the business assets as if they were solely his or her own, the IRS will include the full value of the business in that individual's estate at death. Similarly, if there is an "implied agreement" that the business will pay for the ongoing expenses of the original owner, the IRS will rule that all assets of the business are part of that owner's taxable estate. From the reported cases, the IRS is quite adept at finding implied agreements. One telltale sign of this is when the original owner did not retain sufficient assets to provide for her or his own personal needs.

In other words, a family limited partnership cannot be run solely as an estate tax–avoiding scam. For example, turning your stock portfolio into a "family limited partnership" is unlikely to convince the IRS that there's any legitimate partnership business. However, a family business that combines, say, a stock portfolio and commercial real estate might be acceptable to the IRS.

In the right circumstances—with sound legal advice and a family business that passes IRS muster—establishing a family limited partnership can definitely offer estate tax savings.

SEE AN EXPERT

Expert help is essential. The IRS has issued "Settlement Guidelines" for family limited partnerships and family limited liability companies. If you are considering creating a family limited partnership or family limited liability company, you need to consult an expert who is familiar with these guidelines. Indeed, if you want to use a family limited partnership or family limited liability company in your estate planning, even if that business has been long-established, you must seek the advice of a knowledgeable lawyer. See Chapter 29 for tips on finding one.

Special Rules for Valuing Business Real Estate

Real estate used in a family trade or business or as a family farm can be valued for estate tax purposes at its value for the present use,

rather than at its "highest and best" use. For example, a family farm doesn't have to be valued for its (possibly much higher) worth as a potential location for a shopping center or subdivision, but can be valued on the basis of its worth as a farm. This valuation rule can provide a real break for family businesses. Currently, the value of the real estate can be reduced up to a maximum of $1,090,000 of the difference between "present use" and "best use." This figure is indexed to annual changes in the cost of living so it will rise in future years.

Several requirements must be met for the rule to apply:

- The value of the family business or farm must be at least 50% of the overall estate.
- The value of the real estate of that business must be at least 25% of the overall estate.
- The owner must leave the family business to a family member.
- The deceased or a family member must have used the real estate for the business in five of the eight years preceding the decedent's death.
- There are restrictions on the sale and use of the real estate for ten years (and in some cases 15 years) after the estate tax break. During this time, the family must agree to notify the IRS if the property is sold or no longer used for the business and may be required to repay some or all of the estate taxes if the ownership or use of the real estate changes.

Deferring Estate Tax Payments

If a family business, including a family farm, is part of a taxable estate, estate taxes due on that business interest can be paid in installments over fourteen years, rather than within nine months of the owner's death, as otherwise required. Interest is charged on the amount due, but the interest rate is favorable. The first four installments are interest only; the last ten are principal and interest. In other words, the final payment isn't due until roughly 15 years after the owner's death.

> **EXAMPLE:** Andrew dies in 2014 owning Shortstop Shipping, which has a net worth of $4.5 million. The total net value of his estate is $7.3 million. The personal estate tax exemption for 2014 is $5.34 million. The remaining $1.96 million, attributable to the business, is taxable. The tax payments are interest only for four years, and then interest and principal over the next ten.

Significant income tax savings are permitted for corporate stock redeemed to pay estate taxes assessed against family businesses or farms.

The principal Internal Revenue Code requirement is that the value of the small business must exceed 35% of the total estate or 50% of the taxable estate. Also, installment payments are not allowed for "passive assets"—property the deceased owned, but which was not actively used for a trade or business. For example, if the deceased owned an office park entirely managed and operated by an independent company not owned by the deceased, the office park is a "passive asset" for the purpose of the owner's estate tax.

Gifts of Minority Interests in the Business

Family business owners who face estate tax may be able to reduce or eliminate that tax liability by giving away minority interests in the business before death. Gifts are usually made to children or grandchildren.

The value of a minority interest in a business is reduced for gift tax purposes: Whatever the interest would be worth if it were part of majority control of the business, that interest is worth significantly less as minority ownership. This is called a "valuation discount."

Two separate discounts are normally involved. The first is based on the fact that minority owners do not have voting control over the business. Minority owners cannot manage, sell, or liquidate the business or distribute money to owners. So outside buyers will not pay the same price for minority interests as for majority ones. This is called a "discount for minority interest." The second discount is allowed if the basic small business agreement (partnership agreement, corporate bylaws, or operating agreement) restricts the sale of interests to family members or another narrow group, as many family businesses do. The interest cannot simply be sold to any willing buyer. This is called a "discount for lack of marketability."

The two combined discounts can range roughly from 20% to 60%. There are no statutory rules or IRS regulations governing how valuation discounts are determined, so calculating them is not easy. This is an area where owners may benefit from "aggressive" accounting and hiring "expert" appraisers. But even without skirting the edge of legality, substantial discounts are reasonable, and you can achieve significant estate tax savings.

> **EXAMPLE:** McWilson is the sole owner of the DaaDee Corp., which has 50,000 shares of stock. By the best estimate of McWilson and his accountants, if all shares were sold, they would sell for $2 million. So, at first glance, each share seems to be worth $40. But if the shares are split between minority and majority shareholders, the valuation differs. McWilson takes a 25% valuation discount for the minority shares. Each minority share is valued at $30.
>
> McWilson gives 10,000 shares to each of his two daughters. (In his living trust, he leaves the remaining stock to them equally.) For gift tax purposes, the minority shares are valued at $30. Realistically, each share transfers $40 worth of assets; after all, each daughter will eventually own 50% of the business, and there won't be any distinction then between majority and minority shares. Nevertheless, "reasonable" discounts for minority shares are legal.

If the value of a discounted share of a family business that's given away exceeds the annual gift tax exempt amount (currently $14,000), a gift tax return must be filed. The gift tax return, IRS Form 709, now contains the question "Does the value of an item given reflect … a valuation discount?" If so, the giver must provide an explanation of the factual basis for the discounts and the amount of discount taken.

Under current tax law, the IRS has only three years to challenge a gift or gift valuation disclosed on a gift tax return. After three years have passed, the IRS cannot go back and reopen the valuation issue. So if you make a gift of discounted stock in a family business, file a gift tax return, and when three years pass, you can be sure that, after you die, the IRS can't attack the legality of that gift or the way you valued it.

SEE AN EXPERT
You need a lawyer for gifts of minority interests. If you have a large estate and you want to obtain possible estate tax benefits by giving interests in a business to family members (or anyone else), you must see a lawyer. This is a very tricky and rapidly changing area of the law. In the right circumstances, you can achieve significant estate tax savings. But the IRS is not fond of discounted gifts of a family business, and scrutinizes them closely. You must do it right, and that requires working with a lawyer who knows this subject.

Gifts of Stock Options

This tax reduction ploy is useful only for some top corporate executives who receive stock options as part of their compensation. A stock option is the right to buy a certain amount of stock for a set price in the future.

> **EXAMPLE:** Hardriver receives the right to buy 2,500 shares of stock in Workamorte at $35 a share. Two years later, the stock is selling at $55 a share. Hardriver can exercise the option and buy 2,500 shares at the option price of $35 a share. If Hardriver promptly sells the stock, he makes a profit of $20 per share.

Under IRS rules, only certain types of stock options can be given to family members or family trusts. The IRS has no rules on how to value stock options for gift tax purposes. Very low values can usually be put on them. After all, if the stock never reaches the option price, the option isn't worth anything at all.

> **EXAMPLE:** Jean-Francois, CEO of Blow-Em-Up Movie Productions, receives the right to buy 10,000 shares of company stock at $50. The stock is selling for $42 when he receives the option. American males suddenly tire of watching stuff explode on movie screens. The stock falls to between $13 and $18 and stays there. Obviously, Jean-Francois will not exercise his stock option.

Phony Businesses Don't Fool the IRS

Just a reminder that gifts of discounted interests in a family business work only if the business is legitimate. Some wealthy folks have tried to create family limited partnerships for their vacation homes or investment portfolios. The IRS has refused to accept valuation discounts with these kinds of alleged businesses. Currently the IRS is aggressively litigating a series of cases, claiming the family businesses are shams.

The lawsuits now in progress between the IRS and various inventive givers (and their sly estate tax advisers) should help resolve what is a valid family business, for gift discount purposes. Some extremes are already clear. A family "business" created a few days before death, for the sole purpose of reducing estate taxes by giving away discounted minority interests, is not a valid business. Also, the enterprise must be run as an independent business. The primary owner must keep separate business records and can't mix cash from the business with personal accounts.

With a family limited partnership, the limited partners (the children or grandchildren who receive minority interests) do not have to be actively involved in the business. But again, the basic rule is that the business itself must exist. Some very pricey lawyers are busy right now trying to turn "exist" into "anything goes." It's not likely to be in your or your family's interests to be on the cutting edge of this fight.

Many major U.S. corporations have stock option plans that allow top employees to give options to children, grandchildren, or family trusts. Because the option can be valued so low, the worth of the gift is usually under the annual gift tax exclusion, and no gift tax is assessed. Even if some gift tax is assessed, it is often far below the eventual worth of the option. If the stock price rises significantly, the recipient can make a bundle.

> **EXAMPLE:** Holly, President of Cashotronics, Inc., has the option to buy 2,000 shares of the corporation stock at $70 a share. The corporation is privately held, and there is no market for the stock. However, Holly is sure the company will go public soon, and then the stock will be worth much more.
>
> She gives her option to her adult son, D.J. With the aid of a costly accountant and more costly lawyer, Holly values the option at $4 a share, or a total of $8,000. Since this is under the annual gift tax exclusion, no gift tax is assessed. Three years later, the company goes public, and the market stock price is $160 a share. D.J. exercises the option, buys 2,000 shares at $70 and immediately sells them. His profit is $90 a share, for a total of $180,000.

Gifts of stock options are fancy, high-end stuff, raising many tricky problems. Complicated income tax rules govern taxation of any profits from exercise of the option and subsequent sale of the stock. The stock plan itself must meet complex IRS regulations. Obviously, an expert lawyer is needed here, which is not news to the wealthy folks who benefit from this perk.

Family Business Estate Tax Freezes

A few lawyers still push a sophisticated, on-the-edge (or over it) tax-saving technique called a stock "freeze" for family corporations. It was a common practice until 1987, when Congress enacted restrictive (and confusing) provisions controlling attempted estate freezes.

Estate planning lawyers no longer consider estate freezes desirable for most family businesses. However, a few small loopholes remain, which might work for family business owners if the facts are just right.

Essentially, a freeze involved the creation of two classes of stock for the company: preferred stock (with voting rights to control the business) and common stock (with no voting rights). The owners would give shares of common stock, given as low a value as possible, to their children or grandchildren. They kept all preferred voting stock. Now, for the key: All subsequent appreciation in the worth of the business (if any) was attributed to the common stock. Thus the value of the business, for the controlling owners, would be "frozen" as of the date they gave away the common stock. Because this stock was legally owned by the children, none of the appreciation (or the worth of the common stock given away) was included in the taxable estate of the owner.

Congress attempted to eliminate this ploy. If a lawyer proposes such a freeze to you, be sure you understand exactly why he or she thinks it is legal. Why would the IRS accept the lawyer's scheme?

Avoiding Probate of a Family Business

It's often disastrous for a small business to become enmeshed in probate. Not only is probate costly, but worse, it normally ties up the business under court control for a long time, often over a year. It can be burdensome, even destructive, to have to seek a probate court's approval for business decisions. Would you want a judge supervising your business for months or years? You can plan to avoid probate of your business interest by using either joint tenancy or a living trust. For a number of tax and ownership reasons discussed in detail in Chapters 9 and 10, a living trust is usually the best choice.

Although most business owners should plan to avoid probate, that's not best for everyone. If your business has many debts and creditors' claims, probate may be desirable, because it provides a convenient forum for having those claims resolved. (See Chapter 8 for more on this.) These problems are unusual.

Individual Ownership

For most solely owned businesses, a living trust works fine. The living trust allows the business to be transferred to its new owners promptly, without any risk of loss of control while you live.

EXAMPLE 1: Sam is the sole owner of a New York restaurant. The business is not incorporated. Sam conducts the business under his name "dba (doing business as) The Manhattan Bar and Brasserie," and has filed the appropriate business and tax forms with city licensing agencies. Sam will leave the business to his son, Theodore. Sam creates a living trust and names Theodore to inherit the restaurant. Sam lists the restaurant on Schedule A of the trust: "The restaurant dba The Manhattan Bar and Brasserie … [street address] … and all assets, supplies, accounts receivable, goodwill, or other property of the business." Of course, when Theodore inherits the business, he'll need to complete a new "dba" form.

EXAMPLE 2: Natalie is sole owner of the Stay-Potted plant store. She wants to leave her interest in the store as follows:

- 30% to her close friend Donna
- 25% to her niece Cindy, and
- 15% to each of her three brothers (totaling 45%).

After investigating her options, she decides to incorporate and then transfer the stock of the corporation into a living trust. The trust document provides that each of the beneficiaries receives the percentage of stock she's specified. Natalie also prepares the appropriate corporate records, according to the corporation's bylaws, to approve her actions. She decides she won't worry about management and continuity of the business after she dies. It's up to her beneficiaries. If they agree to run the business and can run it—fine. If that doesn't work out, they can sell the business.

Shared Ownership Businesses

Living trusts also work well if you own your business together with others. Your ownership agreement should specifically permit each owner to transfer his or her interest to a living trust. If the document does not provide for this, you should amend it so that it does. Then, each owner creates his or her own living trust, consistent with any requirements of the ownership agreement (such as the right of surviving principals to buy out the deceased's share), and transfers his or her interest in the business to that trust. The trust then works like any other probate avoidance living trust, as explained in Chapter 9. The business property transferred to the trust is listed on Schedule A, for example as:

"The grantor's shares in the Zeeet Corporation."

"The grantor's partnership interest in the Alphonse-Benjamin partnership."

"The grantor's interest in the 'Go Giants!' Limited Liability Company."

Then, any business asset transferred to the living trust with a document of title must be reregistered in the trustee's name.

EXAMPLE: Vikki and Sloane each own one-half of the stock in Go-Get-'Em, Inc., which owns two apartment houses. Vikki and Sloane each create a living trust for their business interests. Each must do the following to transfer his or her share of the business into the living trust:

- prepare the appropriate corporate records and resolution authorizing and approving the transfer, and
- prepare new corporate shares, listing the living trust (technically, the trustee of the trust) as owner.

Using Lawyers

Some readers will decide that with the aid of this book and other Nolo resources, they can do all of their own estate planning without a lawyer. Others will conclude that they need the help of a lawyer to safely plan their estate. If you're in the second group, read this chapter for my views on how to find an estate planning lawyer, if you don't already know of one, and how to evaluate a lawyer and the level of expertise you'll need.

I also discuss doing some legal research on your own. Even if you'll definitely need a lawyer, that doesn't prohibit doing some legal research yourself, going deeper into one or more topics than this book does. After all, the more you know about the broad legal issues involved in estate planning and the particular legal tools you are considering using in your plan, the more likely you are to make good choices—and the lower your eventual legal bill should be.

Of course, you don't have to do any legal research at all. It does take effort. You may conclude that you have gone as deeply into advanced estate planning as you want by reading and understanding this book. That surely is a reasonable response. After all, unless you really are ready to invest a fair number of hours climbing the estate planning learning curve, you won't acquire enough expertise to creatively challenge and debate a lawyer's technical recommendations.

Hiring a Lawyer

If you do determine that you want an expert's assistance, obviously you don't want to hire a lawyer at random and say "Tell me what to do." As an intelligent consumer, you not only want to gain at least as much knowledge about your problem as you conveniently can, but you also want to invest sufficient time to be sure the person you hire is honest, knowledgeable, and provides good service for your dollar.

Your estate plan should express your intentions. No one knows those intentions better than you. Sometimes, when people think, or fear, that they need a lawyer, what they are really doing is longing for an authority figure (or believing that one is required) to tell them what to do. Keep in mind that only you can decide who should get your property—and how and when they should get it. An estate planning expert is your paid adviser and legal technician, not your mentor.

What Kind of Expert Do You Need?

The first question to decide is whether you need a lawyer, or whether you will be better served by a financial expert such as an accountant or financial planner. Don't just assume a lawyer is your best choice. For example, questions about federal estate taxes or how to calculate tax basis rules on the sale of appreciated property can often be better answered by an experienced accountant. Similarly, for some financial decisions, such as what type of insurance to buy to fund a small business buyout, you may be better off talking to a financial planner. But for most estate planning concerns, you do need to see a lawyer. In the estate planning context, there are basically three categories of lawyers:

- general practice lawyers
- estate planning specialists, and
- highly specialized lawyers working in very difficult aspects of estate planning.

Which type is right for you depends on your estate planning concerns and need. Let's look at each type of lawyer in more detail.

General Practice Lawyers

General practice lawyers handle all sorts of cases; they don't specialize in estate planning. If your needs are basic, such as a garden-variety living trust or will, or a check of some provision of your state's laws, a competent attorney in general practice should be able to do a good job at a lower cost than more specialized attorneys.

Similarly, if your small business needs to customize its partnership agreement, LLC operating agreement, or corporate bylaws to allow for surviving owners to buy out the shares of a deceased owner from his or her inheritors, a general practice lawyer should do fine.

Estate Planning Specialists

For any type of sophisticated estate planning work, you need to see a specialist. Estate planning, as this book may have convinced you, is often a complex matter, and to do a good job, a lawyer needs to be absolutely up to date on many matters, including estate tax law and regulations, the rules governing ongoing trusts, and much more. Whether you need to establish an ongoing trust for estate tax savings, handle issues raised by a second marriage, set up an ongoing gift-giving program while you live, or any one of many other possible complicated matters—you need an expert.

An expert may charge a relatively high fee, but a good one is worth it. Most general practice lawyers are simply not sufficiently educated in estate planning to handle complex matters.

Highly Specialized Lawyers

These lawyers specialize in particularly difficult aspects of estate law. For example, to prepare a "special needs" trust (see Chapter 25), a lawyer must be current on complex federal and state regulations regarding trust property and eligibility for government benefits. Even most estate planning experts don't have sufficient expertise for this. Also consult a specialized estate planning lawyer if you want to protect your or your spouse's assets from the cost of medical care for catastrophic illnesses or disabilities, or if you own property in two or more countries and need an attorney who's expert at multinational estate planning.

Unfortunately, finding a lawyer with the specialized skills you need may not be easy. In some states, such as California, state bar associations certify lawyers as expert estate planners, but even this does not guarantee that they are competent in a specific area of estate planning. You simply have to seek until you find a lawyer with the experience you need.

Locating a Lawyer

How do you find a lawyer? Ours is such a lawyer-ridden society that it's unusual if one hasn't already found you. There is certainly a growing surplus of lawyers. The difficulty, of course, is not just finding a lawyer, but retaining one who is trustworthy and competent, and who charges fairly. In addition, as noted above, many readers will need to find an estate planning expert, not just a general practitioner who says "No problem" when you ask if he or she can prepare, say, sophisticated tax-saving trusts. A few words of advice on how you can find a good lawyer may be helpful.

When looking for a good lawyer, especially an estate planning expert, personal routes are the traditional, and probably best, method. If a relative or good friend who has good business and financial sense has found an estate planning lawyer he or she recommends, chances are you'll like the lawyer too. Failing this, check with people you know in any political or social organization you're involved with, especially those with a large number of members over age 40. Assuming they themselves are savvy, they may well be able to point you to a competent lawyer who handles estate planning matters and whose attitudes are similar to yours.

Another good approach is to ask for help from a lawyer you are personally acquainted with and think well of, even if he or she doesn't work in the estate planning area. Very likely he or she can refer you to someone trustworthy who is an estate planning expert.

Also, check with people you respect who own their own small businesses. Almost anyone running a small business has a relationship with a lawyer, and chances are they've found one they like. Again, this lawyer will probably not be an estate planning expert, but will likely know one, or several.

RESOURCE

Let Nolo take the guesswork out of finding a lawyer. Nolo's Lawyer Directory provides detailed profiles of attorney advertisers, including information about the lawyer's education, experience, practice area, and fees. Go to www.nolo.com.

If you are a member of a legal insurance plan, you may be offered sophisticated estate planning assistance from a referral panel member at a reduced fee. Some of these referrals may be to excellent lawyers. In our experience, however, too often lawyers who sign up to do cut-rate work are not the best alternative. Excellent lawyers, particularly good estate planning experts, tend to have lots of work, and don't need to cut fees to gain clients.

Be cautious when dealing with bar association referral panels. Never assume a listing on a referral panel is a seal of approval. Although lawyers are supposed to be screened about their specialty to get on these panels, screening is usually perfunctory. Often the main qualification is that the lawyer needs business.

As you already know, lawyers are expensive, and expert lawyers are even more expensive. Lawyer's estate planning fees usually range from $200 to $500 per hour, with experts at the higher end of the scale. While fancy office trappings, dull clothes, and solemn (or aggressive) demeanor are no guarantee (or even a good indication) that a particular lawyer will provide top-notch service in a manner with which you will feel comfortable, this conventional style does almost always ensure that you will be charged at the upper end of the fee range. At Nolo, our experience tells us that high fees and quality service don't necessarily go hand in hand. Indeed, many of the attorneys I think most highly of tend to charge moderate fees (for lawyers, that is).

Keep in mind that in any field, including estate planning, there are good high-priced experts and bad ones. It's all too easy to get a mumbo-jumbo–speaking lawyer who confuses you at first, and enrages you later, when you receive an exorbitant bill. Don't be afraid to keep looking until you find a lawyer you like. Many people who have had unhappy experiences with lawyers (and we all know some) wish they had done so.

How Many Lawyers Does a Couple Need?

Sounds like a lightbulb joke, right? Unfortunately, it isn't. Most couples can safely use one lawyer for both spouses' estate planning. However, if there's a potential conflict between different spouses' desires, then perhaps each needs a separate lawyer. For example, in a second or subsequent marriage, if children from one or both spouses' prior marriage(s) don't get along with the other spouse, each spouse may want a separate attorney. (And if you're considering a prenuptial agreement, you'll need the advice of separate lawyers to ensure its validity.) Or, say, the estate lawyer is a good friend of one spouse and the other spouse's children are suspicious that somehow they'll get cheated of their inheritance—or if one spouse tends to be extremely domineering—each spouse may sensibly decide they want independent advice regarding their estate planning. In this case, choosing two lawyers can be a form of insurance against possible later claims of undue influence or unfair representation by a single attorney. Happily, in real life, few couples decide their interests are, or could be, so conflicting that each must pay for a separate lawyer.

Hiring a Lawyer to Review Your Estate Planning Documents

Hiring a lawyer solely to review a will or living trust you've prepared from a Nolo resource sounds like a good idea. It shouldn't cost much and seems to offer a comforting security. Sadly though, it can be difficult to find a lawyer who will accept the job. The reason is that many lawyers feel that by reviewing a document for a relatively small fee, they become just as legally responsible for a client's entire estate plan as if they did all the work from scratch. Or, put more directly, many lawyers see every client as the instigator of a future malpractice claim, or at least a source of later hassles, and simply don't want to get involved for a modest fee.

To counter this mentality and help provide do-it-yourselfers with the coaching and advice they often need, Nolo has advocated unbundling legal services. The idea is that a customer should be able to contract with a lawyer for only the services wanted, and the lawyer should have no broader liability beyond providing those services competently. This approach is becoming more common. But in the meantime, if you have trouble finding a lawyer who will help you help yourself, all you can do is keep trying to find a sympathetic lawyer. It would help if you are prepared to pay a decent fee so that the lawyer can take the time necessary to carefully review your work.

Evaluating a Lawyer

Personally evaluate any lawyer you've been referred to before you agree to hand over your estate planning work. Don't hesitate to question the lawyer, no matter how expert he or she is considered to be. To ask good questions, you need to have done some preparation; you should have at least a rough general idea of what you want to accomplish. Also, you need enough information (gleaned from this book or other sources) to pose intelligent questions and evaluate the lawyer's answers.

It's important that you feel a personal rapport with your lawyer. You want one who treats you as an equal. (Interestingly, the Latin root of the word "client" translates as "to hear, to obey.") When talking with a lawyer on the phone or at a first conference, ask specific questions that concern you. If the lawyer answers them clearly and concisely—explaining, but not talking down to you—fine. If the lawyer acts wise, but says little except to ask that the problem be placed in his or her hands, watch out. You are either talking with someone who doesn't know the answer and won't admit it (common), or someone who finds it impossible to let go of the "me expert, you peasant" way of looking at the world (even more common). You need a lawyer who's open and sympathetic to people who want to actively participate in handling their own legal affairs.

Be sure you've settled your fee arrangement—in writing—at the start of your relationship. Fees depend on the area of the country where you live, generally. I feel that fees for a general practice lawyer in the range of $200 to $300 per hour are reasonable in urban areas, given the average lawyer's overhead. In rural counties and small cities, excellent general help may be available for a little less. Expert estate planning lawyers usually cost more, sometimes a lot more. In addition to the amount charged per hour, you also want a clear commitment from the lawyer concerning how many hours the work will take.

Doing Your Own Research

Learning how to do your own estate planning research can provide real benefits. Of course, legal research isn't for everyone. You have to have the energy, patience, and ability to enter new mental areas, as well as the desire to do so. But for the intrepid, not only are you likely to save money on professional fees, you'll gain at least some sense of mastery over an area of law that concerns you.

Once you understand basic research techniques, some aspects of estate planning law can be fairly easy to research. For example, to find out technical aspects of state laws affecting wills or probate avoidance, you probably only need to check the relevant statutes of your state for the provision you need.

If you decide you want to do your own research, how do you go about it? Begin by finding a good law library or a computer with an Internet connection.

Using a Law Library

There's often a law library in your principal county courthouse. The quality of these libraries varies a lot from state to state and county to county. County law libraries are normally supported by tax dollars or by the fees paid to file court papers. In our experience, county law librarians have been sensitive and, generally, most helpful and courteous to nonlawyers who want to learn to do their own legal research. However, some county law libraries don't have adequate resources for many types of legal research. And, of course, I can't vouch for every law librarian in the country.

If your county library is not adequate, your best bet is a law school library. Those in state colleges and universities supported by tax dollars are almost always open to the public, at least during certain hours.

Once you've found a good law library, you need an introduction to how they work. If you can't hire your own law librarian, the best book explaining how to do your own legal work is *Legal Research: How to Find & Understand the Law,* by Stephen R. Elias and the editors of Nolo (Nolo). It shows you, step by step, how to find answers in the law library, and is, as far as I know, the only legal research book written specifically for nonprofessionals.

Even with the assistance of a sympathetic law librarian and a good research aid, digging into the law can be intimidating at first. I urge you to stay with it. After a while—perhaps sooner than you anticipate—you'll understand the materials and how you can use them.

Legal Information Online

Another way to approach legal research is to use a computer. If you want information about current estate planning issues, such as a recent court decision or a new statute, you'll probably be able to find it somewhere on the Internet. Many public libraries now offer online access, if you're not connected at home or work.

RESOURCE
Finding legal information on the Internet. The Nolo website offers extensive materials on estate planning and is a great place to start your online research. You can find us at www.nolo.com.

How to Approach Research Problems

There's no one standard method for approaching a legal research question. Sometimes, it's prudent to start from the general and move towards the specific. But rather than lay out a number of possible approaches, none of which may work for you, I'll simply refer you again to *Legal Research: How to Find & Understand the Law,* which explores these matters in far greater depth and clarity than any summary could.

Basic Research Sources

Sometimes a good way to dive into legal research is to do some background reading in a good book about a certain aspect of estate planning. This reading can provide an overview of the law applicable to your concerns, possibly provide some initial answers, and refer you to more specific sources.

There are several categories of estate planning background books. In reading these resources, please remember that they are written by estate planning attorneys, for attorneys, and often have predictable prejudices against a do-it-yourself approach. You may need to ignore an author's attitude, or, worse, struggle through wads of legalese, to get to solid legal information.

Background categories include:

- **Overall estate planning.** There are many resources covering estate planning in general. One is the *Forbes Guide to Estate Planning,* 2013 edition. Another is the *T. Rowe Price Estate Planning Guide.* A thorough book, though not entirely up-to-date, is *The CCH Financial and Estate Planning Guide,* by Meyers, Descherer, and Kess (Commerce Clearing House).

- **How-to-do-it estate planning books for lawyers.** Many states have estate planning books designed to show lawyers how it's done. These books contain specific clauses and forms for wills or trusts and many other hands-on materials. For example, in California, Continuing Education of the Bar (CEB) publishes several useful estate planning books, including *Drafting California Revocable Trusts, California Will Drafting, Complete Plans for Small and Mid-Size Estates* and *California Estate Planning.*

Comparable books in New York include: *Stocker and Rikoon on Drawing Wills and Trusts* (Practising Law Institute) and *Blattmachr on Income Taxation of Estates and Trusts,* by Blattmachr (Practising Law Institute).

In other states, the best way to locate this type of book for your state is to ask the law librarian or look up "Estate Planning," or a more specific heading, in the library catalog.

- **Treatises on one area of estate planning law.** For example, for federal estate taxes, there's *Federal Estate & Gift Taxes: Code & Regulations* (CCH). For trusts, there's *Living Trusts: Forms and Practice,* by Bickel (Matthew Bender). There are also a number of popular do-it-yourself tax guides.

Nolo Estate Planning Resources

You can find these estate planning books and software at www.nolo.com.

- *Quicken WillMaker Plus* is software that enables you to prepare many of the estate planning documents you'll need, including a will, financial power of attorney, health care directive (living will), and documents for your executor, the person who handles your estate after you die.
- *Estate Planning for Blended Families: Providing for Your Spouse and Children in a Second Marriage* covers all significant concerns that can arise with planning in a second or subsequent marriage. Included are thorough discussions of planning for children and stepchildren, separating property, choosing executors and trustees, and working with lawyers.
- *Make Your Own Living Trust* offers a complete explanation, including forms, of how to prepare a living trust to avoid probate or save on estate taxes.
- *Nolo's Online Living Trust* is a program that allows you to make an individual or shared living trust online. Just log in, answer questions about yourself and your property, and print. Comes with detailed help and instructions. Find Nolo's Online Living Trust at www.nolo.com.
- *Living Trust Maker*: This software program is very similar to *Nolo's Online Living Trust* (above), except that instead of making your trust online, you use software downloaded to your computer.

- *Quick & Legal Will Book* enables you to prepare a basic will with a minimum amount of work.
- *Nolo's Online Will* offers a customized will you make using an online interactive program—without software and without a lawyer. *Nolo's Online Will* is available at www.nolo.com.
- *Special Needs Trusts: Protect Your Child's Financial Future* shows how to provide for a child with special needs while preserving eligibility for government assistance.
- *Saving the Family Cottage: A Guide to Succession Planning for Your Cottage, Cabin, Camp or Vacation Home* explains how to include succession planning for a vacation home into your estate plan, covering issues that can arise with shared ownership—from choosing the right legal entity for that home to renting it.
- *8 Ways to Avoid Probate* is a thorough discussion of all the major ways to transfer property at death outside of a will.
- *Estate Planning Basics* concisely explains the essential components of estate planning.
- *The Executor's Guide: Settling a Loved One's Estate or Trust* is a comprehensive handbook to help executors and trustees wind up a deceased person's affairs. It can also help you get your estate in shape for your own executor or trustee.
- *The Trustee's Legal Companion* explains the ins and outs of being a trustee. Get detailed

Nolo Estate Planning Resources (continued)

information about what the job of trustee entails, finding and working with legal and tax experts, keeping good records, and avoiding challenges to your actions.

- *How to Probate an Estate in California* explains how to wrap up a basic estate in California without an attorney.
- *Get It Together: Organize Your Records So Your Family Won't Have To* is a complete system you can use to organize your legal documents, financial records, and other important personal information for your executor and other loved ones.
- *Deeds for California Real Estate* explains how to use deeds to transfer California real estate for estate planning purposes.
- *Long-Term Care: How to Plan & Pay for It* is a practical guide that provides all the information you need to help make the best arrangements for long-term care. It shows how to protect assets, arrange home health care, find nursing and nonnursing home residences, evaluate

nursing home insurance, and understand Medicare, Medicaid, and other benefit programs.

- *Social Security, Medicare & Government Pensions: Get the Most Out of Your Retirement and Medical Benefits* provides an invaluable guide through the current maze of rights and benefits for those 55 and over, including Medicare, Medicaid, and Social Security retirement and disability benefits.
- *IRAs, 401(k)s & Other Retirement Plans: Taking Your Money Out* explains when you are allowed, or required, to take money out of your retirement plans.
- *Get a Life: You Don't Need a Million to Retire Well* shares sensible ways for living a fulfilling retirement—ways that have little to do with accumulated wealth and everything to do with quality of life.

On www.nolo.com, you'll also find lots of free legal information, including articles on estate planning.

After You Complete Your Estate Plan

f you are serious about planning your estate, you'll eventually get the job done. What next? Up to you. A sigh of relief? A celebration? Maybe gather those you love, break out your favorite beverage, and offer a toast "To Life!"

But although your big job is complete, you've still got some more to do—storing your documents safely and making any necessary future revisions to your plan. This chapter discusses what you may need to do after you've completed your planning documents.

Storing Your Estate Planning Documents

Completing an estate plan means that you have created some important documents: a will, probably a living trust, quite possibly an ongoing trust, or even several, as well as other forms, such as a durable power of attorney for health care and one for finances. And perhaps you've signed a joint tenancy deed, business ownership documents, or written instructions for your funeral or donations of body parts. Obviously, you want to keep all these documents in a safe place, where you, and your executor or trustee, can readily find them. It's no big secret how to accomplish this. Any secure place can be used for storage: a safe in your house or office, or even a drawer in your home desk or file cabinet.

Some people use a bank safe deposit box. If you do this, you must make sure

that your executor or successor trustee will have ready legal access to that box when it's needed. Check with your bank to see what it requires to allow your executor or trustee to get documents from the safe deposit box. Also check to make sure the safe deposit box isn't sealed, under state law, when one owner dies. (Some states that have estate or inheritance taxes require this.)

While you may want to keep at least some of your estate planning documents private while you live, you also surely want them to be promptly accessible to whoever will handle your affairs at your death. This is especially true for documents that deal with your wishes as to organ transplants and funeral or burial instructions, which must be immediately available. So once you have settled on a storage place, let the person who will wind up your affairs know what you've decided and how to obtain the documents.

What about making copies of your estate planning documents? You may have to produce copies of your living trust for financial institutions, such as a brokerage company, where you have an account you want placed in trust. Whether or not to make copies for personal reasons is up to you. Often people want to give copies to their executor or successor trustee, family members, or friends. If you do need or want copies:

- Photocopy the documents you want people to see or have. These copies are not legal originals, because they are not signed by you. A photocopy of your signature doesn't make a document a legal original.

- Never sign a copy. If you do, it could legally qualify as a "duplicate original." If you later decide to change, amend, or revoke the document, you have to change each duplicate original as well.
- To be extra safe, mark "copy" in ink on each page. This isn't legally required, but it ensures that no one can claim a copy is an original.

Revising Your Estate Plan

Estate plans shouldn't be changed frequently. If impromptu changes ("I'll show her; I'll cut her out of my will") occur often, you have an underlying family or personal problem to examine. Major life events, however, call for estate planning changes. If any of the following events occur, you should review your plan:

- **You sell or give away any property you've specifically mentioned in your will or living trust.** Estate planning transfer devices, such as wills or living trusts, don't become binding until your death. So what happens if you dispose of property but don't change your will or trust? For example, what happens if your will leaves your son your 1988 Chevy, but by the time you die, you've already sold it and purchased a 2014 hybrid? To summarize what can be a complicated area of law: If you leave someone a specific piece of property (say the Chevy) but you no longer own

it when you die, that beneficiary is out of luck. The fact that you own a Honda doesn't help the beneficiary. Lawyers call this "ademption"; people who don't inherit the property in question are often heard to use an earthier term.

- **You get married.** If you don't update your will, your new spouse will have the right to inherit a share of your estate, as determined by state law.
- **You get divorced.** In some states, a divorce ends a former spouse's right to inherit under a will. In other states, it doesn't. Also, property left to a divorced spouse using other estate planning devices may not be affected by a divorce. For example, under federal law, divorce does not automatically cancel the rights of an ex-spouse who had been named as beneficiary of a 401(k) or other employer-sponsored retirement plan. The employee must fill out a form naming a new beneficiary.
- **A child is born.** The rule here is similar to that for marriage.
- **A beneficiary dies.**
- **Your financial situation changes significantly.**
- **You move to a new state.** It is particularly important to review your estate plan if you are married and move from a common law property state to a community property state or vice versa. (See Chapter 3 for a detailed discussion of the issues that may concern you.)
- **You acquire significant property.**

- **You want to change the successor trustee of your living trust or the executor of your will.**
- **You want to change the personal or property guardian you have named for your minor children.** If you have established a child's trust, you'll need to revise your plan if you want to change the person or institution you have named as trustee or custodian for a gift under the UTMA.

If you do decide to change your estate plan, you must decide whether you need, or want, to create entirely new documents or simply modify your existing ones. Which route is better depends both on how complex your changes are and the estate planning document involved.

Living Trusts

Living trusts can be revised fairly easily by:

- **Transferring additional property to your trust.** If you just want to transfer more property to the trust, there should be no problem. A well-drafted living trust has a clause permitting additions of property to the trust after it has been created (called an "after-acquired property" clause). If your trust has such a clause, you can add property by listing it on the trust schedule and taking title to that property in the trustee's name. If you only add property to a trust schedule, you do not need to have the trust notarized again.

  You don't have to name a new beneficiary for this new trust property.

If you don't, it will go to the residuary beneficiary of your trust unless you've provided that "all property" on the trust schedule goes to some other beneficiary.

- **Amending the trust document (not just a property schedule).** For changes that don't necessitate a new document, you can make a formal amendment to your trust. Changes by amendment can include adding or deleting beneficiaries, changing gifts, or naming new successor trustees. You must sign and date the amendment and have it notarized.
- **Making a new trust document.** If you're making wholesale changes to your trust, you'll need to revoke the old trust and prepare a new one, reflecting your current intentions. This is the most complicated method, but is sometimes necessary. You'll have to get the new trust document notarized. Worse, you'll have to reregister property in the trustee's name, as trustee of the new trust as of the date of creation (notarization) of this trust. That's a lot of work.

Wills

There are only two ways to change a formal witnessed will:

- prepare a formal witnessed codicil to the will, or
- destroy the old will and make a new one.

Let's briefly examine each procedure.

Make a Codicil

A codicil is a formal legal method for making changes to a will that has already been drafted, signed, and witnessed. A codicil is a sort of legal "P.S." to the will. It must be typed or printed, with a formal heading. The text of the codicil then identifies the date of the original will and sets out the change made. Following is a sample codicil, without the necessary signature, date, and witness clauses.

Codicil to Will of Beth Thoreau

1. I leave $3,000 to my friend Al Smith.
2. I leave my silver tea set to Bertha Weinstock and revoke my gift of that tea set to Mary Warbler, now deceased.
3. In all other respects, I reaffirm my will dated August 23, 2007.

A codicil must be typed, signed, dated, and witnessed just like a will. Because of this requirement, it can make more sense to prepare an entirely new will, especially if you are using a computer will program. It won't take you any longer to prepare a new computer-generated will than a codicil, and the signing and witnessing requirements for both are the same.

You must sign and date a codicil in the presence of the same number of witnesses who watched you sign the original will, who are told that it's a codicil to your will and who need to sign their names. The witnesses don't have to be the same people

as those for the original will, though it's a good idea to use the original witnesses if they're available. You can find a sample codicil form in *Quick & Legal Will Book,* by Denis Clifford (Nolo).

Make a New Will

If you want to significantly revise your will, it's better to draft a new will and revoke the old one than to use a codicil. A will that has been substantially rewritten by a codicil is an awkward document and can be confusing. The relationship of the codicil to the original will provisions may not always be clear.

If you make a new will, be sure to revoke your old will. You can do this by:

- destroying the will itself (and all copies, if you can get your hands on them)— rip 'em up and throw 'em out, and
- stating in the new will that you revoke all previous wills you have made.

Technically, either one of the acts listed above is sufficient, but I strongly recommend that you do both.

 RESOURCE
Nolo can help you update your will. At Nolo.com you can buy a simple codicil to add to your existing will, or you can create an entirely new will using *Nolo's Online Will.*

Joint Tenancy

If you've established a joint tenancy, are you stuck with it? No. In almost all states, one joint tenant can transform the joint tenancy into a tenancy in common, which eliminates the right of the other co-owners to automatically inherit. However, it takes agreement of all the joint tenants to allow anyone to become the sole owner of the property. If all joint tenants agree to end a joint tenancy, they can sign a document (a deed, for real estate) transferring the property into whatever new form of ownership is desired.

SEE AN EXPERT

Changing a joint tenancy. If you want to transfer your share of joint tenancy property into tenancy in common and the other owners don't consent, you'll need to see a lawyer to learn the procedures required in your state—unless you live in California. In the Golden State, *Deeds for California Real Estate*, by Mary Randolph (Nolo), shows you how to do this.

Pay-on-Death Accounts

You can amend or revoke a pay-on-death account at any time. You can change a beneficiary simply by crossing out the old one and writing in a new one on the financial institution's registration form; sometimes a new, separate form must be completed. You can also end the pay-on-death account simply by closing it or by spending all the money the account contains. If the account is empty when you die, obviously the beneficiary gets nothing.

You cannot safely revoke a pay-on-death account by leaving the property to someone else in your will. Under the law of the great majority of states, a beneficiary under a pay-on-death account prevails over someone who was left the same property by will.

Insurance

If you are the owner of an insurance policy, you can cancel the policy or change the beneficiary of that policy. If you are not the legal owner of the policy, you have no right to cancel the policy or change the beneficiary, even if the policy insures your own life.

Ongoing Trusts

Most ongoing trusts, whether for estate tax saving, property control, or both, do not become irrevocable until the grantor's death. Some, however, such as many charitable trusts or life insurance trusts, become irrevocable upon creation. Once an ongoing trust has become irrevocable, by definition it can't be changed or revoked. Until an ongoing trust is irrevocable, it can be freely changed or revoked by the grantor.

After a Death Occurs

When someone who has created an estate plan dies, someone else (or several someones) must take actions to carry out the deceased person's plan. This is not a book that covers after-death work in depth. That's a subject for another big book. Indeed, Nolo offers just such a book: *The Executor's Guide: Settling a Loved One's Estate or Trust*, by Mary Randolph. Translating legal procedures and jargon into coherent English, the book enables executors and successor trustees to gain a clear understanding of what their jobs actually entail—which isn't terrifying, once the law has been demystified.

This chapter simply offers you summaries of the basic tasks someone may have to handle after a person dies.

Wills

When the will writer dies, the person named as executor is responsible for carrying out the terms of the will. (Some states use the term "personal representative" instead of "executor.") This includes handling probate—normally, by hiring a probate lawyer—and then, once probate is completed, distributing property governed by the will to the beneficiaries named in that document.

If an ongoing trust (including a child's trust or family pot trust) is created in the will, the executor is often also named as trustee of that trust, and so can have continuing duties of managing the trust property. If property is left to a minor under the Uniform Transfers to Minors Act, the executor must turn that property over to the custodian for that gift.

Some executors have additional responsibilities. If a federal or state estate tax return must be filed, it's the executor's legal responsibility to see this is done. Also, in wealthier estates, if a QTIP trust is part of a deceased spouse's estate plan, the executor must decide whether or not to "elect" to have estate tax on the trust property postponed until the surviving spouse dies.

Probate Avoidance Living Trusts

With a living trust designed solely to avoid probate, the successor trustee is responsible, after a grantor dies, for carrying out the terms of the trust. This basically means transferring the trust property to the beneficiaries named in the trust.

Who Serves as Trustee

With a living trust for a single person, the successor trustee takes over promptly once the trust creator dies.

With a basic shared trust made by a couple, the surviving spouse serves as trustee after one spouse's death. (AB trusts are discussed below.) After the surviving spouse dies, the successor trustee is in charge.

If more than one person is named in the trust document as successor trustee, they all serve as cotrustees. This does not, however, mean all trustees must agree on all decisions. Whether all trustees must formally agree on any action taken with regard to the living trust property or whether each trustee can act independently depends on the terms of the trust document.

If more than one successor trustee is named, but one cannot serve, the other remains as trustee. The person named as alternate successor trustee does not take over unless all the people named as successor trustees cannot serve.

A trustee can resign at any time by preparing and signing a written resignation statement. The ex-trustee should deliver the notice to the person who is next in line to serve as trustee. With a well-drafted living trust, any trustee, including the last acting trustee, can appoint someone else to take over if no one named in the trust document can serve.

Usually, it's the last, or alternate, successor trustee who names someone else to act as trustee. The appointment must be in writing, signed, and notarized.

Winding Up a Living Trust Made for One Person

Normally, the job of the successor trustee of a single person's living trust is simply to transfer the trust property outright to the designated beneficiaries. Only if the successor trustee is also trustee of an ongoing trust created in the living trust are continuing duties required of him or her.

Unless there are explicit directions in the trust document, it is not the trustee's responsibility to sell or manage living trust property.

EXAMPLE: Elliot's living trust leaves his house to his children, Clarence and Grace. After Elliot dies, Jamie, the successor trustee, deeds the house from the trust to Clarence and Grace. They can do with it what they wish— live in it, rent it, or sell it. Jamie cannot sell the house and divide the proceeds between the beneficiaries—that's not his decision to make.

Usually, after the grantor dies, the living trust continues to exist only as long as it takes the successor trustee to distribute trust property to the beneficiaries. In many cases, a living trust can be wound up within a few weeks after a grantor's death. But if an ongoing business is involved, it may take longer.

No formal termination document is required to end a living trust. Once the trust property has been distributed, the trust ends.

RESOURCE

Learn more about winding up a living trust. *The Trustee's Legal Companion*, by Liza Hanks and Carol Elias Zolla explains the ins and outs of being a trustee and guides you through the complex tasks that face every trust administrator. Get detailed information about what the job of trustee entails, finding and working with legal and tax experts, keeping good records, and avoiding challenges to your actions.

Winding Up a Shared Living Trust

Coping with what happens when one grantor dies is more complex for a successor trustee who's in charge of a shared living trust. The successor trustee (usually the surviving spouse or mate) must divide the living trust property into two portions. Each portion goes into a new trust entity, as provided for by the original trust document:

- **Deceased spouse's property.** One new trust contains the deceased spouse's share of the living trust property. The terms of this new trust cannot be changed, and the trust cannot be revoked. Property is promptly distributed to its beneficiaries by the successor trustee unless the grantor has provided for its ongoing management, as would be the case for property left to a minor.
- **Surviving spouse's property.** A separate trust which, as a practical matter, is usually a continuation of the original living trust, contains the surviving spouse's trust property. This trust usually includes any of the deceased spouse's share of the living trust property that is left to the surviving spouse. The surviving spouse remains free to amend the terms of this trust, or even revoke it.

Though this may sound complicated, it often isn't. If, as is common, much of the trust property is left to the surviving spouse, that spouse may have little to do beyond distributing a few items to the deceased's other beneficiaries.

When all the property in the deceased spouse's trust has been distributed to the beneficiaries, that trust ceases to exist. No formal termination document is required. In contrast, the surviving spouse's trust remains revocable.

> **EXAMPLE:** Edith and Jacques create a basic shared living trust to avoid probate. They transfer their major asset, their home, which they own together, to the trust, and name each other as beneficiaries. Edith names her son as alternate beneficiary.
>
> When Jacques dies, Edith inherits his half interest in the house. Jacques' trust then ends its existence. Edith's trust remains in effect, and revocable.
>
> Because of the way the trust document is worded, Edith doesn't have to change her trust document to name a beneficiary for the half interest in the house that she inherited from Jacques. Both halves, now consolidated, will go to her son at her death. She may, however, want to amend the trust to make her son the primary beneficiary and name someone else to be alternate beneficiary.

When the surviving spouse dies, the successor trustee named in the trust document takes over as trustee. The process of winding up the surviving spouse's living trust is the same as that for an individual trust.

Property Left to Children

Living trust property left for a child's benefit is normally left in a child's trust, family pot trust, or through the Uniform Transfers to Minors Act. With any of these, the successor trustee must turn the child's property over to the adult manager of the child's property—the trustee of a child's trust or family pot trust or the custodian of an UTMA gift. If the successor trustee serves in one of these capacities as well, he or she must manage the property until it is turned over to the child.

Ongoing Trusts for Estate Tax Savings or Property Management

As discussed, an ongoing trust is one that is irrevocable, usually becoming so on the grantor's death, and generally functioning for an extended period of time. Some ongoing trusts are created in a will, but more often, an ongoing trust is combined with a living trust. First, the trust property avoids probate. Then the ongoing trust becomes operational and may well last for years or decades. As discussed in the chapters covering ongoing trusts, the successor trustee's job will be much more complex here than with a simple probate avoidance trust.

As an example, let's consider an AB disclaimer trust created as part of a living trust and see what happens when one spouse dies. The purpose of this type of trust is to save on overall estate taxes. Both spouses are the original trustees. When a spouse dies, the surviving spouse becomes sole trustee, and the living trust splits into two trusts: the irrevocable Trust A (of the deceased spouse) and the revocable Trust B (of the surviving spouse).

The surviving spouse, as trustee, must first distribute any living trust property the deceased spouse left outside of Trust A to specifically named beneficiaries. Then the trustee must establish and maintain the ongoing Trust A.

A major task here is to figure out how best to divide the couple's property (all that was in the original AB disclaimer trust) between the ongoing Trust A and the surviving spouse's Trust B. Property must be clearly labeled as being owned either by Trust A or by Trust B. Any allocation of equally owned shared trust property is valid, as long as each trust gets 50% of the overall total worth of the AB trust property. Each specific item of property does not have to be split, with half going to each trust. For example, a house, worth (net) $300,000 can be placed in Trust A, as long as other property with a total worth of $300,000 is placed in Trust B.

SEE AN EXPERT
Dividing AB trust property. Deciding how to divide AB trust property on the death of a spouse requires the services of a lawyer or tax accountant. These decisions can have long-term tax consequences, and you can save yourself and your inheritors hassle and expense by getting good advice.

The surviving trustee must prepare two new printed or typed trust schedules. The first lists all property transferred to the irrevocable Trust A. The second lists all property transferred to the surviving spouse's revocable Trust B. The trustee needs to describe the property in enough detail that the IRS, and eventually the final beneficiaries, can tell what property is in each trust.

Establishing the ongoing irrevocable Trust A may require some reregistering of title of some of the deceased spouse's living trust property. For example, if the surviving spouse decides that it is wisest to put all of a shared ownership house in Trust A, a new deed should be prepared to reflect this, listing the trustee of the ongoing trust as the new owner.

> **EXAMPLE:** Moira and Joseph O'Sullivan created the Moira and Joseph O'Sullivan Living Trust. In that trust, each created an AB trust. Joseph dies. Moira, with the help of an accountant, divides the living trust property between her now separate Trust B and the newly operational Trust A for Joseph's property. Property with documents of title transferred into Trust A must be reregistered into the name of the trustee of this new trust. Thus the property would be registered as held by "Moira O'Sullivan, as trustee of the Joseph O'Sullivan Trust A."

An operational Trust A needs a federal taxpayer ID number. The surviving spouse must keep appropriate trust financial records and file a federal trust tax return for Trust A every year. Annual state trust tax returns may also be required, in states with income taxes.

As trustee, the surviving spouse manages the property in Trust A and receives any income it generates. Management can include making sensible investment decisions, which may necessitate the hiring of a professional investment adviser.

The surviving spouse's Trust B goes on as before. It remains revocable and can be changed at any time. The surviving spouse does not need to file a tax return for this trust.

After the death of the surviving spouse, the successor trustee winds up both trusts by distributing all property of both trusts to each trust's final beneficiaries. The successor trustee must file a final tax return for Trust A. The successor trustee files a closing tax return for the second spouse and may also manage any property left in a child's trust or a family pot trust.

Preparing and Filing Tax Returns

It is the responsibility of an executor to file federal estate and state inheritance tax returns, if one or both are required because of the value of the deceased's estate. If most or all property is left by a living trust, however, it's the successor trustee who files any tax returns due. (Of course, the executor and successor trustee are usually the same person.)

A final federal income tax return (and state return, if there's a state income tax) must be filed for the deceased. Legally, this is the responsibility of the executor of the deceased's will. Also, a final federal trust income tax return (and state tax return, if one is required) must be filed for Trust A after both spouses die.

If a federal estate tax return must be filed, it is due nine months after the decedent's death. As we've discussed, estate tax matters can get quite sticky. For instance, for federal estate tax purposes, property can be valued as of the date of death or as of six months after death. The executor will need professional help, and is entitled to pay for it out of the deceased's assets.

The IRS publishes a helpful set of instructions for the estate tax return, *Instructions for Form 706*. Another useful IRS publication is *Introduction to Estate and Gift Taxes* (Publication 950). You can download these publications for free from the IRS website, www.irs.gov.

Trustee's Reports to Beneficiaries

Generally, a trustee is not legally required to make any report of trust income, transactions, or any other aspect of trust management to any beneficiary. There are some exceptions:

- The trustee of any ongoing trust may be required by the terms of the trust to give reports, such as copies of the trust's annual federal trust tax return, to all the trust beneficiaries.
- A few states' laws require the trustee to distribute an annual report to the beneficiaries. For example, Washington law requires distributing "a written itemization of all current receipts and disbursements made by the trustee." (Wash. Rev. Code § 11.106.020.) In most family situations, these laws have little or no impact, because beneficiaries trust the trustee and don't insist on these legal rights.
- A number of states have laws requiring the successor trustee to notify beneficiaries or a state agency when the trust creator dies. I recommend that a successor trustee notify beneficiaries no matter what state the trust's creator lived in.

Collecting the Proceeds of a Life Insurance Policy

How to collect insurance proceeds after the insured person dies is not, strictly speaking, part of estate planning, but nevertheless, people want to be sure their beneficiaries know how to collect these proceeds. Normally, this isn't a problem—they can be collected soon after the insured person's death by submitting an insurance company claim form and a certified copy of the insured person's death certificate to the company. The beneficiary may also have to file a copy of the policy and proof of identity as the named beneficiary, if the insurance company requires it.

How to Obtain a Death Certificate

An executor will need at least several copies of the death certificate. One quick way to obtain them is to ask the mortuary or other institution involved in disposition of the body. Otherwise, there are a couple of ways you can obtain them yourself. You can write the vital statistics office or county health department in the county where the decedent died. Call the office first to find out where to send your request and how much money to enclose.

These days, however, it's often easier to find forms and instructions online. Many county websites offer death certificate request forms that you can print out and send; others allow you to submit your request electronically and pay by credit card. To find out your options, go to the official website of the county where the death occurred. I've found that the easiest way to find a county website is to Google that county and state. For example, when you type "King County Washington" into the Google search engine, the first listing is that county's official website, KingCounty.gov.

Although this is normally routine, there can be several flies in the ointment. In some states with state estate or inheritance taxes, insurance proceeds above a certain amount cannot be released until the tax officials approve. If the insured person owned the insurance policy, the insurance proceeds will be part of her taxable estate, and the state tax officials must first be satisfied that the estate has other sufficient assets to pay its taxes before they authorize release of the proceeds to the beneficiaries.

In other instances, some companies have been known to delay payments for months, so that they can collect interest on the money for a longer time. If this happens to you, a letter to the insurance commissioner of both your state and of the one where the company is headquartered (with copies to the offending company) will normally pry the money loose, pronto.

Obtaining Title to Joint Tenancy Property

The major benefit of joint tenancy is the "automatic right of survivorship." But obviously, the words on a deed to real estate or certificate of title to a car don't magically change on the day one joint tenant takes that last breath. Until someone acts, the legal title will not be changed to the survivor's name. What "automatic right of survivorship" means in this context is that, compared to most legal tasks, it's fairly easy to transfer title to the surviving owner quickly and cheaply, without probate. This is true for all joint tenancies, whether of real estate or personal property.

To get the deceased owner's name off the ownership document so that the surviving joint tenants are on record as legal owners, they must:

- establish that the joint tenant has died by filing a copy of the death certificate with the appropriate government official or recorder of title, and
- file a document establishing that the surviving owners are sole owners to the property.

The surviving owners can hire a lawyer to do this, but this is normally unnecessary because the procedures are routine. If you hire a lawyer, however, be sure the fee charged is a reasonable hourly one. An unfortunate practice in many states is for a lawyer to propose charging one third of what the probate fee would be to transfer joint property to the survivors. Usually, this is far too high a fee; the work is neither complicated nor time-consuming.

For example, to terminate a joint tenancy in real estate, you need to file a certified copy of the deceased's death certificate and a form called an affidavit of death of joint tenant, or something similar, with the county office of property records (often called the county recorder or registry of deeds). The affidavit is a standard legal form, available in many office supply stores. On this form, you state that a joint tenant has died. In some states, such as California, you don't need to complete a new deed. After you record (file) the affidavit and death certificate and any deed required, you can transfer or sell title to the property by signing a deed as "surviving joint tenant."

Tax liens. In some states that have state estate or inheritance taxes, tax liens (legal claims) may be imposed on all of a deceased person's property, and title cannot be transferred until the liens are removed. Removing them may involve posting a bond, filing a final inheritance tax return, or otherwise satisfying the tax authorities that taxes will be paid. It can be a major hassle for the surviving joint tenant. You'll need to locate the governmental agency that imposes and releases these tax liens and see what is required to release them.

Federal estate taxes. Joint tenancy property can also be liable for a proportionate share of a deceased's federal estate taxes, if the estate is large enough to owe them. The taxes due will depend on the size of the taxable estate, which probably won't be determined for some time. But if the surviving owner must wait until the full amount of estate taxes are known (or worse, paid) before obtaining clear title to the joint tenancy property, the practical advantages of the right of survivorship are severely diminished. After all, one purpose of a right of survivorship is to obtain clear title fast. Fortunately, the IRS will usually allow prompt transfer of joint tenancy property if there's an estimate of the value of the property in the estate and a clear indication that there are enough other assets to pay off all estate taxes. The proof required that all taxes due can be paid from the remaining taxable estate will vary depending on the size, complexity, and liquidity of the estate.

Personal Matters

Beyond wrapping up legal and financial affairs, there are usually various personal matters someone must deal with after a death. These can be simple or complex, and can range from returning library books to sorting through mounds of papers and records. Here's a new possible concern: what to do about Internet information by or about the deceased person? You may have to decide whether online accounts, blogs, social networking pages, and other digital information should be removed or maintained. Depending on how much the deceased person used the Internet, this may take a substantial effort.

Some Estate Plans

This chapter presents eight different estate plans, each serving the needs of a person or couple in a different situation. As I stated at the beginning of this book, I don't believe that it makes sense to rely on a formula plan. Instead, you need a personal plan. And due to the changes in your own circumstances or changes in the laws—the estate tax laws, in particular—you may need to update your plan in the coming years. The purpose of this chapter is to illustrate how the estate planning methods discussed in this book can be assembled into a coherent plan.

A Prosperous Couple in Their 60s and 70s

Robert and Teresa Casswell are a prosperous married couple. He's 68, she's 72. Both are retired and live comfortably on their savings, assets, and retirement payments. They live in a common law property state and share ownership of all their property equally. The Casswells have four grown children.

Their property. A house worth $850,000 (all equity; they paid off the mortgage years ago), a summer home worth $400,000 (again all equity), individual retirement plans worth more than $1 million, stocks and mutual funds worth $3.5 million, cash savings of $360,000, works of art valued at $125,000, jewelry valued at $50,000, various investments worth $600,000, and miscellaneous personal property worth a

total of $150,000. Their total estate is worth over $7 million. Of course, they hope the value of their estate will increase by the time either of them dies.

Their estate planning goals. Robert and Teresa each want to leave most of their property to the surviving spouse and then to their four children in equal shares. Each wants to be sure that the survivor has sufficient income and assets to continue to live the affluent kind of life they've had together. They also want to leave smaller gifts to friends, relatives, and charities. They also want to plan to avoid probate and reduce estate taxes to the extent feasible.

Their plan. Robert and Teresa decide to establish an AB disclaimer trust for the bulk of their assets, not including the funds in their individual retirement programs. Each names the other as the beneficiary of his or her retirement program, so that the survivor can "roll over" any funds remaining in the deceased's program into her or his own IRA. Next they transfer their other major assets to the trust. With the AB disclaimer trust, the surviving spouse (as trustee) can decide how much, if any, of the deceased spouse's property to inherit outright, and how much to place in Trust A.

Each spouse names their four children as the final beneficiaries of his or her AB trust.

In their living trust, each spouse also leaves several personal gifts to friends and charities. The successor trustee for the trust, after both spouses die, will be the Casswells' eldest daughter, a stable, savvy woman who lives near them and is respected by the other children. They discuss this with her and mention it to the other children; happily, none of the others object.

After working out these basic ideas about how they want their AB disclaimer trust to work, the Casswells decide to hire a lawyer to help draw up the necessary documents, including basic backup wills, health care directives, and a durable power of attorney for finances.

A Wealthy Couple in Their 70s

Rabia and Alfonso have been married for over 35 years. Rabia is 70, Alfonso is 79. They have two grown children in their early 40s. Rabia has one child, in his late 40s, from a former marriage.

Their property. Rabia and Alfonso's shared estate has a total net worth of $11.4 million. In addition, Rabia has separate property—a rental house worth $180,000 that she inherited from her mother and owns free and clear.

Their estate planning goals. Because Rabia and Alfonso have a large estate, they want to save on estate taxes, leave much of their property for the eventual use of their two children, and also make a gift to charity. Also, Rabia wants to leave a gift to her son from her prior marriage.

Their plan. Each spouse's share of their common property is $5.7 million. Rabia, of course, has an additional $180,000 of her separate property.

First, they create a living trust to avoid probate of their property.

Next, each spouse decides to leave property in an AB disclaimer trust, with their two children as the final beneficiaries. This way, each spouse can make use of his or her own personal estate tax exemption.

Then, each spouse decides that they have enough money to create a generation-skipping trust of $1 million (less any portion of estate taxes due paid from this sum). For Alfonso, this trust is relatively simple. His two children will be the middle generation, and their children (his grandchildren) the final generation. But Rabia wonders if she should also include her son from her first marriage, and his children, as beneficiaries of her generation-skipping trust.

After some reflection and soul-searching, she decides not to. Her son doesn't get along very well with one of her other children, so having both be beneficiaries of the same trust could become problematic. Rabia decides, instead, that she will leave her son a substantial amount of money outright. So, as a part of her living trust, Rabia leaves an outright gift of her separate property home (worth $180,000) and $320,000 from her shared property to her son, a total gift of $500,000. In the trust document, she directs that no estate taxes be paid from this gift.

Finally, each spouse creates a QTIP trust for any property left over after their other trusts have been funded or gifts made. Alfonso names his two children to divide equally all money in his QTIP trust. Rabia distributes the property held by her QTIP trust to her final beneficiaries differently: 40% to each of her children with Alfonso and 20% to her son from the earlier marriage.

Alfonso and Rabia complete their estate plan by each preparing a simple will, health care directive, and a durable power of attorney for finances.

A Single Man in His 60s

Dick Daughterty, a bachelor, wants to leave some of his property to his sister, some to her three children, and much to many friends.

His property. Dick has personal possessions worth $75,000, paintings worth $25,000, a limited partnership interest worth $160,000, stocks worth $47,000, and savings of $165,000. He doesn't own any real estate. His total estate is worth $472,000.

His estate planning goals. Dick is most concerned with who gets his property, not how they get it. He spends considerable time evaluating exactly who gets what, making several lists and numerous revisions before he settles on a plan.

Dick definitely doesn't want his estate to have to pay probate fees. Because his estate is well below the estate tax threshold, he doesn't have to worry about federal taxes.

His plan. Dick creates a probate-avoiding living trust. In his trust, he specifies the many beneficiaries he's chosen, identifying each item of property that goes to each.

Then he transfers all his property, except his savings account, to the living trust. He writes the office of the general partner for the limited partnership and instructs it to reregister his ownership interest in his name as trustee of his trust.

Dick changes his savings account into a pay-on-death account and names his three best friends as equal beneficiaries of the account.

Next, he prepares a basic will, although at present, none of his property will be transferred by will. His will covers the possibility that he may subsequently acquire property that he isn't able to transfer to his trust before he dies.

Then he prepares his health care directives and durable power of attorney for finances. He names his best friend, Al, to be his attorney-in-fact for both, and another friend, Jacqueline, to be alternate attorney-in-fact for both if Al can't serve. Dick is particularly concerned about health care decisions. If he's incapacitated, he wants to be treated by his personal doctors. If he needs to be hospitalized, he wants to be taken to a specific local hospital. And he does not want life support technology used to artificially extend his life if he has a fatal, irreversible disease. So he drafts a health care directive that incorporates all his specific desires, making them legal and mandatory.

Finally, Dick prepares his funeral plan and instructions and gives them to Al, to ensure they're carried out.

A Younger Couple

Mark Ryan and Alicia Lopez are married. He's 43, she's 32. They have two young children. Mark is employed as a carpenter; Alicia works part-time as a proofreader for a publisher. They live in Texas, a community property state.

Their property. They own their house (heavily mortgaged) in joint tenancy. It's their only major asset. They also own two cars, an old Ford and an older Toyota station wagon, the well-used furnishings of their home, personal possessions, such as clothing, books, and electronic equipment, and two savings accounts—one shared account containing $18,000, and another containing $6,000 in Mark's name, an account he had before they were married.

Their estate planning goals. Mark and Alicia's main concern is providing for their children's care, both financial and personal, if both parents die. With total assets worth less than $150,000, they don't need to worry about federal estate taxes. And because their house is owned in joint tenancy, their major asset will avoid probate, unless they die simultaneously.

Their plan. Mark and Alicia decide they don't want to create a probate-avoiding living trust now, as they don't have a lot of property and, statistically, are unlikely to die for many years. They prepare a will, leaving all their non-joint tenancy property, except Mark's savings account, to each other. In their wills, they name their children as alternate beneficiaries, to receive all property covered by the wills

and the house, in case both parents die simultaneously.

Mark and Alicia learn, to their mutual surprise, that they disagree on what should be done with Mark's $6,000 savings account. Alicia believes it should be handled like all their other property; indeed, she points out that Mark can easily convert the account to community property by simply depositing it in their joint account. Mark states that he wants to keep exclusive control over the account, as his own separate property. Further, he wants to leave it to his brother, Herb, a struggling woodworker whom he is close to. Alicia, who has long felt Herb was a no-goodnik, becomes upset that Mark wants to hold out on his own children. After all, if Mark died, she and the kids would need every cent they could get their hands on. As Mark starts to get angry, Alicia realizes they need to slow down and talk it out.

It takes a couple of days, but finally they arrive at a compromise. Mark will transfer $3,000 of his account into their shared account. He can leave the other $3,000 to Herb in his will.

Only after they resolve this issue do Mark and Alicia approach the subject they agree is most important: providing for their two children as best they can if the unlikely occurs and they die simultaneously. They agree on who should be the children's personal guardian and name her in their wills—Alicia's sister Joan, who is willing to do the job.

They also name Joan as the children's property guardian. They decide that some life insurance is necessary, at least until their savings increase and the children are older. They decide to purchase $150,000 term life policies on each of their lives, given that both of them work and the family needs two incomes to get by.

Each establishes a family pot trust in both their wills. If both parents die, the insurance proceeds will be paid to the trust and managed for the children's benefit until they become 18.

Finally, Mark and Alicia each prepare health care directives and a durable power of attorney for finances, each naming the other to make health care or financial decisions in case he or she becomes incapacitated, with Joan as the alternate attorney-in-fact.

A Single Mother in Her 30s

Anne Clark is a single woman who works as an attorney for the Public Defender's Office in Los Angeles. Anne's primary concern is providing for her eight-year-old daughter, Tina.

Her property. Anne's estate consists of money market savings of $90,000, a 403(b) retirement account presently worth $75,000, personal possessions (including her car) worth $80,000, and term life insurance with proceeds of $700,000 payable upon her death. She does not own any real estate.

Her estate planning goals. Anne's goal is simple: to be sure her daughter is cared for if anything should happen to Anne.

Her plan. Anne's first concern is who will raise Tina if she cannot. Tina's father now has a second family and has shown little interest in Tina for several years. To obtain court-ordered child support Anne has twice had to threaten legal action. There is no person who, in Anne's opinion, would be ideal to raise Tina. Anne's older sister says that she'd accept the job, but she's not enthusiastic about it. Plus she lives in New Jersey and has three children and an unstable husband to cope with. So Anne talks to her best friend in Los Angeles, Frederick, about the possibility of caring for Tina. He declares that he'd be pleased to take on the job; he's single, likes Tina, and has always wanted a child.

In her will, Anne names Frederick to be Tina's personal guardian. She includes in the will a detailed statement of why appointing Frederick would be in Tina's best interest, including the reasons why Tina's father is not suitable for the job. Anne also prepares a detailed letter, requesting that Frederick be named as Tina's custodian if Anne becomes incapacitated and unable to care for Tina herself. While not binding, the letter should be persuasive to a judge if something happens to Anne before her death and a custody conflict arises.

Without any other good choice as a backup, Anne names her sister as alternate personal guardian. She's relieved to recall that it's highly improbable that both she and Frederick would be unable to care for Tina.

Anne is healthy and active, so she doesn't have to make a complicated estate plan.

Her two most important assets—the life insurance proceeds and 403(b) money—will pass outside of probate. Anne names Tina as the beneficiary of both assets. For each, she creates an UTMA account, naming Frederick as custodian for any funds Tina receives from either account. Similarly, she makes her money market account a pay-on-death account, naming Tina as the beneficiary through an UTMA account.

She leaves her personal possessions to Tina by her will, having decided that she doesn't have to worry about further probate avoidance: Her will property is not very valuable, and she's unlikely to die for decades. In her will, she creates an UTMA account for any property left to Tina, with Frederick as the custodian.

Because she lives in California, Anne can choose an age Tina must reach, up to 25, for terminating any UTMA accounts. Anne decides that the accounts will end when Tina becomes 21, not wanting to impose restrictions over Tina past the age when she will (Anne hopes) be graduating from college.

Finally, Anne creates health care documents and a durable power of attorney for finances, in each case naming Frederick to act for her if she cannot.

A Widow in Her 80s

Ida Grant, a widow, lives in California. She wants to leave the bulk of her estate to her one child, Carla. She also has a four-year-old Irish terrier, which she loves and wants to provide care for after she dies. Finally, she wants to make a number of small gifts to friends and charities.

Her property. Mrs. Grant's estate consists of a house that she and her husband bought in 1947 for $8,000. It now has a market value of $760,000. Mrs. Grant has household furnishings worth $20,000, a car worth $5,000, stocks worth $70,000, and savings of $180,000. She lives primarily on interest from her savings and Social Security.

Her estate planning goals. Mrs. Grant values simplicity. She wants to transfer her property by the simplest means possible, but she also wants to avoid probate.

Her plan. Mrs. Grant considers transferring her house into joint tenancy with her daughter Carla, whom she trusts absolutely, because this seems to provide the simplest probate avoidance transfer method. However, Mrs. Grant learns there will be serious tax disadvantages if she uses joint tenancy. The IRS will require that a gift tax return be filed because Mrs. Grant is giving a half-interest in the house to her daughter. No tax will actually be paid now because the house's worth is under the gift/ estate tax threshold, but still, it's a hassle to prepare and file the tax return.

Mrs. Grant decides to use a living trust for her house. This allows the house to avoid probate. She names Carla as the trust's beneficiary and successor trustee. She then signs and records a deed transferring the house from herself to herself as trustee of her trust. When listing the house as part of the trust property on the trust schedule, Mrs. Grant includes "all household furnishings," so her daughter will receive this property outside of probate as well.

Mrs. Grant wants to provide care for her dog. When she investigates this possibility, she learns that trusts for animals are legal in California. But she decides to handle the matter informally. Mrs. Grant discusses her concern with Carla, who is far from being a dog lover. Carla suggests that the dog, and a sum of money necessary to care for it, be left to Betty Planquee, a good friend who has said she would accept the responsibility.

Mrs. Grant learns that under California law she can transfer property worth less than $150,000 by her will free of probate. She has her savings in a money market account. She changes that account to a pay-on-death account, naming her daughter as beneficiary, and so avoids probate of that account. Then, using a backup will, she leaves stocks to close friends:

"I leave my stock in A Corp. to my good friend and longtime veterinarian, Arthur Pedronnzi."

"I leave my stock in B Corp. to my good friend and faithful gardener, William Service."

"I leave my stock in C Corp. and my dog, Cherry Blossom, to my friend Betty Planquee."

The residuary clause of her will provides, "I leave all my remaining property subject to this will to my daughter, Carla." Under this clause, any property that remains subject to her will after the stock gifts are made, such as her car, goes to Carla. Because the total amount of property transferred under her will is less than $150,000, no probate is required.

Mrs. Grant doesn't name any alternate beneficiaries. She wants to keep her will simple, and decides that if any of her friends die before her, she wants that money to go to Carla under the terms of the residuary clause. And she doesn't even want to consider the possibility that Carla could die before she does.

Mrs. Grant also prepares a health care directive and a durable power of attorney for finances, naming her daughter Carla in both as her attorney-in-fact, to act for her if she becomes incapacitated and can't make medical or financial decisions herself.

A Couple in Their 60s, in a Second Marriage

Miriam and Ira Bloom are a married couple in their 60s. They live in New Jersey. It's the second marriage for each. Miriam has one child, now 32, from her first marriage; Ira has two, who are 33 and 36, from his first marriage.

Their property. Miriam and Ira share ownership of a $200,000 condominium apartment ($160,000 equity), savings of $80,000, stocks worth $55,000, and miscellaneous furnishings worth approximately $24,000. Each separately owns a car worth roughly $20,000. Ira owns, as his separate property, real estate worth $340,000 ($250,000 equity), partnership interests worth $80,000, and savings of $40,000. Miriam owns a coin collection worth $5,000 and mutual funds worth $485,000.

Their estate planning goals. Both Miriam and Ira want to provide for each other, but each also wants to ensure that their children from their prior marriages are well provided for. Ira's total estate is now worth $552,000. Miriam's is worth $672,000. Neither's estate is large enough to be subject to federal estate taxes, but they do want to avoid probate fees.

Their plan. Miriam and Ira agree that each will leave their shared ownership property outright to the other. Any New Jersey state inheritance taxes assessed against either's estate will be paid from this shared property. Each one's separate property will be left in an AB marital property control trust for the other spouse, with the property in the trust to go ultimately to the deceased spouse's children. Then they see a lawyer to draw up the trust document. The surviving spouse will be the trustee of whichever Trust A becomes operational (containing the separate property of the deceased spouse). Each spouse fully trusts the other to manage his or her trust property, and is confident he or she will conserve the trust principal for their children. But both spouses know that their children are somewhat mistrustful of this arrangement. So the spouses agree that the surviving spouse will send the deceased spouse's children yearly reports of the trust's financial status (a copy of the trust's annual tax return will suffice) to reassure them that the property isn't being squandered.

Because one of Ira's children still needs financial support for education, he places $20,000 of his separate savings in a pay-on-death bank account for her, so she will get money without delay if he dies before she graduates. If the daughter completes her education with Ira's help before he dies, he can then, if he wants to, revoke the informal bank account trust and place the account in his living trust.

The Blooms also each execute health care directives and durable powers of attorney for finances, naming the other spouse as the attorney-in-fact.

Finally, the Blooms prepare simple basic wills.

An Unmarried Couple in Their 40s

Pat and Mercedes have lived together for 13 years. They have no children. They have a written living-together contract, stating that they share ownership of their house and household goods. They've also recorded a deed to the house as tenants in common, with each owning half. In their agreement, they've provided that all other property owned by each of them is separate property.

Their estate planning goals. Each wants to leave his or her interest in the house and furnishings to the other and other items to family and friends. Each wants to avoid probate of all their property. Neither's estate will be subject to federal estate taxes. Finally, each wants to ensure that the other can make medical and financial decisions if one becomes incapacitated.

Their plan. They decide to create a living trust with three distinct property listings: one for their shared property and one for each one's separate property.

Each leaves his or her interest in the their shared property (the house and furnishings) to the other. They prepare and file a deed transferring ownership of their house into their names as trustees of their shared trust.

Then, each leaves gifts of his or separate property to the beneficiaries he or she has chosen. They both complete all paperwork necessary to transfer property to the trust.

Each also prepares a basic will and leaves all property subject to those wills (none right now) to the other.

Finally, Pat and Mercedes each prepare a health care directive and a durable power of attorney for finances, naming the other as attorney-in-fact.

Glossary

Part of the hold that the legal profession has over us has to do with its use of specialized language. It is easy to be intimidated and uncomfortable when we don't know what lawyers and judges are talking about. It is only beginning to dawn on many of us that legal language is sometimes consciously, and occasionally even cynically, used to keep us intimidated, and that the concepts behind the obtuse language are often easily understandable. We'd rather use only plain English throughout this book and eliminate legalistic jargon altogether, but unfortunately we are stuck with a legal system that often creaks into motion best when "magic" (sometimes four-syllabic) words are used. (Lawyers call such words "terms of art.")

If you don't find a confusing term defined here, try Nolo's online legal dictionary at www.nolo.com. Or try a standard dictionary, but be sure to read the entire definition, as specialized legal meanings are often listed last. As a last resort, try *Black's Law Dictionary*, available in all law libraries.

Definitions in quotes and with the symbol (B.) following are taken from Ambrose Bierce's *The Devil's Dictionary*.

AB disclaimer trust. As used in *Plan Your Estate*, a trust giving a surviving spouse (or domestic partner) a choice whether to inherit some or all of the deceased spouse's trust property or to disclaim the property to reduce estate taxes.

Abatement. Cutting back certain gifts under a will when it is necessary to create a fund to meet expenses, pay taxes, satisfy debts, or take care of other bequests that are given a priority under law or under the will.

Abstract of trust. A condensed version of a living trust, which leaves out the key parts of what property is in the trust and who are the beneficiaries. An abstract of trust (also called a certification of trust) is used to prove, to a financial organization or other institution, that a valid living trust has been established, without revealing specifics of property or beneficiaries the person who created the trust wants to keep private and confidential.

Accumulation trust. A trust where trust income is retained and not paid out to beneficiaries until certain conditions occur.

Acknowledgment. A statement in front of a person who is qualified to administer oaths (for example, a notary public) that a document bearing your signature was actually signed by you.

Ademption. The failure of a specific bequest of property to take effect because the property is no longer owned by the person who made the will at the time of his or her death.

Administration (of an estate). The court-supervised distribution of the probate estate of a deceased person. The person who manages the distribution is called the executor if there is a will. If there is no will, this person is called the administrator. In some states, the person is called "personal representative" in either instance.

Adopted child. Any person, whether an adult or a minor, who is legally adopted as the child of another in a court proceeding.

Adult. Any person 18 or older.

Affidavit. A written statement made under oath.

Annuity. Payment of a fixed sum of money to a specified person at regular intervals, usually for life.

Assign. To transfer ownership of something.

Augmented estate. A method used in a number of states with a common law ownership of property system to measure a person's estate for the purpose of determining whether a surviving spouse has been adequately provided for. Generally, the augmented estate consists of property left by the will plus certain property transferred outside of the will by gifts, joint tenancies, and living trusts. In the states using this concept, a surviving spouse is generally considered to be adequately provided for if he or she receives at least one third of the augmented estate.

Autopsy. Medical examination of the body of a deceased person to determine the cause of death.

Basis. A tax term that has to do with the valuation of property for determining profit or loss on sale. If you buy a house (or a poodle) for $20,000, your tax basis is $20,000. If you later sell it for $35,000, your taxable profit is $15,000. A **stepped-up basis** means that you have been able to raise this basic amount from which taxes are computed.

Beneficiary. A person or organization legally entitled to receive gifts made under a legal document such as a will, trust, pay-on-death account, or retirement plan. Except when very small estates are involved, beneficiaries of wills receive their benefits only after the will is examined and approved by the probate court. Beneficiaries of living trusts receive their benefits outside of probate, as provided in the document establishing the trust. A **primary beneficiary** is a person who directly and certainly will benefit from a will or trust. A **contingent beneficiary** is a person who might or might not become a beneficiary, depending on the terms of the will or trust and what happens to the primary beneficiaries. For example, a contingent beneficiary might get nothing until and unless the primary beneficiary dies, with a portion of the trust corpus still remaining.

Bequest. An old legal term for a will provision leaving personal property to a specified person or organization. In this book it is called a "gift."

Bond. A document guaranteeing that a certain amount of money will be paid to those injured if a person occupying a position of trust does not carry out his or her legal and ethical responsibilities. Thus, if an executor, trustee, or guardian who is bonded (covered by a bond) wrongfully deprives a beneficiary of his or her property (say by blowing it during a trip to Las Vegas), the bonding company will replace it, up to the limits of the bond. Bonding companies, which are normally divisions of insurance companies, issue a bond in exchange for a premium, usually about 10% of the face amount of the bond.

Bypass trust. Any trust that creates a life estate for a life beneficiary, with the trust principal going to the final beneficiary when the life beneficiary dies.

Charitable trust. Any trust designed to make a substantial gift to a charity, and also achieve income and estate tax savings for the grantor.

Children. For the purposes of *Plan Your Estate*, children are: (1) the biological offspring of a will maker, (2) persons who were legally adopted by a will maker, (3) children born out of wedlock if the will maker is the mother, (4) children born out of wedlock if the will maker is the father and has acknowledged the child as being his as required by the law of the particular state, or (5) children born to the will

maker after the will is made, but before his or her death.

Child's trust. A trust created for a minor child or young adult.

Codicil. A separate legal document, which, after it has been signed and properly witnessed, changes an existing will.

Common law marriage. In a minority of states, couples may be considered married if they live together for a certain period of time and intend to be husband and wife.

Community property. Eight states follow a system of marital property ownership called "community property," and Wisconsin has a very similar "marital property" law. Very generally, all property acquired after marriage and before permanent separation is considered to belong equally to both spouses, except for gifts to and inheritances by one spouse, and, in some community property states, income from property owned by one spouse prior to marriage.

Conditional gift. A gift that passes only under certain specified conditions or upon the occurrence of a specific event. For example, if you leave property to Aunt Millie provided she is living in Cincinnati when you die, and otherwise to Uncle Fred, you have made a "conditional gift."

Conservator. Someone appointed by a court to manage the affairs of a mentally incompetent person.

Contract. An agreement between two or more people to do something. A contract is normally written, but can be oral if its terms can be carried out within one year and it doesn't involve real estate. A contract is distinguished from a gift in that each of the contracting parties pledges to do something in exchange for the promises of the other.

Creditor. As used in this book, a person or institution to whom money is owed. A creditor may be the person who actually lent the money, or a lawyer or bill collector who is trying to collect the money for the original creditor.

Curtesy. See "Dower and curtesy."

Custodian. A person named to care for property left to a minor under the Uniform Transfer to Minors Act (UTMA) or the Uniform Gift to Minors Act (UGMA).

Debtor. A person who owes money.

Decedent. A person who has died.

Deed. The legal document by which one person (or persons) transfer title (recorded ownership) to real estate to another person or persons. If the transfer is by a **grant deed**, the person transferring title makes certain guarantees or warranties as regards the title. If the transfer is by **quitclaim deed**, the person transferring does not make any guarantees, but simply transfers to the other persons all the interest he or she has in the real property.

Descendant. An offspring, however remote, of a certain person or family.

Devise. An old English term for real estate given by a will. In this book, it is called a "gift."

Disclaimer. The right to refuse to accept property left to you by trust or will. An AB disclaimer trust allows the surviving spouse to disclaim any trust property left to him or her by the deceased spouse, sending the disclaimed property to the deceased spouse's Trust A.

Domicile. The state, or country, where one has his or her primary home.

Donor. A person who gives a gift. A **donee** is a person who receives a gift.

Dower and curtesy. The right of a surviving spouse to receive or use a set portion of a deceased spouse's property (usually one third to one half) in the event the surviving spouse is not left at least that share and chooses to take against the will. Dower refers to the title which a surviving wife gets, while curtesy refers to what a husband receives. Until recently, these amounts differed in a number of states. However, since discrimination on the basis of sex is now illegal, states generally provide the same benefits regardless of sex.

Durable power of attorney. A power of attorney that remains effective even if the person who created it (called the "principal") becomes incapacitated. See "Power of attorney." The person authorized to act (called the "attorney-in-fact" or "agent") can make health care decisions and handle financial affairs of the principal.

Encumbrances. If property is used as collateral for payment of a debt or loan, the property is "encumbered." The debt must be paid off before title to the property can pass to a new owner. Generally, the value of a person's ownership in such property (called the "equity") is measured by the market value of the property less the sum of all encumbrances.

Equity. The difference between the current fair market value of your real and personal property and the amount you owe on it, if any.

Escheat. Property that goes to a state government because there are no legal inheritors to claim it. I put this in here because it's one of our favorite legal words.

Estate. All the property you own when you die. There are different ways to measure your estate, depending on whether you are concerned with tax reduction (the taxable estate), probate avoidance (the probate estate), or net worth (the net estate).

Estate planning. What this book is about— the art of prospering when you're alive, dying with the smallest taxable estate and probate estate possible, and passing your property to your loved ones with a minimum of fuss and expense.

Estate taxes. Taxes imposed on your property as it passes from the dead to the living. The federal government exempts a set dollar amount of property. Taxes are imposed only on property actually owned by you at the time of your death. Thus, estate planning techniques designed to reduce taxes usually concentrate on the legal transfer of ownership of your property

while you are living, to minimize the amount of property you own at your death.

Estate tax threshold. The dollar value of an estate at which estate tax may be due.

Executor. The person named in your will to manage your estate, deal with the probate court, collect your assets, and distribute them as you have specified. In some states this person is called the "personal representative." If you die without a will, the probate court will appoint such a person, called the "administrator" of the estate.

Final beneficiaries. People or institutions designated to receive life estate trust property outright upon the death of a life beneficiary. See "Life beneficiary."

Financial guardian. See "Guardian of the minor's property."

Funding a trust. Transferring ownership of property to a trust, in the name of the trustee.

Funeral. "A pageant whereby we attest to our respect to the dead by enriching the undertaker, and strengthen our grief by an expenditure that deepens our groans and doubles our tears." (B.)

Future interest. A right to property that cannot be enforced in the present, but at some future time.

Generation-skipping trust. An estate tax– saving trust, where the principal is left in trust for one's grandchildren, with one's children receiving only the trust income.

Gift. As used in *Plan Your Estate*, any property you give to another person or organization, either during your lifetime, or by leaving it in a will or living trust after your death.

Gift taxes. Taxes levied by the government on gifts made during a person's lifetime.

Grantor. The person who establishes a trust; also called a "settlor" or "trustor."

Grantor-retained income trusts. Various types of trusts where the grantor retains some interest in the trust property during his or her life.

Guardian of the minor's property. Termed "property guardian" in this book, this is the person you name in your will to care for property of your minor child not supervised by some other legal method, such as a minor's trust. Also called "guardian of the minor's estate" or "financial guardian."

Guardian of the person. An adult appointed or selected to care for a minor child in the event no biological or adoptive parent (legal parent) of the child is able to do so. If one legal parent is alive when the other dies, the child will automatically go to that parent, unless the best interests of the child require someone different, or (in some states) the court finds the child would suffer detriment.

Health care directive. A document in which you state your wishes regarding health care in case you are ever unable to speak for yourself and/or name a trusted person to see that your wishes are carried out.

Hearse. "Death's baby carriage." (B.)

Heirs. Persons entitled by law to inherit your estate if you don't leave a will or other device to pass property at your death.

Holographic will. An unwitnessed will that is completely handwritten by the person making it. While legal in some states, it is never advised except as a last resort.

Incidents of ownership. All (or any) control over a life insurance policy.

Inherit. To receive property from someone who dies.

Inheritance taxes. Taxes a few states impose on property received by inheritors from a deceased's estate.

Inheritors. Persons or organizations who inherit property.

Instrument. Legalese for document; often used to refer to the document that creates a trust.

Insurance. "An ingenious modern game of chance in which the player is permitted to enjoy the comfortable conviction that he is beating the man who keeps the table." (B.)

Inter vivos trusts. See "Living trust."

Intestate. To die without a will or other valid estate transfer device.

Intestate succession. The method by which property is distributed when a person fails to distribute it in a will. In such cases, the law of each state provides that the property be distributed in certain shares to the closest surviving relatives. In most states, these are a surviving spouse, children, parents, siblings, nieces and nephews, and next of kin, in that order. The intestate succession laws are also used in the event an heir is found to be pretermitted (not mentioned or otherwise provided for in the will). See "Pretermitted heir."

Irrevocable trust. Means what it says. Once you set it up, that's it. Unlike a revocable, probate avoidance trust, you can't later revoke it, amend it, or change it in any way.

Issue. Legalese for one's direct descendants —children, grandchildren, and so on.

Joint tenancy. A way to take title to jointly owned real or personal property. When two or more people own property as joint tenants, and one of the owners dies, the other owners automatically become owners of the deceased owner's share. Because of this "right of survivorship," a joint tenancy interest in property does not go through probate.

Lawful. "Compatible with the will of a judge having jurisdiction." (B.)

Lawyer. "One skilled in circumvention of the law." (B.)

Legacy. "A gift from one who is legging it out of this vale of tears." (B.)

Letters testamentary. The term for the document issued by a probate court authorizing the executor to discharge his or her responsibilities.

Life beneficiary. A person who can use trust property and benefit of trust income for his or her life, but who doesn't own the trust property itself (the "principal") and has no power to dispose of the trust property upon his or her own death.

Life estate. The right to use trust property and receive income from it during one's lifetime.

Life insurance trust. An irrevocable trust that owns a life insurance policy; often used to reduce the size of the original owner's taxable estate.

Liquid assets. Assets that can readily be turned into cash.

Living trust. A trust set up while a person is alive and that remains under the control of that person until death. Also referred to as an "inter vivos trust," a living trust is an excellent way to minimize the value of property passing through probate. This is because it enables people (called "grantors") to specify that money or other property will pass directly to their beneficiaries at the time of their death, free of probate, yet also allows the grantors to continue to control the property during their lifetime and even end the trust or change the beneficiaries if they wish.

Living will. See "Health care directive."

Marital deduction. A deduction allowed by federal estate tax law for all property passed to a surviving spouse. This deduction (which really acts like an exemption) allows anyone, even a billionaire, to pass his or her entire estate to a surviving spouse without any tax at all. This might be a good idea if the surviving spouse is relatively young and in good health.

Marriage. A specific status conferred on a couple by the state. In most states, it is necessary to file papers with a county clerk and have a marriage ceremony conducted by an authorized individual in order to be married. However, in a minority of states, called "common law marriage" states, you may be considered married if you have lived together for a certain period of time and intend to be husband and wife.

Mausoleum. "The final and funniest folly of the rich." (B.)

Minor. Persons under 18 years of age. A minor is not permitted to make certain types of decisions (for example, enter into most contracts). All minors are required to be under the care of a competent adult (parent or guardian) unless they qualify as emancipated minors (in the military, married, or living independently with court permission). This also means that property left to a minor must be handled by a guardian or trustee until the minor becomes an adult under the laws of the state.

Mopery. Not genuine legalese, but a humorous facsimile, such as "indicted on two counts of mopery."

Mortgage. A document that makes a piece of real estate the security (collateral) for the payment of a debt. Most house buyers sign a mortgage when they buy; the bank lends money to buy the house, and the house serves as security for the debt. If the owners don't pay back the loan on time, the bank can seize the house and have it sold to pay off the loan.

Net taxable estate. The value of all your property at death less all encumbrances and other liabilities.

Next of kin. The closest living relation.

Ongoing trust. Any trust that is designed to be irrevocable and operational for an extended period of time.

Pay-on-death (POD) designation. A method of providing, on a property account form, who will inherit what remains of that property when you die. Most commonly used for bank accounts.

Personal property. All property other than land and buildings attached to land. Cars, bank accounts, wages, securities, a small business, furniture, insurance policies, jewelry, pets, and season baseball tickets are all personal property.

Pour-over will. A will that "pours over" property into a trust. Property left through the will must go through probate before it goes into the trust.

Power of appointment. Having the legal authority to decide who will receive someone else's property, usually property held in a trust.

Power of attorney. A legal document through which you authorize someone else to act for you. See also "Durable power of attorney."

Pretermitted heir. A child (or the child of a deceased child) who is either not named or (in some states) not provided for in a will. Most states presume that people want their children to inherit. Accordingly, children, or the children of a child who has died, who are not mentioned or provided for in the will (even by as little as $1) are entitled to a share of the estate.

Probate. The court proceeding in which: (1) The authenticity of your will (if there is one) is established, (2) your executor or administrator is appointed, (3) your debts and taxes are paid, (4) your heirs are identified, and (5) the property in your probate estate is distributed according to your will (if there is a will).

Probate estate. All of your property that will pass through probate. Generally, this means all property owned by you at your death less any property that has been placed in joint tenancy, a living trust, a pay-on-death account, or life insurance.

Probate fees. Because probate is so laden with legal formalities, it is usually necessary to hire an attorney to handle it. The attorney will take a substantial fee from the estate before it is distributed to the heirs.

Property control trust. Any trust that imposes limits or controls over the rights of beneficiaries, for any of a number of reasons. These trusts include:
- *Special needs trusts* designed to assist disadvantaged persons with special physical or other needs;
- *Spendthrift trusts* designed to prevent a beneficiary from being able to waste trust principal;
- *Sprinkling trusts,* which authorize the trustee to decide how to distribute trust income or principal among different beneficiaries.

Proving a will. Getting a probate court to accept the fact, after a will maker's death, that the will really is the dead person's will. In many states, this can be done simply by introducing a properly signed and witnessed will. In others, it is necessary to produce one or more witnesses (or their affidavits) in court, or offer some proof of the will maker's

handwriting. Having the will maker and witnesses sign an affidavit before a notary public stating that all will-making formalities were complied with usually allows the will to "prove" itself without the need for the witnesses to testify, or other evidence.

QDOT trust. A trust used to postpone estate tax when a U.S. citizen spouse leaves more than the amount of the personal estate tax exemption in the year of death to a non-U.S. citizen spouse.

QTIP trust. A marital trust with property left for use of the surviving spouse as life beneficiary. No estate taxes are assessed on the trust property until the death of the life beneficiary spouse.

Quasi-community property. A type of property that may be owned by married couples who have moved to California, Idaho, or Washington. (A similar form of property, called "deferred marital property," exists in Wisconsin.) Laws in these states require all property acquired by people during their marriage in other states to be treated as community property at their death.

Real estate. A term used by *Plan Your Estate* as a synonym for the legalese "real property."

Real property. All land and items attached to the land, such as buildings, houses, stationary mobile homes, fences, and trees. See "Real estate." All property that is not real property is personal property.

Recording. The process of filing a copy of a deed with the county land records office. Recording creates a public record of all changes in ownership of property in the state.

Residuary beneficiary. Can have various meanings, including: a person who receives any property left by will or trust not otherwise given away by the document, and a person receiving the property of a trust after the life beneficiary dies.

Residue, residuary estate. All property given by your will or trust to your residuary beneficiary after all specific gifts of property have been made—that is, what's left.

Right of survivorship. The right of a surviving joint tenant to take ownership of a deceased joint tenant's share of the property.

Rule against perpetuities. A rule of law that limits the durations of trusts (except charitable ones). The workings of the rule are very complicated, and have baffled law students for generations. Very roughly, a trust cannot last longer than the lifetime of someone alive when the trust is created, plus 21 years.

Separate property. In community property states, all property that is not community property. See also "Community property."

Spouse. In *Plan Your Estate,* your spouse is the person to whom you are legally married.

Successor trustee. The person (or institution) who takes over as trustee of a trust when the original trustee(s) have died or become incapacitated.

Surviving spouse's trust. In an AB disclaimer trust, the revocable living trust (Trust B) of the surviving spouse, after the other spouse has died.

Taking against the will. The ability of a surviving spouse to choose a statutorily allotted share of the deceased spouse's estate instead of the share specified in his or her will. In most common law property states, the law provides that a surviving spouse is entitled to receive a minimum percentage of the other spouse's estate (commonly one third to one half). If the deceased spouse leaves the surviving spouse less than this share in or outside of the will, the surviving spouse may elect the statutory share instead of the will provision ("take against the will"). If the spouse chooses to accept the share specified in the will, it is called "taking under the will." See "Dower and curtesy."

Taxable estate. The portion of your estate that is subject to federal or state estate taxes.

Tenancy by the entirety. A form of marital property ownership with a right of survivorship between spouses; similar to joint tenancy.

Tenancy in common. A way for co-owners to hold title to property that allows them maximum freedom to dispose of their interests by sale, gift, or will. At a co-owner's death, his or her share goes to beneficiaries named in a will or trust or to the legal heirs, not to the other co-owners. Compare "Joint tenancy."

Testamentary trust. A trust created by a will.

Testate. Someone who dies leaving a valid will, or other valid property transfer devices, dies "testate."

Testator. A person making a will.

Title. Document proving ownership of property.

Totten trust. Another term for a pay-on-death bank account.

Transfer-on-death (TOD). Refers to the right to name a beneficiary in a document of title that allows the beneficiary to receive the property quickly, outside of probate. In all states except Texas, securities (stocks and bonds) can be registered in TOD form. In some states, you can register vehicles in this way or create transfer-on-death deeds for real estate.

Trust. A legal arrangement under which one person or institution (called a "trustee") controls property given by another person (called a "grantor" or "trustor") for the benefit of a third person (called a "beneficiary"). The property itself is termed the "principal" of the trust.

Trust corpus or res. Legalese (in Latin, no less) for the property transferred to a trust. For example, if a trust is established (funded) with $250,000, that money is the corpus or res.

Trust merger. Occurs when the sole trustee and sole beneficiary are the same person. In this case, there's no longer the separation between the trustee's legal ownership of trust property from the beneficiary's interest, which is the essence of a trust. So, the trust "merges" and ceases to exist.

Trustee. A person or an institution who manages a trust and trust property under the terms of the trust.

Trustee powers. The provisions in a trust document defining what the trustee may and may not do.

Uniform Transfers (or Gifts) to Minors Act. A series of state statutes that provide a method for transferring property to minors.

Usufruct. The right to use property owned by another, or receive income from it. Included because it's another of my favorite legal words.

Will. A legal document in which a person states various binding intentions about what he or she wants done with his or her property after death.

Index

A

G

⚖ NOLO *Online Legal Forms*

Nolo offers a large library of legal solutions and forms, created by Nolo's in-house legal staff. These reliable documents can be prepared in minutes.

Create a Document

- **Incorporation.** Incorporate your business in any state.
- **LLC Formations.** Gain asset protection and pass-through tax status in any state.
- **Wills.** Nolo has helped people make over 2 million wills. Is it time to make or revise yours?
- **Living Trust (avoid probate).** Plan now to save your family the cost, delays, and hassle of probate.
- **Trademark.** Protect the name of your business or product.
- **Provisional Patent.** Preserve your rights under patent law and claim "patent pending" status.

Download a Legal Form

Nolo.com has hundreds of top quality legal forms available for download—bills of sale, promissory notes, nondisclosure agreements, LLC operating agreements, corporate minutes, commercial lease and sublease, motor vehicle bill of sale, consignment agreements and many, many more.

Review Your Documents

Many lawyers in Nolo's consumer-friendly lawyer directory will review Nolo documents for a very reasonable fee. Check their detailed profiles at **Nolo.com/lawyers**.

Nolo's Bestselling Books